REVERE FRANKLIN WEIDNER

Annotations on the Revelation of St. John

Contents

Original Publishing Info

ANNOTATIONS
on the
REVELATION OF ST. JOHN THE DIVINE
by
REVERE F. WEIDNER, D. D., LL. D.
*Professor of Systematic Theology in the Chicago Lutheran
Theological Seminary*
New York
The Christian Literature Co.
mdcccxcviii
Copyright, 1898,
By THE CHRISTIAN LITERATURE COMPANY
THE LUTHERAN COMMENTARY
a plain exposition of the
Holy Scriptures of the New Testament
by
SCHOLARS OF THE LUTHERAN CHURCH IN
AMERICA
edited by
HENRY EYSTER JACOBS
Vol. XII

Preface

It was with the utmost diffidence that the writer consented
to prepare a brief commentary on the Book of Revelation.
This was principally due to three reasons: (1) The diverse
views held by interpreters as to its meaning; (2) The fact,
strange as it may seem, that the writer, though familiar with
the different theories concerning the book and its contents,
had never committed himself to any one theory, but in all
his brief discussions of the book, whether in the class-room,
or in public lecture, or in print, had aimed merely at a clear
and correct presentation, in an objective way, of the various
systems of interpretation, or else simply had developed the
teaching of the book in its bearing upon biblical theology; (3)
Because the writer has always had very little sympathy with
those interpreters who maintain that prophecy is merely
history written beforehand, and that all which it reveals of
the future must be as literal as history itself.

Notwithstanding these objections, the writer felt drawn
to the study of this book, not because he had some new
interpretation to offer, but mainly because he himself wished
to obtain a clearer understanding of the revelation which
God has vouchsafed to make of the future of His Kingdom.
As a student of prophecy, especially of the Old Testament,
and as a firm believer in predictive prophecy, he could
not help realizing that so close was the relation between

the Old and New Testaments, that he who accepts the teaching of the Old Testament concerning the Messiah, as fulfilled in Christ's First Advent, must also accept its teaching concerning the kingdom of the Messiah. Particularly so, if the New Testament distinctly teaches another and Second Coming of Christ, in language which exactly harmonizes in all its details with prophecies in the Old Testament, which are universally recognized as not having been fulfilled in His First Advent, and which must, therefore, necessarily refer to His Second Advent.

The aim of the writer has been to follow the clear teaching of Scripture, and he has sought everywhere to interpret the prophecies here recorded, concerning the Second Coming of Christ and the events of the Last Day, in the same way and spirit in which the New Testament writers interpret the prophecies in the Old Testament concerning the Messiah and His First Advent. After repeated study of all the Old Testament quotations found in the New Testament, the writer can come to no other conclusion than this, that the Book of Revelation bears the same relation to the Christian Church to-day as the prophecies of Daniel, Ezekiel, and Zechariah did to the Jewish Church after the Exile, and that if we interpret the Apocalypse in the same spirit as Christ and the writers of the New Testament interpreted these prophecies of the Old Testament, we cannot fall greatly into error. Incorrect as many of the expositions given in these notes possibly may be, still the writer believes that in this direction alone the truth is to be found.

The aim has been to prepare a book for those who wish to make a special study of prophecy, both in the Old and New Testaments. It is remarkable how the thought and language of the book is interwoven throughout with the language of the prophets of the Old Testament, and the reader will be amply repaid for all the care that he gives in looking up each Scripture reference. In fact, this book furnishes a key to the Old Testament itself, and shows how, in many cases, Old Testament prophecy only finds its true fulfilment in the last days.

The book is written altogether in the inductive way. The author did not begin with any preconceived views as to what the outcome would be. Nor has the attempt been made to harmonize what at times may appear conflicting views. These seeming contradictions may after all but be two different aspects of the same event. An attempt has also been made to present in a summary a clear statement of the different interpretations given to the most important visions. The writer has sought to be impartial in his statements, seeking only to follow Scripture teaching, and has nowhere attempted to discuss the topics from a dogmatical standpoint, but simply from a purely exegetical one, but must confess that the more he studies the Apocalypse, and sees the vast divergence of views in the interpretation of the book, the less is he inclined to be over-positive and dogmatic about the true meaning of these wonderful visions. The Apocalypse is a very deep book, and those who are so confident that they alone have fathomed its meaning may some day discover that they have been but like children playing by the shores of the deep sea. "O the depth of the riches both of the wisdom and the knowledge of God! how unsearchable are His judgments, and His ways past tracing out!"

R. F. W.

Chicago Lutheran Theological Seminary,
Epiphany, January 6, 1898.

Introduction

1. *The Authorship and Genuineness of the Book of the Revelation.* It is the almost unanimous opinion of the Early Church that the Apocalypse or the Book of the Revelation was written by the Apostle John, the beloved disciple of Christ. No other book of the New Testament is better authenticated. Papias, a hearer of St. John, born probably 60–70 A. D., bishop of Hierapolis, a city not far from Laodicea (Rev. 3:14), made use of the Apocalypse in a work published about 130–140 A. D. (Euseb. *H. E.* III. 39), and Justin Martyr, writing about 146 A. D., in his *Dialogue with Trypho*, a discussion held at Ephesus, the chief of the Seven Churches in Asia (Rev. 2:1), definitely mentions the Apocalypse of John, saying distinctly that it was the Apostle's (Euseb. *H. E.* IV. 18). This testimony is all the more valuable because this is the only book of the N. T. to which Justin refers by name, and St. John the only writer. It is utterly impossible for Justin Martyr to have been mistaken as to the authorship of the Apocalypse. Irenæus, writing about 180 A. D., refers to the Apocalypse over thirty times, and quotes it as the work of the Apostle John. He was almost a contemporary of St. John, and well acquainted with Polycarp, the favorite disciple of John, and although in later life bishop of Lyons in France, he was born and trained in Asia Minor, and thus his testimony is very valuable. Melito, bishop of Sardis (about 170 A. D.), Appollonius of Ephesus

(about 170–180 A. D.), Theophilus, bishop of Antioch (about 171–183 A. D.), Clemens Alexandrinus (*died* 220 A. D.), Origen (*d.* 254), Hippolytus of Rome (about 225 A. D.),—in fact, all the Ante-Nicene Fathers of the Eastern Church bear testimony that the Apocalypse was written by the Apostle John. Eusebius in his *Church History* has preserved for us the tradition of the Eastern Church from the earliest period respecting the Apocalypse, and the external evidence is most clear and convincing that John the Apostle wrote this book. The conjecture of Dionysius, bishop of Alexandria (247 A. D.), is all that he can adduce against the Apostolic authorship of the Apocalypse (Euseb. *H. E.* VII. 25).[1]

The Early Latin Fathers also give most decided and unanimous testimony to the Apostolic authorship of the Apocalypse, and there is no book of the Bible which has more decisive external testimony in its favor than this one.[2]

The objections against the genuineness of the Apocalypse have all arisen from what is known as internal evidence, turning on divergencies between the Gospel and the Apocalypse (1) in doctrinal views, (2) in spirit and tone, and (3) in style and language. Four different views have been held with reference to the question as to the relation of the Apostle John to the principal works which bear his name:

(1) Neither the Gospel nor the Apocalypse is by John.[1]

(2) The Apocalypse is by John, but the Gospel was not written by the Apostle John.[2]

(3) The Apostle John wrote the Gospel, but not the Apocalypse.[3]

(4) The Gospel, Epistles, and Apocalypse were written by the Apostle John. This is the view adopted by all conservative critics and maintained by Hengstenberg, Ebrard, Hofmann,

Kliefoth, Godet, Luthardt, Alford, Ellicott, Salmon, Lee, Farrar, Meyer, Westcott, Wordsworth, Sadler, Milligan, Simcox, and others.

The objections drawn from internal evidences against the Apostolic authorship of the Apocalypse have been mainly as follows:

(1) The author does not style himself an Apostle, and nowhere does he designate himself as a personal disciple of Jesus. So in substance Luecke, Keim, Harnack, etc. But, in answer, it is sufficient to say that the author describes himself as "the servant" of Jesus Christ (1:1) "who bare witness of the word of God, and of the testimony of Jesus Christ" (1:2), expressions which remind us of John 1:14; 19:35; 1 John 1:2; and the writer also names himself John (1:1, 4, 9; 22:8) in such a way that it can refer to no other than to John the Apostle. Salmon, in favor of the view that the Apocalypse was written by a personal hearer of our Lord, maintains that "echoes of the Gospel records of the words of Jesus are to be found more frequently in this than in any other N. T. book, except perhaps in the Epistle of James" (*Introd.* p. 201), and Zeller of the Tuebingen School held that "among all the parts of the N. T., the only one which can, with any right, claim to have been composed by an Apostle, who was an immediate disciple of Christ, is the Apocalypse."

(2) The author speaks (21:14) in such an objective way of the twelve Apostles that it is scarcely credible that he himself belonged to them. So Harnack, Keim, Ewald, Credner, etc. But the Apostles are spoken of in such an objective way by Paul in 1 Cor. 12:28; Eph. 3:5, and Lee rightly calls attention to the fact that Rev. 21:14 only reflects the teaching of such passages as Matt. 16:18; 19:28; and Eph. 2:20.

(3) The language of the book, we are told, is wholly different from that of the Fourth Gospel and the Epistles of John,—that it is characterized by Hebraizing idioms, irregular constructions, and grammatical inaccuracies. This objection has been developed very fully by Ewald, Luecke, Credner, and De Wette, and answered at length by Lee, Salmon, and Davidson,—the last affirming the Johannean authorship of the Apocalypse, but denying that of the Gospel. Davidson maintains that there are few *real* solecisms *in* the Apocalypse, almost all that are adduced being also found in Greek writers, or in those of the N. T., and he accounts for the strongly Hebraized diction of the book on the ground that the writer expressed Jewish conceptions in Greek, and that John conformed his language to the diction and symbolic features of the prophets Ezekiel and Daniel. Davidson concludes his long examination of the arguments of those who deny the Apostolic authorship of Revelation by maintaining that these objectors "proceeded on principles which, if fairly applied and carried out, would divest John of the authorship of the Epistles generally acknowledged as his, and would equally denude the Apostle Paul of some Epistles which *he* confessedly wrote."[1] In answer to the question, How is it that the Greek of the Gospel is so much better than that of the Apocalypse, if both books were written by the same author? Salmon answers: "I am not sure that the Greek of the Gospel does display so very much wider a knowledge of grammatical forms;" and he quotes with approval Westcott:[2] "To speak of St. John's Gospel as 'written in very pure Greek' is altogether misleading. It is free from solecisms, because it avoids all idiomatic expressions," and Salmon adds: "It is on account of this more restricted range of grammatical

xiii

forms that the Gospel of St. John has been so often used as the first book of a beginner learning a foreign language." Archdeacon Lee maintains that the peculiar style of the Apocalypse "results naturally from the excited condition of prophetic ecstasy," and that "the language of the Apocalypse is more akin to the Hebrew than to the Greek, it being occupied with visions and imagery corresponding to the Hebrew diction of the O. T., especially to its prophetic and sacred forms of speech."[3]

(4) Stress has also been laid on the fact that the entire style, subject-matter, and doctrinal aspect of the Book of the Revelation are so unlike the Gospel and the Epistles, that the same author could not have written the Apocalypse. But Gebhardt[4] has most convincingly shown that no argument against the unity of authorship can be drawn from differences in doctrinal views. Salmon contends that John's Gospel presents no more exalted conception of the Saviour's dignity than that which is offered in the Book of the Revelation, and Lee maintains that "each book is the complement of the other; and both, by their union, make up one perfect whole." Milligan,[1] after he has answered the most important objections urged against the unity of authorship of the Gospel and the Apocalypse, takes up also the positive side, and develops very fully the proof that the two books so closely resemble each other in *language, structure,* and *teaching*, that we must conclude that they have been written by the same author, the Apostle John.

2. *The Unity of the Apocalypse.* Among those who deny that the Apocalypse was written by John the Apostle we find some like Voelter, Weizaecker, Pfleiderer, Harnack, Vischer, and others, who in the spirit and method of negative Higher

Criticism maintain that the Apocalypse is composed of various documents. But there is no foundation whatever for their theories, which have been fully answered by Warfield[2] and Milligan.[3]

3. *The Canonicity of the Apocalypse.* The canonicity of no book of the N. T. is better attested by the Early Church than that of the Apocalypse. Because the Apostolic origin of the book was so universally accepted, it could not be excluded from the books of the N. T. Canon. No one in ancient times ever questioned the inspiration or authority of the Book of the Revelation, except those who were prejudiced against its contents. The full evidence is given by Westcott. It is well known that Luther and some of the Reformers questioned the apostolicity, and therefore also the canonicity, of the Apocalypse, but this was owing to the fact that they did not understand the nature and scope of the book. But if the Apocalypse was written by the Apostle John, its canonicity or right to belong to the New Testament is established.

4. *The Time of Writing.* There is some difficulty in determining the date of the Apocalypse. The majority of modern critical historians and commentators, diverse as may be their views on other points, agree in this, that the Apocalypse, no matter by whom written, was composed between the death of Nero (June 9, 68 A. D.) and the destruction of Jerusalem (August 10, 70 A. D.).[1] But the internal evidence, upon which the main stress is laid in proof of an early date, is not sufficiently convincing to overcome the clear and weighty testimony of the Early Church that John wrote the Apocalypse, in his old age, at the end of Domitian's reign (95 or 96 A. D.), at about the same time that he wrote the Gospel and the Epistles.[2]

In favor of the early date the following arguments, drawn from internal evidence, are urged:

(1) There is no reference in the Apocalypse to the destruction of Jerusalem. If Jerusalem had been destroyed before the book was written, the author could not have failed to notice that event. We answer, such a reference we might expect if the work had been written within five or ten years, but not after the lapse of twenty-five years.

(2) There are many particular passages in the Apocalypse which plainly inform us that the book was written while Nero was Emperor of Rome. But to interpret Rev. 6:9–11 as referring to the persecution of the Christians by Nero,—to assert that 11:1, 2, proves that the temple must have been still standing, and that Jerusalem was in a state of siege at the time of the writing of this book,—to maintain that the *Beast* of 13:1, 18; 17:3, 8–11, was the Emperor Nero,—such a method of interpretation raises historical, exegetical, and dogmatical difficulties which it is utterly impossible to overcome.

(3) The copiousness of the imagery and the energy and passionate ardor of the style bespeak an early and not a late date. But Milligan rightly calls our attention to the fact that the richly poetical blessing of Jacob (Gen. 49) and the Song and Blessing of Moses (Deut. 32 and 33), as well as Psalms 71 and 72, the closing prayers of David, were all written in extreme old age. We must not forget that the imagery is based upon the language of the prophets, and every figure of speech can be traced to the O. T.

(4) The literary differences between the Apocalypse and the Gospel of John are so great that we must allow at least a period of twenty-five years to intervene between the writing of the two works. But this difference has been greatly

exaggerated. Whatever peculiarities there may be, these do not supply any argument in favor of the early date of the book. Milligan, who discusses this point very ably, says: "The grammatical and stylistic eccentricities of the Apocalypse are not the result of ignorance. So far from this, the book displays more than ordinary freedom in the use of the Greek tongue. It is written in a far more difficult style than that of the calm and simple narratives of the Gospel. It is figurative, poetic, impassioned. In various passages, such as the description of the Fall of Babylon in chap. 18, and of the New Jerusalem in chap. 21, it rises to a strain of eloquence unsurpassed by anything that has come down to us from Greek antiquity. No tyro acquiring a knowledge of the language could have penned such a passage.... The grammatical constructions of the Apocalypse arise not from ignorance, but from design, and from the fact that, in an apocalyptic book, the writer naturally employs a style of language which he has come to regard as not merely an appropriate, but as the only appropriate vehicle of visions such as his.... Nor is it strange that it should be so. Every one will admit that the Apocalypse is steeped in the essence of that style of thought by which the Old Testament prophets are marked. Shall not its language also be largely colored in a similar way? The imagery of the Old Testament certainly lived in the mind of the Seer with no less vividness than in the minds of its original authors.... The prophets and their words are in his heart. He breathes their atmosphere, sees with their eyes, hears with their ears, and is in every respect one with them. In these circumstances it is only most natural that their modes of expression should also influence him.[1]" It is not necessary, as Salmon does,[2] to explain the linguistic differences between the Apocalypse and the Gospel by the supposition that John wrote the former book with his own hand, and employed an amanuensis when he wrote the Gospel.

(5) The nature and object of the Revelation are best suited by the earlier date, and thus its historical understanding is greatly facilitated. But this argument rests upon the subjective and, in many cases, on the rationalistic view, that "all interpretations not strictly historical must be excluded" (Harnack), and that the writer refers principally to events in his own age, and that he shared in the popular delusion that Nero was the Antichrist.

(6) The historical notices of the condition of the Seven Churches in Asia reveal a state of affairs pointing to the earlier, and inconsistent with the later, date. But such an argument has little weight. The persecutions mentioned in the letters to the Seven Churches need not necessarily refer to the days of Nero, but are far more suitable to the time of Domitian, a quarter of a century later,—and there has also been such a development of errors, not only in practice but in doctrine (Rev. 2:14, 15, 24), that the days of Domitian alone would allow of sufficient time for such degeneracy.

We cannot therefore accept any of these arguments drawn from internal evidence as establishing an early date for the Apocalypse.

In favor of the later date we have both the unanimous external evidence of the first three centuries and strong internal evidence.

Before the fourth century there is no variation in the external evidence,—all statements supporting the conclusion that the Apostle John was banished to Patmos by the Emperor

xviii

Domitian (81–96 A. D.), some writers placing the exile in the fourteenth year of his reign, in 95 A. D.,—and all agree that the visions of which the Revelation is the record were received in the isle of Patmos,—and Archdeacon Lee adds, "If external evidence is of any value at all, it is of value here; no amount of 'subjective' conjecture, or arbitary interpretation, can set aside the verdict of history." Among the principal witnesses are Irenæus, who could not have been born later than 130 A. D., having been the disciple of Polycarp, a contemporary of the Apostle John himself, whose words have been preserved by Eusebius (*H. E.* V. 8)—"for not a long time ago was *it* (the Revelation) seen, but almost in our generation, at the end of the reign of Domitian;"—Clemens of Alexandria (*died* 220 A. D.); Tertullian (*d.* 220 A. D.); Victorinus, a martyr (303 A. D.) under Diocletian, writing as far as is known the earliest commentary on the Apocalypse, who, commenting on Rev. 10:11, says that "when John said these things he was in the island of Patmos, condemned to the labor of the mines by Cæsar Domitian, and there he saw the Apocalypse;"—Eusebius, bishop of Cæsarea in Palestine (260–340 A. D.); and we may close with Jerome (*died* 420 A. D.), who says of John that "having been banished in the fourteenth year of Domitian to the island of Patmos, he wrote the Apocalypse."[1] All later statements are, at most, but "instances of eccentric speculation" (Lee), as in the case of Epiphanias, bishop of Salamis in the island of Cyprus (*died* 403 A. D.), who places the banishment of John to Patmos in the reign of the Emperor Claudius (41–54 A. D.), but becomes so greatly entangled in the chronology of John's life, that he places his age at ninety, in the year 54 A. D.; on the other hand, a superscription of a Syriac version of the Revelation, of the sixth century, makes the assertion that the Revelation was "given by God to the Evangelist John on the island of Patmos, to which he had been sent by the Emperor Nero," while Theophylact, the famous exegete (*died* 1107 A. D.), also places his exile in the time of Nero, making the strange statement that John wrote his *Gospel* in the island of Patmos, *thirty-two years after the Ascension of Christ.* But all these later speculations have no value whatever. The evidence of Christian antiquity is unanimous that the Apostle was exiled in the reign of Domitian, and that the Apocalypse was written about 95 A. D.

In agreement with this external evidence we have also strong *internal* evidence for the *later* date.

(1) The Apocalypse shows that it was written in the time of great persecution (Rev. 1:9). It is a well established fact that the persecution under Nero was mainly confined to the city of Rome, while that under Domitian was much more widespread. It was in the last year of his reign that Domitian became a persecutor, and it was in the same year, according to ancient tradition, that John saw these visions. The statement, too, that John was *banished* to Patmos, is in accordance with the known practice of Domitian, but not that of Nero,—for we have no record whatever in any ancient writer that Nero resorted to exile as a means of punishment. All this is in favor of the tradition of the Early Church that the Visions were seen by John, and that the Apocalypse was written by him, at the end of the reign of Domitian.

(2) The fact that John sent this book to the Seven Churches in Asia Minor (Rev. 1:4) is also a strong proof in favor of the later date. We have no evidence whatever that John had any dealings with the Churches of Asia Minor before the

destruction of Jerusalem. All the evidence and the whole career of St. Paul are directly opposed to such a view. The first three chapters of the book give most positive evidence that John had long been acquainted with the Seven Churches, and yet it is positively certain that up to 68 A. D., John was not presiding over them. There can be only one solution of the whole problem. The Apocalypse was not written before the reign of Domitian.

(3) The internal condition of the Seven Churches, their degeneracy in Christian faith and practice, gives evidence that the time was much later than that depicted in the Pastoral Epistles and in 1 and 2 Peter. The errors which are so sharply condemned in the letters to Ephesus, Pergamum, Thyatira, Laodicea, and Sardis are such that could not have arisen within a few years, between 62 A. D., the date of Paul's Epistle to the Ephesians, and 68 A. D., the Neronic date which so many insist of giving to the Apocalypse. All this is an evidence of the *late* date of the book.

(4) The early date is intimately connected with the idea that the main subject of the book is the reign of Nero and the destruction of Jerusalem. In fact, it is this erroneous interpretation which has caused so many modern scholars to fix on an early date. But surely the Apocalypse treats of greater topics and issues than those belonging to the reign of Nero.

There is therefore no reason whatever why we should give up the unanimous testimony of the Early Church that the Apocalypse was written by the Apostle John, at the close of the reign of Domitian, about 95 or 96 A. D.

5. *The Place of Writing.* Ancient tradition informs us that John saw the Visions recorded in this book while he was in

the isle of Patmos, condemned to the mines by Domitian Caesar, and that he wrote this book while at Patmos. This matter is of little importance, but the style of the book suggests that it was written in the same ecstatic condition in which the vision was seen. This is also implied in Rev. 10:4; 14:3. The hints given in the book itself also point to Patmos as the place of composition. Compare 1:9, 11, 19; 10:4; 14:13; 19:9; 21:5.

6. *The Persons Addressed.* The Lord Jesus Himself directs John to write in a book what he sees and to "send it to the seven churches, unto Ephesus, and unto Smyrna, and unto Pergamum, and unto Thyatira, and unto Sardis, and unto Philadelphia, and unto Laodicae" (Rev. 1:11), and John's salutation is "to the seven churches which are in Asia" (Rev. 1:4). These seven cities are named in the order in which a messenger would naturally visit them, going north from Ephesus as the principal city, or as they would naturally be enumerated by a person writing from Patmos. There were other churches near Ephesus, probably many—we know at least of those at Colossæ and Hierapolis (Col. 4:13), at Melitus and Troas. No doubt these churches had been the objects of the Apostle's special oversight. But this book is addressed not only to the seven churches in Asia, but also to all those who read and hear the words of the prophecy (1:3).

7. *The Importance of the Study of the Apocalypse.* The great majority of Christians take very little interest in the Revelation of St. John because it seems so obscure and mysterious and very difficult to understand. It is probably the least read book in the Bible. But if God has given this Revelation to His Son Jesus Christ that He might show it unto His servants (1:1), and if a special blessing is promised

to those who read and hear the words of this prophecy (1:3), why should we neglect this most sublime, instructive, and consoling portion of the Scriptures? What the books of Isaiah, Daniel, and Zechariah were to the Jewish Church, the Apocalypse is to the Christian Church. It is true indeed that many of the Jews did not understand the O. T. prophecies of the coming of the Messiah in the flesh, but that was owing to their preconceived ideas of what the Messiah should be when He did come, and so there will also be many professing Christians who will not pay heed to the teaching of the Apocalypse with reference to His Second Coming in glory. That there are so many diverse interpretations of this book is no reason why we should not seek for its true interpretation. But the student should ever bear in mind the warning of a recent writer on this theme: "In studying the Revelation of St. John, humility, calmness, openness to conviction, singleness of desire to ascertain the truth, and charity are even more than usually required" (Milligan).

8. *The Text of the Apocalypse.* As is well known, there are many small differences between the Authorised and Revised Versions of the Book of the Revelation. This is owing to the fact that the Greek text of the Apocalypse from which the Authorised Version was made in 1611 was so imperfect, being based upon few and imperfectly collated Manuscripts.

Erasmus, whose text after all lies at the basis of our Authorised Version, treated this book worse than any other part of the N. T. Owing to the critical labors of Tischendorf, Tregelles, Westcott and Hort, and Weiss, we now have a fairly well determined critical text, and this has been faithfully translated in the English Revised Version, and in the margin the most important readings are also indicated.

9. *The General Aim of the Apocalypse.* No matter how diverse may be the views with reference to the *special* aim of the book, whether it is a prediction of the overthrow of Paganism, or of the downfall of Papal Rome, or of the destruction of some future Antichrist, expositors of every school of interpretation will admit that the great theme of the Book of Revelation is the *personal Coming of the Lord at His Second Advent.* This thought is presented as a prophetic consolation to His Church, and is especially prominent in the introductory chapters of the book, including the letters written to the Seven Churches, and in the last chapter (22:6–21). Sadler maintains that the devout Christian, though he may not understand the real meaning of the visions, may yet gather from the book itself four great truths: (1) The Nearness of the Coming of Christ; (2) The Personal Providence of God; (3) The Ministry of Angels; (4) Christians must be disciplined by suffering and distress. But this raises the important question whether we are to regard the Apocalypse as essentially *predictive* or purely *descriptive.* There are two classes of writers who deny that we have *prediction* in the Apocalypse.

(1) Those who deny prediction *altogether,* and maintain that the events referred to were so near the writer that he required no higher inspiration than keen insight into the signs of the times. Harnack is a representative of this class, who in his article on *Revelation* in the *Encyclopædia Britannica* affirms "that the Apocalypse is the most intelligible book of the N. T.," for "all interpretation not strictly historical must be excluded."

(2) A second class who deny *prediction in the Apocalypse* are those who deny that the subject-matter of the book

refs to *events*. These maintain that the book embraces the whole period of the Christian dispensation, but refers to *principles* and *ideas* instead of events,—that it sets before us great *principles* of God's method of governing both the world and the Church, but has no reference to special events. One of the ablest representatives of this class is Dr. Milligan, who holds what we may call the *Spiritual System* of interpretation. In the *Introduction* to his *Commentary* (1883) he says: "All the symbols are treated as symbolical of principles rather than of events.... The book thus becomes to us not a history of either early or mediæval, or last events written of before they happened, but a solemn warning to Christians that in every age they have to consider the signs of their own time." So likewise in his *Lectures on the Apocalypse*[1] (pp. 185, 187): "The Apocalypse was written not simply to describe the conflict, the preservation, and the triumph of Christ's true people, but to warn against the coming degeneracy of His professing Church.... It contains no continuous history of the Church from the beginning to the end of her historical course. It is not a mere revelation of events that are immediately to precede the Second Coming of our Lord. It is no mere prophecy of the early doom of those enemies of Christian truth whom the Seer beheld around himself. The book is not predictive. It contains no prediction that is not found in the prophecies of Christ. It gives us no knowledge of the future that is not given first by our Lord, and then by others of His inspired Apostles. It is simply the highly idealized expression of the position and fortunes of His 'little flock.' " But such an interpretation of the design of the book fails to present a sufficient motive for its composition, and David Brown[2] keenly asks: "Were these first principles, these elementary truths of all revealed religion, so obscurely expressed and so insufficiently enforced in other parts of Scripture, that it needed a book of such complicated structure and such extreme difficulty of interpretation to make them clearer and more impressive?" He also refers to the novelty of this interpretation and traces it to a two-fold source: (1) the rationalistic criticism of this century which tries to explain away both miracles and prophecy, and (2) to the despair on the part of believing expositors of finding in history any events to correspond with the predictions.

No matter how great the difficulties of interpreting this book may be, this one thing seems certain, that it has to do with events pertaining to the Second Coming of Christ, which still lies in the future.

10. *The Structure of the Apocalypse.* Commentators agree that the book has three main divisions:

1. The Introduction Proper (1:1–3:22).

2. The Revelation Proper, consisting of a series of visions (4:1–22:5).

3. The Epilogue (22:6–21).

The first question to be decided is one that has a most important bearing upon the interpretation of the Apocalypse. Do these visions recorded in Rev. 4:1–22:5 represent one consecutive series of events, or are they to be divided into groups, each of which extends to the end of time? Do not some of these visions start as it were anew, going over the same ground in a different manner and bringing to light a new aspect of the end? Though these groups of visions are closely connected together, so as to form one united whole, one vision often anticipating what is to be shown in another, nevertheless a close study of Old Testament prophecy shows that these visions do not represent a continuous history of the Church or of the end. The book partakes of the same character as the prophecies of Daniel and Zechariah. Wordsworth illustrates this very clearly: "The predictions and visions in the Book of Daniel are like a succession of charts in a Geographical Atlas. The first vision (the *Vision of the Image*, Dan. 2) *anticipates* the end. It represents a prophetic view of all the Four great Empires of the World, following one another in succession, and ending in the consummation of all things, and in the glorious sovereignty of Christ. It is like the map of the two hemispheres which stands first in our books of Geography. By a process of *repetition* and *amplification*, the same four Empires are *afterwards* displayed under another form (the *Vision of the Four Beasts*, Dan. 8), and are delineated with great minuteness of detail; and this representation is also closed with a prophetic view of the establishment of Christ's kingdom and the overthrow of all His enemies. These comprehensive prophecies are followed by other visions, displaying in great fulness *portions* (the *Vision of the Ram and the Goat*, Dan. 8; see also Dan. 11:1–4) of the same periods as those which had been comprised in those comprehensive prophecies; just as the map of the two hemispheres in an Atlas is followed by separate maps, on a larger scale, exhibiting the several countries contained in the habitable globe. The prophecies of Zechariah are framed on the same principle."

It seems, then, that it is best to accept the *recapitulation* theory, that we have several descriptions of the end of the world, and after one vision is finished we apparently begin again, and then the end comes a second time, and then we begin again, and then the end comes a third time, and so on. Each group of visions thus contains a prophecy reaching to the end of the world. How often, in our judgment, we are thus brought to the final consummation, or what seems equivalent to it, the exposition of the text alone can decide, but we cannot greatly err when we reach the conclusion that the prophet at least five times gives us a description of the end:

(1) Rev. 6:12–17 (in its aspect of terror to the wicked);

(2) Rev. 11:15–18 (a description of the final consummation);

(3) Rev. 14:14–16 (the harvest, the ingathering of the Saints); 14:17–20 (the vintage, the ingathering of the wicked);

(4) Rev. 16:17–21 (in its aspect of punishment upon the wicked);

(5) Rev. 20:11–15 (the final judgment of the wicked).

If this can be clearly established, then such an interpretation would favor the view that the five groups of visions—(1) 5:1–8:1; (2) 8:2–11:19; (3) 12:1–14:20; (4) 15:1–16:21; (5) 17:1–20:15—contained in the main body of the book (4:1–22:5), in a general way, refer to events parallel to one another, each one culminating in a vivid description of the final end.

11. *The Different Schools of Interpretation.* It is well known that there are four main systems of interpretation of the Book of Revelation, which from their characteristic tendencies of thought may be called the Spiritual, the Preterist, the Continuous Historical, and the Futurist Systems.

1. *The Spiritual System.* Probably the best exponent of this view is Dr. Milligan, who has written so extensively and so ably on every topic connected with the study of the Apocalypse. He maintains that the book embraces the whole

period from the first to the Second Coming of the Lord, but that this whole period was the Last Time, the Lord's Day, which was to close God's dealings with man in a present world, and to bring to full light the principles upon which the Church was guided to her eternal rest. We have no right in interpreting the Apocalypse to interject into it the thought either of a long or a short development of events. While the Apocalypse thus embraces the whole period of the Christian dispensation, it sets before us within this period the action of great principles and not special incidents. It represents in a highly poetic and symbolic form the general principles that mark the Church's history in the world. The book is written, however, not simply to describe the conflict, the preservation, and the triumph of Christ's true people, but also to warn against the coming degeneracy of His professing Church.[1]

To the same school belongs also Bishop Boyd Carpenter, who in his *Commentary* says: "We are disposed to view the Apocalypse as the pictorial unfolding of great principles in constant conflict, though under various forms. The Preterist may, then, be right in finding early fulfilments, and the Futurist in expecting undeveloped ones, and the Historical interpreter is unquestionably right in looking for them along the whole line of history; for the words of God mean more than one man, or one school of thought, can compass. There are depths of truth unexplored which sleep beneath the simplest sentences. Just as we are wont to say that history repeats itself, so the predictions of the Bible are not exhausted in one or even in many fulfilments. Each prophecy is a single key which unlocks many doors, and the grand and stately drama of the Apocalypse has been played perchance out in one age to be repeated in the next. Its majestic and mysterious teachings indicate the features of a struggle which, be the stage the human soul, with its fluctuations of doubt and fear, of hope and love—or the progress of kingdoms—or the destinies of the world—is the same struggle in all."[2]

This is indeed an excellent way of making a practical application of the great truths taught in the Apocalypse, but surely this is not the only design and aim of the book. Such a system of interpretation if applied to Old Testament prophecy would lead to nothing but uncertain generalities, and give us no insight into the progress of God's kingdom upon earth. For any one who compares the Book of Revelation with the Book of Daniel must see that the same method of interpretation must be applied to both—that the Apocalypse is expressly intended as a sequel and completion of the disclosures in Daniel, and that the great theme of the Apocalypse is the Second Coming of the Son of Man to enter upon His everlasting kingdom.

This spiritual system of interpretation seems to be utterly contrary to the design and aim of predictive prophecy.

2. *The Preterist System.* According to the Preterists the visions of the Apocalypse relate chiefly to the destruction of Jerusalem, and the history of Pagan Rome during the reigns of the Emperors Nero, Galba, Vitellius, Vespasian, Titus, and perhaps Domitian. The prophecies of the book, at least in their primary intention, have been fulfilled. This system claims for itself an exclusive possession of the improved methods of modern research, and holds that the great discovery of modern times in connection with the Apocalypse is the identification of the Emperor Nero with

the beast of chaps. 13 and 18, and maintains that the Babylon of the later chapters is Rome. Renan says: "If the Gospel is the book of Jesus, the Apocalypse is the book of Nero," and Farrar, Gebhardt, and others regard the Nero-hypothesis as the key of the book. Among the most eminent expounders of this view we may mention Grotius, Bossuet, Calmet, Eichhorn, Wetstein, Hug, Herder, Ewald, Luecke, De Wette, Duesterdieck, Bleek, Renan, Reuss, Samuel Davidson, Moses Stuart, Maurice, Cowles, Desprez, Farrar, Hausrath, Gebhardt, and Weiss.

Of all the suggested interpretations of this book this one appears to be the one most unlikely to be true, and Sadler very positively remarks; "I cannot conceive how any persons of ordinary common-sense should have accepted it as it is usually stated *except for some strong reason in the background.*"

3. *The Continuous Historical System.* The expositors adopting this method of interpretation regard the Apocalypse as a progressive history of the fortunes of the Church from the first century to the end of time. According to them the visions are partly fulfilled, partly in course of fulfilment, and a portion still remains unfulfilled. This school includes the great majority of conservative commentators, but they differ widely among themselves in the chronology and application of details. "No system of interpretation has exercised so powerful an influence over those who have concerned themselves with the study of this book. From the thirteenth century until recently it may be said to have had undisputed possession of the minds of men. It pervaded largely the writings even of many who did not accept it as a whole (such as Alford, Auberlen, Isaac Williams). To this day no belief is more commonly entertained than that in

the visions of St. John we may read of the establishment of Christianity under Constantine, of Mohammed, of the Papacy, of the Reformation in the sixteenth century, of the French Revolution,—of not a few, in short, of the greatest movements by which, since the beginning of the Christian era, the Church and the world have been stirred" (Milligan).[1] By far the most elaborate exposition of this view is given by Elliott in his *Horæ Apocalypticæ*, in four large volumes. Among the most distinguished expositors who adopt this view we may mention Luther, Gerhard, Bengel, Mede, Vitringa, Isaac Newton, Bishop Newton, Faber, Elliott, Gaussen, Barnes, Words-worth, Birks, Alford, Lord, Lee, Glasgow, Auberlen, Hengstenberg, Ebrard, Hofmann, and Philippi.

But the objections to this system are fatal to it.

(1) The selection of historical events as the fulfilment of the different prophecies is in a high degree arbitrary.

(2) There is an infinite variety of interpretation and hopeless disagreements among those belonging to the same school. "In almost nothing are they at one; and there is hardly a single vision of the book in regard to which the greatest diversity of interpretation does not prevail among them" (Milligan, p. 134).

(3) Many commentators of this school resort to the most outrageous expositions to maintain the continuity of the prophecy.

On the whole, therefore, we may conclude that this system of interpretation is no more defensible than the other two, though, in the words of Milligan, we may add: "The system has, indeed, been supported by men whom in every other respect it is alike a duty and a delight to honor; but, however numerous or illustrious its defenders, it may be said without exaggeration that its tendency is to diminish the value and to discredit the general acceptance of the Revelation of St. John. The taste, however, for such interpretation is rapidly passing away, probably never to return."

4. *The Futurist System.* The Futurist expositors maintain that the whole book, with the exception of the first three chapters, refers principally to events which are immediately to precede, to accompany, and to follow the Second Advent of Christ. Those who adopt this system of interpretation find the key to the whole book in Rev. 1:19, "Write therefore the things which thou sawest" (the contents of the first chapter), "and the things which are" (the contents of the second and third chapters, referring to the whole Church period on earth), "and the things which shall come to pass hereafter;" i. e. *after these things* (the contents of the main part of the book, chapters 4–21, referring this prophecy to the events that take place after the Rapture of the Saints, after the Church period has come to an end).

In order that the reader may understand what in general is the view held by the Futurists, we insert here the following diagram taken from W. E. Blackstone's *Jesus is Coming.* A careful study of the references, explanations, and notes added to this chart (also taken from the same work, but carefully revised) will enable the student to grasp more clearly and intelligently the Futurist conception of the teaching of the Apocalypse.

EXPLANATION.

•—The birth of Christ, the King of the Jews. Matt. 2:2.
—The death and resurrection of Christ.

A.—Ascension of Christ. Acts 1:9.

D.—Descent of the Holy Ghost. Acts 2.

Church.—Mystical body of Christ. Eph. 1:22, 23; 3:3–6; Rom. 12:4, 5; Col. 1:24–27; 1 Cor. 12:12–27; and the Bride of Christ, Eph. 5:21–23.

De.—Descent of the Lord (1 Thess 4:16) to receive His bride. John 14:3.

R.—Resurrection of the just. Luke 14:14; Acts 24:15; 1 Thess. 4:15, 16; and change of living believers. 1 Cor. 15:23, 51, 52.

Rapture.—Translation of the saints who (like Enoch) are caught up to meet Christ in the air. 1 Thess. 4:17.

M.—The meeting of Christ and His bride. 1 Thess. 4:17.

This is our gathering together unto Him. 2 Thess. 2:1.

And the marriage of the Lamb. Matt. 22:2–10; 25:10: Luke 14:15–24; Rev. 19:7, 8.

So shall we ever be with the Lord. John 12:26; 14:3; 17:24; 1 Thess. 4:17.

It is the Hope of the Church. Phil. 3:20, 21: Tit. 2:13; 1 John 3:2, 3.

And the redemption mentioned in Luke 21:28; Rom. 8:23; Eph. 4:10.

Wherefore, comfort one another with these words. 1 Thess. 4:18.

Thus the Church escapes the tribulation. Luke 21:36:2 Pet. 2:9; Rev. 3:10.

T.—Period of unequalled tribulation to the world (Dan. 12:1; Matt. 24:21; Luke 21:25, 26), during which—the Church having been taken out—God begins to deal with Israel again (Acts 15:13–17), and will restore them to their own land. Isa. 11:11; 60:1–22; Jer. 30:3; 31:1–40; 32:36–44;

Amos 9:15; Rom. 11.

Antichrist will be revealed. 2 Thess. 2:8.

The vials of God's wrath poured out. Ps. 2:1–5; Rev. 6:16, 17; Rev. 14:10; 16:1–21. But men only blaspheme God. Rev. 16:11, 21. Israel accepts Christ (Zech. 12:10–14; 13:6), and are brought through the fire. Zech. 13:9. They pass not away. Matt. 24:34; Ps. 22:30.

Rev.—The Revelation of Christ and His saints (Col. 3:4; 1 Thess. 3:13) in flaming fire (2 Thess. 1:7–10) to execute judgment on the earth. Jude 14, 15.

This is Christ's second coming to the earth. Acts 1:11; Zech. 14:4, 5; Matt. 16:27; 24:29, 30.

J.—Judgment of the nations, or the quick. Matt. 25:31–46; 19:28; Acts 10:42; 1 Pet. 4:5.

Antichrist is destroyed. 2 Thess. 2:8. The Beast and the False Prophet are taken. Rev. 19:20. Gog and his allies are smitten. Ezek. chapters 38 and 39.

Satan is bound. Rev. 20:1–3; Rom. 16:20.

R. T.—Resurrection of the Tribulation Saints, which completes the First Resurrection. Rev. 20:4–6.

Mill'm.—The Millennium. Christ's glorious reign on the earth for 1,000 years (Rev. 20:4) with his Bride. 2 Tim. 2:12; Rev. 5:10; Isa. 2:2–5; 4:1–6; 11:1–12; 25:6–9; Isa. 65:18–25: Mic. 4:1–4; Zeph. 3:14–20; Zech. 8:3–8; Zech. 8:20–23; 14:16–21.

S.—Satan loosed for a little season, and destroyed with Gog and Magog. Rev. 20:7–10; Heb. 2:14.

Res.—The Resurrection of Judgment. Rev. 20:12–15; John 5:29; Dan. 12:2.

J. W. T.—Judgment at the Great White Throne of all the remaining dead. Rev. 20:11–15.

Death and Hell destroyed. Rev. 20:14; 1 Cor. 15:26.

E. E.—Eternity, or rather, The *aions* to come. Eph. 2:7.

ADDITIONAL NOTES

The Raptnre and the Revelation. The Futurists draw a sharp distinction between Christ coming for His saints at the *Rapture* (1 Thess. 4:15–17; John 14:3), and His coming with His saints to end the Tribulation and to destroy Antichrist, at the time of the *Revelation*, which ushers in the Day of the Lord. According to them the *Rapture* may occur at any moment (Matt. 24:42), but the *Revelation* cannot occur until Antichrist be revealed, and all the times and seasons which point to that great Day of the Lord in Daniel and the Apocalypse be fulfilled. At the *Rapture* the Church, like Enoch, is taken out of the world, and thus escapes the Tribulation which overtakes the ungodly and precedes the *Revelation* (Matt. 24:29, 40).

The Church and the Millennial Kingdom. Most of the Futurists also distinguish sharply between the *Church* militant, which was begun on the Day of Pentecost, and ends at the *Rapture*, before the Tribulation begins, and the *Millennial Kingdom*, which is to begin with the *Revelation*, at the close of the Tribulation (see *Chart*). Of course, it can readily be seen that all Futurists believe in the *pre-millennial* coming of Christ, and, according to the view of the great majority, this millennial kingdom shall consist in the personal reign of Christ on earth, "in the regeneration when the Son of man shall sit on the throne of His glory" (Matt. 19:28), when "the kingdom of the world shall have become the kingdom of our Lord and of His Christ" (Rev. 11:15; Dan. 7:14), "and the saints of the Most High shall have received the kingdom" (Dan. 7:18–27; Luke 12:32). Combining the prophecies contained in Isa. 11:1–16; Jer. 23:3–8; 32:36–44; chapters 34, 36, and 37 of Ezekiel; Rom. 8:21–23; and especially Isa. 60:1–22, they maintain that restored Israel and Jerusalem are to be the very central glory of this *Millennial Kingdom.*

The Tribulation. Most Futurists hold that the Tribulation or time between the Rapture and the Revelation covers a period of seven years (Dan. 9:27; Rev. 11:3, 7 with 13:5), at the beginning of which those Jews who shall have returned to Palestine in unbelief and are rebuilding their temple (Isa. 66:1, 2; Rev. 11:1, 2), enter into a seven years' covenant with the Antichrist (Dan. 9:27; John 5:43). At the end of three and a half years he is revealed as the Man of Sin (Dan. 9:27; 2 Thess. 2:3; Rev. 11:7; 13:1), kills the two witnesses who had been prophesying during this time (Rev. 11:3–7), stops the daily sacrifice which had been resumed (Dan. 9:27; 11:31; 12:11), and has his own image set up in the Holy Place (Matt. 24:15; 2 Thess. 2:4; Rev. 13:14, 15). Then follow, during the last three and a half years (Dan. 7:25; 9:27; Rev. 13:5), the treading under foot of the Holy City (Dan. 9:26; Luke 21:24; Rev. 11:2), and the time of the "great tribulation, such as hath not been from the beginning of the world until now, no, nor ever shall be" (Jer. 30:7; Dan. 12:1; Matt. 24:21; Rev. 13:14–17), which, under the Antichrist (Dan. 7:21–25; 2 Thess. 2:2; Rev. 13:1–8) and his prophet (Rev. 13:11–17; 19:20), shall come upon all the world (Rev. 13:15–17; 20:4). A third part of Israel will be brought through this tribulation (Zech. 13:8, 9), and for the elect's sake, the days of this culminating tribulation shall be shortened (Matt. 24:22), by the *Revelation* of Christ (2 Thess. 1:7; 2:8). The terrible character of this period, they maintain, can be learned from chapters 24–28 of Isaiah, and many, especially from the remnant of Israel, will accept of Christ, and become His witnesses, and be slain by Antichrist. These are known as the tribulation saints who are to be raised at the close of the great tribulation as the gleanings of the great harvest of the first resurrection (Rev. 20:4–6).

The Resurrection. The great majority teach that there is a *first Resurrection* of believers including the Old Testament saints, of those "that are Christ's, at His coming' (1 Cor. 15:23), who are raised at the Rapture, when Christ comes to meet them in the air (1 Thess. 4:17), but to these shall be added the *gleanings* of the first Resurrection, those who believe and suffer during the tribulation (Rev. 13:15), who will be raised at the time of the *Revelation*, when Christ comes to destroy Antichrist, that they may take part in the millennial kingdom (Rev. 20:4–6). The second Resurrection, or the Resurrection of Judgment (John 5:29), occurs after the Millennium, and includes all the remaining dead (Rev. 20:12–14).

The Judgment. As a rule the Futurists maintain that "the day of Judgment" covers a long period of years, that the Judgment of Rewards for believers probably begins at the Rapture, and that the Judgment upon the ungodly is ushered in with plagues at the time of the *Revelation* (2 Thess. 1:6–10; Rev. 19:11–21) and closes in fire (Rev. 20:10–15), between which a long season of "the sure mercies of David" (Isa, 55:3; Acts 13:34), or the Millennium intervenes. Many distinguish between four judgments, which they maintain probably occur in the following order:

(1) The Judgmant of Rewards for the Saints. This takes place in heaven, probably in connection with the Rapture of the Saints (1 Thess. 4:13–18). Here belong such passages as

1 Cor. 4:5; 2 Cor. 5:10; Rev. 22:12; Eph. 6:8; 1 Cor. 3:8; 2:9. The saints receive their reward before the Judgment upon the nations occurs (Matt. 25:31–46). See also 1 Pet. 4:17, 18.

(2) The Judgment of the Nations that are upon the earth at the *Revelation.* This is the Judgment of the *quick* or of the living (Acts 10:42; 2 Tim. 4:1; 1 Pet. 4:5). When Christ comes to destroy Antichrist at the Revelation, He comes also to execute judgment upon the living nations (1 Cor. 6:2; Jude 14, 15; Matt. 25:31–46). Then follows the Millennium.

(3) The Judgment of the Dead at the Great White Throne (Rev. 20:12–15). See also Matt. 10:15; 11:21–24; 12:41, 42; 2 Pet. 2:9; 3:7; Rom. 2:5–16.

(4) The Judgment of Angels (1 Cor. 6:3; 2 Pet. 2:4; Jude 6; Rev. 20:10; Matt. 25:41).

Such, in general, with many divergencies in matters of detail, is the view held by modern Futurists. Among those who more or less agree with this method of interpretation we may mention De Burgh, Maitland, Benjamin Newton, Todd, Seiss, Lincoln, Kelly, Peters, Richter, and in general the followers of Darby (Plymouth Brethren) and allied schools of prophetic teaching. This, in general, has also been the traditional explanation of the Apocalypse during the first four centuries of the Christian Church. Simcox in his Commentary on the English text of Revelation (as well as on the Greek text), published in the Cambridge Series, gives an excellent summary of this traditional view, which we here condense:

"From the time of Tertullian and Hippolytus—not to say of Justin and Irenæus—we have a consistent expectation of the course of events that will precede the last Judgment.... The Roman Empire was to be broken up into ten kingdoms, bearing (we must understand from Daniel) the same relation to it that the Hellenized kingdoms of the East bore to the Empire of Alexander. Among these kingdoms will arise a new Empire, reviving the old pretensions of Rome to world-wide instead of merely local dominion; but instead of resting on law, patriotism, and submission to the will of Providence, this new Empire will have no other basis than the self-will, the self-assertion, at least the self-deification, of its Ruler. He will come 'in the spiritual power' of Epiphanes and of Nero: he may be called Nero in the sense in which our Lord is in prophecy called David, or His forerunner Elias. He will be a man free from coarse vices, such as hinder the consistent pursuit of any aim, but equally free from any restraint imposed by the fear of God, or by regard for human opinion. Claiming for himself the honor due to God and the supreme obedience due to His Law, he will persecute the Christian Church: his persecution being so relentless, so systematic and well-directed, that the Church would be exterminated did not God supernaturally interpose to 'shorten the days.' But, while persecuting Christianity, he will extend a more or less hearty patronage to Judaism, being possibly himself of Israelitish birth. Having in some sense revived the Roman Empire, he will yet show himself an enemy to the city of Rome, which will be finally destroyed, either by his armies or by the direct act of God; and he will, perhaps on occasion of this destruction, choose Jerusalem for his seat of Empire. To this end he will restore the Jews to their own land: he will perhaps be recognized by them as their Christ: he will restore their Temple, but will make it serve rather to his own glory than to that of the Lord God of Israel....

xl

"So far, his career has apparently been unchecked. Now God sends against him two prophets—probably Moses and Elijah, or Enoch and Elijah—who, by their words and miracles, to some extent counteract his, But they will be put to death in his persecution, and then his power will appear finally established: but only for a few days. God will raise them from the dead, and call them up into heaven: and by this miracle, together with the preaching that preceded their death, the Jews will be converted. Elijah will have fulfilled his destined work, of 'turning the hearts of the fathers to the children,' i. e. of God's old people to His new....

"Still Antichrist's universal empire appears scarcely shaken by the secession of the one little nation of Israel: he will assemble the armies of the world for its reconquest, and it will seem far easier for him to reduce his second capital than the first. But when in the Land of Israel, he and his army will be met and destroyed, not in a carnal battle with the forces of Israel after the flesh, but by the power of God in the hand of His Son....

"Here, according to what seems to be the oldest form of the tradition, and certainly that standing in closest relation to the Apocalypse, follows what is popularly called the Millennium, The whole reign of Antichrist lasted, apparently, but three years and a half; the divine triumph after his overthrow will last for a thousand years. This will begin, perhaps, with the appearance of the Lord Jesus on earth, certainly with the resurrection of the Marytrs, Prophets, and other chief Saints. Whether these remain on earth or no, the condition of the earth is made such that it shall not be an unworthy abode for them. Moral evil, if not annihilated, at least has its power broken. Jerusalem remains what Antichrist had made it—the spiritual and temporal metropolis of the world; but this world-wide power is now in the hands, not of God's enemy, but of God Himself: and the world under the rule of Jerusalem realizes the most glorious prophetic descriptions of the kingdom of God.…

"Yet this kingdom of God is not the final and eternal one.… Not only does the natural order of the world go on—with deaths and (what shocked fourth century feeling most) marriages and births occurring; but there must be some root of moral evil remaining, to account for the end of this age of peace. The devil will at last for a short time recover his power: while the central regions of the world remain faithful to God, the outlying ones are stirred up to revolt against Him, and press in to crush His kingdom by the brute force of numbers. They are on the point of success—nearer to it, perhaps, than their predecessor Antichrist had been—when they are, like Antichrist, overpowered by the direct interposition of God. Then, all God's enemies being subdued, comes the end of all things—the General Resurrection of the Dead, the final Judgment, and the Eternal Kingdom of God."

The reader cannot avoid noticing that those who adopt this system of interpretation have attained the conviction that we ought, in general, to study and interpret prophecy in the same way as we do the historical and doctrinal books of the Bible, and to insist on the grammatico-historical meaning and symbolical teaching of the Apocalypse, and not to spiritualize all its statements. They maintain that if we are to be guided by the fulfilment of the prophecies of the Old Testament concerning the Messiah, and consider how in every case referring to the first Advent they have been *literally* fulfilled, surely no fault ought to be found with those who believe that the direct and positive assertions of God's Word concerning the Second Coming of Christ, as recorded in the Old and New Testaments, will also be literally fulfilled, in so far as they do not come in conflict with the nature of God's kingdom as revealed in the New Testament.

A careful examination of the pages of the following commentary will show in how far the writer regards the general principles underlying the Futurist System to be correct.

12. *The Numerals of the Apocalypse.* The study of the *numbers* used in Scupture is not as dry a field as most people imagine. Mahan, who has so fully discussed the numerals of Scripture, says:[1] "God is indeed a wonderful Numberer. There is no such thing as chance in God's world—no such thing as confusion. Everything is numbered, everything is in its place, everything comes up in its time and season. Upon nature and upon history there is the stamp of symmetry and proportion.... The Bible informs us that our steps are numbered; that our days are numbered; that the hairs of our head are all numbered; nay, that God numbereth the drops of rain; that the righteous are numbered to life; that the wicked are numbered to the sword; that earthly kingdoms are numbered; and, in short, that there is nothing without number, save only 'His understanding,' of which the Psalmist declares 'there is no number.'" In the same spirit Lee[2] remarks: "Number and proportion are essential and necessary attributes of the Kosmos; and God, as a God of order, has arranged each several province of Creation—even to the minutest particular ('the very hairs of your head are all numbered,' Matt. 10:30)—according to definite numerical relations (Ps. 147:4; Isa. 40:26). Not only where the thought transcends the limits of man's understanding (Gen. 13:16;

xliii

Jer. 33:22; Rev. 7:9), but also in the province of human freedom (Job 14:16; Ps. 56:8), all has been divinely disposed according to number and proportion, order and design; and should such dispositions not admit of being computed by human faculties, or should God reveal them in mystery, they are nevertheless capable of being represented not only by means of ideal types and symbols, but also by numerical relations.... Numbers, like words, are but the signs of ideas; and if we can ascertain the idea corresponding to a particular sign, we have the meaning of that sign. It is this underlying idea alone on which the numerical symbolism of Scripture depends." The symbolical meaning of numbers in Scripture deserves more study and attention than it has received in recent years. Inexplicable as it may seem, certain numerals in Scripture occur so often in connection with certain classes of ideas, that we are naturally led to associate the one with the other. This is especially true of the numbers three, seven, eight, twelve, forty, and seventy.

Certain numerals, in their most literal application, symbolize certain great principles, and their meanings have come down to us with a most remarkable unanimity of opinion.

1. *One* is in all languages the synonym of unity.

2. *Two* is the number of certainty or assurance (Deut. 17:6; 19:15; John 8:17). There were *two* tables of Commandments (Ex. 32:15); *two* Testaments; the Apostles and the Seventy were sent forth "by two and two" (Mark 6:7; Luke 10:1); there are *two* witnesses, *two* olive trees, *two* candlesticks (Rev. 11:3; Zech. 4:3).

3. *Three* is the number of *essential* perfection. It is "the numerical 'signature' of the Divine Being, and of all that stands in any real relation to God. It is but natural, indeed,

that the essential character of the *Triune God*, as He has revealed Himself, should be impressed upon His works. All, in short, in which the Divine completes itself has the stamp of *three*. There are *three* dimensions of space; time is *past, present, future;* the universe offers to the view, *sky, earth*, and *sea;* ... the benediction is *three*-fold (Num. 6:24–26); and above all, there is the *thrice Holy* of Isa. 6:3" (Lee).

4. *Four* is the number of the *Cosmos*, the world in its universality and order. Lee: "*Four* is the 'signature' of Nature, of the created, of the world as a *Cosmos*, as the revelation of God so far as Nature can reveal Him." We have the *four* rivers of Paradise (Gen. 2:10); the *four* corners of the earth (Isa. 11:12; Ezek. 7:2; Rev. 7:2; 20:8); the *four* winds (Dan. 7:2; Zech. 2:6; Matt. 24:31; Rev. 7:2); the *four* living creatures (Rev. 4:6, 8; 5:6; 6:1; 7:11, etc.); the *four* Gospels, etc.;

5. *Six* is the number of earthly imperfection or secular completeness. Its concentrated power is seen in 666,—six units, six tens, and six hundreds,—the number of Antichrist (Rev. 13:18)—of the earthly as opposed to the divine power.

6. *Seven* is the number of spiritual perfection. As *three* and *four* make *seven*, this number is spoken of as "the note of union between God and the world" (Lee). "It is the number of religion, the 'signature' of Salvation, Blessing, Peace, Perfection" (Lee). Its root idea is that of *rest*, or Sabbath, for "on the seventh day God finished his work which he had made" (Gen. 2:2). *Seven* is the sacred number of the Old as well as of the New Testament. Genesis begins with *seven* days, and the Apocalypse ends with a series of *sevens*. We have *seven* days of creation, *seven* days of the week, *seven* years of plenty and famine; *seven* is the keynote of all the festivals and of sacrifice; on the *seventh* day Jericho was encompassed

xlv

seven times; *seven* is the number of clean beasts (Gen. 7:2, 3) taken into the Ark, and *seven* times was Naaman to wash in the Jordan (2 Kings 5:10),—in fact, the number occurs continually throughout the whole Old Testament. Even more significant is its usage in the New Testament, above all in the Apocalypse,—witness the *seven* Spirits before the throne, the *seven* churches, the *seven* candlesticks, the *seven* angels, the *seven* seals, the *seven* trumpets, the *seven* bowls, and so throughout.

Thus we see that the number *seven* is manifestly a favorite in Scripture, being impressed with the seal of sanctity as the symbol of everything closely connected with God, and there can be no question that the number is associated with the idea of *the spiritual as* distinguished from the worldly.

7. The *half of seven* is used in the O. T. to signify a time of tribulation. It appears in various forms both in the Old and New Testament. The famine in Elijah's time lasted three and a half years (1 Kings 17:1; Luke 4:25; James 5:17); the same period is the "time and times, and half a time" of Dan. 7:25 and Dan. 12:7; "the half of the week" referred to in Dan. 9:27. This same period of time appears in Revelation under the form of forty-two months (Rev. 11:2; 13:5), or 1,260 days (Rev. 11:3; 12:6), or "a time and times, and half a time" (Rev. 12:14). The *two witnesses* also lay dead "three days and a half" (Rev. 12:9, 11). This *broken number* is therefore a symbol of great significance, and has been taken to be the "signature" of the broken covenant or of suffering and disaster.

8. *Eight* is the number of renewal, regeneration, and resurrection. The *eighth* day is the day of circumcision; it is the great day of the Feast of Tabernacles, which is the type of the Incarnation; it is, above all, the day of the resurrection,

"the Lord's Day."

9. *Ten* is the symbolical representation of absolute perfection and complete development whether referred to God or to the world. It is the "signature" of a complete and perfect whole. *Ten* is the number of the Commandments; the Holy of Holies was a cube, each side being of ten cubits; *ten* times *ten*, or 100, is the number of God's Flock (Luke 15:4, 7); and the cube of *ten*, or 1,000, is the length of the reign of the saints (Rev. 20:4). The *tenth* generation means "for ever" (compare Deut. 23:3 with Neh. 13:1). *Ten* is also the number of worldly completion, symbolizing perfect power. The *ten* Egyptian plagues symbolized the complete outpouring of divine wrath; the fourth beast of Daniel had *ten* horns (Dan. 7:7, 24); the Red Dragon of the Apocalypse has *ten* horns (Rev. 12:3), as well as the First Beast or Antichrist (Rev. 13:1).

10. *Twelve* is emphatically the number referring to the kingdom of God, the "signature "of God (*three*) multiplied by the "signature "of the world (*four*). Lee holds that while *seven* is the sacred number of Scripture, *twelve* is the number of the Covenant People in whose midst God dwells, and with whom He has entered into Covenant relations. *Twelve* are the tribes of Israel: there were twice *twelve* courses of the priests; four times *twelve* cities of the Levites; *twelve* is the number of the Apostles; twice *twelve* is the number of the Elders who represent the Redeemed Church; the woman of Rev. 12:1 had a crown of twelve *stars* on her head; the New Jerusalem has *twelve* gates (Rev. 21:12), the wall of the city has *twelve* foundations (21:14), and the tree of life bears *twelve* names of fruits (22:2).

13. *The Year-Day Theory of Interpretation.* It is a favorite theory with many commentators, especially of the Contin-

uous Historical School, that in the predictions of Daniel and of St. John each *day* represents a natural *year*. This view has been supported by adducing as proof Num. 14:34 and Ezek. 4:4–6, where the expression "each day for a year" occurs. But these passages do not in any way apply, for they both occur in plain narrative and are not in any way prophetical, although the last passage is found in a prophetical book. Those who hold this view add as their final argument the prediction of the *seventy weeks* in Dan. 9:24–27, which evidently indicates seventy *weeks* of years, or 490 years,—"each day for a year." But Lee correctly calls attention to the fact that the literal rendering is seventy *sevens*, and that the exact meaning of this, whether it denotes "a seven (of days)," or "a seven (of years)," or "a seven (of some other period of time)," must be determined by the context alone. Keil on Dan. 9:24 remarks: "Hofmann and Kliefoth are in the right when they maintain that *sevens* does not recessarily mean *year-weeks*, but an intentionally indefinite designation of a period of time measured by the number seven, whose chronological duration must be determined on other grounds." The whole context, however, of Dan. 9:24 seems to point to the interpretation of seventy *sevens* (of years). When Daniel wishes to speak of "a seven of days" he does so in language which cannot be mistaken (Dan. 10:2, 3). There is therefore no reason whatever why we should accept the year-day theory with reference to the numbers used in the Apocalypse, and though all these numbers may have a symbolical meaning, it is perfectly biblical to regard the 1,260 days as literal days, the 42 monthe as literal months, the 3½ years as literal years, and the 1,000 years as literal years, though we by no means contend that such is necessarily the

xlviii

true interpretation. The saying of Christ is still true, "It is not for us to know times or seasons which the Father hath appointed by his own authority" (Acts 1:7). The more one studies the Apocalypse, and sees the vast divergencies of views in the interpretation of the book, the less inclined is one to be over positive about things. The Apocalypse is a very deep book. What Mahan affirms of the Bible as a whole we would in a special sense confess of the Apocalypse: "Though there are those who imagine they can touch bottom in it, yet it may be in such cases that they are really like children sporting on the sands. It is easy to sound the sea where the sea and shore meet; but if we launch farther out; if we venture forth as it were into the silence of the deep; if we reach that point where the horizon bends around us in a circle of infinity, where a whole heaven above smiles upon a whole heaven beneath, then we feel it is high time to put up our fathoming lines, and, confessing our ignorance, to be content with adoration" (*Palmoni*, p. 128).

14. *Select Literature.* The literature on the Apocalypse and allied topics is of immense extent. The mere list of special works on this book given in Darling's *Cyclopædia Bibliographica*, published in 1859, covers 52 columns, and if we include the list referring to special topics connected with the book, it covers over 70 columns. It will be our aim to designate a few books, limiting the number to 25, which we regard as most helpful in the study of the Apocalypse. In this list all the different schools of interpretation will be represented by leading authorities, and a brief characterization of each work named will be given.

1. Alford, Henry. *The Greek Testament*: with a critically revised text, a digest of various readings; marginal references

to verbal and idiomatic usage; prolegomena; and a critical and exegetical Commentary. For the use of theological students and ministers. Four vols. New edition. Boston, 1880.

The commentary on Revelation with the prolegomena covers 270 pages of the fourth volume. Alford is always judicious, biblical, and scholarly, and makes large use of German authorities. He maintains that some of the prophecies are already fulfilled, some are now fulfilling, and others await their fulfilment in the yet unknown future. In the main he represents the Continuous Historical School, but in many points he disagrees with them. The author was the Apostle and Evangelist St. John, and he wrote the book at the close of the reign of Domitian, about the year 95 or 96 A. D. Alford accepts literally the first resurrection and the millennial reign. "I have again and again raised my earnest protest against evading the plain sense of words, and spiritualizing in the midst of plain declarations of fact. That the Lord will come in person to this our earth; that His risen elect will reign here with Him and judge; that during that blessed reign the power of evil will be bound, and the glorious prophecies of peace and truth on earth find their accomplishment:—this is my firm persuasion, and not mine alone, but that of multitudes of Christ's waiting people, as it was that of His primitive Apostolic Church, before controversy blinded the eyes of the Fathers to the light of prophecy." He offers no explanation of the two witnesses, nor any solution of those periods of time, so remarkably pervaded by the half of the mystic seven. "I have never seen it proved, or even made probable, that we are to take a day for a year in apocalyptic prophecy; on the other hand, I have never seen it proved, or made probable, that such mystic periods are to be taken literally, a day for a day." He offers no solution of the prophetic number of the beast (Rev. 13:18): "Even while I print my note in favor of the *Lateinos* of Irenæus, I feel almost disposed to withdraw it. It is beyond question the best solution that has been given; but that it is not *the* solution, I have a persuasion amounting to certainty." The first beast represents the secular power antagonistic to the Church of Christ, and in the second beast he recognizes the sacerdotal persecuting power,—in all its forms, Pagan, Papal, and Protestant,—leagued with and the instrument of the secular. In the last chapters he takes almost the same position as the Futurists, interpreting the text in the main in a literal manner. His commentary is worthy of careful study, even if many of his interpretations cannot be accepted.

2. Auberlen, Carl August. *The Prophecies of Daniel and the Revelations of St. John*, viewed in their mutual relation. With an exposition of the principal passages. With an Appendix by Roos. Edinburgh, 1856.

This is not a commentary, but consists of a series of essays on topics, connected with the prophecies of Daniel and of St. John. The last 200 pages are devoted especially to the Revelation of John, and the discussion centres around the Two Beasts, the Woman, and the Millennium. He maintains that the book was written shortly before the destruction of Jerusalem, and that the Book of Daniel forms its basis. Its object is not to give a detailed description of Church history (in opposition to the church-historical view as represented by Bengel, Elliott, and Gaussen), but with Hofmann, Hengstenberg, and Ebrard, he maintains that its aim is to represent the great epochs and leading principal powers in the development of *the kingdom of God*, viewed in its relation to the world-kingdoms. In the main, Auberlen belongs to the Continuous Historical School, but with many divergencies of interpretation. The Woman of Rev. 12. is the congregation of God in its purity, the Church of believers of the Old and New Testaments; in Rev. 17. this woman has become the Great Harlot, the Apostate Church, unfaithful to her Lord; in 19:7 and 21:9, the woman is the transfigured, perfect Church, the bride of the Lamb, ready for the marriage feast. "Woman, harlot, bride, these are the three aspects of the Church.... The woman is the invisible Church; the harlot the visible Church. Both are the Church militant; whereas the Bride is the Church triumphant." We must carefully distinguish between Christ's coming to establish His kingdom of glory upon earth, and His coming to the final judgment; there will be a *personal* Antichrist; the millennial kingdom and the first resurrection are to be taken literally and as still future.

This able work, written from a strictly evangelical standpoint, ought to be carefully mastered by every student of the Apocalypse, and the book has exercised a deep and widespread influence throughout all theological circles.

3. Bengel, John Albert. *Gnomon of the New Testament.* Revised and edited by Rev. Andrew R. Fausset. Five vols. Edinburgh, 1860.

Bengel is a leading representative of the Continuous Historical School, to which belong such distinguished writers as Mede, Vitringa, Hengstenberg, Ebrard, Auberlen, Elliott, Gaussen, Wordsworth, Alford, Barnes, Lord, and Glasgow. In general, this view regards the Apocalypse as a prophetic compendium of Church History, and supposes that the exalted Saviour has revealed therein the chief events of all centuries of the Christian era, in detail, and with chronological accuracy. Bengel adopts the general Protestant interpretation in vogue since Luther's time, and the only new feature in his commentary is his definite chronological system, as he himself says: "I have nothing new except the definite durations of prophetic times." His chronological system lies at the basis of his whole theory, and became to him the key to his interpretation of the Apocalypse. The entire duration of the world from the creation to the final judgment is 7,777 years, and the millennial kingdom was to begin on June 18, 1836. He himself says: "Should the year 1836 pass without bringing remarkable changes, then there must be some great error in my system." The result has proved the existence of this error.

The chief importance of Bengel's system consists in this, that he brought to light again the primitive Christian doctrine of the millennial kingdom, which had been mis-apprehended for nearly fifteen centuries. He laid the foundation for a dogmatic development of eschatology, and his world-chronology assisted greatly in promoting the idea of an organic historical development of the kingdom of God.

4. Boyd Carpenter, W. *The Revelation of St. John the Divine.* Edited by Charles John Ellicott. London and New York.

This is the last volume of what is known as the *Handy Commentary* edited by Bishop Ellicott. Dr. Boyd Carpenter, Bishop of Ripon, is a good representative of the Spiritual School of interpretation. (See *Introduction*, p. xxv.) He says: "It is hard to believe, with the Preterist, that the counselling voice of prophecy should have spoken only of immediate dangers, and left the Church for fifteen centuries unwarned; or, with the Futurist, to believe that eighteen centuries of the eventful history of the Church are passed over in silence, and that the whole weight of inspired warning was reserved for the few closing years of the dispensation. Nor, on the other hand, can we be thoroughly satisfied with the Historical School, however ably and learnedly represented.... A mistake into which this system falls is that of bringing into prominence the idea of *time*.... We are not to look for any indications of *time* in the visions of the Apocalypse.... These carefully selected numbers, always bearing a relationship to one another, and so selected that a literal interpretation of them is almost precluded, are beyond doubt symbolical, and thus in harmony with the whole character of the book.... We are disposed to view the Apocalypse as the pictorial unfolding of great principles in constant conflict, though under various forms."

This little work of 280 pages is more helpful than some more pretentious volumes.

5. Currey, G. *The Revelation of St. John the Divine*.

This work covers about 150 pages of the second and last volume of the Commentary published on the New Testament by the Society for Promoting Christian Knowledge, London. On the whole, Dr. Currey belongs to the Continuous Historical School, but in many points he has brought out the teaching of the Apocalypse more clearly. The Seven Epistles predict in direct words the same future events which in the Visions are symbolically portrayed, and these Visions do not present a consecutive series of events, but each group extends to the end of time, the one following starting as it were afresh, going over the same ground in a different manner. We are to be on our guard against literal interpretations, which have misled so many expositors. The "short time" of 12:12 is the same as the 1, 260 days, or "three times and a half," reaching from the Ascension to the Second Advent. Brief as is this Commentary, we have always consulted it with profit.

6. De Burgh, W. *An Exposition of the Book of the Revelation.* Fifth edition. Dublin, 1857.

De Burgh is one of the best representatives of the Futurist School. The Seals are still in the future; in fact, the whole Apocalypse after the Epistles of the Seven Churches is solely occupied with the events of the Last Times. Israel is the literal Israel, the Temple is to be rebuilt, the periods of time are to be literally interpreted Dan. 9:27 refers to the time of Antichrist, and the duration of his power is seven years, half of which time Antichrist is in covenant with the Jews (Dan. 11:23, 32), and during the latter half turns against them. In our notes we will continually refer to the views of this commentator.

7. Duesterdieck, Friedrich. *Critical and Exegetical Handbook to the Revelation of John.* Translated from the third edition of the German, and edited, with Notes, by Henry E. Jacobs. New York, 1887.

Though Duesterdieck belongs to the Preterist School, and even denies that the Apostle John is the author of the Apocalypse, tracing it to the Presbyter John, still this work, on account of its exegetical faithfulness and clear summary of the history of interpretation, is one of the best commentaries that has ever appeared on this book,—and we say this, though we may not agree with him in most of his conclusions. He maintains that the Presbyter John wrote the work before the destruction of Jerusalem, and though the book is canonical, trustworthy, "and inspired," he thinks that the writer in some points evidently makes statements not warranted by the analogy of Scripture, and thus gives evidences of "natural limitation." We must confess our indebtedness to Duesterdieck on every page.

8. Ebrard, J. H. A. *Die Offenbarung Johannis.* (Vol. 7 of *Olshausen's Commentary.*) 1853.

Ebrard belongs to the same Continuous Historical School as Hofmann, Auberlen, and Hengstenberg, though some commentators (as Lee) would place all four under the Spiritual School, because they lay stress upon the spiritual application of the contents of the Apocalypse to all the various conditions of the kingdom of God on earth, during its successive struggles against the prince of this world. According to Ebrard the prophecies in the Apocalypse are divided into four divisions, differing both in contents and form. The first vision, including the first three chapters, represents Christ in His relations to the Church, the *Seven Churches* having a typical significance for the later Church; the second vision, that of the seven seals and the seven trumpets (chaps. 4–11), represents Christ in His relation, as Ruler of the world, to the powers of the world and nature; the third, the vision of the dragon and the beast out of the sea (chaps. 12–14), represents the relation between the godless, who stand under the prince of this world, and the Church of Christ (the seven heads of the beast are seven world-monarchies, the sixth head being the Roman world-power which corresponds with the beast that ascended out of the sea—the Papacy being the beast that ascends out of the earth, the false prophet); the fourth vision (chap. 15 to the end) containing the final development and consummation. Ebrard therefore refers the visions of the twelfth and thirteenth chapters to distinct events in Church history, but those of the seventeenth to the nineteenth chapters to events occurring in the times of Antichrist immediately preceding the Second Advent. The 42 months or 1,260 days of Rev. 11:2, 3; 12:6; and 13:5 are a mystical term for the entire period from the destruction of Jerusalem by Titus to the conversion and restoration of the Jewish nation, while the three and a half days of 11:9, 11, are identical with the three and a half times of Daniel (Dan. 7:25) and of Rev. 12:14, equivalent to three and a half years, the period of Antichrist, which forms the transition between the Church-historical period and the millennial kingdom. He regards the 1,000 years as a mystical number,—"when the whole long period, from the ascension of Christ to His Second Coming, is represented symbolically, as half a prophetic week of three and a half years, and the period of the visible existence of the kingdom of God upon earth as a thousand years; we have therein an indication that the period, after the result of the preceding ages has been gained, will be very much longer than the period of conflicts. The time when Christ's kingdom will exist on earth will be the true New Testament time, in the strict sense of the word; the present period of the oppressed and militant Church is of a duration which appears insignificant when compared with it."

The work of Ebrard is very suggestive, and his exposition may be characterized as an attempt to combine Hofmann's views with those of Elliott and Gaussen.

9. Elliott, E. B. *Horæ Apocalypticæ*. A Commentary on the Apocalypse critical and historical; including also an examination of the chief Prophecies of Daniel. Four vols.

Fifth edition. London, 1862.

Elliott has given us the most important work in English representing the Continuous Historical School. His historical interpretation ends with the pouring out of the *sixth* vial (Rev. 16:12). The remaining predictions belong to the future. The work is marked by its strong anti-papal character. Gaussen, in enumerating "the most successful commentators" on Revelation, mentions "Irenæus, Hippolytus, and Jerome; afterwards the Waldenses and Wiclifites; afterwards Mede, Vitringa, Newton, Cressener; and, in modern times, Faber, Cunninghame, Irving, Bickersteth, Birks, and *the excellent Elliott*." In the judgment of some Elliott shows a more remarkable knowledge of the history of the Saracens, of the development of the Papacy; and of the progress of the Lutheran Reformation in Germany, than of the teaching and meaning of the Apocalypse. In our summary of the history of interpretations we refer constantly to the views of Elliott, and every commentator on Revelation must master his work.

10. Gebhardt, Hermann. *The Doctrine of the Apocalypse, and its relation to the Doctrine of the Gospel and Epistles of John.* Edinburgh, 1878.

This work, though not strictly a commentary, is a most valuable contribution to the better understanding of the teaching of the Apocalypse, even if we cannot always accept the conclusions which he draws from the facts he presents. Gebhardt maintains that the Apostle John wrote the Apocalypse toward the end of the year 68, or early in 69 A. D. As he belongs to the Preterist School he refers the first beast, the Antichrist, to the Emperor Nero. The woman of 17:18 is the Rome of Nero's time. The work is worthy of careful study, as representing the evangelical Preterist view.

11. Hengstenberg, E. W. *The Revelation of St. John*, expounded for those who search the Scriptures. Translated from the original by Patrick Fairbairn. 2 vols. Edinburgh, 1851, 1852. Second German edition, 1862.

Hengstenberg belongs to the Continuous Historical School, and though in many points there is a general agreement between him and Auberlen, Hofmann, and Ebrard, in other points he diverges most widely from them. The Apostle John wrote the Apocalypse in the time of Domitian. The contents of the book contain prophecies relative to the world and Church history, most of which have already been fulfilled. The *First Beast* is the God-opposed world-power; the *Head wounded to death* is the Roman world-power; the great *Battle* of Rev. 19. denotes the Christianization of the Germanic nations; the millennial kingdom is past,—"the commencement of the millennial kingdom coincides with the Christianization of the Germanic nations, and *the millennium itself is (to speak roughly) identical with the German Empire, which lasted a thousand years."* Since the year 1848 we are living in the times of Gog and Magog, that "short space of time during which Satan is loosed again." Valuable and suggestive as this work of Hengstenberg is, it is marked in many cases by the most arbitrary exegesis.

12. Kliefoth, Theodor. *Christliche Eschatologie.* Leipsic, 1886.

Whatever Kliefoth has written on the Book of the Revelation and topics connected with it is worthy of the most careful study. His Commentary on the *Revelation of John* appeared in 1874, in three volumes, but his latest views are given in his *Christliche Eschatologie.* His Commentaries on

Daniel (1868), Ezekiel (1861–1865), and Zechariah (1862) must also be compared. A small abridgment of Kliefoth's *Christliche Eschatologie*, prepared by Witte, appeared in 1895, under the title *Lehre von den Letzten Dingen*.

13. Lange, John Peter. *The Revelation of John*. Enlarged and edited by E. R. Craven. New York, 1874.

This well-known work has considerable merit, though its value lies largely in its clear and condensed abstract of the different views of commentators. The notes added by the American editor greatly enhance the value of the book.

14. Lee, William. *The Revelation of St. John*. (In *Speaker's Commentary*.)

This work is found in Vol. IV. of the *Speaker's* or the *Bible Commentary*, covering pp. 405–844. It is noted for its excellent introduction and the clear synopsis of the various systems of interpretation. Although Lee, in the main, adopts the views of the Continuous Historical School, he prefers to class himself among those who adopt the *Spiritual System* of interpretation. He maintains that the Apocalypse must be understood throughout in a symbolical sense, and yet in the same breath calls attention to the fact that "the symbolical interpretation of this book has, from the earliest times, been carried to an extravagant excess, and to the most inconsistent conclusions." On the whole, this commentary takes the very highest rank among its class.

15. Luthardt, C. E. *Die Lehre von den letzten Dingen*. Third edition. Leipsic, 1885.

The last 85 pages of this work contains a translation and a brief commentary upon the Book of the Revelation. Luthardt is a Futurist, and on the whole favors a literal interpretation. We often refer to him in our notes.

16. Maitland, Charles. *The Apostles' School of Prophetic Interpretation*. With its history down to the present time. London, 1849.

Though not a commentary this work very ably presents the fundamental principles underlying the Futurist System. Maitland maintains that we must accept, in the main, the teaching of the Early Church concerning the Apocalypse, because "there had been handed down to the ancients, side by side with the written word, an unwritten explanation of the leading prophecies contained in it." With the primitive writers he holds that when a symbol is accompanied by an inspired explanation, that explanation embodies its true and final meaning; he maintains that the prophetic style is never found to affect *the times,*—for from Genesis to Revelation there is no instance in which a prediction containing a set time has been fulfilled in any other measure of time; that a scrupulous adherence to the language of Scripture will be found our only safety; that the year-day theory involves a plain and obvious fallacy, for all the numerals of time in the Apocalypse are to be taken literally, a day for a day, and a year for a year.

17. Milligan, William. *Revelation*. Covering 161 pages of Vol. IV. of the *Popular Commentary on the New Testament*, edited by Philip Schaff. New York, 1883.

Dr. Milligan is also the author of *Lectures on the Apocalypse* (third ed., London, 1892) and *Discussions on the Apocalypse* (third ed., London, 1893), both of which books originally constituted his Baird Lectures on the *Revelation of St. John*, published in 1886. He also wrote the commentary on *Revelation* in the *Expositor's Bible* (London and New York. 1889). Dr. Milligan is the best representative of the Spiritual

System of interpretation, and all of his works are marked by sound scholarship and sober exegesis. Especially valuable are his *Lectures* and *Discussions on the Apocalypse*. We have never consulted his works without profit, though we may not be able to accept the great majority of his interpretations.

18. Plummer, A. *Revelation*. In the *Pulpit Commentary*.

This volume of 585 closely-printed pages contains the labors of seven students of the Apocalypse. Principal Randell writes the introduction and the exposition is mainly by Dr. Plummer. In the main the comments represent the Continuous Historical School. There is a greater harmony in the presentation of the views than one would naturally expect. The exposition is strictly exegetical, and the volume takes a high rank among commentaries of its class.

19. Sadler, M. F. *The Revelation of St. John the Divine*. With notes critical and practical. London, 1893.

The writer of this commentary represents the most evangelical wing of the Church of England. The Apostle John wrote the Apocalypse about 95 or 96 A. D., while on the isle of Patmos; the visions are not a continuous history of the Church, but the final consummation is described six or seven times. He utterly rejects the Preterist interpretation. He regards Elliott's *Horæ Apocalypticæ* the most elaborate and exhaustive exposition of the Continuous Historical scheme, and he adds: "I have constantly referred to this work, giving specimens of its (I really must say) outrageous expositions to show the reader how little reliable a system can be which has to resort to such expedients to maintain its continuity." He cannot however adopt the view of the Futurists, but thinks "the present time in which we live must be under the opening of the seals." According to him all the horse riders under the seals run together; "if the effects of the fifth angel-trumpet be the rise and progress of Islamism, and the sixth the rise and progress of the Turkish power, then this may be taking place now and a large portion of mankind may be affected by it;" "if the two *beasts* of chap. 13. be the fierce and ferocious world-power, and the milder and more cultured world-power of Bishop Boyd Carpenter and others, then of course the warfare is going on now, and we are living in it;" he is uncertain about the pouring out of the vials,—"if they are synchronous they immediately precede the Second Coming;" "with respect to the vision of what is called the millennium, in chap. 20, Christ has certainly reigned ever since *all things were put under his feet at* His Ascension. He has reigned in order to discipline His elect, that they may be ready for Him when He comes at the last; and His saints may have reigned under Him, not visibly, but effectually—effectually for the purposes for which He has ordained their reign."

20. Simcox, William Henry. *The Ravelation of St. John the Divine*. With Notes and Introduction. Cambridge, 1890.

The volume belongs to the Cambridge Bible for Schools and Colleges. Simcox has also written the notes on *Revelation* in the Cambridge *Greek Testament* for Schools and Colleges, the Introduction and Appendixes, covering over 90 pages, being virtually the same in both editions. He accepts the early date of the Apocalypse, and tries to unite the Preterist and the Futurist schemes of interpretation. He thinks that the Apocalypse "was written *specially* for the Church of the Apostles' own age, and for the Church of the last age of all: we need not therefore expect to find any intermediate age of affliction, or any intermediate enemy of the truth, indicated with such individualizing detail as Nero and his persecution on the one hand, or Antichrist and his on the other." There was an imperfect and inadequate fulfilment of the prophecies of Antichrist in this book in the persons of Nero and Domitian, but we must look for a more complete fulfilment at the last times. "We may thus recognize an element of truth in the two rival schemes of interpretation commonly called the *preterist* and the *futurist*—that which sees in the Revelation only a prediction or forecast of events near the Seer's own time, and now past, and that which sees a prediction of events wholly or almost wholly future, and only to be fulfilled in the few last years of the world's existence.... Revelation may be regarded as a picture of the persecution of the Church, 'in type' by such emperors as Nero and Domitian, 'in truth' by the Antichrist of the last days, and a prophecy of Christ's victory over both enemies, the type and the antitype." The work, small as it is, is a valuable contribution to the literature of the Apocalypse.

21. Seiss, J. A. *The Apocalypse.* A series of special Lectures on the Revelation of Jesus Christ. With a Revised Text. 3 vols. Phila., 1869–1880.

These fifty-two lectures of Dr. Seiss are strictly exegetical, models of what expository lectures ought to be, and the ablest presentation in a popular form of the view in general advocated by the Futurist School. The Seven Epistles refer to the *present Church Period*, extending from John's time to the Rapture of the Saints, which is liable to occur at any time. The occurrence of this event is indicated at the beginning of the fourth chapter. Then comes *the great Judgment Period*, which embraces all the events connected with the opening of the seven Seals, the sounding of the seven Trumpets, and the pouring out of the seven Bowls of Wrath, as contained in chapters 4–19. The length of time covered by this period is at least 40 years, most likely 70 years, if not more. The termination of this period is the visible manifestation of Christ, with His glorified Saints, for the destruction of Antichrist and his armies, and the binding and confinement of Satan. Then comes *the great Millennial Period*, the thousand years during which Satan is bound. It dates from the destruction of the Antichrist. It is the following up of the victory of the battle of the Great Day, resulting in the enthronement of all the glorified saints with their Lord in the invincible rulership of the world, which rule never terminates, but finally opens out into an eternal reign over the redeemed and renewed earth. This Millennial Period ends with the loosing of Satan for a brief space, his leading astray of certain remote peoples who think to throw off the dominion of Christ and His glorified Saints, the quick destruction of these rebels by fire from heaven, the consignment of Satan to his final perdition, the recall of all the unsanctified dead before the great white throne for their final sentence, and the complete and everlasting removal of all sin, all death, and all curse from the face of the earth. *The Eternal State* immediately follows the Millennial Period. It begins with the completion of the new heavens and earth, the coming of the heavenly Jerusalem into its place, and the final establishment of Christ and His glorified ones in their everlasting dominion over the redeemed world and its populations. Thenceforward everything proceeds in undisturbed and ever-augmented blessedness, world without end.

22. Todd, J. H. *Six Discourses on the Prophecies relating to*

Antichrist, in the Apocalypse of St. John. Preached before the University of Dublin, at the Donnellan Lecture, 1841. Dublin, 1846.

Todd represents the Futurist School. The revelations made at the opening of each seal all portray the circumstances of our Lord's Second Coming, representing that event under various aspects. The Trumpets announce judgments which are to be regarded as *literal* visitations which will usher in the great tribulation of the last times. Jerusalem shall be inhabited again by the Jews, the Temple rebuilt, the duration of Antichrist's dominion shall be 1,260 days, during which time two literal witnesses are to prophesy. The seven Bowls of wrath do not bring us to the "great day of final account, but to the fall of Babylon and the consequences of that event which are immediately to usher in the Day of Christ's Coming." Babylon is Rome, but not Rome as it is now, but Rome as it shall be in that future time to which the prophecy refers.

23. Vaughan, C. J. *Lectures on the Revelation of St. John*. Fifth edition. London, 1882.

This volume contains a series of 38 Lectures delivered in the years 1861 and 1862 in the Parish Church of Doncaster, England. In general Dean Vaughan represents the Continuous Historical School, though he may better be classed as belonging to the Spiritual School. He follows largely in the footsteps of Alford and Hengstenberg, though with many divergencies of intrepretation. Of Alford's *Commentary on Revelation* Vaughan remarks: "It has appeared to me that this part of Dean Alford's elaborate work on the Greek Testament is the most valuable and instructive of his contributions to the sacred literature of our age." He further says: "The human author to whom I owe most in regard to this labor—without whom indeed I should probably not have undertaken it—is Hengstenberg. To him I owe much, very much, both of the general and of the particular treatment here adopted. His very language has now and then, I doubt not, incorporated itself unawares in mine." These lectures are expository and models of their kind.

24. Weiss, Bernhard. *Die Johannes-Apokalypse*. Textkritische Untersuchungen und Textherstellung. Leipsic, 1891.

This is a very valuable contribution to the Textual Criticism of the Apocalypse, and the first 156 pages are devoted to a critical discussion of the variations of the three representatives of the oldest Text (Codex Sinaiticus, A, C), and of the two best representatives among the Uncials of the later Text (P, Q). Then follows the emended Greek Text, accompanied with brief, but very valuable notes, covering pages 157–225. Weiss as a Preterist maintains that the Apocalypse was manifestly written before the destruction of Jerusalem, and that it mainly refers to that event.

25. Williams, Isaac. *The Apocalypse, with Notes and Reflections*. New edition. London, 1889.

It is difficult to decide to what class the devout Williams belongs, but it is probably best to place him among the Spiritual School of Interpreters, though at times he favors the Continuous Historical method of interpretation, and at other times the Futurist. His work is noted for its mystical and symbolical interpretations, which are constantly brought forward, from the ancient commentators, especially Victorinus, Tichonius, Primasius, Andreas, Arethas, Œcumenius, Bede, and Berengaudus. For a devotional commentary we know of no better work on the Apocalypse. It is biblical, spiritual, and deeply mystical in its tendencies.

26. Wordsworth, Christopher. *The New Testament in the Original Greek*. With Introductions and Notes. New edition. Two vols. London, 1877.

The Commentary on Revelation covers the last 130 pages of the second volume. He also is the author of *Lectures on the Apocalypse*, being the Hulsean Lectures for 1848 (third London edition, 1852; second London edition reprinted, Phila., 1852), and *The Greek Text of the Apocalypse* from the most ancient Manuscripts, London, 1849. Wordsworth belongs to the Continuous Historical School. The Apocalypse was written by St. John on the isle of Patmos about 95 A. D. The Seals represent a prophetic view of the History of the Christian Church, from the first Advent of Christ to the end of the world; the six Trumpets represent judgments of God warning men to prepare for the sounding of the *Seventh Trumpet*, which will convene them to the General Judgment at the Last Day (the *first* Trumpet sounded in the fourth century, the *second* represents the incursions of the Barbarians, the *third* the heresies of the fifth century, the *fourth* the apostasies and defections in the seventh, the *fifth* Mohammedanism, etc.); the First Beast is the *Roman Papal Power*, the Second Beast represents teachers of unsound doctrine, the Papal clergy and Roman Hierarchy. The whole exposition is marked by a strong anti-papal tendency, and is one of the best productions of the Continuous Historical School. In our notes we will constantly refer to the views of Wordsworth.

For some of these works we might have substituted others, but each commentary has been selected for some special reason. It does not follow because we do not include in this list the works of Barnes, Beck, Birks, Bisping, Bleek, Blunt, Brown, Burger, Cowles, Cumming, Darby, Dennett, Desprez, De Wette, Fuller, Garland, Glasgow, Godet, Grant, Hofmann, Huntingford, Irving, Kellogg, Kelly, Lincoln, Low, Luecke, Maurice, Mede, Murphy, Newton, Pember, Plumptre, Pond, Rinck, Scott, Snell, Terry, Tregelles, Trench, Trotter, West, Whedon, and Zuellig, that these have no merit. Helpful as many of these are, the student will find the best representatives of each school of interpretation included in the list given.

15. *Analysis of the Apocalypse.* Many commentators see a seven-fold structure in the book. According to Hengstenberg the Book of Revelation naturally divides itself into Seven groups of Visions.

1. The Seven Epistles (2, 3).

2. The Seven Seals (4–8:1).

3. The Seven Trumpets (8:2–11.).

4. Satan and his subordinates in conflict with the Church (12–14.).

5. The Seven Vials (15, 16).

6. The Overthrow of Satan and his subordinates (17–20).

7. The Glories and the Happiness of Heaven (21, 22).

The Analysis of Farrar is in substance the same, save that the headings of 4, 6, and 7 are changed as follows:

4. The Seven Mystic Figures (12–14).

(1) The Sun-clothed Woman (12:1–6).

(2) The Red Dragon (12:7–12).

(3) The Man-child (12:13–17).

(4) The First Beast from the Sea (13:1–10).

(5) The Second Beast from the Land (13:11–18).

(6) The Lamb on Mount Zion (14:1–13).

(7) The Son of Man on the Cloud (14:14–20).

6. The Doom of the Foes of Christ (17–20.).

7. The Blessed Consummation (21, 22).

We believe that the following analysis will bring out very clearly the scope and aim of the Book.

I. *The Prologue* (1:1–20).

1. The Inscription (1:1–3).

2. The Salutation (1:4–8).

3. The Place and Time of the Vision (1:9–11).

4. The Vision of the Son of Man (1:12–16).

5. The Apostle's Commission (1:17–20).

II. *The Epistles to the Seven Churches* (2:1–3:22).

6. The Epistle to the Church in Ephesus (2:1–7).

7. The Epistle to the Church in Smyrna (2:8–11).

8. The Epistle to the Church in Pergamum (2:12–17).

9. The Epistle to the Church in Thyatira (2:18–29).

10. The Epistle to the Church in Sardis (3:1–6).

11. The Epistle to the Church in Philadelphia (3:7–13).

12. The Epistle to the Church in Laodicea (3:14–22).

III. *The Vision of God on His Heavenly Throne* (4:1–5:14).

13. The Vision of the Divine Majesty (4:1–8).

14. The Unceasing Hymn of Praise (4:9–11).

15. The Book with Seven Seals (5:1–7).

16. The Adoration of the Lamb (5:8–14).

IV. *The Opening of the Seven Seals* (6:1–8:1).

17. The Opening of the First Seal (6:1, 2).

18. The Opening of the Second Seal (6:3, 4).

19. The Opening of the Third Seal (6:5, 6).

20. The Opening of the Fourth Seal (6:7, 8).

21. The Opening of the Fifth Seal (6:9–11).

22. The Opening of the Sixth Seal (6:12–17).

67. Symbolic Proclamation of Babylon's Fall (18:21–24).

XII. *The Vision of the Second Advent* (19:1–21).

68. The Song of Triumph in Heaven (19:1–8).

69. The Blessedness of those bidden to the Marriage Supper of the Lamb (19:9).

70. The Angel forbids John to worship him (19:10).

71. The Vision of the Second Advent (19:11–16).

72. The Victory over the Beast and the False Prophet (19:17–21).

XIII. *The Events Culminating in the Final Consummation* (20:1–15).

73. The Binding of Satan (20:1–3).

74. The Millennial Kingdom of Christ (20:4–6).

75. The Final Victory over Satan (20:7–10).

76. The Final Judgment of the Wicked (20:11–15).

XIV. *The New Heavens and the New Earth* (21:1–22:5).

77. The Vision of the New Heavens and the New Earth (21:1–8).

78. The Vision of the New Jerusalem (21:9–27).

79. The Paradise of God (22:1–5).

XV. *The Epilogue* (22:6–21).

80. An Assurance of the Truth of the Apocalypse (22:6, 7).

81. The Testimony of John Himself (22:8, 9).

82. The Final Message of the Angel (22:10, 11).

83. The Testimony of Jesus (22:12–17).

84. Conclusion (22:18–21).

This analysis and the interpretation which we have been led to adopt shows that with Hengstenberg, Farrar, and others, we divide the Apocalypse into Seven Groups of Visions, of which the five following the Seven Epistles, and preceding the Final Consummation, by a process of *repetition* (or recapitulation) and amplification, five times give us a description of the times of Antichrist and the Second Coming of Christ, or blended with it a description of the Final Consummation. These various groups of Visions may therefore be arranged as follows:

1. The Visions of the Seven Epistles (1–3).
2. The Visions of the Seven Seals (4–8:1).
3. The Visions of the Seven Trumpets (8:2–11:18).
4. The Visions culminating in the Harvest and Vintage (12–14).
5. The Visions of the Seven Bowls of Wrath (15, 16).
6. The Visions of the Doom of the Foes of Christ (17–20).
7. The Visions of the New Heavens and New Earth (21, 22).

* * *

[1] Dionysius, in the spirit of modern Higher and Literary Criticism, utterly ignored the external and ecclesiastical testimony for the Apostolic authorship, and subjected the book to severe criticism, and as he assumed the genuineness of the Gospel and the First Epistle of John, he questioned the genuineness and authorship of the Apocalypse on account of its divergence from both these writings in spirit and in style.

[2] For the presentation of the evidence in detail, see Westcott, *On the Canon of the N. T.* Index II. Fifth ed., 1881. Luecke, Alford, and Lee discuss the evidence most fully in their Commentaries.

[1] So Keim, Volkmar, Scholten, Holtzmann, Pfleiderer,

Harnack, and the advanced school of negative critics.

[2] So Baur, Schwegler, Zeller, Hilgenfeld, Davidson, Edwin A. Abbott, and the Tuebingen School in general.

[3] Schleiermacher, Luecke, Credner, De Wette, Bleek, Ewald, Neander, Mangold, and Duesterdieck assign the Apocalypse to the doubtful and mysterious "John the Presbyter."

[1] Davidson, *Introduction to the N. T.*, vol. 3, pp. 561–584.

[2] *Introduction to the Gospel of John*, p. 50, in *Bible Commentary*.

[3] *Commentary on Revelation*, pp. 454, 455.

[4] *The Doctrine of the Apocalypse*, and its Relation to the Doctrine of the Gospel and Epistles of John. Edinburgh, 1878.

[1] In his *Discussions on the Apocalypse*, pp. 180–266. London, 1893.

[2] See *Presbyterian Review*, April, 1884.

[3] See *Discussions on the Apocalypse*, pp. 27–74, 1893. Simcox in his *Commentary on Revelation* (Cambridge Bible for Schools and Colleges), pp. 155–174, gives a somewhat too appreciative notice of the Vischer-Harnack theory "of the supposed Jewish origin of the Revelation of St. John." The same Excursus, with a few additions, is also republished in Simcox's Commentary on the Greek Text of the *Revelation*.

[1] So Neander, Gieseler, Luecke, Ewald, De Wette, Reuss, Duesterdieck, Renan, Weiss, Auberlen, Stier, Gebhardt, Davidson, Cowles, Bishop Lightfoot, Stanley, Schaff, Westcott, Farrar, Simcox, and others.

[2] So the great majority of the older commentators, and among moderns, Elliott, Alford, Hengstenberg, Ebrard, Lange, Hofmann, Godet, Lee, Van Oosterzee, Sadler,

Wordsworth, Milligan, Warfield, David Brown, and others.

[1] *Discussions on the Apocalypse*, pp. 186, 192, 196.

[2] *Introduction*, p. 220.

[1] The full evidence is given by Lee, Milligan, and others.

[1] Third edition. London, 1892.

[2] In his *Structure of the Apocalypse*, pp. 28, 29. New York, 1891.

[1] See *Lectures on the Apocalypse*, pp. 146–192.

[2] Isaac Williams and Dean Vaughan also take a spiritual view of the whole book.

[1] *Lectures on the Apocalypse*, p. 127.

[1] See M. Mahan's *Palmoni*; or the Numerals of Scripture. A Proof of Inspiration, p. 134. Also his *Mystic Numbers:* A key to Chronology. A Test of Inspiration. Both works are found in the second volume of his collected works. New York, 1875.

[2] See the *Introduction* to his Commentary.

1

Revelation 1

1. The Inscription (1:1–3)

The first three verses may be regarded as the superscription to the whole book, setting forth the prophetic character of the Apocalypse and commending it to the Church. In this Preface we have a statement (1) from whom this Revelation comes (1:1), (2) of the fidelity with which it is reported (1:2), and (3) of the blessing which follows a faithful reception of the same (1:3).

1. The Revelation of Jesus Christ, which God gave him to shew unto his servants, *even* the things which must shortly come to pass: and he sent and signified *it* by his angel unto his servant John.

The Revelation. The Greek work is *Apocalypse*, whence the name so often given to this book. This word is frequently used in the N. T. and means the uncovering or unveiling of what was before concealed. Nothing is gained by those interpreters who wrongly insist that "the Revelation of

Jesus Christ, which God gave him," means "the appearing of Christ," His Second Advent, His *Parousia*, for this is the great theme of the whole book, and it is concerning this that this Revelation is made *by* Jesus Christ through an angel unto John. **Of Jesus Christ.** It is Jesus Christ, the risen and ascended Lord, who makes this revelation to John, for it is Christ's distinctive office as a prophet to make known to the Church the mysteries of God (Matt. 11:27). **Which God gave him.** At the time when Christ ascended on high, and according to His human nature was exalted at the right hand of God,—when the Father "made him to sit at his right hand in the heavenly places, far above all rule, and authority, and power, and dominion, ... and put all things in subjection under his feet, and gave him to be head over all things to the church" (Eph. 1:21, 22). This does not in any way conflict with Christ's statement as recorded in Matt. 24:36; Mark 13:32. It was in His state of humiliation, speaking as a mere man, that Christ tells us that no one knoweth the day and the hour of the Second Coming of the Son of man, "not even the angels of heaven, neither the Son" (according to His human nature in the state of humiliation), "but the Father only." But it is different now in His state of exaltation, for Christ has now entered upon the full use of all the divine attributes, so that now His human nature forever participates in the Omniscience of His divine nature. The Father as the First Person of the Trinity is forever the fountain of all knowledge, grace, and glory, but what the Father has He gives to the Son (John 5:26, 27). We are not to suppose that the Son in His exalted and glorified condition did not know the things here revealed, and that the Father by a special act had to make them known to His Son. **To shew unto his servants.**

2

Most probably *his* refers to Jesus Christ, not to God. In this case *servants* would denote all Christians, and not, as some maintain, the *prophets* only. **Even the things.** It is best to omit *even* as in the margin of R. V., making this clause the direct object of *to shew*. The R. V. in the text regards this clause as a further description of the "Revelation which God gave," but incorrectly. **Which must shortly come to pass.** The two Greek words translated *shortly* have been the cause of much discussion. The Preterists, who maintain that the predictions of this whole book were fulfilled within a comparatively short time after the Apostle wrote, insist that their interpretation is already corroborated here—for it is distinctly stated that these things must *shortly*, i. e. before long, *come to pass*. Many of the Historical School, who look upon the series of visions as embodying a continuous history from the Ascension to the Second Advent, accepting this translation *shortly*, interpret, "before long," i. e. as time is computed by God understood in the light of 2 Pet. 3:8,—not that the events are close at hand,—and reference is made to the same Greek words translated *speedily* in Luke 18:8, where the context shows that long delay is implied. Some of the Historical Interpreters and most of the Futurists insist that we should translate *quickly*, i. e. swiftly, as referring to the rapidity with which the events prophesied, at the appointed time, shall come to pass. Alford is probably right when he observes "that these words cannot with any fairness be used as furnishing a guide to the interpretation of the prophecy. They are far rather to be regarded as a prophetic formula, … used in order to teach us how short our time, and the time of this our world, is." **He sent.** That is, Jesus Christ sent. **And signified it.** Not *it*, the Revelation, but better, as in the

3

margin of the R. V., *them*, i. e. "the things which must shortly come to pass." Milligan: "The word *signified* must be allowed to stand in all its own obsolute solemnity and force. It is by no means improbable that in this word there is special reference to 'signs,' to the figures which are to be used in the book, and which need to be interpreted. The word may indicate not only prophetic intimation (John 12:33; 18:32; 21:19; Acts 11:28), but the manner in which such intimation was usual among the prophets (see especially Ezekiel and Zechariah), that is, by 'signs,' significant acts, and parabolic words." **By his angel.** Just as the law was given "through angels," by the hand of Moses (Gal. 3:19), and as Daniel and Zechariah received interpretations of their visions through angels (Dan. 8:16; 9:21; 10:11, etc.; Zech. 1:19; etc.), so this whole revelation was given to John through mediation, though only here and there does an angel actually appear as the interpreting angel (17:1, 7; 19:9; 21:9; etc.), and it is difficult to decide whether one particular angel acts as interpreter, or whether different angels act as spokesmen throughout the book. **Unto his servant John.** The Apostle John who wrote this prophecy. See *Introduction*.

2. Who bare witness of the word of God, and of the testimony of Jesus Christ, *even* of all things that he saw.

John does not here refer to his Gospel, as some maintain, but he uses "the epistolary aorist," in the sense "who bears witness," in this present work. John here gives us a guarantee of the faithfulness with which this revelation made to him has been recorded. This prophecy is called **the word of God,** because it proceeds from God, and **the testimony of Jesus Christ,** because He as "a faithful witness" (1:5; 3:14) made it known to John. Wordsworth: "St. John thus intimates that

4

what he writes in the Apocalypse is not from *himself,* but from *God;* that it is not from any private imagination, but that it is the testimony of Christ; and that he writes *whatever he saw* in the visions of God."

3. Blessed is he that readeth, and they that hear the words of the prophecy, and keep the things which are written therein: for the time is at hand.

The Apostle pronounces a blessing upon two classes of persons: (1) upon the public reader in the church or congregation, whom he, regards faithful, and (2) upon those who hear and mind the things of this prophecy. Just as the Law and the Prophets had been read in the synagogue, so the Gospels and Epistles came to be read in the Churches generally, in the course of the second century. To **keep the things which are written** in this prophecy is to observe them in such a way that our practical conduct shall be governed by them. **He that readeth, and they that hear,** are only blessed if they mind "the several exhortations to repentance, faith, patience, obedience, prayer, watchfulness, stedfastness, which are scattered up and down in the prophecy" (Alford). **For the time is at hand.** The appointed time when these things shall come to pass.

2. The Salutation (1:4–8)

This salutation divides itself into three parts: (1) the address and greeting to the Seven Churches of Asia (1:4, 5*a*); (2) a doxology of adoration (1:5*b*, 6); (3) the announcement of Christ's glorious victory at His coming,—the great theme of the book (1:7, 8).

4. John to the seven churches which are in Asia: Grace to

5

you and peace, from him which is and which was and which is to come (*which cometh*); and from the seven Spirits which are before his throne.

These **seven churches** are named in 1:11. By **Asia** is meant Proconsular Asia (1 Cor. 16:19), the western part of what we now call Asia Minor. Its capital was Ephesus, where John resided after 70 A. D., and exercised his office of oversight over the neighboring churches. There were more than seven churches in this district, but John evidently had special oversight over these. Tertullian already calls our attention to the fact that if we trace the history of their origin we shall find that John was the founder of most of them. Seven is the number of perfection, and many commentators consider these seven churches to represent "the Holy Church throughout all the world." Chrysostom writes, "The seven churches are all churches on account of the seven Spirits." Augustine maintains "that by the seven is signified the perfection of the Church universal; and that by writing to the seven he shows the fulness of one." "Through these seven churches," says Bede, "he writes to every church. For by the number seven is denoted universality." We may, at least, with the devout Isaac Williams, affirm that John writes, "first to the seven metropolitan churches, and in them to all the other churches in the Lydian Asia, the patriarchate of St. John; and from thence to all churches then in the world; and thence to those of all time." **Grace to you and peace.** All spiritual blessings have their source in the *grace* of God, and the effect of the reception of divine grace is that state of blessedness known as *peace*. So also in 1 Pet. 1:2; 2 Pet. 1:2; 2 John 3, in which latter passage "mercy" is added. **From him which is and which was and which**

is to come. The grammatical inaccuracy in the Greek here, after a preposition governing the genitive, adds to the sublimity of the language. The Father is here described by a paraphrase, reminding us of Ex. 3:14, as *He who is and He who was and He who comes.* The whole phrase is used as an indeclinable noun, the name of Him who is absolute and unchangeable. It is highly probable that God the Father is here described in His covenant relation to His people as *Jehovah.* On the clause *which is to come*, Milligan remarks: "God is here contemplated as the redeeming God, and that as such He comes, and will come, to His people. The Son is never alone even as Redeemer.... When He comes the Father comes, according to the promise of Jesus (John 14:23). As, therefore, throughout this whole book the Son is the 'coming' One, so the same term is here properly applied to the Father." **And from the seven Spirits.** These *seven Spirits which are before His throne* (3:1; 4:5; 5:6) represent the *Holy Spirit* as seven-fold in His operations, because in the One Spirit is all fulness and perfection. Compare the "seven eyes" of Zech. 3:9; 4:10. It is said that they are "before his throne," because connected with God's authority and government. Duesterdieck: "These seven Spirits belong to God and Christ Himself in a way other than can be conceived of any creature. But they cannot be regarded mere attributes.... Essentially, nothing else can be understood than 'the Spirit' who speaks to the churches (2:7, 11, 29), and the Spirit of Christ (3:1; 5:6) who makes men prophets (see also 14:13; 22:17)." Alford: "The seven Spirits betoken the completeness and universality of working of the Holy Spirit, as the seven churches typify and indicate the whole Church." These seven Spirits are not the seven principal angels (Gabriel, Michael, Raphael, Uriel,

7

Sealthiel, Jehudiel, Barachiel), as has been inferred by some.

5a. And from Jesus Christ, *who is* the faithful witness, the firstborn of the dead, and the ruler of the kings of the earth.

This greeting to the seven churches is given in the name of the three Persons of the Trinity, first from the Father, then from the Holy Spirit, and here the salutation is from the Son. We might have expected the Son to be spoken of before the Spirit, but the reason the Son is placed last is because John wishes to call especial attention to the works of the Son, and His Coming in glory (1:5–8), the great theme of the book. Three things are here affirmed of the risen and exalted Lord. **Who is the faithful witness.** The insertion of *who is* in the text indicates that we have here another grammatical peculiarity, all the three designations of Christ being in the nominative. This gives prominence to these three titles given to our Lord. Christ was indeed a *faithful witness* while on earth and sealed His testimony by His death as a faithful *martyr,* but it is probably better to refer this title *here* to His exalted condition, for all three titles refer to His glorified state. Christ's witness is the absolute truth of God, and whatever He has revealed to John will most surely come to pass (3:14; 19:11; 21:5; 22:6). **The firstborn of the dead.** St. Paul speaks of the risen Christ as "the firstfruits of them that are asleep" (1 Cor. 15:20), "the firstborn *from* the dead" (Col. 1:18), and as Christ is now "alive for evermore and has the keys of death and of Hades" (1:18), this title reminds believers of the glorious fact that Christ will also raise them from the dead (John 6:40, 44, 54; 1 Cor. 6:14; 2 Cor. 4:14). **The ruler of the kings of the earth.** Christ indeed attained this kingly power through His death and resurrection at the time of His exaltation (Matt. 28:18; Phil.

8

2:9–11; Eph. 1:20–23), but the manifestation of this will take place at the time of the Second Advent (6:15; 17:14; 19:16). Compare Ps. 89:27; Isa. 55:4. In the three titles given to Christ in this verse we may see a reference to His three-fold office as prophet, priest, and king.

5b, 6. Unto him that loveth us, and loosed us from our sins by his blood; and he made us *to be* a kingdom, *to be* priests unto his God and Father; to him *be* the glory and the dominion for ever and ever. Amen.

The Apostle now breaks forth in a doxology of praise to Christ for His inestimable love for us. **That loveth us.** Christ loves us now even amidst the glory of His exalted state, and this love continues forever. **And loosed us from our sins.** The *aorist* points to a definite time when this took place. It was when Christ purchased us with His blood (5:9) by His death on the cross. See notes on 1 Pet. 1:18, 19; 2:24. The reading *washed is* not so well attested, although there is only the difference of one letter between the two original Greek words. If this were the true reading, this *washing* from our sins would have taken place at the time of our baptism. **He made us a kingdom.** The change from the participial to the direct construction is after a Hebrew idiom. It is not said here that believers are made "kings," but we are made "a kingdom." This is the correct reading. Collectively believers form the kingdom of God. On the Futurist conception of *the kingdom* see *Excursus* I. The Apostle now passes to the individual designation of believers,—they are **priests unto his God and Father.** In the kingdom, sharing its privileges, each Christian is a *priest*. So likewise Peter (quoting exactly the Greek of Ex. 19:6, which, however, is a correct rendering of the Hebrew *a kingdom of priests*) speaks of *a royal priesthood,*

9

calling it royal, because the Church is a *kingdom*, of which all the members are priests. See also Rev. 5:10. For the nature of this Universal Priesthood of believers see notes on 1 Pet. 2:5. Duesterdieck: "The priesthood of all the redeemed lies in this, that they come immediately to God, offer to Him their prayers, and further give themselves peculiarly to Him in holy obedience and spiritual service." **To him be the glory and the dominion.** Ascribed to Jesus Christ. This two-fold doxology becomes three-fold at 4:11, fourfold at 5:13, and seven-fold at 7:12, the article in each case preceding each noun, thereby expressing universality.

7. Behold, he cometh with the clouds; and every eye shall see him, and they which pierced him; and all the tribes of the earth shall mourn over him. Even so, Amen.

Behold, he cometh with the clouds. A graphic prophetic summary of the contents and great theme of the Apocalypse. This is the *coming to judgment* prophesied of in Dan. 7:13, and so clearly foretold by Christ Himself (Matt. 24:29, 30; Mark 13:26; Luke 21:27, "Immediately after the tribulation of those days ... they shall see the Son of man coming in the clouds of heaven with power and great glory"). Compare also Mark 14:62; Matt. 26:64. His coming "with the clouds" does not denote so much the glory of His coming as the terror of that Great Day. It is an unquestionable fact that the coming of Christ is here described as a visible appearance in connection with great events taking place on the visible world. **Every eye shall see him.** For He shall come openly and visibly (Matt. 24:30; Acts 1:11). Absolutely all will see Him, believers and unbelievers (Matt. 25:32), the living (Luke 18:7, 8) and the dead (1 Thess. 3:13), but here John especially refers to the

10

fact that all unbelievers, with shame, confusion, and terror, shall behold Christ at His coming *to judgment*. **They which pierced him.** "Those who were His murderers, whether the Jews who delivered Him to be crucified, or the Romans who actually inflicted His death" (Alford). Ebrard thinks the reference is to converted Israel, which is probably the true explanation. Indirectly this statement is based upon John 19:37 and Zech. 12:10. The fact that John in these two passages (*here* and John 19:37) deliberately rejects the reading of the Greek Bible and renders the original Hebrew of Zech. 12:10 by the same Greek word, is almost a demonstration of the common authorship of the Gospel and the Apocalypse. **And all the tribes of the earth shall mourn.** That is, all the unbelieving Gentiles on the earth at the time of Christ's coming to destroy Antichrist. This *mourning* and wailing shall be one of dismay, in fear for themselves in regard to the consequences of His coming, not of penitence. So also Matt. 24:30. Milligan rightly remarks that this whole verse "corresponds with the object of the book, and the coming of Jesus is described as that of One who comes to overthrow His adversaries and to complete His triumph." **Even so, Amen.** The fulfilment is doubly assured,—the Greek and Hebrew forms being united as in 2 Cor. 1:20. This strong asseveration answers to the "Thus saith the Lord" of the prophets.

8. I am the Alpha and the Omega, saith the Lord God, which is and which was and which is to come, the Almighty.

Alford, although granting that it is our Lord who speaks in 1:17 and 22:13, maintains that we must understand these words as being uttered by the Eternal Father, on account of the titles here given to God. Probably, however, it is better to

11

ascribe them to the Lord Jesus, who here identifies Himself with the Lord Jehovah the God of Hosts of the O. T., so that these words are spoken by Him of Himself, as undoubtedly they are in 22:13. Nor need we be surprised that He who is of one essence with the Father should affirm of Himself these divine titles. Wordsworth: "These words, applied by Christ to Himself (21:6; 22:13; 1:17, 18), and compared with the declarations of *Jehovah* (Isa. 41:4; 44:6; 48:12), are also a plain assertion of Christ's divinity and co-eternity with the Father." **The Alpha and the Omega.** The first and last letters of the Greek alphabet, denoting "the first and the last" (1:17; 22:13), "the beginning and the end" (21:6; 22:13). All that can be said is said when Jehovah has spoken. **The Almighty.** This title occurs nine times in the Apocalypse; elsewhere in the N. T. only 2 Cor. 6:18. The same Greek word is used in the Greek Bible to translate *Shaddai* (Job 5:17) and *Elohe Tsebhaoth*, God of hosts (Jer. 5:14; 15:16; 44:7; Amos 3:13; 4:13). This eighth verse only emphasizes the certainty of the fulfilment of verse 7, that Christ shall be victorious over all His enemies.

3. The Place and Time of the Vision (1:9–11)

The Introductory Vision (1:9–20) readily divides itself into three parts, (1) the statement of the place and time of the Vision (1:9–11), (2) the description of the appearance of Christ in His Glory (1:12–16), and (3) the commission given to John by Christ Himself (1:17–20).

9. I John, your brother and partaker with you in the tribulation and kingdom and patience *which are* in Jesus, was in the isle that is called Patmos, for the word of God and the testimony of Jesus.

12

I John. So also 22:8, after the prophetic style of Daniel (9:2; 12:5). **In the tribulation and kingdom.** The fellowship of John with his readers was not simply an outward one, but *in Jesus*, and this implied that as true believers both the readers as well as John himself were experiencing that "in the world ye have tribulation" (John 16:33), and "that through many tribulations we must enter into the kingdom of God" (Acts 14:22). The order of words and the construction are peculiar, but although *the kingdom* in a certain sense has already come, the thought of John here evidently is, the tribulation is present, the kingdom in its blessed fulness is still future, and they who would attain it must endure with **patience.** We are reminded of the exhortation of James, "Be patient therefore, brethren, until the coming of the Lord.... Stablish your hearts: for the coming of the Lord is at hand." (See notes on James 5:7, 8.) Only hearts strong and steadfast in the faith can endure tribulation and wrong patiently, with longsuffering. **Patmos.** A rocky island, one of the Sporades, lying in that part of the Ægean called the Icarian Sea, about 30 miles from land, just visible from Miletus. The Apostle John was banished to this island during the last year of the reign of Domitian (81–96 A. D.), probably to work in the *mines,* evidently marble quarries,—from which he was recalled to Ephesus the year following by the Emperor Nerva. **For the word of God.** This does not mean, as so many moderns would have us believe, that John went to Patmos for the purpose of receiving this *revelation,* or for the purpose of preaching the Gospel. The construction is the same as in 6:9; 20:4, and there can be but one true meaning. We have here a plain statement of what was the *cause* of John's exile. It was because he had been faithful in proclaiming "the word

13

of God and the testimony of Jesus."

10. I was in the Spirit on the Lord's day, and I heard behind me a great voice, as of a trumpet.

I was in the Spirit. That is, fell in a state of ecstasy. Four times do we meet with this expression in the Apocalypse, and always at a crisis in the development of the visions (*here;* 4:2; 17:3; 21:10). Christ speaks of David "in the Spirit" (Matt. 22:43), "in the Holy Spirit" (Mark 12:36), calling Him Lord, and to be *in the Spirit* is evidently the same as being in that ecstatic state in which Peter was, when "in a trance he saw a vision" (Acts 10:10, 11; 11:5), into which Paul fell while praying in the temple at Jerusalem (Acts 22:17), and in which he was when "he was caught up into Paradise, and heard unspeakable words" (2 Cor. 12:4). **On the Lord's day.** Undoubtedly here used, though for the first time, to designate the first day of the week, the day of the Lord's Resurrection. Many of the Early Fathers used the Greek expression, here employed, of the first day of the week. Futurists only injure their cause when they insist that this expression refers to "the Day of the Lord's Coming." It raises the suspicion that all their arguments rest on no firmer foundation. It is surprising that any Greek scholar should ever be found to agree with them. **I heard behind me.** So also Ezek. 3:12, "Then the spirit lifted me up, and I heard behind me the voice of a great rushing." Duesterdieck suggests that *behind me* refers "to the unexpected, surprising utterance of the divine voice." **A great voice.** This loud voice was like the sound of a trumpet. Milligan maintains that this trumpet is not the trumpet of festal proclamation (Num. 10:10; Joel 2:15), but the trumpet of war and judgment, "therefore not merely one with a strong and clear sound, but

14

with a sound inspiring awe and terror, and corresponding in this respect to the distinguishing characteristic of the Lord in the further details of the vision."

11. Saying, What thou seest, write in a book, and send *it* to the seven churches; unto Ephesus, and unto Smyrna, and unto Pergamum, and unto Thyatira, and unto Sardis, and unto Philadelphia, and unto Laodicea.

Saying. We have a right to infer that this voice comes from Christ Himself (1:17, 18). **What thou seest.** All the visions which Christ gave to John and which are recorded in this book. **Write in a book.** Twelve times is the command given to John in the Apocalypse to write (*here;* 1:19; 2:1, 8, 12, 18; 3:1, 7, 14; 14:13; 19:9; 21:5), and there is no reason why John should not have written down these visions at the time that he received them. **Send.** When the roll is written, covering the whole contents of the Apocalypse, it is to be sent *to the Seven Churches*. The seven churches are named in the order in which a messenger starting from Patmos or from Ephesus would successively visit them,—going north from Ephesus to Smyrna and Pergamum, then inland to Thyatira, southward to Sardis, and southeasterly to Philadelphia and Laodicea. These seven churches, though historical, evidently represent the universal Church in all countries and ages. See notes on 1:4.

4. The Vision of the Son of Man (1:12–16)

12. And I turned to see the voice which spake with me. And having turned I saw seven golden candlesticks.

John turns round to see the one who uttered the "great voice," and sees seven golden candlesticks or *lampstands,* and

15

Christ Himself in the midst of them (1:13). Probably he saw the lampstands first, and then the form of the Lord appeared among them. In the tabernacle there was one golden candlestick with seven branches (Ex. 25:31, 32), although it seems that Solomon had made ten for the Temple (1 Kings 7:49). Here, however, John sees seven golden candlesticks, "for the one golden candlestick of the Law (Ex. 25:31; Zech. 4:2) becomes seven in the Church universal" (Williams). There is nothing here to indicate whether the seven golden candlesticks of the Apocalypse are to be considered as single or as seven-branched, but analogy would suggest the latter. Alford: "Here there are *seven* separate candlesticks, typifying as that *one* of the Tabernacles, the entire Church, but now no longer bound together in one outward unity and one place. Each local church has now its candlestick to be retained or removed from its place according to its own works." These candlesticks are figures of particular churches throughout the world, together making the Church universal, fed by the Oil of Holy Scripture, and illuminating the world (After Wordsworth).

13. And in the midst of the candlesticks one like unto a (*the*) son (*Son*) of man, clothed with a garment down to the foot, and girt about at the breasts with a golden girdle.

The whole description of these verses (1:13–16) aims to set forth the majesty and glory of Christ's appearance. **In the midst of the candlesticks.** To typify that the candlesticks (churches) are supplied with the oil of divine grace by Christ Himself, from whom all light-bearing power comes, and who is present with His churches, and watches over them. **Like unto the Son of man.** So Daniel describes Christ (Dan. 7:13). Probably John in vision saw Christ standing, not

16

walking, as in 2:1. **Clothed with a garment down to the foot.** A garment of supreme dignity, typifying that Christ was both a High Priest and a King,—for a long white linen robe, reaching down to the feet, was worn by priests as well as by kings. We are reminded of the prophecy of Zechariah (6:12, 13), "Behold, the man whose name is the Branch ... he shall sit and rule upon his throne; and he shall be a priest upon his throne." We see Christ here as the King-Priest arrayed in the apparel of kingly and priestly dignity. **Girt about ... with a golden girdle.** The golden girdle may typify the kingly office. Probably the best explanation is given by Boyd Carpenter: "The girdle is not around the loins, as though ready for action and toil (Luke 12:35), but it is worn as by one who rests from toil in the 'repose of sovereignty.' The girdle is of gold, not interwoven with gold, as was the high priest's girdle (Ex. 28:8), but pure gold, the emblem of a royal presence. Compare Isa. 11:5; Dan. 10:5; Eph. 6:14." Possibly Isa. 22:21 may shed some light upon this passage, "I will clothe him with thy robe, and strengthen him with thy girdle, and I will commit thy government into his hands." Milligan: "We have before us not only a Priest but a King, One who is already a Priest upon His throne, a Priest after the order of Melchizedek. But the thought of the King is prominent."

14. And his head and his hair were white as white wool, *white* as snow; and his eyes were as a flame of fire.

White as white wool, as snow. Most generally interpreted as a symbol of purity, holiness, and glory (Isa. 1:18). This doubtless is true, but evidently there is also a reference to Christ as the Eternal One, "the first and the last" (1:17, 19), for the same attributes are here ascribed to Christ as Daniel

17

assigns to "The Ancient of Days" (Dan. 7:9), "whose eternity is designated by the whiteness of his hair" (Duesterdieck). **His eyes ... a flame of fire.** So also 2:18; 19:12. Fire in Scripture is the symbol of divine wrath. This symbolizes "omniscience combined with holy wrath directed against all that is unholy" (Duesterdieck.)

15. And his feet like unto burnished brass, as if it had been refined in a furnace; and his voice as the voice of many waters.

Like unto burnished brass. The exact meaning of the Greek word, *chalco-libanos*, here used is not certain,—probably *white brass*, i. e. *brass* heated in a furnace to a *white* heat. The whole imagery takes us back to Dan. 10:6, "his eyes as lamps of fire, and his arms and his feet like in color to burnished brass, and the voice of his words like the voice of a multitude." Compare also Ezek. 43:2, "And behold, the glory of the God of Israel came from the way of the east: and his voice was like the sound of many waters; and the earth shined with his glory." Milligan: "All the features of this description are those of majesty, terror, and judgment,—*white ... as snow*, absolute purity,—*eyes ... flame of fire*, penetrating and consuming fire,—*his feet*, from the treading of these burning feet no ungodly of any nation shall escape,—*the voice of many waters*, the voice not simply loud and clear, but of irresistible strength and power, a voice the rebuke of which no enemy shall be able to withstand."

16. And he had in his right hand seven stars: and out of his mouth proceeded a sharp two-edged sword: and his countenance was as the sun shineth in his strength.

In his right hand seven stars. These stars represent "the angels of the seven churches." See notes on 1:20. Christ

18

is here represented as holding in His right hand, as His own property, these seven stars (2:1). This is written for the consolation of believers in all the churches, for Christ will protect and keep His own (John 10:28). Alford: "Now that He *holds them in* His hand (2:1), He appears as their Guardian, their Provider, their Nourisher; and, we may add, their Possessor." **Out of his mouth proceeded a sharp two-edged sword.** Also 2:16; 19:15, 21. Compare Isa. 11:4, "he shall smite the earth with the rod of his mouth, and with the breath of his lips shall he slay the wicked;" 2 Thess. 2:8. This sword is the Word of God which proceeds out of His mouth (Eph. 6:17; Heb. 4:12). Many see in the *two edges* the Law and Gospel. This is the weapon with which Christ will subdue His enemies (Rev. 2:16; 2 Thess. 2:8). It is probably best to refer this passage here principally to the destroying and punishing power of the Word, convicting, judging, and condemning. Duesterdieck: "Of the power of the Word of God, preached by Christ's ministers, striking the conscience and otherwise divinely efficacious (Heb. 4:12; Eph. 6:17), there is nothing said here. The sword from the mouth of Christ is directed against His enemies both within (2:12, 16) and without (19:15, 21) the Church." **His countenance ... as the sun shineth.** His face shone with the brilliancy of the sun, when its light is at the strongest. The dazzling glory of the Sun of Righteousness is intolerable to human eyes. This signifies that the eyes of sinful man cannot look upon the holiness and righteousness of the Son of man when He comes to judgment.

19

5. The Apostle's Commission (1:17–20)

17. And when I saw him, I fell at his feet as one dead. And he laid his right hand upon me, saying, Fear not.

As one dead. The effect of the divine appearance upon John was one of mortal terror (Isa. 6:4; Dan. 8:17), for it is a dreadful thing for sinful man to stand face to face with God. **He laid his right hand upon me.** The same all-powerful right hand which held the stars, and which on earth had brought so many blessings, also brought assurance and comfort to John, and evidently raised John to his feet (Ezek. 2:1, 2).

18. I am the first and the last, and the Living one; and I was dead, and behold, I am alive for evermore, and I have the keys of death and of Hades.

In this verse we have three clauses describing the glorious attributes which belong to the risen and glorified Christ. The first clause, **I am the first ... and the Living one,** refers to the eternal pre-existence of the Son, and to His unchangeable existence. We are not to explain *the first and the last* as the first in glory, the last in humiliation, but the reference is to His eternity, as in Isa. 41:4; 44:6; 48:12. The expression occurs three times in the Apocalypse (*here;* 2:8; 22:13). See also notes on 1:8. That Christ should assume this attribute proves that He is one with the Father in power, essence, glory, and eternity. Christ, as the personal Son of God, is absolutely *the Living one* from all eternity. The second clause, **I was dead ... alive for evermore,** has reference to His work of Redemption. He *became dead* refers to His state of Humiliation, but having risen from the dead, now in His state of Exaltation, He is *alive for evermore.* The last clause, **I have**

20

the keys of death and of Hades, refers to Christ's rule as the exalted king. Wordsworth: "Christ holds the keys of Death, both of natural and spiritual death; of *Natural Death*, as He proved by raising the dead, and by giving to His Apostles the power of raising the dead, and by raising Himself from the dead (John 5:21). He holds the keys of *Spiritual Death*. He quickens the soul, dead in trespasses and sins, by His Word and Sacraments; and as the appointed Judge of the quick and dead, He will condemn the wicked at the Last Day to that spiritual death which is called in the Apocalypse *the Second Death* (20:6, 14; 21:8)." Death is not the same as Hades, and is here personified and regarded as having gates, and the place of death, which also appears closed in with gates, is Hades. In 6:8; 20:13, 14, Hades is in like manner combined with death. The invisible world into which all souls went at death, *before* Christ's resurrection, is known in Scripture as *Sheol* (O. T.) or *Hades* (N. T.). It embraced two parts, the place or state of bliss, and the place or state of misery.

After Christ's resurrection, and especially His triumph over Satan, Hades as such remained the abode of all evil angels, including the souls of the ungodly dead (Rev. 20:13), and it is reserved as the fore-hell into which all the souls of unbelievers *now* enter until the day of judgment. But at Christ's glorious descent unto Hades as the risen God-man (1 Pet. 3:19; 4:6), great changes were wrought in the condition of the souls of the saints. That part of Hades known as Paradise before Christ's resurrection has now yielded up its captives, for the Lord Jesus "hath led captivity captive" (Eph. 4:8, 9). Christ has snatched all the blessed dead from Hades, and ever since Christ's resurrection from the dead and ascension into heaven, the souls of the blessed dead,

21

according to the constant testimony of the N. T. Scriptures, are in heaven with Christ, under the throne of His glory, and the souls of all believers who now die enter immediately into heaven (not into Hades), to be with Christ in joy and glory,—there in blessedness to await the Second Coming of Christ and their glorious resurrection, when with body and soul reunited they shall enter upon their eternal glory. (See *Lutheran Commentary on General Epistles*, pp. 147, 156, 157, 181.) Milligan is therefore right when he maintains: "Neither *death* nor *Hades* is to be understood in a natural sense. The one is not simply death, but death as a terrible power from which the righteous have escaped; the other is a region peopled, not by both the righteous and the wicked, but by those alone who have not conquered death. Both words thus describe the condition of all who are out of Christ, and are not partakers of His victory. Yet, however they may be opposed to Him, He has the keys of the prison within which they are confined." (See *Excursus* II. on *Hades*.)

19. Write therefore the things which thou sawest, and the things which are, and the things which shall come to pass hereafter.

Write therefore, with full assurance that all the things which I shall reveal to you will come to pass, for I have all the power (1:18). This word *therefore* supplies the practical application, and the whole verse refers us back to 1:11. **The things which thou sawest.** Probably referring to the vision recorded in 1:12–18. Others, however, do not limit it to this vision, but would include the whole series of visions. **The things which are.** Some (Bleek, De Wette, Ewald, Alford, Wordsworth) would translate *what it signifies*, but it is far better to translate as in the text. *The things which are*, which

22

concern the present state of the churches, as described in the seven Epistles (Rev. 2 and 3). **The things which shall come to pass hereafter,** or *after these.* Which are described in the visions recorded in Rev. 4–21. It is difficult to decide whether by *the things which shall come to pass* are meant the visions recorded in Rev. 4–21, or the events typified by these visions,—in either case the teaching is the same,—but it is probably best to see in this verse the indication of a three-fold division of the Apocalypse: (1) 1:12–18, a past vision; (2) ch. 2, 3, the present vision; and (3) ch. 4–21, the future visions.

20. The mystery of the seven stars which thou sawest in my right hand, and the seven golden candlesticks. The seven stars are the angels of the seven churches: and the seven candlesticks are seven churches.

We now have the explanation of the vision of the seven stars (1:16) and of the seven golden candlesticks (1:12). **The mystery.** Probably governed by *write* of 1:19; others would take it *absolutely.* **In my right hand.** Greek *upon,* i. e. resting on the Lord's right hand, equivalent to the *in* of 1:16. **The seven stars are the angels.** In the typical language of Scripture a "star" is the symbol of highest dominion (Num. 24:17; Isa. 14:12; Matt. 2:2), as well as of faithful or false teachers (Dan. 12:3; Jude 13). By the *angel* of the church, therefore, is not to be understood "a guardian angel" (Reuss, Alford, Weiss), nor "the personified spirit of a congregation" (De Wette, Luecke, Duesterdieck, Gebhardt, Lange), nor "the collective presbytery" (Hengstenberg), but the chief minister or pastor, the individual person or bishop who presided over the church. Many Church of England commentators (Trench, Wordsworth, Sadler, Lee) insist that the word *angel* here designates *the Bishop* in the modern sense of the word, but this cannot be satisfactorily shown. **The seven candlesticks are seven churches.** See notes on 1:12, 13. A candlestick or lampstand is a striking emblem of a visible church or congregation. It is a light-holder, aiming to preserve and make visible the light that is in it.

Revelation 2

6. The Epistle to the Church in Ephesus (2:1–7)

Four views may be held as to the character of these seven churches and the significance of these Epistles. 1. That we have here *merely* seven letters to seven historical churches, describing the condition of each church at the close of the first century, without any prophetic reference to the future condition of the church, and only valuable for instruction and reproof. This may be called the *Historical* view.

2. That these letters have no proper historical character, no such churches existing at this time, but *prophetically* represent (*a*) *merely* seven consecutive periods of Church History down to the end, or (*b*) seven tendencies existing synchronically in the Church, immediately before Christ's return, a favorite theory (with many modifications) of a few extreme Futurists. This has been called the *Prophetic* view.

3. That there were seven churches existing when the letters

were written, but that these were typical of seven periods of Church History, succeeding one after another. No two writers, however, are in harmony as to the exact time covered by each of these seven periods which are thus prefigured, although many are agreed that Ephesus represents a picture of the Church at the end of the Apostolical Age, whilst Laodicea pictures it as it shall be in the period preceding the Second Advent. The views of those who adopt this theory are substantially the same as those presented by Vitringa (*died* 1722), and may be presented in the following tabular form:

(1) *Ephesus.* The Church of First Love.

From John to the Decian Persecution. 250 A. D.

(2) *Smyrna.* The Persecuted Church.

From the Decian to Diocletian Persecution. 312 A. D.

(3) *Pergamum.* The Confessing Church.

From the Diocletian Persecution to Charlemagne. 800 A. D.

(4) *Thyatira.* The Church united to the State.

From Charlemagne to the rise of the Waldenses. 1200 A. D.

(5) *Sardis.* The Church of Uncompleted Works.

From 1200 A. D. to the Reformation. 1517 A. D.

(6) *Philadelphia.* The Faithful Church.

From the Reformation to the Present Time.

(7) *Laodicea.* The Professing but Lukewarm Church.

Lukewarmness before the Second Advent.

This is known as the *Historico-Prophetical* view.

4. A fourth view accepts the historical character of these Epistles, but differs from the preceding in that it regards the seven churches as representing the Universal Church,

and that "they are prophetic types of churchly conditions which shall hold good until the end of the world, ... seven life-pictures contained side by side through all the ages of the Church,—now one, and now another, predominating,—one prevailing at this place and another at that" (Lange). So, with many others, Milligan: "We have not merely before us seven letters to seven individual churches, ... but we have a representation or picture of the Church at large.... The seven churches selected are preferred to others, because they appeared to the Apostle to afford the best typical representation of the Church Universal." This fourth view seems to be most in harmony with the aim and teaching of the Apocalypse,—at least all are agreed "that the words contained in these Epistles are applicable to and intended for the guidance, warning, and encouragement of the whole Church Universal, and its several parts, throughout all time" (Alford). Lee also remarks: "That the teaching of the seven Epistles is *applicable* for reproof or for encouragement throughout all future time is firmly to be maintained; but that *definite* periods of the Church are here predicted, or that the Epistles refer severally to *successive* aspects of the Divine Kingdom, may well be doubted." See also notes on 1:4, and on the Epistles themselves.

The plan of the seven Epistles is the same in all, and all rest on the same fundamental thought—the Coming of the Lord, as announced in 1:7. In each we find—

1. A command to write.

2. A glorious title of our Lord.

3. An address to the angel of the church.

(*a*) A testimony and admonition.

(*b*) A prophetic announcement.

27

4. The conclusion.

(*a*) An appeal.

(*b*) A promise.

1. To the angel of the church in Ephesus write; These things saith he that holdeth the seven stars in his right hand, he that walketh in the midst of the seven golden candlesticks.

The angel. Although the address of each Epistle is a personal one, to the presiding pastor, yet it is addressed also to the church represented as a whole, for each congregation has a character of its own. We do not positively know who was the presiding pastor or bishop of Ephesus at this time. Timothy, who had been appointed bishop or overseer at Ephesus about 62–67 A. D. (1 Tim. 1:3), may still have been living. A tradition (though not one on which we can implicitly rely) speaks of his martyrdom about the time the Apocalypse was written (96 A. D.). Ignatius, writing to this same Ephesian church (107–116 A. D.), speaks of "Onesimus, who is your bishop." **In Ephesus.** Ephesus was the chief city of Ionia, lying near the sea, between Miletus and Smyrna, noted for its commerce and Grecian culture, "the light of Asia." Here Paul had labored during three years (Acts 18:19–19:20; 20:31), and it had also been the chief seat of John's later ministry. It contained the magnificent temple of Diana, which was regarded as one of the seven wonders of the world (Acts 19:27), the skill of Praxiteles having contributed to its beauty. **He that holdeth the seven stars.** The titles given to our Lord in these Epistles are taken mainly from the imagery of the preceding vision. (See notes on Rev. 1:16.) Christ not only *has* the stars in His right hand, but He *holds* them, indicating the power with which He protects and supports His people, for no one shall snatch those who believe in Christ and follow Him out of His hand (John 10:28). **He that walketh** Christ is not only *in* the midst of the candlesticks (1:13), but He *walketh* in the midst of them, as if trimming the lamps and supplying them with oil (Lev. 24:2–4), this designating His living and actual presence among the churches. Milligan: "Not one of their backslidings or errors escapes His notice; they have no weakness which He will not strengthen, no want which He will not supply."

2. I know thy works, and thy toil and patience, and that thou canst not bear evil men, and didst try them which call themselves apostles, and they are not, and didst find them false.

The address to the angel of the church follows, embracing verses 2–6. The angel or chief pastor or bishop is addressed as the representative of the church, thus emphasizing the responsibility of the pastor's office. The first two verses (2, 3) seem to contain seven points of commendation. (1) **I know ... thy toil and patience.** In five of these Epistles does Christ proclaim His divine *omniscience* and His ever-watchful observation of what is done in the churches, by the statement, *I know thy works* (2:2, 19; 3:1, 8, 15), and it is implied in the other two Epistles (2:9, 13). By *works* is meant the external activity in general, whereby the Church manifests her inner life, and these works are here more accurately defined as consisting of *toil* and *patience*. It was especially difficult for believers to lead a holy life in the profligate and idolatrous city of Diana, and it required *toilsome labor*, which means more than simply labor in the service of the Lord. The *patience* displayed, too, was not one simply of a passive kind, but that *active endurance* which patiently bore whatever suffering was inflicted by

29

a hostile world. We may also include the interpretation suggested by Wordsworth: "The angel is praised because he unites *active toil* with *patient endurance;* and because he exercises godly discipline in the correction of errors, and yet practises Christian forbearance towards the erring. A lesson to pastors and churches." (2) **Thou canst not bear evil men.** They would not tolerate men who in their very nature and character brought disgrace upon the Christian name. It was at Ephesus that St. John himself rushed out of the bath in which Cerinthus the heretic was. (3) **And didst try them which call themselves apostles.** St. Paul had warned the elders of Ephesus against the false teachers that should arise among them (Acts 20:29, 30), and they had profited by his warning and had been zealous for pure doctrine. St. Paul speaks of heretical teachers who claimed to be Apostles (2 Cor. 11:13–15). These false teachers are not to be identified with the Nicolaitans of verse 6. (4) **And didst find them false.** It was found that these false teachers were liars. Possibly they were Judaizing Christians sent from Jerusalem, trying to subvert the Gospel of Christ, or else deluded fanatics claiming apostolic inspiration.

3. And thou hast patience and didst bear for my name's sake, and hast not grown weary.

(5) **Thou hast patience.** In practising Christian forbearance towards the erring,—or probably better in patient endurance under suffering. (6) **And didst bear for my name's sake.** Thou didst suffer for my sake. Milligan: "They had borne the burden laid upon them because of the 'name' of Jesus." (7) **And hast not grown weary.** Thou toilest, but dost not feel the toil (Wordsworth). Apparently greater praise could not have been bestowed upon the Ephesian church.

30

Milligan: "The chief point of commendation in the state of the Christians at Ephesus is their instinctive discernment and rejection of false teachers, and their zeal for the true doctrine of Christ as handed down by His commissioned and inspired Apostles. Around this all else that in their case was worthy of commendation centred."

4. But I have *this* against thee, that thou didst leave thy first love.

Now follows the deserved reproof. Wordsworth: "The Church is addressed as a Bride (2 Cor. 11:2), and she is reproved for having abated the fervor of her early love to God." In what particular the Ephesian church had left her first love is not stated, but evidently "the love of first conversion had waxed cold, and given place to a lifeless and formal orthodoxy" (Alford). The case of too many professing Christians now.

5. Remember therefore from whence thou art fallen, and repent, and do the first works; or else I come to thee, and will move thy candlestick out of its place, except thou repent.

To the reproof of verse 4 is added a three-fold exhortation ("remember, repent, reform"), with a threatening of judgment. **From whence thou art fallen.** The first love of the Ephesian church is regarded as a height from which she has fallen. **Repent.** The tense indicates that this repentance is to take place quickly, once for all. The spiritual condition of the church was in a sad state. **Do the first works.** Manifest the fruits of your first love. Simcox: "Do again what love made thee do, that thou mayest learn to love again." **Else I come to thee.** In a special visitation of judgment. **And will move thy candlestick out of its place.** That is, I will remove thy light, and thou shalt cease to exist as a church.

31

From a letter written to this same church by Ignatius, Bishop of Antioch, not many years after the date of the Apocalypse, we learn that this warning here given was not unheeded, and he specially praises this church for not allowing false teachers to sow their pernicious seed, and for tolerating no heresy,—but at the same time the letter gives evidence that the church seems to be still in danger of waxing cold in their love, for Ignatius says: "All this ye know, if your faith and your love be perfect in Christ; for faith and love are the beginning and end of life—faith the beginning, love the end; and both, when fitly joined together, are of God." But the church at Ephesus, planted by St. Paul and nourished by St. John, did not remain faithful to her trust. Those who have visited the ruins of that once famous city have borne witness to the literal fulfilment of this threatened judgment.

This warning declares an important doctrinal truth. Any particular *candlestick* may be removed; that is, any one *congregation* may fail. But the light of the Christian Church will never be extinct; because Christ, who is the Light of the world, is ever walking in the midst of the candlesticks, and He has promised to be with His Church always, even unto the end of the world (Matt. 28:20), and to send the Holy Ghost to *abide* with her for ever (John 14:16). (After Wordsworth.)

6. But this thou hast, that thou hatest the works of the Nicolaitans, which I also hate.

Note the tender compassion of Christ, who does not leave this church without another word of praise. Very little is definitely known of the sect of the Nicolaitans. Irenæus and others of the Early Fathers describe them as deriving their name from Nicolas, one of the seven deacons (Acts 6:5), and as leading dissolute and licentious lives—but some of the

Fathers deny that Nicolas himself was responsible for their tenets and practices. (See notes on Rev. 2:15.) It is sufficent to know, as Œcumenius maintains, that they were "most impious in doctrine, and in their lives most impure." Note that the hatred is not directed against *the persons* but against the *works* of these evil men.

7. He that hath an ear, let him hear what the Spirit saith to the churches. To him that overcometh, to him will I give to eat of the tree of life, which is in the Paradise of God.

He that hath an ear. This sentence occurs in each of the *Seven Epistles* (2:7, 11, 17, 29; 3:6, 13, 22), marking the importance of the message. What the Spirit here says to any *one* church is designed for *all* the churches of the world. The idea is, we are not only to *hear* but to *give heed.* The same expression was often used by Christ while still on earth (Matt. 11:15; 13:9, 43; Mark 4:9, 23; Luke 8:8; 14:35). **The Spirit saith.** "The revelation of Christ can be designated also as an address of the Holy Ghost, because He is the Spirit of Christ (Rom. 8:9, 10), and speaks in Christ's name (John 16:13, 14)" (Duesterdieck). The working of the Son and of the Spirit is never separated. **To him that overcometh.** A phrase also repeated in each of the Seven Epistles, but in each case its meaning is somewhat different because each church has a different form of temptation. And here we may observe one point of especial notice in these Epistles to the churches, that in each not only the angel of the church is addressed, and the church collectively, but also each individual in the church. **To eat of the tree of life.** This tree of life is not to be regarded as the Gospel, nor the Holy Spirit, nor Christ Himself (so already Bede and Calovius, and Ebrard, Milligan, and others), but the reference undoubtedly is to the tree of life, bearing

33

twelve manner of fruits, that shall be in the New Jerusalem (Rev. 22:2, 14, 19; Ezek. 47:2), the antitype of the tree of life which was in the first Paradise (Gen. 2:9). (So most modern commentators.) The language and imagery is from Gen. 2:9; 3:22. What this tree of life is, whether it is an actual tree, or only typifies the continual and heavenly nourishment of eternal life in its full fruition, we need not speculate. **Which is in the Paradise of God.** This word *Paradise* occurs three times in the Greek Bible of the O. T. to translate the Hebrew for "garden" (Gen. 2:8; 3:1; Ezek. 28:13). It is also found three times in the Greek N. T. (Luke 23:43; 2 Cor. 12:4; Rev. 2:7), and always translated *Paradise.* It is always used of the place or abode of the children of God. The first time we read of Paradise it was on *earth*, the abode of God's children before the Fall. When we hear of it the second time, it is no longer on earth, but it has been transferred to the upper part of Hades, *under the earth*, but it is still the abode of the children of God, whither the souls of all the saints descended before Christ's death and resurrection (Luke 23:43). When we read of it again, after Christ's victory over death, Satan, and Hades, it has been transferred to heaven (2 Cor. 12:4), into which *now*, since Christ's ascension, all the souls of the dying saints enter, to await their glorious resurrection; and this Paradise shall again be found on earth, but on *the new earth*, for after the consummation of all things the tree of life shall stand in the Paradise of God (Rev. 2:7; 22:2), and God shall tabernacle with His people (Rev. 21:3).

7. The Epistle to the Church in Smyrna (2:8–11)

8. And to the angel of the church in Smyrna write; These things saith the first and the last, which was dead, and lived *again.*

Angel of the church. See notes on Rev. 1:20. It is highly probable that Polycarp, the disciple of St. John, was already bishop of Smyrna at this time. We know that Polycarp suffered as a martyr 168 A. D., and that he then declared that he had served Christ eighty-six years. Ignatius writes to him as bishop of Smyrna some ten years after the date of the Apocalypse. **Smyrna.** Smyrna was about forty miles north of Ephesus, lying on an excellent harbor of the Ægean Sea, and was one of the most wealthy cities of Asia Minor, and is flourishing even to this day, being the centre of the trade of the Levant. The Christian Church at Smyrna, it is said, is the only one of the seven churches which is still existing. **The first and the last.** The titles which Christ here gives to Himself are taken from the vision recorded in the first chapter. See notes on Rev 1:18. **And lived.** The *aorist* tense marks the historical fact of the resurrection. Simcox: "The attributes of *death* and *life* are here especially ascribed to Christ, because the message He sends is a promise of life to them who die for His sake."

9. I know thy tribulation, and thy poverty (but thou art rich), and the blasphemy of them which say they are Jews, and they are not, but are a synagogue of Satan.

I know thy tribulation. Probably arising from the persecutions of the heathen, instigated, as we may infer from this verse, by the Jews. There is extant a letter written, nearly a century later, by the church of Smyrna, giving an account of the persecution in which Polycarp suffered martyrdom (168 A. D.), in which they relate that the *Jews* took an active part in hastening the death of Polycarp by collecting the wood for the fire,—and even after he had been burned, they tried to hinder the Christians from gathering up his remains for burial. **And thy poverty.** For most of the Christians were poor, and what they did have was taken from them by their persecutors. **But thou art rich.** Rich in faith and good works. **The blasphemy of ... Jews.** It is evident that these revilers and slanderers were real Jews and not simply Judaizing Christians. This blasphemy no doubt also included a reviling of Christ Himself. Christ in His gracious compassion knew what they had to endure from these Jews who reviled them with such bitter and relentless hatred. But these Jews are no longer worthy of the honorable name by which they call themselves. They are no longer "the synagogue or congregation of the Lord" (Num. 16:3; 31:16), but they are become **a synagogue of Satan,** because they do the works of Satan.

10. Fear not the things which thou art about to suffer: behold, the devil is about to cast some of you into prison, that ye may be tried; and ye shall have tribulation ten days. Be thou faithful unto death, and I will give thee the crown of life.

This verse contains an exhortation to endure fearlessly and faithfully the fresh persecutions which would immediately arise. This tribulation shall proceed from **the devil,** but only indirectly, for he would make use of human agents, the heathens and Jews, the persecutors spoken of in the last verse. **Into prison.** Persecution generally begins with imprisonment (Acts 8:3; 12:4; 16:23; 26:10). **That ye may be**

36

tried. Satan seeks their ruin, for he hopes that those cast into prison may fall away. Christ permitted this trial that their faith might be *proved* and redound to their glory. **Ten days.** We are not to interpret (1) ten years (Faber, Birks, etc.), nor (2) the ten persecutions of the Christians (Stier, Ebrard, etc.). nor (3) a very long time (Bede, etc.), nor (4) of persecution carried to its full extent, *complete* (Milligan, Plumptre, etc.), but (5) it is probably best to take the number ten—like nearly all the other numbers in the Alpocalypse—in the symbolical sense as denoting *a short time* (De Wette, Trench, Alford, etc.). Compare Gen. 24:55; Num. 11:19; 1 Sam. 25:38; Dan. 1:12. Perhaps, however, the prediction may be interpreted literally, and may have been fulfilled when Polycarp suffered martyrdom. At least this was written for their consolation, that the tribulation should last only a short and limited time, *ten days.* **Be thou faithful unto death.** Some therefore had to manifest their faith by enduring a martyr's death. In the letter written by the church at Smyrna, referred to in the last verse, we read: "The devil devised many things against the martyrs, but, thanks be to God, he did not prevail over *them all*," thus signifying that the devil did prevail over some,—but that others like Polycarp *were faithful unto death*, for "Polycarp by his patience overcame the unrighteous ruler, and received the crown of Immortality." All this proves that the Apocalypse was known to the church at Smyrna. **I will give.** Christ throughout these Epistles asserts that He is the distributor of rewards (2:7, 11, 17, 26, 23; etc.). **The crown of life.** Eternal life itself is the crown. The expression occurs only *here* and James 1:12 (which see). In 2 Tim. 4:8 we read of "the crown of righteousness," and in 1 Pet. 5:4 (which see) of "the crown of glory." It is not necessary to decide whether

37

Christ had in view the *diadem* of the king, or the *wreath* of the victor, but probably it is best to think of the *victor's crown.*

11. He that hath an ear, let him hear what the Spirit saith to the churches. He that overcometh shall not be hurt of the second death.

In the conclusion we have the same appeal as in 2:7 (which see). **Shall not be hurt of the second death.** Notice that the promise to him that overcometh, in each of the Seven Epistles, always corresponds to the work done. By being *faithful unto death* they will by death gain a crown of life and escape *the second death.* This **second death** (also 20:6, 14; 21:8) is eternal death, the everlasting misery of the body and soul of the wicked, after their resurrection, in Gehenna, the place of final punishment. (See *Excursus* II. on *Hades.*)

8. The Epistle to the Church in Pergamum (2:12–17)

12. And to the angel of the church in Pergamum write;
   These things saith he that hath the sharp two-edged sword.
   We do not know who was bishop of Pergamum. (See notes on Rev. 1:20.) **Pergamum.** This important city, the seat of a Roman supreme court, was situated about fifty miles north of Smyrna, distinguished for the temple of Æsculapius, the god of medicine, which, on account of the many cures performed there, vied in glory with the temple of Diana at Ephesus, and the sanctuary of Apollo at Delphi. It had also been famous for its large library of 200,000 volumes, which, however, had been removed to Alexandria by Antony and Cleopatra to increase the glory of the Alexandrian library. We know nothing of the origin of the church at Pergamum.

The title by which Christ is described, as having **the sharp two-edged sword,** is taken from the vision recorded in 1:16 (which see).

13. I know where thou dwellest, *even* where Satan's throne is: and thou holdest fast my name, and didst not deny my faith, even in the days of Antipas my witness, my faithful one, who was killed among you, where Satan dwelleth.

The church at Pergamum had been more severely tried than any other, and Satan had succeeded in stirring up persecution more effectually than anywhere else, for he had proceeded so far as to shed martyr's blood. "Whether this may have been owing to the fact of the residence of the supreme magistracy at Pergamum, or to some fanatical zeal of the inhabitants for the worship of Æsculapius, or to some particular persons dwelling there especially hostile to the followers of Christ, must remain uncertain" (Alford). One thing, however, was certain, that Satan had taken up his abode in Pergamum, and had there set up his **throne.** This points with peculiar emphasis to the temptations and dangers which the Christians at Pergamum had to encounter. Milligan: "In a city, where science itself was the very pillar of witchcraft and idolatry, where licentiousness and wickedness of every kind prevailed, Satan had been enabled to put forth against the bodies of the Christians every evil which envy at their souls' escape from him suggested." **Thou ... didst not deny my faith.** Christ speaks of them as still *holding fast his name,* i. e. Christ Himself personally as their Saviour, nor did they in the hour of their great temptation deny faith in Him and fall away. This commendation is all the more emphatic by the fact that they remained faithful even in the days when persecution meant death. Of the martyr **Antipas** nothing

39

historical is known. Later traditions make him to have been a bishop of Pergamum, and by command of Domitian to have been burned to death in the interior of a brazen bull, made red-hot. It is strange to what extremes commentators may go in trying to find a symbolic meaning for the name *Antipas.*

14. But I have a few things against thee, because thou hast there some that hold the teaching of Balaam, who taught Balak to cast a stumblingblock before the children of Israel, to eat things sacrificed to idols, and to commit fornication.

Though Christ had commended the church so highly, He now reproves them for **a few things,** *few* as compared with the things approved in verse 13. The church had not used her power of *discipline,* but still permitted those who taught false doctrine and led immoral lives to remain members of the church. Two classes of errorists in both doctrine and life are referred to in this and the next verse. **That hold the teaching of Balaam.** Some of the professing members of the church not only approved of Balaam's teaching, but followed it. Balaam is a strange character. His history is given in Num. 22:1–24:25; 31:8–16; Josh. 13:22. (See notes on 2 Pet. 2:15, 16.) **Who taught Balak to cast a stumblingblock before the children of Israel.** According to our text this *stumblingblock* consisted of two things: The Israelites were enticed (1) *to eat things sacrificed to idols,* and (2) *to commit fornication.* The counsel of Balaam to Balak was to entice the Israelites to fornication and to the idolatrous worship of Baal-peor, by means of the women of Moab (Num. 31:16; 25:1–3). The Israelites not only did eat of the sacrifices made to their gods, but "bowed down to their gods" (Num. 25:2), and "committed whoredom with the

40

daughters of Moab" (Num. 25:1). The name Balaam ever after became typical of one who played the part of a teacher and of a seducer from the true and holy worship of God (2 Pet. 2:15; Jude 11). As Pergamum was noted for its idol-worship and the impure character of its heathen festivals, we can readily see how this *teaching of Balaam* brought forth its bitter fruits, in idol-worship and carnal sensuality,—for we have a right to infer that these false members of the church had fallen into these grievous sins. All of which only brought out more prominently the sin of the church in Pergamum in not exercising *church discipline.* What a lesson to many a Christian congregation of the present day!

15. So hast thou also some that hold the teaching of the Nicolaitans in like manner.

This verse describes still another class of errorists that were permitted to remain in the church in Pergamum. They taught false views of Christian liberty, and led immoral lives, following in this the example of the Nicolaitans (see notes on 2:6). **In like manner** with the Balaamites of verse 14, they were guilty of the same grievous sins, and there evidently was a close affinity between the Balaamites and the Nicolaitans, although it is best to regard them as two distinct sects. No matter what differences there may have been in their false theories, they practically reached the same goal of profligacy and immorality, transgressing the very fundamental principles underlying the Christian religion (1 Cor. 8:7–13; Acts 15:29).

16. Repent therefore; or else I come to thee quickly, and I will make war against them with the sword of my mouth.

We have here an admonition to the church to repent. This repentanee on the part of the bishops and the members of the church would manifest itself in a two-fold way, by seeking to convert these errorists from their evil way, or by exercising church discipline. If the church would not be zealous for purity of doctrine and life, then Christ Himself would quickly visit them in punishment. But if they repented, Christ gives the gracious promise that the truth shall be victorious, for He Himself shall aid in a special manner, and give efficacy to the word of God, so that these errorists shall be overcome.

17. He that hath an ear, let him hear what the Spirit saith to the churches. To him that overcometh, to him will I give of the hidden manna, and I will give him a white stone, and upon the stone a new name written, which no one knoweth but he that receiveth it.

See notes on 2:7, 11. **To him will I give of the hidden manna.** Pure, holy, and heavenly food as contrasted with the polluted meats offered to idols. This *bread of heaven* may be Christ's peculiar gift of Himself (John 6:48–58), to be the nourishment as well as the reward of His faithful ones. This *manna* is *hidden*, because "our citizenship is in heaven" (Phil. 3:20), and our spiritual life "is hid with Christ in God" (Col. 3:3), and will not be fully enjoyed until we enter upon our future glory (1 John 3:2). **A white stone.** White is the color of victory and of purity. Of the many interpretations given of the *white stone* we believe that given by Victorinus, Erasmus, Calovius, Vitringa, Wordsworth, and others to be the most satisfactory. "In ancient courts of justice, the acquittal of the criminal was declared by a majority of *white stones*, cast into the judicial urn. Christ, the Redeemer of the world, the Judge of the quick and dead, will pronounce the acquittal of him that overcometh, at the Great Day of Assize. This white stone is not only a stone of *acquittal*, but it is a passport of *admission* to the spiritual banquet of the life eternal in the heavenly Jerusalem" (Wordsworth). **And upon the stone a new name written.** This is evidently the *new* name bestowed upon the believer, descriptive of his character, position, and glory in the New Jerusalem. It is a name *which no one knoweth but he that receiveth it,* "because no one can enter into Christ's presence by means of the merits *of others;* every one must give an account of himself to God, and be rewarded according to his own works (Rom. 14:12)" (Wordsworth). "Jacob, after he had wrestled with the angel, received the new name of Israel. Wouldst thou know what new name thou art to receive? Overcome. Till then thou wilt ask in vain; but then thou shalt soon read it on the white stone" (Bengel).

9. The Epistle to the Church in Thyatira (2:18–29)

18. And to the angel of the church in Thyatira write;

These things saith the Son of God, who hath his eyes like a flame of fire, and his feet are like unto burnished brass.

Angel. We do not positively know who was bishop of Thyatira. (See notes on Rev. 1:20.) Some from ancient times have held that Carpus (not the one mentioned in 2 Tim. 4:13) was bishop, while others call the bishop of Pergamum by that name. **Thyatira.** This city was situated on the river Lycus, about forty miles southeast of Pergamum, and its chief trade was the dyeing of purple. Whether the church was founded by the Lydia mentioned in Acts 16:14, 15, who was baptized with her household at Philippi, we cannot positively determine. **The Son of God.** For the description which Christ gives of Himself, see notes on 1:14, 15. The most remarkable part of it is that He designates Himself *the Son of God.* This does not conflict with 1:13, where John says that he saw "one like unto the Son of man," for Christ is both God and Man. Our Lord thus designates Himself here, probably because in verse 27 there is reference to Ps. 2:7–9, where the glory of the Son is predicted. The *Son of God* with His eyes of flame penetrates everything, and nothing impure shall escape from the treading of those burning feet.

19. I know thy works, and thy love and faith and ministry and patience and that thy last works are more than the first.

Thy works. See notes on 2:2. These works are defined as manifesting themselves in a four-fold way. **Thy love ... faith ... ministry ... patience.** Two groups of works are mentioned, in such order that the members of the first group correspond to those of the second. *Love* shows itself in *ministry; faith* in *patience* or endurance (Milligan). This *love* was both to God and men; this *ministry* displayed itself in loving service to all that needed it,—the sick, the poor, the orphan, the aged. *Faith* is to be taken in its general sense, not *faithfulness*, and proved itself in faithful and persevering *patience* amidst all trying and suffering. **Thy last works are more than the first.** In this there was a great contrast between this church and that at Ephesus (2:5). There was progress in all the works of this church.

20. But I have *this* against thee, that thou sufferest the woman Jezebel, which calleth herself a prophetess; and she teacheth and seduceth my servants to commit fornication, and to eat things sacrificed to idols.

This church, like the one in Pergamum, was careless in exercising *church discipline.* **Thou sufferest the woman Jezebel.** A particular woman is meant; her name may

44

have been Jezebel, but probably not. The wickedness of this woman, however, marked her as another Jezebel, like that Sidonian queen, the wife of Ahab, who introduced the worship of Baal, and caused the children of Israel to commit fornication (2 Kings 9:22). This woman pretended to be a prophetess and taught false doctrines closely related to those of the Balaamites (2:14), and to those of the Nicolaitans (2:15), for the practical end was the same—immorality and apostasy. Many authorities, some ancient, read *thy wife* Jezebel. This reading would make this false prophetess the wife of the bishop. Some interpret this passage *figuratively*, making Jezebel the name of a heretical party, her sin of *fornication* designating idolatry and worldly alliances, *her children* (2:23), disciples. In accordance with this view we find the comment of Wordsworth: "The heresy here reprehended is that of those who said that it was not necessary to *suffer martyrdom* for Christ; and that, provided men had knowledge, there was no sin in *eating* things *offered to idols*, and in complying with all the requirements of the idolatrous persecutors of the Church." It is far better to retain the literal meaning. Lange correctly says: "Jezebel was a religious fanatic, who claimed to be a prophetess and had founded a school of Antinomianism, in which an impure intercourse of the sexes was reduced to a religious system, and clothed in the garb of pious enthusiasm. The name is symbolical, but not the sex. It should be observed that the seduction to fornication occupies the foremost place, and that more stress is laid upon it than upon the eating of idolatrous sacrifices."

21. And I gave her time that she should repent; and she willeth not to repent of her fornication.

God had delayed His righteous judgment upon this woman,

and the time for repentance was still at hand, but she had become so hardened in her evil ways, that there was no hope for repentance. **She willeth not to repent.** A remarkable statement showing the freedom of the will in things that are evil.

22. Behold, I do cast her into a bed, and them that commit adultery with her into great tribulation, except they repent of her works.

From the bed of shame and infamy she should be cast upon a bed of sickness and suffering. Some think that this *bed* denotes the final punishment in Gehenna or Hell. It will surely overtake her, but this is not the meaning here. Those who shared in her deeds shall also suffer punishment, which is described as a *great tribulation.* **Except they repent.** The *they* may include not only the parties in her adulteries, but those in the church who tolerated her wicked ways (see verse 24).

23. And I will kill her children with death; and all the churches shall know that I am he which searcheth the reins and hearts: and I will give unto each one of you according to your works.

Her children. We need not interpret, her actual children of fornication, for it is strictly biblical to call all those who share the evil deeds of Jezebel (verse 22) *her children.* **With death.** The *great tribulation* which overtakes these adulterers terminates with the punishment of death,—possibly with a reference to the punishment visited upon such guilty ones (Lev. 20:10). **All the churches shall know.** Not only in Asia Minor, but in all the world, wherever this Epistle shall be read. **Which searcheth the reins and hearts.** This is an attribute ascribed to the righteous God, "for the righteous

46

God trieth the hearts and reins" (Ps. 7:9). These two words "reins and heart" include the whole inner and secret life of man. Christ as the Son of God, "with his eyes like a flame of fire" (2:18), penetrates our innermost thoughts, and when the Lord cometh "he will both bring to light the hidden things of darkness, and make manifest the counsels of the hearts; and then shall each man have his praise from God" (1 Cor. 4:5). **Unto each one of you according to your works.** Addressed here specially to these guilty followers of Jezebel, but true of all whether believers or unbelievers (Rom. 2:6–11).

24. But to you I say, to the rest that are in Thyatira, as many as have not this teaching, which know not the deep things of Satan, as they say; I cast upon you none other burden.

This is addressed to the faithful in the church at Thyatira, to those not infected either by the false doctrine or the impure life of Jezebel and her followers. These faithful ones are described by two marks, in what follows. **The deep things of Satan, as they say.** It is probably best to refer *they say* to these false and immoral teachers, who, like the other gnostic sects of this and a later period, professed to initiate their followers in the depths of the profoundest mysteries. Some of them in their impious recklessness may have pretended to fathom even *the deep things of Satan*, and may have "taught that it was a duty for the true gnostic to dive into all the gulfs of sensuality, and that he could not be hurt thereby, any more than gold by mud, and some of them even did not hesitate to adore the Evil One himself, such as the *Ophites*, or Serpent-Worshippers, and the *Cainites*. Indeed, the enormities committed by them, while pretending to superior spiritual knowledge of things, are too monstrous

47

to be recorded" (Wordsworth).

Another interpretation is that this saying of the false teachers only includes *the deep things*, or possibly the deep things of God, but that the Lord in indignation substitutes *of Satan.* (So Calovius, Bengel, Ewald, De Wette, Alford, Duesterdieck, and others.) A few would even refer *as they say* to *the faithful Christians*, and that these called *the deep things* of the heretics, *the deep things of Satan.* But evidently this is not what is here meant. **I cast upon you none other burden.** To what burden does Christ refer? Many answers have been given. (1) Some would refer it to the Christian obligation of "abstaining from the pollution of idols and from fornication" (Acts 15:20, 28, 29), the very points here at issue (Alford, Lee, Stern, Hengstenberg, Duesterdieck, Simcox, and others); (2) others refer it to the previous suffering implied in the patience of verse 19 (De Wette, Bisping, and others); but the context implies (3) that it refers to the trouble which the church will have of excommunicating Jezebel and her followers (2:20) (Lange, Milligan, and others).

25. Howbeit that which ye have, hold fast till I come.

In addition to exercising strict church discipline, so that I have nothing against thee (2:20), **hold fast** thy present faithfulness, so highly commended (2:19). **Till I come.** The reference is to the Second Advent, but the uncertainty of the time is expressed by the little Greek word *an*, which is untranslatable in English.

26. And he that overcometh, and he that keepeth my works unto the end, to him will I give authority over the nations.

He that overcometh and ... keepeth. In this letter the promise to the victor precedes the proclamation to hear what the Spirit saith to the churches. (See notes on 2:7, 11,

17.) Here the victory consists in remaining faithful unto the end. **My works.** Which belong to me,—not only those which I command. Note how essential to the Christian life are personal purity and holiness,—the believer must closely walk in the footsteps of Christ, and aim at a perfect Christian development. **I will give authority over the nations.** In scriptural language this can only refer to the time of the *Parousia* or Second Advent, when the nations are given to Christ for His inheritance (Ps. 2:8, 9), and He begins His rule in the midst of His enemies (Ps. 110:2, 5, 6), and when the saints shall reign with Christ in His kingdom. The reign of the saints is prominent in the Apocalypse (3:21; 5:10; 20:4; 22:5). There are many references in Scripture to the time when and the manner in which the saints shall exercise this authority (Ps. 149:5–9; Dan. 7:22, 27; Matt. 19:28; 1 Cor. 6:2). See *Excursus* I. on *The Kingdom of God.*

27. And he shall rule them with a rod of iron, as the vessels of the potter are broken to shivers; as I also have received of my Father.

All these promises do not refer to this present life, but to the future. The same power that Christ has received of the Father (Ps. 2:8, 9), and which He Himself will exercise over His enemies (Rev. 12:5; 19:15), He will confer upon His victorious servants (Luke 22:29). The victor shall share in the glory of the Messiah's kingly rule, and Christ shall *shepherdize* the nations "with as absolute a mastery as is expressed in crushing a potsherd" (Simcox).

28. And I will give him the morning star.

A difficult passage. This *morning star* does not designate the devil, with reference to Isa. 14:12; nor the king of Babylon (Zuellig); nor the bright glory, the heavenly *doxa*, with which

49

the victor is to be endowed (De Wette, Duesterdieck); nor does it symbolize the full dawn of the new day of Jesus Christ (Lange, Luthardt); but it is far better, from the title which Christ gives to Himself in 22:16, to regard this *morning star* as the Lord Jesus Himself, displayed in all His heavenly beauty before the hearts of His people, as their proper portion and hope. He gives Himself to His people, as the sum of every spiritual blessing (Trench), the fruition of His glorious presence (Plumptre), sharing with them His royal dominion (3:21). (So Calovius, Bengel, Ebrard, Lee, Milligan, and others.)

29. He that hath an ear, let him hear what the Spirit saith to the churches.

On this formula see notes on 2:7.

3

Revelation 3

10. The Epistle to the Church in Sardis (3:1–6)

1. And to the angel of the church in Sardis write;

These things saith he that hath the seven Spirits of God, and the seven stars: I know thy works, that thou hast a name that thou livest, and thou art dead.

The angel. See note on Rev. 1:20. The name of this bishop we do not know. During the middle of the second century (170 A. D.) it was the residence of the learned Melito, who wrote a commentary on the Apocalypse (Eusebius, *H. E.* IV. 26). **Sardis.** This ancient capital of Lydia, the residence of its kings, including Croesus, was situated upon the river Pactolus, the golden sand, about fifty miles due east of Smyrna and twenty-three miles due south of Thyatira. It was noted for its riches and its luxury, famous for its manufacture of Persian carpets, and also on account of a magnificent temple of the goddess Cybele, the rites of whose worship were noted for their impurity. **He that hath the seven Spirits of God.** These *seven Spirits* represent the Holy Spirit as seven-fold in His operations. (See notes on Rev.

1:4.) This phrase illustrates the doctrine of the procession of the Holy Ghost from the Father and the Son. Christ is here spoken of as having the Spirit, not so much because in the days of His flesh He was anointed with the Spirit above measure (John 3:34), "but because, as the Son of God, the Spirit of God is His Spirit (Rom. 8:9), and because He sends the Spirit (John 15:26; 20:22; Acts 2:33), who acts as His representative (John 15:26)" (Craven). **And the seven stars.** See notes on 1:16, 20; 2:1. "Since *the stars are the angels of the seven churches* (1:20), we must see in this combination a hint of the relation between Christ, as the giver of the Holy Spirit, and as the author of a ministry of living men in His Church (Eph. 4:7–12; John 20:22, 23; Acts 1:8; 20:28)" (Trench). **Thou hast a name that thou livest.** A reputation of being a Christian church, but this is contrary to the real facts of the case, for **thou art** spiritually **dead.**

2. Be thou watchful, and stablish the things that remain, which were ready to die: for I have found no works of thine fulfilled before my God.

Watchful. Very expressive in Greek, the present participle being used,—*become watching*, i. e. "awake and watch." **Stablish the things that remain.** Most modern commentators incorrectly refer this phrase to *persons*, the members of the church which remain (Duesterdieck, De Wette, Ebrard, Trench, etc.). The context, however, implies that the things that remain refer to "those thy remaining few graces which in thy spiritual deadly slumber are not yet quite extinct." (So Alford, Bengel, Ewald, Milligan, etc.) **I have found no works of thine fulfilled.** Many ancient authorities read *not found thy works.* For they have not reached the standard which God requires, nor hast thou fulfilled thy duties to which as a church thou wast called. **Before my God.** These works may have appeared praiseworthy in their own eyes and in those of the world, but not before God.

3. Remember therefore how thou hast received and didst hear; and keep *it,* and repent. If therefore thou shalt not watch, I will come as a thief, and thou shalt not know what hour I will come upon thee.

Remember ... how thou ... didst hear. Sardis had kept *what* she had received, for the doctrine of the church was not heretical,—but she had lost *the manner* in which she had once received the Gospel, and the *manner* in which she heard and gave heed to the doctrine. **Keep** the divine truth which *thou hast received and didst hear,* and **repent,** for if the truth is maintained it has in itself power to work true repentance. The aorist imperative (*repent*) implies "a quick and decisive act of amendment" (Alford). **If thou shalt not watch.** In the aorist, "if thou shalt not awake and become watchful." **I will come as a thief.** This does not here refer to Christ's Second Advent, but to some special punishment which He would suddenly and unexpectedly visit upon the church at Sardis, in case they did not repent of their coldness, their want of spirituality, and of their hypocrisy.

4. But thou hast a few names in Sardis which did not defile their garments: and they shall walk with me in white; for they are worthy.

A few names. Bengel calls our attention to the fact that these few faithful Christians had not separated themselves from the church in Sardis, notwithstanding its dead state. **Which did not defile their garments.** Who had not sullied the purity of their Christian life by falling into the impure sins so common among the heathen. **They shall walk with**

me in white. White is the color of victory, innocency, and purity, and white garments are peculiar to those in heaven (6:11; 7:9; 19:8). "They, who in their earthly lives have kept their garments undefiled, will walk with Christ (John 17:24) in white garments, since, thus adorned, they will live in the state of immortal glory, before the throne of God and of the Lamb, in the full and blessed enjoyment of His fellowship" (Duesterdieck). **For they are worthy.** Not in the Roman Catholic sense *of merit*, as if they had earned this reward by their own powers. But there is a fitness and propriety in thus rewarding them. Calovius reminds us that "Christ alone, by faith, renders them worthy."

5. He that overcometh shall thus be arrayed in white garments; and I will in no wise blot his name out of the book of life, and I will confess his name before my Father, and before his angels.

He that overcometh. See notes on 2:7. The overcoming in this Epistle has especial reference to their victory over the flesh and the worldly spirit. **Thus.** As those mentioned in the preceding verse. **In no wise blot his name out of the book of life.** This expresses the certainty of the salvation of those who overcome. Whether a name once written in the Book of Life can be blotted out depends on the meaning we assign to "being written in the book of life" (13:8; 17:8). If we identify this with the *eternal choosing* of the believer in Christ (*election* in the sense as used in 1 Pet. 1:1, 2) (see notes on Rev. 13:8; 17:8), there can be no blotting out, for this election of God is in itself unchangeable and eternal (see notes on 1 Pet. 1:1, 2; 2 Pet. 1:10). But if we maintain that a man is written in the Book of Life only when he becomes an heir of the kingdom through faith in Christ, simultaneously with his calling and conversion, or his admission into the Church by baptism, then this name may be blotted out. But this is not the question here. What we are told is, not that some names shall be blotted out, but that certain names shall in no wise be so. This *book of life* is conceived of in Scripture as containing a register of all those who are to inherit eternal life (Ex. 32:32, 33; Ps. 69:28; Isa. 4:3; Ezek. 13:9; Dan. 12:1; Luke 10:20; Phil. 4:3; Rev. 3:5; 13:8; 17:8; 20:12, 15; 21:27). **I will confess his name.** The promise to the victor includes three things: (1) glorious apparel; (2) certainty of salvation; (3) public recognition. "The promise implies that in the great day the Judge will expressly acknowledge the name thus written in the book of life, as belonging to one of His" (Alford). **Before my Father.** Matt. 10:32, "Every one who shall confess me before men, him will I also confess before my Father which is in heaven." **Before his angels.** Luke 12:8, "Every one who shall confess me before men, him shall the Son of man also confess before the angels of God."

6. He that hath an ear, let him hear what the Spirit saith to the churches.

See notes on 2:7. The usual exhortation with which the last four Epistles end.

11. The Epistle to the Church in Philadelphia (3:7–13)

7. And to the angel of the church in Philadelphia write;

These things saith he that is holy, he that is true, he that hath the key of David, he that openeth, and none shall shut, and that shutteth, and none openeth.

The angel. See notes on 1:20. The *Apostolic Constitutions* (VII. 46) speaks of "Demetrius as bishop of Philadelphia." Some have identified him with the Demetrius of 3 John 12. **Philadelphia.** A city in Lydia, at the foot of Mount Tmolus, about twenty-eight miles southeast of Sardis, built by Attalus Philadelphus (whence its name), king of Pergamum, died 138 B. C. A letter written by Ignatius to this church is still extant. Though frequently visited by earthquakes, the city still exists, "a living monument of the faithfulness of Divine promises in the midst of ruins" (Lange). **He that is holy ... true.** The three-fold description here given of Christ is in harmony with 1:12–18, but takes this special form with reference to the contents of this Epistle. Christ is the one absolutely *holy* (*hagios*). separated from all evil, and hating evil, an attribute belonging to God alone; He is also the *true*, i.e. "the actual and genuine Messiah, heir and Lord of the truly abiding theocracy" (Duesterdieck). This is evidently the meaning of *true* in its relation to the context, although others maintain that it means *truthful, or faithful, or perfect.* Christ is the *true* Messiah, for He has **the key of David.** The *key* is the symbol of authority and power in the kingdom of God, and this power is exercised by Jesus Christ. In Isa. 22:20–22 we read that *the key of the house of David* was laid upon *the shoulder* of Eliakim (2 Kings 18:18), as a steward, but now it is held by Jesus the Messiah. It is not necessary to draw a distinction between *the key of David and the key of the house of David*, as some do, for both designate the kingdom of David, and this kingdom in Scripture language is the kingdom of Jesus Christ. This key is not the key of *knowledge*, "the power to open the understanding of the Scriptures (Luke 11:52; 24:32)," nor so much the key of *discipline* (although this is included),—but rather the key of *power*, for Christ as the Supreme Lord admits into the kingdom and excludes from it,—as it is emphatically expressed in the latter part of the verse.

56

8. I know thy works (behold, I have set before thee a door opened, which none can shut), that thou hast a little power, and didst keep my word, and didst not deny my name.

I know thy works. See notes on 2:2. A word of commendation and consolation. **I have given before thee a door opened.** The context shows that the meaning is, the church will have an opportunity to do successful mission work. "He has opened a door before his faithful and stedfast church, through which a multitude of still unbelieving Jews are to enter (3:9)" (Duesterdieck). The Greek word *given*, translated *set*, "is deliberately chosen to bring out the fact that every advantage we possess; every privilege we enjoy, every victory we gain, is the gift of Christ" (Milligan). **Thou hast a little power.** This phrase marks the first of three good qualities now affirmed of this church. The church had not failed; it had some power. We are not to understand as if this meant that there was a spiritual weakness in the church, but it refers rather to the smallness of the church, and its poverty in comparison with the richer Jewish synagogue. **And didst keep my word.** Making open confession of the same before the Jews and the heathen. **Didst not deny my name.** Even in the time of the greatest trial and tribulation.

9. Behold, I give of the synagogue of Satan, of them which say they are Jews, and they are not, but do lie; behold, I will make them to come and worship before thy feet, and to know that I have loved thee.

Of the synagogue of Satan. The partitive genitive, i. e. *certain persons from out of the synagogue.* These were Jews, but on account of their enmity towards their Messiah, they had no right to the honorable name, but were rather a *synagogue of Satan.* See notes on 2:9. **To come and worship.**

The mission of this church among the Jews shall be very successful. Just as in the O. T. it is prophesied that the Gentiles shall be converted and come unto Zion (Ps. 72:9; Isa. 2:3; 49:21–23; 60:14–16; Zech. 8:20–23), so here it is predicted that the Jews shall in their conversion come to the Church of Christ, and seek to enter the kingdom, which He, who has the key of David, has set up. This conversion of the Jews, here at Philadelphia, may be a type of the future conversion of the Jews in connection with the events of the Last Day. **To know that I have loved thee.** Duesterdieck here sees a reference to the life of Christ as manifested by His death upon the cross. But the interpretation of Alford suits the context better: "It is the love, bestowed on the Philadelphian church, in signalizing its success in the work of Christ, that these converted enemies shall recognize."

10. Because thou didst keep the word of my patience, I also will keep thee from the hour of trial, that *hour* which is to come upon the whole world, to try them that dwell upon the earth.

The word of my patience. Thou didst obey the word which teaches thee to endure with patience, even as I endured and suffered. **I will keep thee from the hour of trial.** A special promise given to the church at Philadelphia as a reward for their faithful endurance under trial. This does not mean that they shall be preserved *in* trial, as was the promise to Peter (Luke 22:32), but preserved *from* this great trial and temptation. **Which is to come upon the whole world.** If we take this in its historical sense, we have here the prediction of a general persecution of the Church which shall be visited upon all Christians, but from which the church at Philadelphia shall be exempt. The object would then be **to try them that dwell upon the earth,**—that is, to believers it would be a trial, making manifest their fidelity,—to unbelievers a temptation, leading to still greater hardening of hearts. But the context proves that Christ is here pre-eminently referring to the great tribulation which shall come before His revelation to destroy Antichrist.

11. I come quickly: hold fast that which thou hast, that no one take thy crown.

I come quickly. This is written for the comfort and encouragement of the church at Philadelphia, for the time of Christ's coming to reward her was near at hand. **Hold fast that which thou hast.** The strength, the faithfulness, and patience under trial, described in verses 8–10. **That no one take thy crown.** The crown of life, which is the victor's reward. See notes on 2:10. For unless thou perseverest unto the end thou mayest fail to win what seems almost within thy grasp.

12. He that overcometh, I will make him a pillar in the temple of my God, and he shall go out thence no more: and I will write upon him the name of my God, and the name of the city of my God, the new Jerusalem, which cometh down out of heaven from my God, and mine own new name.

Overcometh. See notes on 2:7. **A pillar in the temple of my God.** The glorified Church in the heavenly Jerusalem is here represented as a temple, the inner sanctuary (*naos*), and the saints compose the living stones of the same, and some even are rewarded as occupying important places, as *pillars* in the temple of God. The image used of the Church *militant* (1 Cor. 3:16; Eph. 2:19–22; 1 Pet. 2:5) is here transferred to the Church *triumphant.* Futurists lay stress upon this passage as setting forth "the pre-eminence of the victorious saints of the present dispensation, in the future æon of blessedness and glory" (Craven). **He shall go out thence no more.** This emphasizes the permanence of the reward given to the victorious saints, and to the stedfastness and purity with which they shall serve God in their exalted and responsible offices. **I will write upon him the name of my God.** Upon the forehead of the victor (14:1; 22:4), not upon the pillar. Possibly this name of God is *Jehovah*,—at least it signifies that the one who bears it belongs to God. **Of the city of my God.** This would signify citizenship. Some have thought it might *be Jehovahshammah*, "The Lord is there" (Ezek. 48:35). Christ Himself, however, calls the city **the new Jerusalem,** and describes it as that which **cometh down out of heaven.** See notes on 21:2, 10. **And mine own new name.** This *new* name is not the one mentioned in 19:16, *King of kings, and Lord of lords*, which is known to all, nor the one given in 19:13, *The Word of God*, but that incommunicable name referred to in 19:12, "which no one knoweth but he himself." "He who bears the new name of the Lord is thereby designated as eternally belonging to the Lord as though with the Lord's own signature" (Duesterdieck). These three names "express in one way or another the relation of the victorious believer to God as his Father, to Christ as the Revelation of the Father, and to the privileges and joys of citizenship in the kingdom made known to us in the Father and the Son" (Milligan).

13. He that hath an ear, let him hear what the Spirit saith to the churches.

He that hath an ear. See on 2:7.

12. The Epistle to the Church in Laodicea (3:14–22)

14. And to the angel of the church in Laodicea write; These things saith the Amen, the faithful and true witness,

the beginning of the creation of God.

The angel. See on 1:20. An ancient tradition makes the Archippus mentioned in Col. 4:17 the bishop to whom this letter was addressed. **Laodicea.** One of the renowned cities of Asia, rich in manufactures and commerce, situated in Phrygia, on the river Lycus, in the neighborhood of Hierapolis and Colossæ, about forty-five miles southeast of Philadelphia, and one hundred and fifteen east of Ephesus. A Christian church already existed in 62 A. D., at the time that Paul wrote his letter to the Colossians (Col. 2:2; 4:13, 15, 16), and it appears that Paul had appointed Archippus as their first bishop (Col. 4:16, 17). The second bishop is said to have been Nymphas (Col. 4:15), and the third Sagaris, who was martyred about 165 A. D. **The Amen.** Christ is *the Amen*, a title evidently taken from Isa. 65:16, "He who blesseth himself in the earth shall bless himself in the *God of Amen*," translated *God of truth*, "and he ... shall swear by the *God of Amen*." The titles here given to Christ imply the absolute certainty of what He here affirms. Compare 2 Cor. 1:20. **The faithful ... witness.** See on 1:5. His testimony is trustworthy and absolutely true. **The beginning of the creation of God.** Compare the parallel passage in Col. 1:15, 16, "the firstborn of all creation." This does not mean "the first of all God's works, the first creature of God," as the Arians taught, but "the principle, the original source, of the creation of God," the active principle of creation. Duesterdieck very correctly asks: "How could Christ have caused even the present Epistle to be written, if He Himself were a creature? How could every creature in heaven and earth worship Him (5:13), if He Himself were one of them?" He then adds: "In the *Alpha* lies the fact that Christ is the

61

beginning of the creation, while in the *Omega* lies the fact of Christ's *coming* to *make* an end of the visible creation." See also notes on 1:8, 18. Lee: "Christ is the source not only of the first Creation, but also of the *new* Creation, which springs from Him as the Second Adam:—*Behold, I make all things new* (21:5)."

15. I know thy works, that thou art neither cold nor hot; I would thou wert cold or hot.

The *hot* are those who are filled with a fervent zeal for the Lord. Many understand the *cold* to be those hostile and actively opposed to Christ, as Saul was as long as he was a persecutor (so Duesterdieck, De Wette, Alford, Milligan), but it is probably better to regard the *cold* those unbelievers who have "hitherto been untouched by the power of grace" (so Bengel, Trench, Lee, Lange, Ebrard, and others). Trench: "The *lukewarm* is one who has tasted of the good gift ... but in whom the grace has failed to kindle more than the feeblest spark. The publicans and harlots were *cold*, the Apostles *hot*, the Scribes and Pharisees (Luke 7:36–50) *lukewarm*. It was from among the *cold*, and not the *lukewarm*, that Christ drew recruits."

16. So because thou art lukewarm, and neither hot nor cold, I will spew thee out of my mouth.

This figure is evidently taken from the nauseating effect of lukewarm water when taken into the mouth. See also Lev. 18:28; 20:22. It implies utter rejection on the part of Christ. Wordsworth: "Heathen ignorance is *better* than Christian indifference. There is more hope of influencing those who have no knowledge of the Gospel, than those who have a little knowledge, and are self-satisfied in it.... Men are not so liable to be led astray by open unbelievers as by indifferent

Christians."

17. Because thou sayest, I am rich, and have gotten riches, and have need of nothing; and knowest not that thou art the wretched one and miserable and poor and blind and naked.

A graphic description of the inner nature of *lukewarmness.* It consists in self-sufficiency and self-righteousness, indolence and indifference, and self-deception. Notice that the three expressions affirming their wealth form a climax. The context shows that these Laodiceans were boasting of their spiritual riches,—but it is very likely that they were also rich in earthly goods, and no doubt worldly prosperity had been the main cause for making this church *lukewarm.* **The wretched one.** The most deplorable state of all is that of those who seem and deem themselves religious, and in their self-satisfied and self-deceived condition are unconscious of their spiritual needs, and do not realize their lost condition.

18. I counsel thee to buy of me gold refined by fire, that thou mayest become rich; and white garments, that thou mayest clothe thyself, and *that* the shame of thy nakedness be not made manifest; and eyesalve to anoint thine eyes, that thou mayest see.

I counsel thee. "There is a deep irony in this word. One who *has need of nothing,* yet needs counsel on the vital points of self-preservation" (Alford). **To buy.** "That one who is *poor* should be advised to *buy gold* and *raiment* and *ointment,* might of itself show what kind of buying is meant, even if Isa. 55:1, *Buy ... without money* and *without price,* had not clearly defined it. Yet notwithstanding such clear warning not to go wrong, the Roman Catholic expositors have here again handled the Word of God deceitfully, and explained, as Lyra, *to buy,* i. e. *with good works*" (Alford). **Of me.** Your only

63

Saviour. If we should aim to particularize and to distinguish between the three *spiritual blessings* with which this church needed to be endowed, we might refer the **gold refined by fire** to the merits of Christ resulting from His passive obedience and suffering, which avails for the forgiveness of sins,—the **white garments that thou mayest clothe thyself** to the righteousness of Christ, obtained through His active obedience and fulfilment of the law, apprehended by faith,—and the *eyesalve* to the anointing of the Holy Ghost (1 John 2:20, 27), who opens our eyes and hearts to see the wondrous things of God's kingdom. These three *blessings* correspond to *the poor, blind*, and *naked* of verse 17, although the order is different.

19. As many as I love, I reprove and chasten: be zealous therefore, and repent.

I reprove and chasten. In this way Christ's love is manifested to this church. He *reproves* (or *convicts*) by bringing them to a knowledge of their sins and guilt, and *chastens*, i. e. educates and disciplines them by means of fatherly eorrection. **Repent.** Repent from your lukewarmness and indifference. This applies both to the bishop and to the members of the congregation. This verse evidently predicts that outward afflictions shall be visited upon the Laodiceans (Heb. 12:6).

20. Behold, I stand at the door and knock: if any man hear my voice and open the door, I will come in to him, and will sup with him, and he with me.

The verse calls attention to Christ's continual presence, and emphasizes His readiness to forgive every one who repents of his sins. **I stand at the door and knock.** This door is the door of the heart, and Christ knocks at every

64

signal manifestation of His providence, and whenever the Word of God reaches us. Some would explain the figure by a reference to Luke 12:36 and Cant. 5:2, but it is a question whether there is here any reference to the marriage supper of the Lamb. It is better to limit this verse entirely to the blessed communion of the truly penitent with the Lord in this life. **And open the door.** This passage does not teach Synergism or Pelagianism, as if the sinner had power by his own strength to receive Christ, "as though men could open the door of their heart when they would, as though repentance was not itself a gift of the exalted Saviour (Acts 5:36). They can only open when Christ knocks, and they would have no desire at all to open unless He knocked" (Trench). While the Word of God is enlightening the intellect, the Holy Ghost is working inwardly, stirring up the conscience, awakening the heart, and bringing about penitence and faith. **Will sup with him, and he with me.** This figure expresses the most intimate communion. It is best to understand this of the spiritual blessings of this life. Compare John 14:23, "If a man love me, he will keep my word: and my Father will love him, and we will come unto him, and make our abode with him." Alford: "This blessed admission of Christ into our hearts will lead to His becoming our guest, ever present with us,—and then the guest Himself becomes the host, because He is the Bread of Life,—and thus we are ever in close union with Him, partaking ever of His fulness, until we sit down at His table in His kingdom."

21. He that overcometh, I will give to him to sit down with me in my throne, as I also overcame, and sat down with my Father in his throne.

He that overcometh. See notes on 2:7. **To sit down with**

me in my throne. A promise that shall receive its fulfilment in the life of glory hereafter. See notes on 2:26, 27. **As I also overcame.** The reference is to Christ's resurrection, ascension, and exaltation at the right hand of God.

22. He that hath an ear, let him hear what the Spirit saith to the churches.

See notes on 2:7.

Wordsworth calls especial attention to the fact that in each of the Epistles the special warning or promise "is appropriately adopted and adjusted to the attribute under which Christ presents Himself to each church in succession. It is also accommodated to the special *difficulties* and *dangers* which have been overcome, or are to be overcome by that particular church. There is also a gradual *scale of ascent* in the dignity and blessedness of the promises made by Christ to them *that overcome.*"

Isaac Williams: "(1) The variety of circumstance and of trial in the case of these churches is so great that it seems to comprehend the state of every church that can arise,—so that every church that would understand itself will find itself in that mirror. In every case an individual is addressed, as well as his church, for good or evil.... (2) The fact that the church and its angel or bishop are so blended as to have rendered it matter of question which is addressed, is in itself instructive, as proving that as the bishop, so is the church in the long run; as the church, so the bishop.... (3) These seven Epistles are to the churches of all time what the parables of the Gospel are to individuals—a glass in which they may detect themselves, and the judgment of God. It is, in fact, beholding themselves 'in the mind of Christ.' Hence this, their searching depth of application to all times, has led to those fanciful interpretations which suppose them successive historic periods until the end."

4

Revelation 4

13. The Vision of the Divine Majesty (4:1–8)

W e now come to the second of the three great divisions of the Book of Revelation (4:1–22:5). Chapters 4 and 5 form a kind of introduction to the events which are afterwards recorded. They unfold to us the scene in heaven in relation to the judgments which are about to take place on earth. In chapter 4. St. John in a vision beholds the absolute majesty and holiness of God.

1. After these things I saw, and behold, a door opened in heaven, and the first voice which I heard, *a voice* as of a trumpet speaking with me, one saying, Come up hither, and I will shew thee the things which must come to pass hereafter.

After these things. This marks that John now beholds a new vision, following the one recorded in 1:10–3:22. **I saw.** In his ecstatic state, for St. John was "in the Spirit" (1:10) during the entire revelation (1:10–22:16). **A door.** For heaven is regarded as a house, the temple of God, in which

He is enthroned (Ps. 11:4; 18:6; 29:9). **Opened.** "Observe the *perfect* participle, the door had been opened and was *standing open.* The veil of the heavenly Holy of Holies had been removed by Christ (Heb. 10:19, 20), and heaven was laid open to view" (Wordsworth). **The first voice ... as of a trumpet.** The voice which he had heard at first (1:10), probably that of Christ Himself. **Come up hither.** Into heaven, through the open door. **The things which must come to pass after these things.** After the things referred to in the Seven Epistles. See 1:19.

2. Straightway I was in the Spirit: and behold, there was a throne set in heaven, and one sitting upon the throne.

I was in the Spirit. Although John had been previously in an ecstatic state, a fresh outpouring of the Spirit is now given here (cf. Ezek. 11:1, 5). John is transported in vision through the open door up into heaven, where he can see things occurring in heaven and on earth. We are reminded of St. Paul's vision (2 Cor. 12:1–4). **A throne set.** John sees two things, *a throne set,* occupying a certain fixed position, and *one sitting upon the throne.* This *throne* is the symbol of God's established government. Although men may not recognize it on earth, in heaven it is manifest to all. It is difficult to decide whether "He who sitteth upon the throne" is the Father, as distinguished from the Son (5:6; 6:16; 7:10) and from the Holy Spirit (4:5), or the Triune God. It is probably best to refer the title to the Triune God on account of the Trisagion in 4:8, and the parallel vision in Isaiah (6:1–3), where the reference unquestionably is to the Trinity. "God is here introduced to us as He is in Himself, and not according to that separation of *hypostases* or personalities revealed to us in other passages of Scripture" (Milligan). "The references in

69

4:5 and 5:6 to the Second and Third Persons of the Trinity do not oppose this view; neither does the doxology in 4:11" (Lee).

3. And he that sat *was* to look upon like a jasper stone and a sardius: and *there was* a rainbow round about the throne, like an emerald to look upon.

Like in vision to a jasper and a sardine stone. "The entire form of the enthroned one appears in the two-fold, yet united, brilliancy of the jasper and the sardius, just as the entire form of the Lord, in 1:16, was in appearance like intense light of the sun" (Duesterdieck). The jasper and the sardius were the *last* and the *first* stones in "the breastplate of judgment" (Ex. 28:17–20). It is difficult to decide what gem is exactly meant by the *iaspis* (jasper) of John, as some, from the passage in 21:11, "a stone most precious, as it were a jasper stone, clear as crystal," identify it with the diamond. The bright sparkliug whiteness of the jasper (21:11) makes it a symbol of the holiness and glory of God. The sardius was of a fiery red color, our carnelian, and this gem is the symbol of the justice and wrath of God as manifested towards all ungodliness and unrighteousness. "The double brilliancy of the two stones shining through one another is to be regarded as a profound designation of the essential unity of the holiness and righteousness of God" (Duesterdieck). **A rainbow ... like an emerald.** The bow that John saw *round about the throne*, forming a complete circle, surrounding the throne vertically, had the form of a rainbow, but instead of having seven colors, it was *emerald green*, "the color even more refreshing and more directly symbolizing grace and mercy. So far at least we may be sure of as to the symbolism of this appearance of Him that sitteth on the throne: that the brightness of His glory and fire of His judgment is ever girded by, and found within, the refreshment and surety of His mercy and goodness. So that as Duesterdieck has well said, 'This fundamental vision contains all that may serve for terror to the enemies, and consolation to the friends, of Him that sitteth on the throne' " (Alford).

4. And round about the throne *were* four and twenty thrones: and upon the thrones *I saw* four and twenty elders sitting, arrayed in white garments; and on their heads crowns of gold.

Round about the throne four and twenty thrones. Evidently lower and smaller than the grand central throne. **Four and twenty elders.** These elders are not *angels*, for two things mark them, white robes and crowns of gold, the rewards of conflict, endurance, and victory (3:4, 5; 2:10). "They are representatives of the entire congregation of all believers, to whom, as to these elders, belong the holiness and glory indicated by the white robes, and the royal dominion by the thrones and crowns" (Duesterdieck). These elders represent the triumphant Church in heaven, including both the Old and the New Testament saints. In the O. T. the elders were the representatives of the Church (Ex. 4:29; 12:21; etc.), as well as in the New Testament (Acts 20:17; 21:18; etc.), and these *twenty-four* elders evidently symbolize the twelve Patriarchs, representing the Old Testament Church, and the twelve Apostles, representing the New Testament saints. "This follows (1) from 5:8–10; (2) from Matt. 19:28; Luke 22:30 (Eph. 2:4–6); (3) from 21:12, 14, where the Twelve Tribes and the Twelve Apostles are conjoined; (4) from the union of the Old and New Covenants in 15:3; and (5) from the functions, distinctly representative, of the elders, as

71

described in 5:5, 8; 7:13" (Lee). **Sitting.** Implying the attitude of rest and honor in the kingdom already come. **Arrayed in white garments.** Inplying that all their sins have been washed away and that they are clothed in robes of purity, the robes of priests. **And on their heads crowns of gold.** For they are "priests of God and of Christ, and shall reign with him" (20:6; 5:10).

5. And out of the throne proceed lightnings and voices and thunders. And *there were* seven lamps of fire burning before the throne, which are the seven Spirits of God.

These *lightnings and voices and thunders* ever proceeding out of the throne represent the sovereignty and almighty power of God (Ex. 19:16; Ps. 29:3–8), and indicate that God's throne is a throne of judgment. "These *seven lamps of fire burning before the throne* of God indicate nothing else than that the eyes of the Lord are 'as a flame of fire' (1:14), and that the Holy Spirit is to be regarded chiefly as illuminating, seeing, and searching all things (1 Cor. 2:10), and for that very reason everywhere active in His holy judgments" (Duesterdieck). See notes on 1:4 and 1:14.

6. And before the throne, as it were a glassy sea like unto crystal; and in the midst of the throne, and round about the throne, four living creatures full of eyes before and behind.

What John saw before the throne of God appeared to him as a sea of glass clear and pure as crystal. Many attempts have been made to explain the significance of this symbol—nearly all different. As examples of the more probable, Ebrard thinks that as the stormy sea represents the mass of the nations in their ungodly state (17:15), so here the pure and calm sea designates "creation in its true relation to the Creator;" Alford maintains that by this figure is signified "the purity, calmness, and majesty of God's rule;" Luthardt, on the other hand, sees in this symbol "the fulness of the divine life (22:1), which is nothing but peace and calm, in contrast with the stormy disquietude of the life of the world (13:1; Dan. 7:2);" Wordsworth: "*Sea* in this Book represents the element of *tumult* and *confusion* in the lower world (13:1). But here, by way of contrast, there is in the *heavenly* Church a sea *of glass*, expressive of smoothness and brightness; and this *heavenly sea* is of *crystal*, declaring that the calm of heaven is not, like earthly seas, ruffled by winds, but is *crystallized* into an *eternity of peace;*" Milligan: "In the *glassy sea* of this verse we have an emblem of the course of Providence by which God conducts those who place themselves in His hands to their final rest in His immediate presence." Probably it would be better to lay more stress upon the bearing of the symbol upon *the righteous judgments of God*, to indicate the depth and purity of divine justice. In Ps. 36:6 the *judgments* of God are spoken of as "a great deep," and in strict harmony with this explanation, those who sing the song of Moses and of the Lamb (15:2–4),—"Great and marvellous are thy works, O Lord God, the Almighty: righteous and true are thy ways ... for thy righteous acts have been made manifest,"—are represented as standing "by the glassy sea mingled with fire, having harps of God" (15:2). **In the midst ... and round about the throne.** From Isaiah's vision (6:1, 2) we may infer that the *four living creatures* stood above, and not on the same level as the throne, one in the centre of each side of the throne. "They stand so free as to be able to move (15:7); and because they have manifestly turned with their faces towards the throne, John can see that they are 'full of eyes before and behind' " (Duesterdieck). In these *four living creatures* we

73

have a combination of the Seraphim of Isaiah (6:2, 3) and the Cherubim of Ezekiel (1:5, 6; 10:5, 12).

7. And the first creature *was* like a lion, and the second creature like a calf, and the third creature had a face as of a man, and the fourth creature *was* like a flying eagle.

Each one of the living creatures in Ezekiel's vision (1:6, 10) had all four faces, while here each one has but one face. The greatest diversity of opinion exists among commentators as to the significance of these four symbols. Most of these explanations are extremely fanciful or mere surmises. Many of the ancient commentators (Augustine, Jerome, Bede), and some moderns (Williams, Wordsworth, and others), maintain that these four living creatures designate the Four Evangelists, or the Four Gospels (Matthew the *man*, Mark the *lion*, Luke the *calf*, John the *eagle*). others, *the four* Patriarchal Churches (Alexandria, Jerusalem, Antioch, Constantinople); others, the *four* mysteries of the faith (the Incarnation, Passion, Resurrection, Ascension); or, the *four* great Apostles (Peter, James, Matthew, Paul); or, the *four* cardinal virtues; or, the attributes of God (wisdom, power, omniscience, creation); or, *the four* faculties of the human soul, etc. But it is best with the great majority of our ablest modern commentators of all schools to regard these four cherubic forms as representing the whole animate creation. "We have thus the throne of God surrounded by His Church and His animated world; the former represented by the twenty-four elders, the latter by the four living creatures" (Alford). "These four forms are to be taken as the heads of the four classes of animated creation—rational beings, birds, tame animals, and wild animals. That is, we have here, ideally represented, the collective, living creation on which the judgments of the first four seals (6:1–8) are inflicted—each of the Living Creatures inviting the Seer to behold. So also, when the wrath of God is poured out on the created universe (15:7; 16:1–21), one of the Living Creatures gives to the ministering Angels the Seven Vials. The number *Four*, too, is the recognized *signature* of the assemblage of created life; it is, in fact, the *signature* of the world (7:1; 21:13)" (Lee).

8. And the four living creatures, having each one of them six wings, are full of eyes round about and within: and they have no rest day and night, saying, Holy, holy, holy, *is* the Lord God, the Almighty, which was and which is and which is to come (or *which cometh*).

We must understand the *six wings* in the same way as the six wings of the Seraphim in the vision of Isaiah (6:2), "each one had six wings; with twain he covered his face, and with twain he covered his feet, and with twain he did fly," as representing the dependent and ministerial relation in which each living creature stands to its Creator,—for this statement in Isaiah indicates *awe*, for the Living Creatures dare not look upon God; *humility*, for they stand in His presence; *obedience*, for they are ready to execute His commands (After Bengel). **Full of eyes round about and within.** The statement of verse 6 is repeated in order to emphasize the fact that the eyes were *round* the outside of each wing, and up the *inside* of each when expanded, and on that part of the body beneath the wing. So also in Ezek. 1:18; 10:12. These *eyes* signify the wakeful activity with which they celebrate their ceaseless praise of God. **Holy, holy, holy.** We are reminded of the hymn of praise sung by the Seraphim (Isa. 6:3). This *Trisagion*, thrice repeated attribute of holiness, has ever been rightly understood by the Church to refer to the Blessed Trinity.

Lee: "It is generally admitted that the Four Living Creatures here, and in Ezek. 1:5, are of the same character as the *cherubim* of the Tabernacle of Moses (Ex. 25:20; 37:9), and of the Temple of Solomon (1 Kings 6:23–26). When the different descriptions are compared, it results that the figure of the Cherub had no fixed, definite form; and that the conception was that of a symbolical image." Cremer (*Lexicon*): "They are usually the signs and tokens of majesty, of the sublime majesty of God, both in His covenant relation and in His relation to the world (Ps. 99:1); and, therefore, it is that they are assigned so prominent a place, though no active part in the final scenes of sacred history (Rev. 6:1–7).... They do not, like the angels, fulfil the purposes of God in relation to men; they are distinct from the angels (Rev. 5:11). We are thus led to conclude that they materially represent the ideal pattern of the true relation of creation to its God."

14. The Unceasing Hymn of Praise (4:9–11)

9. And when the living creatures shall give glory and honor and thanks to him that sitteth on the throne, to him that liveth for ever and ever (Gr. *unto the ages of the ages*).

This adoration is paid to the Triune God, *to him that sitteth on the throne* (see 4:2, 3). The future implies a continued repetition of the act, which the regular subjunctive would not suggest.

10. The four and twenty elders shall fall down before him that sitteth on the throne, and shall worship him that liveth for ever and ever, and shall cast their crowns before the throne, saying.

It has been remarked "that the living creatures only cele-

brate and declare; the elders worship with understanding."
All God's works will praise Him, as represented by the four
living creatures (4:9), but only the redeemed, as represented
by the twenty-four elders, recognize in the fullest sense
their dependence and debt to their King and Lord. Three
acts of worship and homage on the part of the elders are
described, "falling down," "worshipping," and "casting their
crowns before the throne." Though made kings (5:10), yet
they cast down their crown before God as attributing all
true kingship to Him, the one and only Potentate, in whose
presence no creature whatever has any glory or honor of its
own (Ps. 115:1). "If the beings who dwell so near about His
throne act so reverentially towards Him, how much more
humbly does it behoove us to conduct ourselves, who dwell
in cottages of clay! Were our hearts penetrated with a just
dread of Him, we should also come to possess an assurance
of His favor, confidence in Him, desire after Him, delight in
Him, and a more zealous endeavor to do what is pleasing in
His sight" (Bengel).

11. Worthy art thou, our Lord and our God, to receive the
glory and the honor and the power: for thou didst create all
things, and because of thy will they were, and were created.

"Here the praise of the elders refers not to redemption
itself,—which first occurs in 5:9, 10,—but to the power and
glory of God revealed in creation, so that the words of the
elders stand in beautiful harmony with the praise of the
four living creatures, representing the *entire* living creation
(4:7–9), as well as with the significance of the entire vision"
(Duesterdieck). **Our Lord and our God.** Probably the
our of these twenty-four elders representing the Redeemed
Church marks that the redeemed ones are standing in a more

77

intimate relationship to God than the four living creatures. The elders substitute the word *power* for the *thanks* of the four living creatures, not that they fail in gratitude, but because "in this ascription of praise they look on creation from without, and that thanksgiving which creation renders for its being becomes in their view a tribute to Him *who called them into being*, and thus a testimony to His creative power" (Alford). **Because of thy will they were.** *They existed*, in contrast to their previous non-existence. The existence of all things was owing to the will of God, and the manner by which all things came into existence was by the definite act of creation at a definite time, for all things **were created.** As is well known this verse is the Eucharistic Hymn of the Ancient Liturgies.

5

Revelation 5

15. The Book with Seven Seals (5:1–7)

The general vision recorded in the fourth chapter still continues in this fifth chapter, only that there is a progress in the vision, a particular scene now appearing. In the fourth chapter we beheld God as the Creator and Governor of all things, in this we behold Christ as the Redeemer of His people.

1. And I saw in the right hand of him that sat on the the throne a book written within and on the back, close sealed with seven seals.

The Greek is *"on the right hand,"* i. e. the book lay on the open hand, implying "that *on God's part* there was no withholding of His future purposes as contained in this book" (Alford). This *book* was a scroll, written on both sides (Ezek. 2:9, 10), so that every part of the roll was covered with writing, indicating that we have here the complete record of God's counsels respecting the earth (4:1, "the things which must come to pass hereafter") and the judgments which shall be visited upon it (6:1–11:18). As Ezekiel's book contained the judgments on the foes of Jerusalem, this book contains those upon the foes of Christ's Church. The *close-sealing* with *seven seals* indicates the mysterious character of the contents, and the completeness of the sealing, which can only be opened by the Lamb of God (5:5, 7, 9). Sixteen interpretations as to what is meant by this Roll and its contents have been enumerated by Todd (*Lectures on the Apocalypse*), among which we may mention the more prominent: It is the Old Testament; it is the whole Bible; it is Christ Himself; it is the title deed of man's inheritance; it is the book of divorce giving an account of the rejection of the Jews; it is the book of God's purposes and providence; it is the Apocalypse; it is that part of the Apocalypse containing the judgments to be visited on the foes of Christ and His Redeemed Church. It is best to regard this last as the most natural interpretation, and that its contents extend not only to what is written from 6:1 to 8:1, but that it includes the seven seals and the seven trumpets (6:1–11:18).

2. And I saw a strong angel proclaiming with a great voice, Who is worthy to open the book, and to loose the seals thereof?

A strong angel ... with a great voice. For his voice penetrated heaven, earth, and Hades (5:3). "That an *angel* raises the cry may remind us of the interest taken by angels in the plan of redemption and in the fortunes of the Church (1 Pet. 1:12)" (Milligan). **Worthy.** In the sense of having the moral qualifications.

3. And no one in the heaven, or on the earth, or under the earth, was able to open the book, or to look thereon.

As in Phil. 2:10, the whole universe is here designated under its three divisions. No one of created beings could be found even to attempt to open the book, for there was not one, from Gabriel downwards, who had the requisite qualifications to undertake the task.

4. And I wept much, because no one was found worthy to open the book, or to look thereon.

He wept, probably because he thought that this would put an end to further revelations. "Without tears the Revelation was not written, neither without tears can it be understood" (Bengel).

5. And one of the elders saith unto me, Weep not: behold, the Lion that is of the tribe of Judah, the Root of David, hath overcome, to open the book and the seven seals thereof.

This *one* "of the elders" represented the twenty-four elders, and therefore the whole Church of the Redeemed in heaven, who knew what Christ had done for them as their Redeemer, and that all power was given unto Him in heaven and on earth (Matt. 28:18). Christ, "the Lamb that hath been slain" (5:6, 12), is here designated as *the Lion that is of the tribe of Judah*, with reference to Gen. 49:9, 10, "for it is evident that our Lord hath sprung out of Judah" (Heb. 7:14), and *the Root of David, with* reference to Isa. 11:1, 10, "for Jesus Christ, the Son of God, was born of the seed of David according to the flesh" (Rom. 1:1–3). **Hath overcome.** The *aorist* in Greek. He *overcame* once for all, at the time of His Resurrection, Ascension, and Exaltation at the right hand of God, and by virtue of His great victory it is in His power *to open the book and the seven seals thereof.*

6. And I saw in the midst of the throne and of the four living creatures, and in the midst of the elders, a Lamb standing,

81

as though it had been slain, having seven horns, and seven eyes, which are the seven Spirits of God, sent forth into all the earth.

The words seem to indicate that the Lamb was standing immediately before the middle point of the throne. The Greek word is *arnion*, "a little lamb," not *amnos*, "a lamb," as in other passages (John 1:29, 36; 1 Pet. 1:19; Acts 8:32), and also in Isa. 53:7 ("as a lamb that is led to the slaughter," the very passage to which reference is here made),—and no doubt this *diminutive* is used to give prominence to the idea of innocence and meekness. **Standing.** For the Lamb is *living*, but it bears its death-wounds still on its body, the marks of its sacrificial death showing that it has once been slain. **Having seven horns.** The symbol of perfect power,—the horn being the well-known emblem of might (1 Sam. 2:10; Ps. 112:9; 148:14; Dan. 7:7, 20, 21; 8:3, 4; Rev. 17:3), and seven the number of perfection (Matt. 28:18). **And seven eyes.** The symbol of perfect knowledge, expressly interpreted as designating **the seven Spirits of God, sent forth into all the earth.** See notes on 4:5; 3:1, and 1:4. "That Christ *has* these spirits (this Spirit) of God is symbolized here by the seven eyes of the lamb, just as before the throne of God the same Spirit appears as seven lamps (4:5). Because Christ has the Spirit, He knows everything, even things upon earth, whither the Spirit is sent,—the doings of His enemies, and the state of His own people" (Duesterdieck).

7. And he came, and he taketh *it* out of the right hand of him that sat on the throne.

To raise the question whether the Lamb also had hands is to miss the whole aim of the symbol. "St. John sees the Lamb not merely take the roll, but keep it. It is His,—His by the

82

right of the victory He has won" (Milligan).

This has a special significance if we understand the book to contain the judgments which are to be visited upon the earth in connection with Christ's coming to destroy Antichrist. It is not simply as divine Son of God, but also and principally as victorious Saviour and King of His people, that Christ takes the book. "His worthiness has been established in conflict and temptation (John 14:30; Heb. 2:9; 4:15)" (Boyd-Carpenter).

16. The Adoration of the Lamb (5:8–14)

8. And when he had taken the book, the four living creatures and the four and twenty elders fell down before the Lamb, having each one a harp, and golden bowls full of incense, which are the prayers of the Saints.

The Lamb shares in the divine glory of Him that sitteth on the throne (4:9–11). The phrase *having each one a harp and golden bowls,* according to grammar, the context, and the symbolical significance, applies only to the elders. Each of the elders, the representatives of the Redeemed Church, has a harp in one hand, with which they accompany their song of praise (compare 14:2, 3; 15:2), and each one has a golden bowl in the other hand. These bowls or censers are full of incense, and this incense represents **the prayers of the saints.** Who these saints are, that are spoken of, is not revealed, though as these twenty-four elders represent the Redeemed Church in heaven, and in person offer the praises and thanksgivings of the glorified saints, it is most probable that this incense cannot refer to the prayers of the Redeemed Church in heaven, but most likely to the prayers of the saints on earth, who are passing through the great tribulation in connection with the revelation of Antichrist (compare 6:9–11; 8:3–5; Luke 18:7, 8). "It is to be noted, on the one hand, that the elders do not pray for themselves, that for themselves they praise; and on the other, that they are not intercessors for the saints on earth, that they but offer to the Lamb the prayers of the suffering saints" (Milligan).

9. And they sing a new song, saying, Worthy art thou to take the book, and to open the seals thereof: for thou wast slain, and didst purchase unto God with thy blood *men* of every tribe, and tongue, and people, and nation.

This song is that of the twenty-four elders alone. It is *new* because it celebrates a special occasion, the worthiness of the Lamb to open the seals; *new*, because its theme is new, the glory of a completed redemption; *new*, because it is sung for the first time by the Redeemed Church in heaven. **Thou wast slain, and didst purchase.** The work of Redemption is the great theme of this song. The tenses point to the definite act when Christ purchased us by His death on the Cross. (See notes on 1 Pet. 1:18, 19.) **Unto God.** For Christ, through the eternal Spirit, offered Himself without blemish unto God (Heb. 9:14), and gave Himself up for us, as an offering and a sacrifice to God (Eph. 5:2). **Of every tribe ... and nation.** The thought here is not that Christ has died for all men, which is indeed true (Rom. 5:15–19; Heb. 2:9; 2 Cor. 5:15; 1 Tim 2:6; 1 John 2:2), but that the Redeemed Church in heaven has been gathered out from every quarter of the globe,—universality being indicated by the mention of four sources from which they come.

10. And madest them *to be* unto our God a kingdom and priests; and they reign upon the earth.

There are three particulars mentioned here. The first two are already included in John's doxology of praise to Christ (see notes on 1:6). We here have the important addition, "and they reign upon the earth." This is probably the correct reading, though the weight of ancient authority seems to be almost equally divided between the present and the future, *they shall reign.* The tense does not really affect the meaning. The song of the elders anticipates the opening of the seals, the visitation of the judgments upon the earth, the destruction of Antichrist, and the establishment of Christ's kingdom. Most commentators refer this *reigning* to the present condition of the Church. So Alford: "The present is not to be rendered as future, but keeps its own meaning (the whole aspect and reference of this heavenly vision being *not future,* but *present:* the world and Church as now existing, cf. Eph. 2:6). The Church even now, in Christ her Head, reigns on the earth." The weakness of the position of all those accepting this view lies in this, that they take it for granted that these visions *do not* refer to the future. The *Futurists* maintain that this passage refers to the personal reign of the Redeemed Church hereafter with Christ, at the time of the establishment of His kingdom. "They shall reign as kings, not in worldly power on the earth as it is now; but when restored to that state originally designed for man (Gen. 1:26, 27), over *the new earth* (Rev. 22:5)" (Burger). It is best to refer this reigning to the time of the Millennium. (See *Excursus* I.)

11. And I saw, and I heard a voice of many angels round about the throne and the living creatures and the elders; and the number of them was ten thousand times ten thousand, and thousands of thousands.

The order of the three choral songs recorded in this chapter

85

is very significant. First we hear the song of praise by the Redeemed Church in heaven (5:9, 10), then the song of the angels (5:11, 12), and finally the song of Creation itself (5:13), closed with the *Amen* of the four living creatures.

John now sees innumerable hosts of angels whose song he hears. Although angels are not themselves partakers of redemption (Heb. 2:16), they take the deepest interest in the history of salvation (Luke 15:10; Eph. 3:10; 1 Pet. 1:12; Heb. 1:14). This statement of the number of the angels, as in Dan. 7:10, only indicates their actual innumerability, "myriads of myriads," "the innumerable hosts of angels" (Heb. 12:22).

12. Saying with a great voice, Worthy is the Lamb that hath been slain to receive the power, and riches, and wisdom, and might, and honour, and glory, and blessing.

Notice that this ascription of praise by the angels to the Lamb is *seven-fold;* so also is the ascription which is addressed by the angels to *God* in 7:11, 12. Notice that only *one* article is prefixed to the seven nouns. "These seven words of praise must be expressed as though they were a single word, because they all stand with one another after a single article" (Bengel).

13. And every created thing which is in the heaven, and on the earth, and under the earth, and on the sea, and all things that are in them, heard I saying, Unto him that sitteth on the throne, and unto the Lamb, *be* the blessing, and the honour, and the glory, and the dominion, for ever and ever (Gr. *unto the ages of the ages*).

Every animated creature, including the angels and the glorified saints, and the whole inanimate creation, join in this universal chorus celebrating the glory of God and the Redeemer,—for the time has come for Christ to enter upon His universal kingdom (Phil. 2:10, 11; Heb. 8:9–12). "The chorus proceeds from universal nature, from all created things without exception. It is the harmony of the universe in the thought of the completion of God's purposes, in the perfect execution of that which He originally contemplated in Jesus Christ.... At last the regeneration of the world has come: and in one burst of song all created things send up their shout of triumph and their hymn of praise" (Millligan).

14. And the four living creatures said, Amen. And the elders fell down and worshipped.

As the Four Living Creatures, representing the entire living creation, had begun this series of hymns (4:8), so now they pronounce the *Amen* to Creation's chorus of praise. The Elders, representing the Redeemed Church in heaven, can only in silent adoration fall down and worship God and the Lamb.

6

Revelation 6

17. The Opening of the First Seal (6:1, 2)

1. And I saw when the Lamb opened one of the seven seals, and I heard one of the four living creatures saying as with a voice of thunder, Come.

We still have a continuation of the general Vision to which chapters 4 and 5 were preparatory and introductory. The opening of these seals unfolds to us the events which shall take place on earth in the future, preparatory to, and in connection with, the great day of the Lord's Revelation to destroy Antichrist. This sixth chapter contains a description of the opening of the first six seals and of their contents. Notice that on the breaking of a seal John does not *read the contents of the book*, but *sees a Vision* disclosing the contents. The key to these visions is Matt. 24, in which our Lord also declares the signs of His coming. It is with this sixth chapter that the great differences between commentators begin.

This *voice of thunder* evidently belonged to each one of *the four living creatures*, although mentioned only in the case of the first that speaks. As *the four living creatures* represent Creation, it seems very fitting that the opening of the first four seals, which represent the judgments which shall in the future overtake the earth, should be introduced by them. The great majority of commentators maintain that the cry *Come* is addressed to John, having accepted the gloss *and see*, which some of the ancient authorities have added to the text; others think that these invitations (6:1, 3, 5, 7) are addressed to the respective Riders, but it is better (with Alford, Hofmann, Kliefoth, Milligan, and others) to regard it as addressed to Christ Himself (as in 22:17, 20). The remarks of Alford are suggestive: "It is a cry addressed, not to John, but to the Lord Jesus: and as each of these first four seals is accompanied by a similar cry from one of the four living creatures, I see represented in this four-fold *Come* the groaning and travailing together of creation for the manifestation of the sons of God, expressed in each case in a prayer for Christ's coming: and in the things revealed when the seals are opened His four-fold preparation for His coming on earth. Then at the opening of the fifth seal the longing of the martyred saints for the same consummation is expressed, and at that of the sixth it actually arrives."

2. And I saw, and behold, a white horse, and he that sat thereon had a bow; and there was given unto him a crown: and he came forth conquering, and to conquer.

Everything that underlies this verse expresses the victorious conqueror,—*the white horse*, the rider with *the bow* and *crown*, his going forth *conquering, and to conquer.* The imagery of these horses and riders is evidently closely related to that in the visions of Zech. 1:7–11; 6:1–8. But the great question

89

is, Who is this Rider and what is here represented? Most commentators answer, The Son of God riding forth in the power of His Gospel, or *Christianity* personified. But to maintain, that because the Lord Himself came out of heaven on a white horse (19:11), it is also Christ who here appears on the white horse, is to overlook the plainest teachings of the vision. The horses and riders in the seals that follow give us the keynote to a better solution, for all agree that these represent three great judgments that shall overtake the earth, *war, famine,* and *pestilence.* The first seal also represents a *judgment,* the oppression and devastation of a *conqueror,* who shall bring in his train the plagues that follow. The rider *had a bow,* setting forth his warrior character, and a crown *was given to him,* suggesting that he is not a monarch when he first appears, but will obtain a crown by his energy and victories. As all four seals usher in *judgments* that shall come upon the earth as opposing Christ and His reign, it is highly probable that this first Rider represents a false Christ (Matt. 24:5), whom God may use, as a blind instrument, to punish the nations of the earth. It may be that we have here the counterpart of "the first beast" of Rev. 13:1–10. It is also highly probable that the Seal Visions represent the circumstances of our Lord's *Revelation* to destroy Antichrist under different aspects, many of them being synchronous. "Many think that this Rider is Christ, or at least the representative of Christ's kingdom. But is it possible that when He has come, the plagues that follow should come after Him? or why should the living creatures continue to cry to Him to come, if He be come already? It would be more credible that the first Rider is a *false* Christ, just as Matt. 24:5 precedes verses 6, 7" (Simcox).

18. The Opening of the Second Seal (6:3, 4)

3. And when he opened the second seal, I heard the second living creature saying, Come.

The vision which followed the opening of the first seal has ended, but we need not infer that the rider of the first horse will have finished his career of conquest before the rider of the second horse makes his appearance upon earth. It is most likely that the judgments represented by these horses and their riders will all appear simultaneously on the earth in connection with the events accompanying the Revelation of Antichrist.

4. And another *horse* came forth, a red horse: and to him that sat thereon it was given to take peace from the earth, and that they should slay one another: and there was given unto him a great sword.

The color of each horse corresponds to the mission of its rider,—here *red*, to indicate war and *bloodshed.* In agreement with this, it is given to this rider to take peace out of the earth, for "ye shall hear of wars and rumours of wars: for nation shall rise against nation, and kingdom against kingdom; but the end is not yet" (Matt. 24:6, 7), and the inhabitants of the earth, opposed to Christ and His kingdom, shall kill one another,—and of all this *the great* sword given to the rider is the symbol. Nearly all expositors are united concerning the general meaning of this vision, but apply it differently. Milligan correctly remarks; "The *earth* out of which peace is taken is the ungodly world, and the slaughtering of which we read is not produced by the attacks of the wicked on the good, but by those of the former on one another." All these judgments belong to the days immediately preceding the

91

Revelation of Christ to destroy Antichrist.

19. The Opening of the Third Seal (6:5, 6)

5. And when he opened the third seal, I heard the third living creature saying, Come. And I saw, and behold, a black horse; and he that sat thereon had a balance in his hand.

The color *black* implies *mourning*, sadness, and *want*; the *balance* is the symbol of scarcity, bread being doled out by weight. Compare Ezek. 4:16, 17, "they shall eat bread by weight, and with carefulness; and they shall drink water by measure, and with astonishment: that they may want bread and water."

6. And I heard as it were a voice in the midst of the four living creatures saying, A measure of wheat for a penny, and three measures of barley for a penny, and the oil and the wine hurt thou not.

Famine is to follow in the footsteps of war and bloodshed. A *choinix measure* (less than a quart) of wheat, usually sold for an eighth of a denarius, and sufficient for a man's daily nourishment, will then cost a *denarius*, the amount a laboring man can earn in one day (Matt. 20:2), and the daily pay of a soldier. A man can then only earn enough to buy choice food for himself, to say nothing of his many other wants, or of the wants of his family. He may indeed buy three measures of barley for the same sum, but that in itself is an evidence how hard the times will be. This famine, in accord with Christ's own words, shall immediately precede His own Coming (Matt. 24:7). But there is to be a limit even to this famine. God takes pity upon the needs of His creatures, and limits the effects of the famine by sparing the oil and the wine, which in Eastern lands are as needful to the poor as to the rich. Alford: "By this third seal we learn that Famine—the pressure of want on men, not sweeping them away by utter failure of the means of subsistence, but keeping them far below the ordinary standard of comfort, and especially those who depend on their daily labor—will be one of the four judgments by which the way of the Lord's coming will be opened. This seems to point, not so much to *death* by famine, which belongs to the next vision, as to agrarian distress with all its dreadful consequences."

20. The Opening of the Fourth Seal (6:7, 8)

7. And when he opened the fourth seal, I heard the voice of the fourth living creature saying, Come.

Each one of the four living creatures (4:7), representing living creation, invites Christ to come. See notes on 6:1.

8. And I saw, and behold, a pale horse: and he that sat upon him, his name was Death; and Hades followed with him. And there was given unto them authority over the fourth part of the earth, to kill with sword, and with famine, and with death (or *pestilence*), and by the wild beasts of the earth.

This horse has the color which agrees with his mission. The word translated *pale* indicates the greenish pallor of fear and of death, *livid*, the color of a corpse in incipient decay. The signification of this vision is expressly given,—the Rider was *Death*. Hades, the place and condition belonging to Death and Satan, where all the souls of the ungodly are (see notes on 1:18, and *Excursus* II. on *Hades*), is here personified and represented as accompanying Death, ready to engulf and detain all the souls of the ungodly which perish by the

93

judgments symbolized by this fourth seal. A fourth part of all the ungodly shall perish. Mention is here made of the *four sore judgments* also enumerated by Ezekiel (14:21), the *sword, famine, pestilence,* and *wild beasts;*—the *famine,* the result of the *sword; pestilence,* that of *famine;* and the *wild beasts* multiplying because of the deserted places. By *death* in the text is evidently meant death by *the pestilence.*

21. The Opening of the Fifth Seal (6:9–11)

9. And when he opened the fifth seal, I saw underneath the altar the souls of them that had been slain for the word of God, and for the testimony which they held.

The character of the vision now changes. John sees an altar in heaven, and underneath it the souls of martyrs whose blood has been shed on account of their faithful testimony to the Word of God. They are symbolically represented as *underneath* the altar, because they had offered themselves to the Lord as a sacrifice. The imagery is taken from the O. T. ritual. The souls of the martyrs correspond to the blood of the sacrifice poured out beneath the altar (Lev. 4:7; 8:15). These souls are those who, like in 20:4, have been slain on earth during the persecutions which accompany the manifestation of Antichrist.

10. And they cried with a great voice, saying, How long, O Master, the holy and true, dost thou not judge and avenge our blood on them that dwell on the earth?

It is the blood of the martyrs that calls to God for vengeance upon the ungodly inhabitants, that dwell on the earth. And the martyrs may rightly expect a judgment, for God is *holy* and *true.* The opening of this seal discloses to us the great

94

tribulation which shall overtake believers in connection with the manifestation of Antichrist. To these events Christ also refers in Matt. 24:9–11, 21, 24; especially Luke 18:7, 8, "And shall not God avenge his elect, which cry to him day and night, and he is long suffering over them? I say unto you, that he will avenge them speedily. Howbeit when the Son of man cometh, shall he find faith on the earth?"

11. And there was given them to each one a white robe; and it was said unto them, that they should rest yet for a little time, until their fellow-servants also and their brethren, which should be killed even as they were, should be fulfilled.

A white robe designates victory, innocence, and purity. See note on 3:4. The bestowal of the white robe designates that they receive their glory and blessedness, and await their glorious resurrection. They however receive the promise that the judgment of the Lord shall soon (*rest yet for a little time*) overtake the ungodly world, but the end is not yet. There are still other faithful ones who will offer up their lives during this period of tribulation. Possibly two classes arc here referred to, *their fellow-servants* and *their brethren.* These have not yet *fulfilled their course* (accepting the margin of the Revised Version as possibly the correct reading). Bengel writes: "These first martyrs were chiefly from Israel; *their fellow-servants*, future martyrs from the Gentiles, and *their brethren*, martyrs of Israel." But this cannot be positively decided.

22. The Opening of the Sixth Seal (6:12–17)

12. And I saw when he opened the sixth seal, and there was a great earthquake; and the sun became black as sackcloth of hair, and the whole moon became as blood.

This Seal brings us to the very eve of the final consummation, for in this vision we see disclosed to us the events of the great day of the Lord's Coming. We have here only a fuller description of what Christ Himself revealed to us in Matt. 24:29, 30. "The most striking features of earlier prophecies are also combined here—Isa. 2:19; 34:4; 50:3; Ezek. 32:7, 8; Hos. 10:8; Joel 3:20, 21; Nah. 1:6; so the ancient and most modern expositors" (Lee). This sixth Seal is "one of the clearest and most magnificent descriptions of the Day of Judgment which is to be found in the Bible" (Todd). **A great earthquake.** The vengeance for which the martyrs prayed for under the fifth Seal has now come. See Matt. 24:7. **Sackcloth.** The sun appears as a great black orb (Isa. 50:3). **Whole moon.** The *full moon* looks like blood, suggesting the thought of wild devastation.

13. And the stars of the heaven fell unto the earth, as a fig tree casteth her unripe figs, when she is shaken of a great wind.

Compare Matt. 24:27; Luke 21:25, 26. The imagery is taken from Isa. 34:4. **Unripe figs.** Probably the winter figs, which almost always fall off unripe. See also Nah. 3:12. "As to the stars falling to the earth, Scripture describes natural phenomena as they would appear to the spectator, not in the language of scientific accuracy; and yet, whilst thus adapting itself to ordinary men, it drops hints which show that it anticipates the discoveries of modern science" (Fausset).

14. And the heaven was removed as a scroll when it is rolled up; and every mountain and island were removed out of their places.

Compare Isa. 34:4, "the heavens shall be rolled together as a scroll: and all their host shall fade away, as the leaf fadeth from off the vine." **Every mountain ... removed.** "The whole earth is broken up by a change as total as any of those previous ones which have prepared it for its present inhabitants" (Alford). The confusion and destruction are complete.

15. And the kings of the earth, and the princes, and the chief captains, and the rich, and the strong, and every bondman and freeman, hid themselves in the caves and in the rocks of the mountains.

The Day of Judgment has come. Terror seizes upon all the enemies of Christ and His kingdom. "The significant classification (given in this verse) proves how no kind of earthly greatness or power, the previous cause of insolent assurance, can afford any protection whatever. Kings share the anguish with the humblest slaves" (Duesterdieck). **In the caves.** For the imagery see Isa. 2:19. Millligan: "The righteous have no place in this enumeration; but the ungodly without exception, whatever their rank or station, are divided into seven groups in order to indicate that none escape."

16. And they say to the mountains and to the rocks, Fall on us, and hide us from the face of him that sitteth on the throne, and from the wrath of the Lamb.

Compare Isa. 2:10, 19; Hos. 10:8; Nah. 1:6; especially Luke 23:30, "Then shall they begin to say to the mountains, Fall on us; and to the hills, Cover us." So great is their terror of the impending judgment of wrath, that all the ungodly long for death and annihilation, rather than face their God and His Lamb.

17. For the great day of their wrath is come; and who is able to stand?

"The expression *the great day* depends upon Joel 2:31; 1:15; 2:1, 2; Isa. 63:4–6; and the question *Who is able to stand?* on Nah. 1:6; Mal. 3:2" (Duesterdieck).

Alford correctly remarks: "We are thus brought to the very threshold itself of the great day of the Lord's Coming. It has not yet happened; but the tribes of the earth are troubled at its immediate approach, and those terrible signs with which all Scripture ushers it in have taken place. We are now then arrived at the time described in Matt. 24:30: the coming itself of the Son of Man being for a while kept in the background, as hereafter to be resumed. He is seen, as it were, coming, but before the vengeance is fully accomplished, the elect of God then living on the earth must be gathered, as Matt. 24:31, out of the four winds of heaven, from among the inhabitants of the earth. To this ingathering the sealing in our text is the necessary preliminary."

Fausset calls attention to the fact that Matt. 24 plainly forms a perfect parallelism to the six seals, not only in the events, but also in the order of their occurrence: Matt. 24:3, the first seal; 24:6, the second seal; 24:7, the third seal; 24:7*b*, the fourth seal; 24:9–28, the fifth seal, with its persecutions; 24:29, the sixth seal.

For a brief presentation of the various interpretations given to the *First Six Seals*, see *Excursus* III.

7

Revelation 7

The seventh chapter contains two episodes that intervene between the opening of the sixth and seventh Seals. Although the great day of the wrath of God and of the Lamb has been anticipated in the opening of the *sixth* Seal (6:12–17), that day with its woes will only befully described at the opening of the *seventh* Seal. Before that day fully approaches, our attention is called to two classes *who are able to stand before the face of the Lord and the Lamb at that great day* (6:17): (1) the servants of God who are sealed (7:1–8,) and (2) the saints who have come out of the great Tribulation (7:9–17).

23. The Sealing of the Servants of God (7:1–8)

1. After this I saw four angels standing at the four corners of the earth, holding the four winds of the earth, that no wind should blow on the earth, or on the sea, or upon any tree.

Angels, as ever, are servants of God and of the heirs of salvation, fulfilling His Word (Ps. 103:20; Heb. 1:14). There

99

is no reason why we should attempt to allegorize, as so many do,[1] the particular statements of this verse. These angels are here represented as the executors of God's judgments, "to whom it was given to hurt the earth and the sea" (7:2),—now indeed restraining the disturbing winds (7:3), but in God's own time executing vengeance upon the ungodly world.

2. And I saw another angel ascend from the sunrising, having the seal of the living God: and he cried with a great voice to the four angels, to whom it was given to hurt the earth and the sea.

John sees *another angel*, not Christ, as maintained by Bede, Calovius, Hengstenberg, and others. He ascends from the horizon, *from the sunrising*, whence rises the source of light, life, and blessing upon the earth (Duesterdieck, Hengstenberg, Ebrard, Lee, etc.), "as naturally agreeing with the glorious and salutary nature of his employment (Ezek. 43:2; Matt. 4:2)" (Alford). This angel has a *seal* in his hand belonging to the *living* God, to that God who has and is the *giver* of life (Duesterdieck, Bengel, Hengstenberg, Kliefoth, Lee, etc.). We cannot infer from the context what the *mark* of the seal is. Some (Bede, Grotius, etc.) regard it the sign of the cross; others (De Wette, Ebrard, etc.) propose the name of God and of the Lamb. He cried with a *great voiee*, not because he was so anxious to restrain the four angels who were just ready to unloose the winds (Bengel), nor to emphasize the command (Hengstenberg), but probably that the call might penetrate to the four corners of the earth (7:1) (Duesterdieck).

3. Saying, Hurt not the earth, neither the sea, nor the trees, till we shall have sealed the servants of our God on their foreheads.

100

The angels were not to let loose the winds which they held and which would bring judgments upon the world and its inhabitants, until the servants of God, who would have to endure the great tribulation, were sealed. Some maintain that the purpose of this sealing is to prevent these servants of God from experiencing these trials which are to come upon the earth (so Vitringa, Stern, Bengel, De Wette, Bleek, Hengstenberg, Ebrard, Alford, etc.), but it is far better to regard this *sealing* not as a preservation and protection *from tribulation*, but preservation from *Apostasy* under tribulation. Duesterdieck rightly remarks: "The servants of God do not remain entirely untouched by all the sufferings whereby judgment comes upon the world.... The sealing of those who already are servants of God designates nothing else than the immutable firmness of their *election* (Matt. 24:22–24), which is not to be affected even by the *trial* of the last great *tribulation*. Striking analogies to this interpretation of the *sealing* are 2 Cor. 1:22; Eph. 1:13; 4:30. To the servants of God, therefore, upon whose forehead the seal of the living God is impressed, the divine warrant is thereby given that in the greatest tribulations they remain the servants of God, until they have been preserved in their fidelity unto the end, and are victoriously conducted to eternal glory in God's kingdom." **Till we shall have sealed.** The plural indicates that the angel had associates, but we are not to think of the four angels holding the four winds. That these *servants of God* are Jewish Christians will appear from the next verse. They are sealed *on their foreheads* as the noblest and most conspicuous part of the human body. The act of sealing is assumed as taking place between this and the next verse.

4. And I heard the number of them which were sealed, a

hundred and forty and four thousand, sealed out of every tribe of the children of Israel.

We are not to take the number 144,000 literally, as if just 12,000 of each of the twelve tribes were sealed, no more or no less. The number is symbolical and designates perfection and completion. It signifies a perfect number reserved for the kingdom. They were sealed *out of every tribe of the children of Israel.* It is one of the important questions in the interpretation of this book whether Israel is here to be understood in the literal or spiritual sense. There is no reason why we should identify it with spiritual Israel, "the Israel of God" (Gal. 6:15, 16), as consisting of Jewish and Gentile Christians. It is far better to take it in its literal sense as Rom. 11, and in answer to the arguments presented by Mede, Vitringa, Hengstenberg, Wordsworth, Alford, Gebhardt, Philippi, Kliefoth, Beck, and others, we simply answer, it is not so written *here.* These 144,000 represent Jewish believers chosen out of the literal Israel. So in substance Bengel, Williams, Ebrard, Godet, Duesterdieck, Auberlen, Burger, Fausset, and, in general, all Futurists. They are the believing Jews who shall faithfully resist the seductions of Antichrist during the time of the great tribulation.

5. Of the tribe of Judah *were* sealed twelve thousand:
Of the tribe of Reuben twelve thousand:
Of the tribe of Gad twelve thousand:
6. Of the tribe of Asher twelve thousand:
Of the tribe of Naphtali twelve thousand:
Of the tribe of Manasseh twelve thousand:
7. Of the tribe of Simeon twelve thousand:
Of the tribe of Levi twelve thousand:
Of the tribe of Issachar twelve thousand:

8. Of the tribe of Zebulun twelve thousand:

Of the tribe of Joseph twelve thousand:

Of the tribe of Benjamin *were* sealed twelve thousand.

Commentators call our attention to various interesting points in this catalogue:

(1) As to the number 12,000, fixed for each of the twelve tribes. This indicates "that the Lord knoweth and sealeth His own: that the fulness of their number shall be accomplished and not one shall fail" (Alford); "that in the divine gifts of grace all have like share, but no one from any one right" (Duesterdieck).

(2) In no two places in the Bible are the names and order of the catalogue of the Twelve Tribes the same. "With the exception of Judah being placed first, the order of the tribes here given does not seem to follow any assignable principle" (Alford).

(3) The tribe of Dan is omitted. Three reasons have been assigned for this: (*a*) From this tribe the Antichrist was to come. So the Church Fathers, Bede, Stern, and others, relying on Gen. 49:17; (*b*) Because Dan had been given to idolatry (Judg. 18:1–31). So among others, Wetstein, Vitringa, Hengstenberg, Wordsworth; (*c*) Because it had died out long already before the time of John. So Duesterdieck, Grotius, Ewald, De Wette, Ebrard, Alford, and others. Bossuet thinks that the name of Dan is omitted here merely in order to preserve the number Twelve, Joseph appearing twice—once in his own person (7:8), and once in the person of Manasseh (7:6).

(4) Levi is included. Bengel: "Since the Levitical ceremonies have been abandoned, Levi again is found on an equal footing with his brethren. All are priests; all have

103

access, not one through the other, but one with the other."
So Duesterdieck, Milligan, and others.

(5) Instead of *Ephraim*, we have the name *Joseph*. Compare
Num. 13:11. Some think this is due to the fact that throughout the O. T. history Ephraim was peculiarly "untheocratic,"
a symbol of opposition to faithful Judah (Isa. 7:17; Jer. 7:15).
So Duesterdieck, Milligan, Wordsworth, and others.

Synopsis of Interpretations. Grotius and the Preterists in
general refer this to the Jewish Christians who fled from
Jerusalem to Pella at the time of the siege and destruction of
Jerusalem.

The Continuous Historical School interpret this sealing variously, some referring it to the Jewish and Gentile
converts succeeding the age of Constantine; others to the
Albigenses and Waldenses; or to the Reformation; or to the
times succeeding the fall of Bonaparte (1815). Others again
refer it to the sealing of the Redeemed going on all the time
that the Church is on earth.

The view of the Futurists in general may be represented
by Fausset, who remarks: "It is clear though *Israel* may
elsewhere designate spiritual Israel, *here*, where the names
of the tribes one by one are specified, these names cannot
have any but the literal meaning. The second advent will
be the time of *the restoration of the kingdom to Israel,* when
the times of Gentiles shall have been fulfilled and the Jews shall
at last say, 'Blessed is he that cometh in the name of the
Lord.' The period of the Lord's absence has been a blank
in the history of the Jews as a nation.... Israel, at the eve of
the Lord's coming, shall be found re-embodied as a nation;
for its tribes are distinctly specified (Joseph, however, being
substituted for Dan; whether because Antichrist is to come

104

from Dan or because Dan is to be Antichrist's especial tool, Gen. 49:17; Jer. 8:16; just as there was a Judas among the twelve). Out of these tribes *a believing remnant* will be preserved from the judgments which shall destroy all the antichristian confederacy (6:12–17), which remnant shall faithfully resist the seductions of Antichrist, while the rest of the nation, restored to Palestine in unbelief, are his dupes and at last his victims."

Another able writer of this school says: "The difference between this sealing and that of believers now with the Holy Ghost will be at once perceived by the instructed reader. Believers of this dispensation are sealed immediately in the forgiveness of sins, and they are sealed unto the day of redemption (Eph. 4:30). The 144,000 of this chapter are sealed with the seal of the living God for preservation through the judgments that will fall upon the world, and which will constitute for Israel the day of Jacob's trouble (Jer. 30:4–9; Matt. 24:21, 22)."

24. The Triumph of the Tribulation Saints (7:9–17)

9. After these things I saw, and behold, a great multitude, which no man could number, out of every nation, and of *all* tribes and peoples and tongues, standing before the throne and before the Lamb, arrayed in white robes, and palms in their hands.

This innumerable multitude which are seen in *heavenly glory* are described in 7:14 as those "which came out of the great tribulation." They are not to be regarded as exactly identical with the 144,000 sealed ones of 7:1–8, for they

105

include more than these. The former could be numbered, but these are innumerable; the former referred to the Jewish Christians alone, this innumerable number not only consists of these, but includes also those servants of God among the Gentiles who have victoriously passed through the great tribulation of the days of Antichrist. The sealing of the 144,000 is represented as taking place before the judgments were visited upon the world, and *here* this scene implies that the days of tribulation are passed. Duesterdieck gives us the true explanation of the relation of these two visions to each other and of their meaning: "In the tribulation with which the Lord comes in judgment upon unbelieving Israel, the 144,000 servants of God are to be kept in security, even though they are to suffer; thus the vision, 7:1–8, looks towards what the seventh seal is to bring upon unbelieving Israel (8:1–11:14). But that also the servants of God from the Gentiles, together with the 144,000 sealed from Israel, are to come out of great tribulation, and to enter glory as faithful warriors of Christ, the other vision states, 7:9–17, which thus refers to the tribulation with which the Lord shall visit Babylon."

Out of every nation ... and tongues. Including Jews and Gentiles. **Standing before the throne.** "The standing before the throne of God and of the Lamb (7:15; 22:3) points to the eternal communion with God and the Lamb, whose heavenly glory and blessed joy are also expressed by white robes, and palm branches in the hands of those who have finished their course." The *white robes* are the attire of victory, the emblem of purity and righteousness. See notes on 3:4 and 6:11. The *palms* are signs of peace and festal joy.

10. And they cry with a great voice, saying, Salvation unto

our God which sitteth on the throne, and unto the Lamb.

They cry. *Present* tense, indicating their unceasing praise.
With a great voice. In the intensity of their joy and
gratitude. They praise *God* as the ultimate Author of their
salvation, and *the Lamb* as their Mediator. "This *salvation* is
not victory in general, but the entire sum of the salvation
which the blessed now perfectly possess, since they have been
removed from all want, temptation, sin, and death, and have
come into the presence of their God" (Duesterdieck).

11. And all the angels were standing round about the
throne, and *about* the elders and the four living createres; and
they fell before the throne on their faces, and worshipped
God.

These angels were the innumerable hosts of angels spoken
of in 5:11, which see. As in 5:14 the elders fall prostrate and
worship, so here the angels do the same, as they join in the
celebration of the great theme of redemption.

12. Saying, Amen: Blessing, and glory, and wisdom, and
thanksgiving, and honour, and power, and might, *be* unto
our God for ever and ever. Amen.

The song of praise, uttered by the tribulation saints in
7:10, is now confirmed by an *Amen* (see 5:14), and then the
angels themselves take up the strain of praise. Here as in
5:12 the doxology of the angels is seven-fold, but the words
and the order differ. Here the article in an emphatic way is
prefixed to each of the nouns, while in 5:12 it belongs only
to the first noun. The remark of Lange is suggestive: "*The
Amen* which the angels utter proclaims the unison of the
whole spirit-world with that redemption of which the earth
is the scene (Col. 1:20); and their present understanding of
the great fact so long hid from their gaze (Eph. 3:10; 1 Pet.

107

1:12) is expressed in their *doxology*. In accordance with their universal standpoint, they merge the praise of the Lamb in the general praise of God."

13. And one of the elders answered, saying unto me, These which are arrayed in white robes, who are they, and whence came they?

One of the twenty-four elders (5:4), who represent the Redeemed Church in heaven (4:4), appropriately acts as interpreter of this vision. "The form of a dialogue, with its dramatic vividness, serves to emphasize the point under consideration. The elder presents the two points concerning which one unacquainted would naturally ask first" (Duesterdieck). Both inquiries are answered in the next verse.

14. And I say (Gr. *have said*) unto him, My lord, thou knowest. And he said to me, These are they which come out of the great tribulation, and they washed their robes, and made them white in the blood of the Lamb.

My Lord. An address, *here*, of proper respect. **Thou knowest.** Compare Ezek. 37:3. "I do not know it, yet it may be heard from you, as you know it" (so Duesterdieck, Bengel, Ewald, De Wette, Hengstenberg, etc.). **These are they which come out of the great tribulation.** This is the tribulation announced by the Lord in Matt. 24:21, which shall come upon the world, and through which the ungodly as well as believers who are on the earth at that time must pass during the evil times of Antichrist. Those who come out of this *great tribulation* are the sealed Jewish Christians of 7:1–8, and those Gentile Christians who shall remain faithful during those terrible times which shall try the saints before the coming of the Lord. Daniel already prophesied of this *time of trouble* (Dan. 12:1), "And there shall be a

108

time of trouble, such as never was since there was a nation even to that same time; and at that time thy people shall be delivered, every one that shall be found written in the book." Our Lord, using almost the same phraseology, speaks of the same tribulation (Matt. 24:21) and calls it a *great tribulation,* and it is immediately to precede the coming of the Son of Man (Matt. 24:29, 30). **They washed their robes, and made them white in the blood of the Lamb.** There is no reference here to the blood of martyrs, as if there was a cleansing power in martyrdom. "Observe, we must not separate the two acts *washing* and *making white,* as Hengstenberg, interpreting the former of forgiveness of sins, the latter of sanctification: the latter is only the result of the former: they washed them, and by so doing made them white. The act was a life-long one,—the continued purification of the man, body, soul, and spirit, by the application of the blood of Christ in its cleansing power" (Alford). "It is the delicate feature of correct ethics," remarks Duesterdieck, "that they who, in this earthly life, have washed their robes white in the blood of the Lamb appear in the future life, arrayed in white garments" (3:4; 19:8).

15. Therefore are they before the throne of God; and they serve him day and night in his temple: and he that sitteth on the throne shall spread his tabernacle over them.

This entire passage (7:15–17) can only refer to the glorious condition of the Redeemed in heaven after the final consummation of all things. Though in reality *these saints* have not yet passed through the *great tribulation,* the vision puts them into their condition of the final glory, and discloses to us what the final issue of glory shall be. **Therefore.***On this account,* because they washed their robes white in Christ's

109

atoning and purifying blood. **They serve.** The life of glory in heaven is one of continued service of God. **Shall spread his tabernacle over them.** "It is exceedingly difficult to express the sense of these glorious words, in which the fulfilment of the O. T. promises, such as Lev. 26:11; Isa. 4:5, 6; Ezek. 37:27, is announced. They give the fact of the dwelling of God *among* them, united with the fact of His protection over them, and assuring to them the exemption next to be mentioned" (Alford). "We have here a description of the eternal, immediate, and personal presence of God enthroned in His glory, and the holiness and blessedness of believers perfected therein" (Duesterdieck).

16. They shall hunger no more, neither thirst any more; neither shall the sun strike upon them, nor any heat.

This whole passage is based upon Isa. 49:10, which ends with the prophecy, "for he that hath mercy on them shall lead them, even by the springs of water shall he guide them." Compare the next verse.

17. For the Lamb which is in the midst of the throne shall be their shepherd, and shall guide them unto fountains of waters of life: and God shall wipe away every tear from their eyes.

Compare Isa. 49:10, quoted under the last verse. The elder here designates the Lamb as the one who, as the *Mediator* and *Redeemer* of the flock, feeds His own, and leads them into living fountains of waters. The latter part of the verse is based upon Isa. 25:8, "He hath swallowed up death for ever; and the Lord God will wipe away tears from off all faces." "It is not without many tears that they come out of great tribulation (7:14); but when they have overcome, God Himself shall dry their tears, and change their weeping into joy" (Duesterdieck).

* * *

[1] Refering *winds* to "wars and calamities," the *earth* to "Asia," the *sea* to "nations and to peoples," the *trees* to "kings and great men," etc.

8

Revelation 8

25. The Opening of the Seventh Seal (8:1)

1. And when he opened the seventh seal, there followed a silence in heaven about the space of half an hour.

After the Lamb had opened six of the seven seals, as recorded in chapter 6, and before the seventh was opened, two comforting visions were seen, as recorded in chapter 7 in view of the approaching judgments which will precede and usher in the coming of Christ, as more fully revealed by the opening of the seventh seal. The first six seals bring in preliminary judgments, constituting perhaps the "beginning of travail" (Matt. 24:8). The seventh seal will introduce *the great tribulation*, partly anticipated already under the sixth seal (6:12–17). **A silence in heaven.** Expressing the solemnity of the crisis which has now arrived, "the earnest adoring expectation with which the blessed spirits and the angels await the succeeding unfolding of God's judgments" (Fausset).

26. The Sounding of the First Trumpet (8:2–7)

2. And I saw the seven angels which stand before God; and there were given unto them seven trumpets.

Seven particular angels are meant, but we need not think of *archangels*. These *trumpets* were given unto them to proclaim the judgments described in 8:7; 8:8, 9; 8:10, 11; etc. "They are trumpets of war and battle, like those whose sound brought down the walls of Jericho, or those whose blast struck terror into the hosts of Midian (Judg. 7:22)" (Milligan). The entire series of trumpet-visions is developed out of the seventh seal.

3. And another angel came and stood over (or, *at*) the altar, having a golden censer; and there was given unto him much incense, that he should add (Gr. *give*) it unto the prayers of all the saints upon the golden altar which was before the throne.

This *angel* is not to be identified with Christ. This *altar*, called also in this verse the *golden altar*, is the same as that mentioned in 6:9, under which were seen the souls of the martyrs. The Greek word for *censer* is elsewhere translated *incense*, but evidently here a *vessel* for incense is meant. **There was given unto him much incense.** "The angel does not provide the incense; it is *given to him* by Christ, whose meritorious obedience and death are the incense, rendering the saints' prayers well-pleasing to God. It is not the saints who give the angel the incense; nor are their prayers identified with the incense; nor do they offer prayers to him. Christ alone is the Mediator, through whom, and to whom, prayer is to be offered" (Fausset). There is no reference here to the Roman Catholic doctrine of intercession by angels or by saints. The significance of this act of *incensing* the prayers of the saints was already suggested

113

by Calovius, that he might render these prayers of the saints *pleasing to God.* Christ's merits alone can thus *incense* our prayers. Here in the text the special reference is to the prayers of the saints who must pass through the great tribulation now to be disclosed, for the Lamb from whom comes the incense is about to execute judgment upon the earth.

4. And the smoke of the incense, with (or, *for*) the prayers of the saints, went up before God out of the angel's hand.

The whole imagery suggests that the saints' prayers on earth and the angel's incensing in heaven are simultaneous, and that God will graciously hear the prayers of His saints during the great trials which come upon the earth by means of the judgments disclosed by the seven trumpets.

5. And the angel taketh (Gr. *hath taken*) the censer; and he filled it with the fire of the altar, and cast it upon (or, *into*) the earth: and there followed thunders, and voices, and lightnings, and an earthquake.

The angel, after having shaken the incense on the altar (see verse 3), while the smoke of the incense was ascending, fills his censer with glowing coals taken from the altar, and casts the hot ashes towards the earth, thus signifying that the answers of the saints are heard, and that the fire of God's vengeance is about to descend upon the earth and its ungodly inhabitants. The immediate consequence of the casting down of these glowing coals on the earth are *thunders, and voices, and lightnings, and an earthquake,* the symbolic precursors of the divine judgments coming upon the earth, which the seven trumpets now begin to sound.

6. And the seven angels which had the seven trumpets prepared themselves to sound.

See notes on 8:2. They raised their trumpets to their

114

mouths and stood ready to sound them.

7. And the first sounded, and there followed hail and fire, mingled with blood, and they were cast upon (or, *into*) the earth: and the third part of the earth was burnt up, and the third part of the trees was burnt up, and all green grass was burnt up.

Commentators call our attention to the fact that the judgments indicated by the *first four trumpets* affect *natural objects*, while the last *three*, the *woe-trumpets* (8:13; 9:12), are expressly said to be inflicted on men (9:4, 15). The language of these judgments is evidently reproduced from the plagues of Egypt,—five, in fact, six out of the ten exactly corresponding,—for we have the hail and fire, reminding us of the *seventh* plague (Ex. 9:24), the water turned to blood of the *first* plague (Ex. 7:19, 20), the darkness of the *ninth* plague (Ex. 10:21; Rev. 8:12), the locusts of the *eighth* plague (Ex. 10:12; Rev. 9:3), and the infliction of death of the *tenth* (Ex. 12:29; Rev. 9:18). These trumpets are not to be regarded so much a *recapitulation* of the six seals, as of the *sixth seal*, for they only disclose more fully the terrors that are coming upon the earth in connection with the destruction of Antichrist.

In a vision John saw the judgments that followed the sounding of the first trumpet come upon the earth—hailstones and balls of fire fell in a shower of blood. Compare also Joel 2:30. In Ex. 9:24 we read, "The Lord sent thunder and hail, and fire ran down unto the earth,"—but nothing is said of the blood. The effect upon the earth was also seen by John. In Ex. 9:24 the devastation was wrought by the hail, but *here* fire is the prevailing element of destruction. Terrible and fearful as is this first judgment, two-thirds of the earth and of the trees

115

escape, but all the green grass is scorched and consumed. To explain this imagery symbolically or allegorically, as so many do, that "the third part" means simply "a large part," the *trees* "the great ones of the earth," the *green grass* "general prosperity," or "the people," is, as Duesterdieck rightly remarks, "an undertaking which, since it has no foundation in the text, can lead to nothing but arbitrary guess-work." So likewise all attempts of the Preterists to refer it to events preceding the destruction of Jerusalem, or of the Continuous Historical interpreters to refer it to the wars under Trojan and Hadrian (Bengel), to the invasion of the Goths (Elliott, Barnes, Wordsworth), to the pestilence and famine under Decius and Gallus (Vitringa), to early heresies (Stern, Gaertner), to spiritual famine (Ebrard), are equally unsatisfactory. Those who think we ought not to look for any historical fulfilment of these prophecies (like Milligan, Alford, Lee, and others) are not agreed, however, what mystical, or allegorical, or symbolical, or spiritual, or moral fulfilment is to be given to any one of these judgments. But why attempt to explain away the plain significance of this trumpet of judgment? If the ten plagues of Egypt were historical and were visited upon the enemies of God's people, why may we not expect a repetition of these judgments in the days of Antichrist? And although we may not fully understand what special form these judgments may assume, their reality, the certainty of their coming, and their terribleness are here clearly disclosed.

116

27. The Sounding of the Second Trumpet (8:8, 9)

8. And the second angel sounded, and as it were a great mountain burning with fire was cast into the sea: and the third part of the sea became blood.

The imagery reminds us of Jer. 51:25, where we also read of "a burnt mountain," or volcano. Probably we may understand a fiery mass or *meteor* falling into the sea, causing putrescence and pestilence. In the first plague of Egypt (Ex. 7:20, 21) *all* the water turned into blood, but *here* a *third part of the sea* becomes blood.

9. And there died the third part of the creatures which were in the sea, *even* they that had life; and the third part of the ships was destroyed.

This trumpet is specially distinguished from the first in that its judgments are visited on the sea instead of on the land. Symbolical interpreters take these *living creatures* to be "men living in the *sea* of this world," and *the ships* to be *churches*, while most commentators allegorize and see in this trumpet the devastation of war, some like the Preterists referring it to the distresses of the Jewish-Roman war (Grotius), others, of the Historical School, to later events in the history of the Roman Empire,—no two agreeing in the interpretation of details. But it is far better to accept the plain signification of the text, as describing a great pestilence and the ruin of many ships, including commercial means of prosperity, for the text contains nothing allegorical. It is highly probable that these *first two* judgments will be held back until the servants of God in the days of Antichrist will be sealed, for the command was, "Hurt not the earth, neither the sea, nor the trees, till we shall have sealed the servants of God on their foreheads"

(7:3). These judgments therefore bring us down to the very eve of Christ's coming to destroy Antichrist, and still lie in the future.

28. The Sounding of the Third Trumpet (8:10, 11)

10. And the third angel sounded, and there fell from heaven a great star, burning as a torch, and it fell upon the third part of the rivers, and upon the fountains of the waters.

One blow follows another until finally the Lord comes, and as the judgments of God are sent forth they deepen in intensity. The first two judgments affected nature, and *man* only indirectly, but this *third* judgment brings about the death of many men. This judgment differs altogether from the preceding. Whether this *great star, burning as a torch*, is a meteor, or comet, we cannot tell; at least John saw it in the form of a *falling star.* In its fall it scattered its sparks, and the fragments fell upon a third part of *the fresh* water on the earth.

11. And the name of the star is called Wormwood: and the third part of the waters became wormwood; and many men died of the waters because they were made bitter.

The *star* is called *Wormwood* (Greek *absinthe*), because it made the water bitter as wormwood, and by its poisonous bitterness John saw that it brought death to many men. It is not said that all who drank died. "The consideration that wormwood is no deadly poison is not at all pertinent, because it is not natural wormwood that is here treated of" (Duesterdieck). There shall come a time, when as a divine punishment men will again drink "of the waters of Marah" (Ex. 15:23–25), for which there is no healing, and in many

118

cases death shall result, as in the days of Elisha (2 Kings 2:19–21).

Many expositors refer this trumpet to *heresies* (Bede, Williams, Wordsworth, Stern, etc.), more definitely still, Pelagius (de Lyra), Origen (Luther), Arius (Bengel, Vitringa, etc.); others, as the Preterists, refer it to events contemporaneous with John; still others, as the Historical School, see in it events affecting the history of the Roman Empire, as the invasion of the barbarians, Attila, the scourge of God (Elliott, Keith, etc.), or the Vandals (Isaac Newton), etc. All this only proves how arbitrary these methods of interpretation are, and how hopeless to solve the problem of the Apocalypse from their standpoint.

29. The Sounding of the Fourth Trumpet (8:12)

12. And the fourth angel sounded, and the third part of the sun was smitten, and the third part of the moon, and the third part of the stars; that the third part of them should be darkened, and the day should not shine for the third part of it, and the night in like manner.

This fourth trumpet brings us to the disturbances which shall take place in the heavenly bodies, parallel to Matt. 24:29, and to the sixth seal (6:12, 13). This miraculous eclipse of the sun, moon, and stars is a sign of the coming day of judgment (Amos 8:9). This plague is in many respects of the same character as the ninth plague of Egypt (Ex. 10:21). For the third of the day the sun shall not shine, and for the third of the night neither moon nor stars. Symbolical interpreters refer this fourth trumpet either to political confusion or to the obscuring of spiritual truth, as the heresy of Eutyches (de

119

Lyra), Islam (Stern), Novatus (Luther), etc. Others refer it to the incursions of the nations.

30. Introduction to the Three Woe-Trumpets (8:13)

13. And I saw, and I heard an eagle, flying in mid heaven, saying with a great voice, Woe, woe, woe, for them that dwell on the earth, by reason of the other voices of the trumpet of the three angels, who are yet to sound.

John saw an eagle flying in that part of the sky where the sun is at noon, *in mid-heaven*, that it might be seen, and its far-sounding, menacing cry might be heard, by all. It is best, as in Deut. 28:49; Hos. 8:1; Hab. 1:8, to regard the eagle as a symbol of judgment "that hasteth to devour" (Hab. 1:8). Its piercing cry proclaims the greatness of the three woes that are yet to come upon the world, which are now to be announced more fully by the last three trumpets. We need not ask who or what this eagle signifies. This episode in the main vision only calls attention to the greatness of the woes that are yet to come. The Preterists see in it the eagle of the Roman legions (Herder, Boehmer, etc.); Williams sees in it St. John himself; Wordsworth, a special messenger, probably Christ Himself; Elliott (as Joachim formerly) thinks the eagle to be Pope Gregory the Great protesting against the title *universal* Bishop. Is it a wonder that men regard the Apocalypse an enigma with such interpreters as guides? (See *Excursus* IV. on the *First Four Trumpets*.)

120

9

Revelation 9

31. The Sounding of the Fifth Trumpet, or the First Woe (9:1–12)

1. And the fifth angel sounded, and I saw a star from heaven fallen unto the earth: and there was given to him the key of the pit of the abyss.

This star, not *falling*, but *having already fallen* out of heaven unto the earth, to whom *the key of the pit of the abyss* was given in order that he might bring an infernal plague upon those who "have not the seal of God on their foreheads" (9:4), is not to be regarded as a *good* angel (Bengel, Bleek, De Wette, etc.), but according to the analogy of Isa. 14:12: Luke 10:18; Rev. 10:9, as an *evil* angel (so Bede, Vitringa, Alford, Todd, Duesterdieck, and others). Some indeed take this angel to be Satan himself, and identify him with "the angel of the abyss" of 9:11, but of this we have no hint in the text. In the power of God this evil angel is the instrument of carrying out God's purpose with reference to the ungodly world, for there was

121

given to him the key of the *bottomless* pit. If the four previous judgments were judicially inflicted by God, this judgment, though still under God's control, is diabolical in its origin and nature. This *abussos*, here and in 9:2, 11; 11:7; 17:8; 20:1, 3; Luke 8:31, denotes the present abode of the devil and his angels, as distinguished from Gehenna, *the lake of fire and brimstone* (Rev. 20:10), which will be their abode after the final judgment of all things. It is evidently included in *Hades* or *Sheol*, the present abode of all the souls of the ungodly dead. (See *Excursus* II. on *Hades.*)

2. And he opened the pit of the abyss; and there went up a smoke out of the pit, as the smoke of a great furnace; and the sun and the air were darkened by reason of the smoke of the pit.

In vision it appeared to John as if this *abyss* was under the earth, having a shaft, after the manner of a well, leading to it, and this well or pit was shut down by a cover and locked. The angel receives the key, unlocks the shaft or well leading down to the abyss, and behold, a smoke like that of a great furnace (Gen. 19:28, the destruction of Sodom and Gomorrah) rushed forth obscuring the light of the sun.

3. And out of the smoke came forth locusts upon the earth; and power was given them, as the scorpions of the earth have power.

John sees, under the covering of the smoke, and *out of the smoke*, infernal locusts coming out of the pit and swarming upon the earth, and they differed from *earthly* locusts in that God gave them power to sting like earthly scorpions, such as are referred to in Deut. 8:15. These *infernal* locusts are able to hurt men, while common locusts are not.

4. And it was said unto them that they should not hurt

122

the grass of the earth, neither any green thing, neither any tree, but only such men as have not the seal of God on their foreheads.

They are thus sharply distinguished from all common locusts which only injure the very things which these infernal locusts are not to touch. These locusts are sent forth as a plague upon a special class of men—those who have not received the seal of God on their forehead (7:3). As the sealed ones of 7:3–8 evidently are believers among the Jews, there are some who maintain that these *unsealed ones* upon whom the plague falls must be *unbelieving Israel*, but of this there is no hint in the text. The plague shall fall upon all, whether Jews or Gentiles, who *have not the seal of God on their foreheads*, and of this plague the saints are not partakers.

5. And it was given them that they should not kill them, but that they should be tormented five months: and their torment was as the torment of a scorpion, when it striketh a man.

But God sets a limit to the evil effect of the stings of the infernal locusts (9:10), for their sting does not inflict death, but instead brings with it great bodily torment, as when men are stung by scorpions. For five long months the dreadful sufferings upon the unsealed will continue.

6. And in those days men shall seek death, and shall in no wise find it; and they shall desire to die, and death fleeth from them.

As the vision represents prophetically what shall come to pass in the days of Antichrist, so John in this verse in plain prophecy describes the terrible effect of the plague. Their longing to die arises from the excruciating pain of the sting of the infernal locusts. Compare Jer. 8:3, "and death shall be chosen rather than life by all the residue that remain of this evil family." "A terrible counterpart to the *desire* of the Apostle springing from the holiest hope (Phil. 1:23)" (Duesterdieck).

7. And the shapes (Gr. *likenesses*) of the locusts were like unto horses prepared for war; and upon their heads as it were crowns like unto gold, and their faces were as men's faces.

We have now a description of the appearance of these infernal locusts. This resemblance of locusts to horses (Joel 2:4) has often been noticed by travellers. Especially is this true when the horse is equipped for war. **Crowns like unto gold.** Alford: "Just as the wings of some of the beetle tribe might be said to blaze with gold and gems." **As men's faces.** Even the common locust has a distant resemblance to the human countenance, but these demoniacal locusts bear this resemblance in a still more remarkable manner.

8. And they had hair as the hair of women, and their teeth were as *the teeth* of lions.

An Arabic proverb compares the antennæ of locusts to the hair of women. Whether these miraculous locusts had antennae like the natural locusts, or whether this hair was attached to the other parts of the body, we cannot tell. Joel (1:6) already uses the same image of the natural locusts.

9. And they had breastplates, as it were breastplates of iron; and the sound of their wings was as the sound of chariots, of many horses rushing to war.

The *thorax* of these infernal locusts is stronger than that of the natural locusts, for it is as if of iron. These demoniacal locusts have wings as natural locusts, and the noise of their wings is like the sound produced by the whirling of many chariot-wheels and the noise of the hoofs of swift horses, all rushing headlong to war (Joel 2:5). It is said that natural locusts in their flight make a most fearful noise.

10. And they have tails like unto scorpions, and stings; and in their tails is their power to hurt men five months.

The special difference between the demoniacal locusts and natural locusts is here stated. They have tails like scorpions and have the power *to sting*, which natural locusts do not have, and it is this sting, not their bite, which causes such great torment for five months (9:5, 6).

11. They have over them as king the angel of the abyss: his name in Hebrew is Abaddon, and in the Greek *tongue* he hath the name Apollyon (that is, *Destroyer*).

These infernal locusts differ also from the natural locusts in having a king, because these latter "have no king" (Prov. 30:27). This *angel of the abyss* is not to be identified with Satan, but is rather a chief among Satan's angels, serving under him, and who is here distinctly mentioned as the king of the locusts rising from the abyss. Some regard him in a special way as the overseer of the abyss (Bengel, Ewald, De Wette, Duesterdieck). His name is given as *Abaddon*. This is a Hebrew word meaning *destruction*. In Job 26:6 it is conceived of as part of Sheol, and in Job 28:22 it is coupled with death, just as Death and Hades are in Rev. 6:8. It is especially regarded as a place of punishment for the wicked ("a fire that consumeth unto Abaddon," Job 31:12) (Ps. 88:11); "Sheol and Abaddon are before the Lord" (Prov. 15:11), and "are never satisfied" (Prov. 27:20). We may safely identify it with *the abyss* of the N. T., and just as Hades of the N. T. corresponds to Sheol of the O. T., so Abaddon of the O. T. and the abyss of the N. T. are regarded as that special place in Sheol or Hades where the devil and his angels and all demoniacal power have

125

their sway. The *angel of the abyss*, the king of these infernal locusts, very appropriately therefore bears the name *Abaddon.* The Greek equivalent for Abaddon or Destroyer is *Apollyon.*

12. The first Woe is past: behold, there come yet two Woes hereafter.

These are the words of John, who thus tersely concludes the first woe, and strikingly calls attention to the two that are yet to follow.

As to the significance of this fifth trumpet there is no reason why we should depart from its plain meaning. This first woe as a terrible judgment will fall upon the ungodly immediately preceding the Second Advent of our Lord, and still lies in the future. Duesterdieck remarks: "He who, like Hebart (*Die zweite sichtbare Zukunft Christi*, Erlangen, 1850), looks for the literal fulfilment of all these visions, expecting, for instance, the actual appearance of the *locusts* described in 9:1–11, certainly does more justice to the text than any allegorist." Hebart himself says (quoted by Lange): "The fact that such creatures have never yet been seen should not make us conclude that they never can or never will come. In the last times many things, till then unheard of, shall come to pass—much thitherto unseen shall greet mortal vision."

*Synopsis of Interpretation.*Alford very properly remarks: "There is an endless Babel of allegorical and historical interpretation of these *locusts from the pit.* The most that we can say of their import is, that they belong to a series of judgments on the ungodly which will immediately precede the second advent of our Lord: that the various and mysterious particulars of the vision will no doubt clear themselves up to the Church of God, when the time of its fulfilment arrives; but that no such clearing up has yet taken place, a very few hours of research among histories of apocalyptic interpretation will serve to convince any reader who is not himself the servant of a preconceived system."

I. *The Preterists.*—The *fallen star* of 9:1 is "the demon Nero" (Volkmar): the locusts are the Roman wars in Judea (Grotius, Wetstein, Herder, etc.).

II. *The Continuous Historical School.*—(1) In general Mohammed and the ravages of Mohammedanism. So Mede, Elliott, Barnes, Wordsworth, Isaac Newton, Bishop Newton, Daubuz, Keith, Faber, Williams, Doddridge, Frere, Scott, etc. (2) Heretics (Bede and many others), Roman Catholics as well as Protestants, each one applying the prophecy to the heretics of his own day. The Roman Catholic writers (Bellarmine) see in the *locusts* Luther and the Protestants, while the Protestant writers (Ussher, Forbes, etc.) apply the prophecy to the Pope, the monks, and the inquisition. Stern sees in the fifth trumpet all kinds of *heresy*, from the end of the fourth century, including the Pantheists of our own day.

III. *The Futurists.*—Some think that these locusts symbolize evil spirits, their appearance being still in the future (the ancient opinion); others think that literal locusts are intended (De Burgh, etc.). The torment is to continue five literal months (Todd, etc.). Fausset remarks: "I agree with Alford, De Burgh, etc., that these *locusts from the abyss* refer to judgments about to fall on the ungodly immediately before Christ's second advent. None of the interpretations which regard them as past are satisfactory. Joel 1:2–7; 2:1–11, is strictly parellel, and expressly refers (2:11) *to the day of the Lord great and very terrible*; Joel 2:10 gives the portents accompanying the day of the Lord's coming, *the earth quaking, the heavens trembling, the sun, moon, and stars withdrawing*

127

their shining; Joel 2:18, 31, 32, also point to the immediately succeeding deliverance of Jerusalem.... De Burgh confines the locust-judgment to *the Israelite land,* even as the sealed in Rev. 7. are Israelites.... I incline to agree with him."

IV. *The Spiritual System.*—This is best represented by Milligan, whose summary we give: "All application to the host of the Mohammedans may be at once dismissed. The woe falls upon the whole world, not merely upon a part of it, and it is not permitted to affect the Redeemed Church. At the same time it cannot find its fulfilment in mere war, or in the calamities which war brings. The woe is obviously spiritual."

32. The Sounding of the Sixth Trumpet or the Second Woe (9:13–21)

13. And the sixth angel sounded, and I heard a voice from the horns of the golden altar which is before God.

This voice John heard coming from between the four horns of the golden altar already previously mentioned (see notes on 8:3; 6:9). Alford: "The voice probably proceeded from the altar itself, represented as uttering the cry of vengeance for the blood shed on it; compare 6:9, with which cry of the martyred saints the whole series of retributive judgments is connected."

14. One saying to the sixth angel, which had the trumpet, Loose the four angels which are bound at the great river Euphrates.

Alford calls attention to the fact that this whole imagery has been the cross of interpreters, and ventures to point out "amidst the surging tumult of controversy" three points of "apparent refuge to which we *must not* betake ourselves." (1) We are not to identify these angels with the four angels spoken of in 7:1–3, as Bede, Elliott, and others do. Certainly not, for their mission and locality is totally distinct. (2) We need not decide whether there are good or bad angels. But Bossuet, Hengstenberg, Wordsworth, and others maintain that they are *good* angels, and some of the early commentators even go so far as to suggest that their names were Michael, Gabriel, Uriel, and Raphael. On the other hand, it is far better to regard these as *evil* angels, chiefs among Satan's angels, who in the power of God are compelled to carry out His purposes in the punishment of the ungodly world. This is seen from the fact that they *were bound* and that they lead forth with them an innumerable infernal army, that has its origin in the abyss, for they bring with them "fire and smoke and brimstone" (9:17, 18). So in general, Bede, Bengel, Ebrard, Ewald, Stern, Stuart, Williams, Duesterdieck, and others. (3) There is nothing in the text to prevent "the great river Euphrates" from being taken in a literal sense. At least John in his vision sees these four angels standing bound at the great river Euphrates, whence all the chastisements on Israel have always come. Todd calls our attention to the fact that "it was the almost universal opinion of the ancients that Antichrist shall arise from this region," and he himself thinks that the region of the Euphrates shall hereafter become the scene of the last great struggle between the Prince of this world and the people of God. The *Preterists* either understand the Euphrates literally as the frontier of the Roman Empire (Grotius, Ewald, Renan, etc.), or as referring to the Tiber, because Babylon is Rome (14:8) (Wetstein, Hammond, and others). Most of the *Historical* School also take the Euphrates *literally*, referring this trumpet to the invasions of the Tartars and Turks, who dwelt beyond the Euphrates. So in general Mede, Vitringa, Elliott, Daubuz, Faber, Forbes, Isaac Newton, Bishop Newton, Keith, Doddridge, and others. But this judgment lies in the future instead of in the past, and it is highly probable that we have come to the days of the beginning of Antichrist.

15. And the four angels were loosed, which had been prepared for the hour and day and month and year, that they should kill the third part of men.

These four angels have been appointed of God to carry out His purpose of punishment upon the ungodly world, and at a certain appointed time—the very *hour* determined upon—it shall begin. One third part of the ungodly shall perish, in the same proportion as the *creatures, trees*, and *ships* in 8:7, 9, 11, 12 suffer. To give a synopsis of the surprising chronological calculations which have been based upon this verse by the *Historical* interpreters would not be very edifying.

16. And the number of the armies of the horsemen was twice ten thousand times ten thousand: I heard the number of them.

Compare Ps. 68:17, "the chariots of God are twenty thousand, even thousands upon thousands." We are not to be surprised at the vastness of their armies, two hundred millions, for John himself heard the number of them. Lee: "Two armies are described in the Apocalypse: (1) that which is described here and in 16:14, 16; 20:8, and of which the aspect has been foreshown in Ezek. 38:4, 15; and (2) in opposition to this host, the Armies of Heaven of which we read in 19:14." Jacobs (in Duesterdieck) calls attention to the fact that Beck would interpret this immense number of a

130

future literal army, explaining it by a universal war involving all races of men, analogous to the migrations of nations, the first appearance of Mohammedanism, the Crusades, and illustrating its probability by referring to the now estimated one thousand millions of the earth's inhabitants. But Fausset more correctly than Beck remarks: "The hosts here are evidently, from their number and their appearance (9:17), not merely *human* hosts, but probably *infernal*, though constrained to work out God's will." This whole vision undoubtedly belongs to the period in connection with the manifestation of Antichrist.

17. And thus I saw the horses in the vision, and them that sat on them, having breastplates *as* of fire and of hyacinth and of brimstone: and the heads of the horses are as the heads of lions: and out of their mouths proceedeth fire and smoke and brimstone.

John now describes more particularly the horses and their riders as he beheld them in his vision. It is best to refer the breastplates to both *horses* and *riders*, and their breastplates were of three colors. One part of the host was covered with breastplates red like fire, another part with those of a dark red or bluish red like hyacinth, and the rest with those of a light yellow, such a color as would naturally be produced by the fumes of brimstone,—corresponding to the fire, smoke, and brimstone coming forth from the mouths of the horses. These horses had a monstrous appearance, for their heads were as *the heads of lions*, possibly "in the size of the mouths and the length of the manes" (Duesterdieck).

18. By these three plagues was the third part of men killed, by the fire and the smoke and the brimstone, which proceeded out of their mouths.

131

The fire and the smoke and the brimstone are here expressly designated as *three plagues* whereby these armies are to kill one third of all the ungodly.

19. For the power of the horses is in their mouth, and in their tails: for their tails are like unto serpents, and have heads; and with them they do hurt.

The power of the horses lies in their mouth, because out of the mouth proceed these plagues which kill one third part of men. But these horses also inflicted great pain with their tails, for these ended in the heads of serpents, and with them they did bite, and brought much suffering upon mankind, just as the locusts tormented men with their scorpion bites (9:5). That all this imagery describes a judgment of plagues coming upon the earth in connection with the days of Antichrist is plainly evident, but to attempt to set forth the exact character of these plagues would be the height of presumption, for no one knows. According to the analogy of 14:10; 19:20; 21:8, the fire, smoke, and brimstone give evidence of the infernal character of the plagues. The *Preterists*, as a rule, refer the whole vision to events connected with the destruction of Jerusalem, while the *Historical* interpreters see in it events which took place in connection with the inroads of the Turks and Saracens. Luther, Calovius, and others have specially in view the erroneous doctrine of the Turks,—Calovius sees the *Koran* proceeding from the mouths of the horses. Elliott sees in these tails of the horses the horsetails borne as symbols of authority by the Turkish Pashas, of which view Alford tersely says: "I will venture to say, that a more self-condemnatory interpretation was never broached." In fact, the variety of interpretation is endless, and all equally unsatisfactory.

The remarks of Todd, who represents the *Futurists*, are

suggestive: "It must be observed that the four angels are said to have been bound at or in the river Euphrates, and we are therefore probably to look to that region as the scene of this great judgment; inasmuch as the prophecy seems distinctly to assert that from thence shall issue the great multitude of horsemen who are to be the instruments of the predicted massacre, wherein the third part of men shall be slain. This conclusion is in exact conformity with the inferences to which we were led from a consideration of the prophecies of Daniel, namely, that the countries in the region of the Euphrates, once the seat of such mighty empires, are destined at some future period to recover their political power, and to become the scene of the last great struggle between the princes of the world and the people of God."

20. And the rest of mankind, which were not killed with these plagues, repented not of the works of their hands, that they should not worship devils (Gr. *demons*), and the idols of gold, and of silver, and of brass, and of stone, and of wood; which can neither see, nor hear, nor walk.

That this judgment of plagues fell only on the ungodly, and aimed at their repentance, is clearly indicated by this verse. But man in those antichristian days will not accept the loving forbearance of God (2 Pet. 3:9), but continue in their old sins, which are more particularly described as demon-worship and idolatry, for "the Spirit saith expressly, that in later times some shall fall away from the faith, giving heed to seducing spirits and doctrines of demons" (1 Tim. 4:1). The sins are the same as those against which Israel was warned and into which Israel fell (Deut. 4:28; Ps. 106:34–40; Acts 7:41). **Which neither see.** Compare Ps. 115:4–7; 135:15–17; 1 Cor. 10:19, 20.

133

21. And they repented not of their murders, nor of their sorceries, nor of their fornication, nor of their thefts.

We have here a characterization of the terrible state of society in the times immediately preceding the manifestation of Antichrist. Luthardt remarks: "These are the chief sins of heathenism. Such moral corruption will occur at the end, in spite of advanced culture; for culture of itself does not promote morality, but, as history teaches, may be employed as well in the service of ungodliness and immorality." On the word *fornication* Bengel comments: "Other crimes are committed by men at intervals; *fornication* alone is perpetual with those who are lacking purity of heart."

10

Revelation 10

33. The Vision of the Little Book (10:1-11)

The sixth trumpet has sounded which brought with it the destruction of a third part of the ungodly by the demoniacal armies from the East, but before the seventh is heralded with its accompanying woe (11:14), there is an interval consisting of two episodes, the vision of the Little Book (10:1-11) and the measuring of the Temple (11:1-13), similar to what occurs between the opening of the sixth and seventh seals (7:1-8; 7:9-17). The events indicated by these episodes are closely connected with the events signified by the sixth trumpet, for it is not until their close that the proclamation is made: "The second woe is past: behold, the third woe cometh quickly" (11:14).

1. And I saw another strong angel coming down out of heaven, arrayed with a cloud; and the rainbow was upon his head, and his face was as the sun, and his feet as pillars of fire.

This strong angel (*another* in contrast with the one spoken of in 5:2) is not to be identified with Christ Himself. Lange:

"This angel, in the might and victorious confidence of his appearance, reminds us of the archangel Michael." There is a general unanimity among commentators that *the cloud* characterizes the angel as a messenger of divine judgment, *the rainbow* indicating the sign of God's covenant of mercy, his face shining *as the sun* the divine glory with which he was invested, and *his feet as pillars of fire* intimating the fire of judgment. Alford: "The symbols with which this angel is accompanied, as those which surrounded the throne of God in 4:2, 3, betoken judgment tempered with mercy."

2. And he had in his hand a little book open: and he set his right foot upon the sea, and his left upon the earth.

This book was in the angel's *left* hand (10:5), and in comparison with the book of 5:2 was a *little* book, for it contained but a small portion of God's purposes, and it was *open*, for God was ready to disclose its contents. The fact that the angel stands *with his right foot upon the sea, and his left upon the earth*, indicates that God's power, whose messenger he is, extends in judgment over the whole earth.

3. And he cried with a great voice, as a lion roareth: and when he cried, the seven thunders uttered their voices.

We have a right to infer that this *outcry* of the angel was of a threatening character, but the nature of its contents we do not know. Bengel would refer the cry to the contents of 10:6. That the seven thunders brought to the ears of John some intelligible revelations may be clearly inferred from the next verse.

4. And when the seven thunders uttered *their voices*, I was about to write: and I heard a voice from heaven saying, Seal up the things which the seven thunders uttered, and write them not.

The remarks of Alford are very suggestive: "Many speculations have been raised as to the purport of the utterances of the seven thunders, and the reason for concealing them. From the very nature of the case, these must be utterly in vain.... It is matter of surprise and grief therefore, when we find historical interpreters of our day explaining them of the papal anathemas of the time of the Reformation.... Thus much we may infer; from the very character of thunder,—that the utterances were of fearful import: from the place which they hold, that they related to the church: from the command to conceal them, first, encouragement, that God in His tender mercy to His own does not reveal all His terrors: secondly, godly fear, seeing that the arrows of His quiver are not exhausted, but besides things expressly foretold, there are more behind not revealed to us." Hofmann imagines that the seven thunders disclosed the blessed mystery of the new world; Vitringa sees in them the seven crusades; others, seven future acts of God; or, seven terrible judgments on the persecutors of the Church.

5. And the angel which I saw standing upon the sea and upon the earth lifted up his right hand to heaven.

He does not lift up both hands as the angel in Dan. 12:7, because the little book lay open on his left (10:2). To lift up the hand toward heaven, as God's dwelling place, was customary in taking a solemn oath (Gen. 14:22; Ex. 6:8; Num. 14:30).

6. And sware by him that liveth for ever and ever (Gr. *unto the ages of the ages*), who created the heaven and the things that are therein, and the earth and the things that are therein, and the sea and the things that are therein, that there shall be time (or, *delay*) no longer.

137

This formal designation of God as the Creator of all things is appropriate, because the subject of the angel's oath, the consummation of the mystery of God (10:7), can only be brought about by that Almighty Power who made all things (Alford, Duesterdieck, Fausset, and others). **There shall be time no longer.** This does not mean that time shall end and eternity begin, but there is evidently an allusion to the answer given to the cry of the souls of the martyrs, "that they should rest *yet for a little time*, until their fellow-servants also and their brethren, which should be killed even as they were, should be fulfilled" (6:11). Alford correctly remarks: "This whole series of trumpet-judgments has been an answer to the prayers of the saints, and now the vengeance is about to receive its entire fulfilment: the appointed delay is at an end."

7. But in the days of the voice of the seventh angel, when he is about to sound, then is finished the mystery of God, according to the good tidings which he declared to his servants the prophets.

The moment that the seventh trumpet shall sound, the mystery shall be made clear, for the fulfilment comes in the days when it sounds. This verse is an anticipation of 11:15–18. This finishing of the mystery of God is the glorious consummation of God's kingdom, when "the kingdom of the world shall have become the kingdom of our Lord, and of his Christ; when he shall reign for ever and ever" (11:15),—the great theme of all O. T. prophecy. It is the time when Christ shall enter upon the possession of His rightful inheritance (1 Cor. 15:24–28). These good tidings God revealed unto His servants the prophets (Amos 3:7), especially to the prophet Daniel, and they have everywhere

138

spoken of Christ's coming kingdom.

There are many who maintain that the days of the seventh trumpet, mentioned in this verse, are identical with the three and a half times spoken of in Dan. 7:25; 12:7, known as the times of Antichrist, and referred to in Rev. 11:2; 13:5, as "forty and two months."

8. And the voice which I heard from heaven, *I heard it* again speaking with me, and saying, Go, take the book which is open in the hand of the angel that standeth upon the sea and upon the earth.

Bengel suggests that this voice (10:4) belonged to Christ, as in 1:11. John is commanded to go and take the little book out of the hand of the strong angel, who represented God's power of judgment over all the world.

9. And I went unto the angel, saying unto him that he should give me the little book. And he saith unto me, Take it, and eat it up; and it shall make thy belly bitter, but in thy mouth it shall be sweet as honey.

It seems that according to John's vision he now left heaven to be near the angel standing on earth and sea. The significance of the angel's command to eat the book can be learnt from Ezek. 2:9–3:3, where Ezekiel was also commanded to eat the roll, and thus received the contents of the prophecy in his heart (Ezek. 3:10), and then go and speak unto the house of Israel (Ezek. 3:1). By eating the book John is made able to proclaim its contents. **It shall make thy belly bitter.** When the contents of the book were fully revealed to him, though at the time of eating (the time of the reception of the revelation) it might taste *sweet as honey*,—as in the case of Ezekiel's roll (Ezek. 3:3), who, however, after eating it sat down astonished seven days in great bitterness

139

(Ezek. 3:14, 15) when the contents of the roll were fully revealed to him, that "there was written therein lamentations, and mourning, and woe" (Ezek. 2:10).

10. And I took the little book out of the angel's hand, and ate it up; and it was in my mouth sweet as honey: and when I had eaten it, my belly was made bitter.

See notes on last verse. John had the same experience as Ezekiel. John Gerhard: "The pleasure of the mouth is a symbol of the pleasure which the godly derive from the revelation of divine mysteries before they fully perceive them. The bitterness of the belly is a symbol of the pain which they derive from the consideration of the persecution to be described in the succeeding prophecy, which Antichrist will exercise against the Church at the end of the world."

11. And they say unto me, Thou must prophesy again over (or, *concerning*) many peoples and nations and tongues and kings.

They say. The expression is very indefinite. Auberlen remarks that the *third person plural*, as in Dan. 7:5, 13, refers to angels. **Thou must prophesy,** Because such is God's will. **Again.** Not after his return from exile, nor as referring to the composition of John's Gospel, but to proclaim the contents of the book which he has eaten, and which evidently is given in that part of the Apocalypse which begins at Rev. 12. **Concerning many peoples ... kings.** This prophecy is evidently found in the Apocalyptic visions beginning with Rev. 12, and contained in the following chapters of the book.

Synopsis of Interpretation. We meet in this chapter with as many variations of interpretations as elsewhere. The *Historical* Interpreters refer it either to the propagation of Christianity in general (Primasius, Bede, etc.), or to the

Reformation (Elliott, Keith, Daubuz, etc.). The scheme of
Elliott reads almost like a life of Luther annotated with
illustrations from Revelation. The Preterists as a rule see
in it the Prelude to the destruction of Jerusalem. As to
details of interpretation: (1) *The strong angel.* Many take
this angel to be Christ (so Bede, Aretas, Mede, Calovius,
Hengstenberg, Wordsworth, etc.); others, an angel (so Stern,
Bengel, De Wette, Lange, Duesterdieck, Alford, Sadler, Boyd
Carpenter, Simcox, Fausset, and others); others, the Emperor
Justinian (de Lyra), or evangelical preachers (older Protestant
expositors), or Luther (Daubuz), or the French Revolution
(Cunninghame); etc. (2) *The sea and earth* (verse 2). C.
à Lapide and Alcazar refer this to the Gentiles and Jews
to whom the Gospel is preached; Bengel sees Europe and
Asia; Hengstenberg, the *sea* of peoples, and the cultivated
earth; Keith, England (sea) and Germany (earth); etc. (3)
There shall be time no longer (verse 6). Cessation of time
(so Bede, Aretas, Œcumenius, Williams, etc.); there shall
be no longer delay, but the beginning of the fulfilment has
come (so Calovius, Vitringa, C. à Lapide, Ewald, De Wette,
Hengstenberg, Duesterdieck, etc.); no longer a season of
grace (Ebrard, Wordsworth); a *chronus* of years (Bengel), thus
making the end of all things in the year 1836, counting
from 725 A. D.; etc. (4) *The contents of the little book*
(verse 10). The contents of 11:1–13, the fate of Jerusalem
(the Preterists, Grotius, Wetstein, Ewald, etc.); the *Codex
Justinianus* (de Lyra); the New Testament (Aretas, etc.); the
Old Testament (Bede); judgments on the degenerate Church
(Hengstenberg); the special commission to Luther and the
preachers of the Reformation (Elliott, etc.); what is written in
the Apocalypse itself, and that, too, in the part which follows

Rev. 10. (Grotius, Calovius, Vitringa, Bengel, Ewald, De Wette, Hengstenberg, Fausset, etc.); the contents of Rev. 11. (Ebrard); the testimony of the Two Witnesses (De Burgh); summed up in 11:1–13, including a reference to Antichrist, announcing the conversion of Israel (Godet); "the little roll of St. John concerns the power which is called the *Little Horn*, by Daniel (7:8, 20), namely, the spiritual power of Rome" (Wordsworth); etc.

Summary. As has been expounded in our notes, we believe that this episode refers to the future, and indicates that after the judgments announced by the sixth trumpet have come upon the ungodly world, the beginning of the final consummation will soon come, and this *little* book contains the judgments which shall immediately come upon the world and the Church in connection with the times of tribulation in the days of Antichrist. The remarks of Fausset, "the eating of the book (10:10, 11), as in Ezekiel's case, marks John's inauguration to his prophetical office—here to a fresh stage of it,—the revealing of the things which befall the holy city and the Church of God—the subject of the rest of the book," and of Lee, "John's new consecration now places him side by side with Ezekiel, Daniel, and Zechariah; and points to the change in the Apocalyptic announcements introduced by Rev. 11:1–14, and beginning at Rev. 12:1," cannot be far from indicating the true idea underlying this whole chapter.

11

Revelation 11

34. The Measuring of the Temple (11:1, 2)

We come now to the second of the two episodes separating the sixth and seventh trumpets. (See notes introductory to the tenth chapter.) John is commanded to perform a symbolic action such as we read of that the prophets of the Old Testament also at times performed (Amos 7:7–9; Ezek. 40–43; Zech. 2:1–4). It is unquestionably one of the most difficult passages to explain in the whole Apocalypse. It seems to be of an anticipatory character, giving us a general glimpse of the events to occur in the times of Antichrist, which are described more in detail in the visions beginning with chapter 12. It is properly a compendium of the more detailed prophecies which follow. And Alford correctly remarks: "We cannot understand this prophecy at all except in the light of those that follow: for it introduces by anticipation their *dramatis personæ*."

1. And there was given me a reed like unto a rod: and one

said (Gr. *saying*), Rise, and measure the temple of God, and the altar, and them that worship therein.

There was given me. By *whom* is not said, probably an angel, possibly by Christ, who seems to be the speaker in 11:3 (Bengel). In 21:15 and Ezek. 40:3 the reed is in the angel's hand. **A reed.** To serve as a measure (Ezek. 40:3; Rev. 21:15). The reed was straight as a *rod of iron* (2:27). **Saying.** Indefinite,—the participle being out of construction. He who gives the *reed* is the speaker. **Arise.** This does not imply that John had been sitting or kneeling, but simply calls to action. **Measure.** The form of the vision is the same as that in Ezek. 40:3 and Zech. 2:1, which see. The two most probable explanations of the significance of this measuring are (1) that it signifies separation for preservation or exemption from destruction (so many of most diverse schools, as Duesterdieck, Hengstenberg, etc.); (2) that it denotes *to rebuild* as in Ezek. 40, whether literally in the future, or allegorically by the restoration of the true Church. It is probably best, after the O. T. type given us in Ezekiel, with Bengel, Godet, De Burgh, Todd, and Futurists in general, to refer this measuring to the rebuilding of the temple. **The temple of God.** This *naos* is that part of the sacred temple (*hieron*) which contained the *sanctuary*, including the Holy Place and Holy of Holies. The *Futurists* maintain that we are now transferred to Jerusalem, which will have been rebuilt by the Jews, while in unbelief, after their return to their own land, for we read *here* of the temple, the altar, the worshippers in the temple, the holy city, of Gentiles in contrast with Jews, and of their conquest of the city. The *Preterists* (Duesterdieck, Renan, Reuss, etc.) understand all this, too, in a literal sense, but refer it to the temple and

144

Jerusalem of John's own time, and maintain that when John wrote the Apocalypse the temple was still standing, and that the symbolism of the whole chapter refers to the capture of the city and the destruction of the temple by Titus. **The altar.** The altar of incense, which alone stood in the sanctuary (*naos*). **And them that worship therein.** Godet takes those who worship in the sanctuary to be the body of faithful Jews, who refuse to worship Antichrist at the time of his reigning in Jerusalem. So in substance also Fausset: "The measurement of the holy place seems to me to stand parallel to the sealing of the elect of Israel under the sixth seal. Literal Israel in Jerusalem, and with the temple restored (Ezek. 40:3–5, where also the temple is measured with the measuring reed 41–43.), shall stand at the head of the elect church. The literal temple at Jerusalem shall be the typical forerunner of the heavenly Jerusalem, in which there shall be all temple, and *no* portion exclusively set apart as *temple....* The temple shall be rebuilt on the return of the Jews to their land. Antichrist shall there put forward his blasphemous claims. The sealed elect of Israel, the head of the elect Church, alone shall refuse his claims."

2. And the court which is without the temple leave without (Gr. *cast without*), and measure it not; for it hath been given unto the nations: and the holy city shall they tread under foot forty and two months.

Only the *sanctuary* (*naos*) is to be measured,—all the rest of the temple is to be rejected,—and the reason is added—by God's appointment the court and the holy city Jerusalem "shall be trodden down of the Gentiles, until the times of the Gentiles be fulfilled" (Luke 21:24).

The view of the Futurists is very clearly stated by Todd:

145

"The act of measuring the temple denotes its restoration
to the worship of God and to the offices of Divine service.
The testimony which this prophecy, literally understood, has
given us is clearly this, that, at the time predicted, Jerusalem
shall be inhabited again, and the temple rebuilt; that after this
restoration the city shall be taken and sacked by the Gentiles,
the outer court also of the temple seized and profaned, but
the sanctuary itself and a remnant of them that worship
therein graciously preserved in the midst of the surrounding
desolation, which desolation shall be of very limited duration,
three years and a half.... There is nothing impossible, nothing
inconsistent with faith or reason, nothing which can furnish
the smallest justification to us for departing from the natural
meaning of the words." And Sadler, who also quotes Todd,
remarks, "Now it is to be remembered that all this may be if
God continues in the future to take an interest in Jerusalem
as He has done in the past." Sadler himself also says: "We
have reason to believe that the restored temple and altar will
be rebuilt in Jerusalem before the Second Advent and the
consummation, and in this case, i. e. on this explanation,
the court which is without, which is to be left unmeasured,
will be the court of the restored temple, which will be under
the power of Antichrist." **Forty and two months.** Nearly
all commentators are agreed that this period occurs in three
forms in this book: (1) here and in 13:5 as 42 months; (2) in
11:3 and 12:6 as a period of 1,260 days; and (3) as "a time, and
times, and half a time" (12:14), which last designation is also
found in Dan. 7:25; 12:7. There are many commentators
who identify these three periods, but the remarks of Alford
are suggestive: "*Equal* as they certainly seem to be, we have no
right to suppose them, in any two given cases, to be *identical,*

146

unless the context requires such a supposition. For instance, in these two verses (11:2, 3), there is strong temptation to regard the two equal periods as coincident and identical: but it is plain that such a view is not required by the context; the prophecy contains no note of such coincidence, but may be very simply read without it, on the view that the two periods are equal in duration, but independent of one another." Alford is probably correct. It is probably best, on the basis of Dan. 9:27, "he shall make a firm covenant with many for one week," to regard the whole of Antichrist's reign to extend over seven years, dividing it into two periods of 3½ years each, "for the half of the week he shall cause the sacrifice and the oblation to cease" (Dan. 9:27). During the first half of the week (3½ years), Antichrist is in covenant with the unbelieving Jews (Dan. 9:27) and the two witnesses are prophesying (Rev. 11:3), and then in the midst of the week, at the end of the first 3½ years, Antichrist shall reveal himself as the man of sin (2 Thess. 2:3), as the beast coming out of the sea (Rev. 13:1), stop the daily sacrifices (Dan. 9:27; 12:11), slay the two witnesses (Rev. 11:7), begin to tread under foot the holy city (Rev. 11:2), begin to wear out the saints of the Most High (Dan. 7:25), and enter upon the full exercise of his diabolical authority for the last 3½ years preceding his destruction by the coming of Christ at His Revelation. If this explanation be correct then the first half of Daniel's week (Dan. 9:27), and the 1,260 days during which the two witnesses are prophesying, are identical, while the second half of Daniel's week (Dan. 9:27) corresponds to the 42 months of the treading under of the holy city (11:2),—to the time and times and half a time of Dan. 7:25,—and to the 42 months of authority exercised by the beast (13:5).

35. The Prophesying of the Two Witnesses (11:3–14)

3. And I will give unto my two witnesses, and they shall prophesy a thousand two hundred and threescore days, clothed in sackcloth.

The article (in Greek) seems to imply that two personal and well-known individuals are designated as the witnesses. That which is given to them is power and authority to *prophesy.* Like prophets of old they proclaim the impending judgments of God, preaching repentance, and above all bear testimony to Christ. The fact that they were *clothed in sackcloth* shows that they preached repentance and the approaching judgment (Jer. 4:8; 6:26; Jonah 3:5). The period of their prophesying was during the first half of Daniel's week, before the beast was manifested as the Man of Sin (11:7; 13:1), for when they had finished their testimony at the beginning of the second half of Daniel's week, Antichrist made war with them, and killed them (11:7). (See notes on last verse.)

4. These are the two olive trees and the two candlesticks (Gr. *lampstands*), standing before the Lord of the earth.

We have here a further description of the character of these two witnesses. This whole verse is based upon the prophetic symbolism of Zech. 4:1–14. Zechariah beholds a golden candlestick, and seven lamps thereon, and two olive trees on either side thereof. The purpose of the vision was to encourage Zerubbabel and the high-priest Joshua not to put their trust in the arm of flesh but in the Spirit of Jehovah (Zech. 4:6). The *two olive trees* are explained by the angel as being "the two sons of oil that stand by the

148

Lord of the whole earth" (Zech. 4:14), evidently designating Zerubbabel and Joshua as these "two sons of oil," although some commentators suggest that the prophets Zechariah and Haggai are meant. In the Apocalypse the symbolism of Zechariah is transferred to these two witnesses, only that here they are called not only *the two olive trees*, but also *the two candlesticks* (in Zechariah we have only one candlestick). Like the two anointed ones in Zechariah these two witnesses are God's testifying servants and prophesy for Christ, and the fact that they *stand before the Lord of the earth* implies that they come not in their own might or power, but in the power and Spirit of God (Zech. 4:6).

5. And if any man desireth to hurt them, fire proceedeth out of their mouth, and devoureth their enemies: and if any man shall desire to hurt them, in this manner must he be killed.

As these two witnesses are sent by God they are endowed with miraculous powers. The nature of these miracles is described in this and the following verse. Just as the opponents of Moses were consumed by fire (Num. 16:35), and fire came down from heaven at the word of Elijah and consumed the two companies sent by the king of Samaria (2 Kings 1; 10–12), so these two witnesses shall destroy with fire all who seek to hurt them.

6. These have the power to shut the heaven, that it rain not during the days of their prophecy: and they have power over the waters to turn them into blood, and to smite the earth with every plague, as often as they shall desire.

Just as Elijah for three years and six months had power to shut the heaven, that it rained not (1 Kings 17:1; James 5:17), so these two witnesses have the same power for the same length of time; and like Moses they also have power over the waters to turn them into blood (Ex. 7:19, 20), and to smite the earth with plagues, only that the power given to the two witnesses shall be greater than that given to Moses, for these have unlimited power "to smite the earth with *every* plague, *as often as they shall desire."*

7. And when they shall have finished their testimony, the beast that cometh up out of the abyss shall make war with them, and overcome them, and kill them.

The two witnesses shall prophesy 1,260 days, or three and a half years, during the first half of Daniel's week (Dan. 9:27). Then *the beast* shall make war with them, and succeed in killing them. This is the first mention of *the therion*, or wild-beast, although we have a fuller description of *the beast* in later visions, in chapters 13. and 17. This beast is spoken of by Daniel as that horn of the fourth beast which "made war with the saints and prevailed against them" (Dan. 7:21). The infernal nature of *the beast* can be seen from his rising *out of the abyss* (*here* and 17:8). (On *abyss* see notes on 9:1, 11.) This beast is evidently Antichrist, who now manifests himself in all his disabolical power as the Man of Sin (2 Thess. 2:3–9). (See notes on 11:2.)

8. And their dead bodies (Gr. *carcase*) *lie* in the street of the great city, which spiritually is called Sodom and Egypt, where also their Lord was crucified.

This dishonor shown to their dead bodies is in great contrast to their later glorification (11:11–13). There is no reason why we should not regard Jerusalem itself as the scene of this dishonor. For in the times of Antichrist Jerusalem can rightly be called Sodom and Egypt (Isa. 1:9; Ezek. 16:48), by reason of its corruptions. In the same Jerusalem where Christ

150

was crucified, there the two witnesses suffer a martyr's death and dishonor. Fausset: "This identifies the city as Jerusalem, though the Lord was crucified *outside* of the city. Eusebius mentions that the scene of Christ's crucifixion was inclosed within the city by Constantine; so it will be probably at the time of the slaying of the two witnesses.... The difficulty is, how can Jerusalem be called 'the great city,' i. e. Babylon? By her becoming the world's capital of idolatrous apostasy, such as Babylon originally was, and then Rome has been; just as she is here called also *Sodom and Egypt*.... Whence it follows that Jerusalem shall be the last capital of the world-apostasy, and so receive the last and worst visitation of all the judgments ever inflicted on the apostate world, the earnest of which was given in the Roman destruction of Jerusalem."

9. And from among the peoples and tribes and tongues and nations do *men* look upon their dead bodies (Gr. *carcase*) three days and a half, and suffer not their dead bodies to be laid in a tomb.

Antichrist will then have possession of the city, and the treading under foot of the holy city by the Gentiles shall have made its beginning by this time (see notes on 11:2). The comment of Simcox on this verse is suggestive: "There seems no reason why we should not follow the traditional view, and understand this chapter as foretelling a sign which shall literally come to pass in the last days. The prophets Moses and Elijah will appear upon earth—or at the least two prophets will arise in their *spirit and power*: the scene of their prophecy will be Jerusalem, which will then be re-occupied by the Jewish nation. Antichrist (under whose patronage, it is believed, the restoration of the Jews will have taken place) will raise persecution against them, and kill them: but they will rise from the dead, and *then*, and not till then, the heart of Israel will turn to the Lord."

10. And they that dwell on the earth rejoice over them, and make merry; and they shall send gifts one to another; because these two prophets tormented them that dwell on the earth.

The followers of Antichrist will greatly rejoice at the downfall of these two witnesses who forever had been preaching repentance and judgment,—and so they will make merry and show their gratification by sending mutual gifts to one another as on festival occasions,—for were not these men who had continually been tormenting them with all manner of plagues now happily out of the way! Fausset: "The antichristianity of the last days shall probably be under the name of philosophical enlightenment and civilization, but really man's deification of himself. Fanaticism shall lead Antichrist's followers to exult in having at last seemingly silenced in death their Christian rebukers."

11. And after the three days and a half the breath of life from God entered into them, and they stood upon their feet; and great fear fell upon them which beheld them.

But the Lord will avenge His faithful servants. The language very closely resembles that used in the vision of the dry bones of Ezekiel, where we read, "And the breath came into them, and they lived, and stood up upon their feet" (Ezek. 37:10). When the followers of Antichrist will see that these two witnesses are raised from the dead, great fear, such as fell on the soldiers guarding Christ's tomb at His resurrection (Matt. 28:4), will overcome them.

12. And they heard a great voice from heaven saying unto them, Come up hither. And they went up into heaven in the

cloud; and their enemies beheld them.

The narrative is very simple. The risen witnesses heard the heavenly voice, and immediately they ascended into heaven, in a cloud, just as Christ Himself had ascended (Acts 1:9), visibly,—but these two witnesses will go up into heaven *in the sight of their enemies.*

13. And in that hour there was a great earthquake, and the tenth part of the city fell; and there were killed in the earthquake seven thousand persons (Gr. *names of men, seven thousand*): and the rest were affrighted, and gave glory to the God of heaven.

The very hour of the glorification of the two witnesses brings with it the punishment of God upon the followers of Antichrist. A great earthquake destroys a tenth part of Jerusalem, and slays 7,000 persons. So great is the effect of the whole scene,—the terror occasioned by the earthquake, and the fear caused by the manifestation of God's power in the resurrection and ascension of the two witnesses,—that *the rest,* the remnant of the Israelites who were not killed, were converted, and gave glory to God. It is highly probable that at this time the conversion of the 144,000 sealed ones of 7:4 will take place.

*Synopsis of Interpretations.—*I. *The Preterists.* All these, whether of the Rationalistic type (Grotius, Wetstein, Herder, Eichhorn, Reuss, Renan, etc.), or the Ordinary Preterists (Hammond, Stuart, Duesterdieck, etc.), no matter how differently they may explain the various details of the vision, at least agree in this, that this episode was fulfilled in the destruction of Jerusalem, 70 A. D. Lee and Duesterdieck give good summaries of the different news. Grotius refers the chapter to the destruction of Jerusalem by Hadrian; the

153

two witnesses are a Hebrew-speaking and a Greek-speaking church at Jerusalem: the *Beast* is Barchochab. In the *two witnesses* Herder, Eichhorn, and others see two High Priests, Ananus and Jesus, put to death in Jerusalem by the Zealots; etc.

II. *The Continuous-Historical View.* This large class, which includes some of the ablest commentators of the past, will perhaps be best represented by Elliott, who has written so voluminously upon this subject. This episode can refer to nothing else than the Reformation and the causes which led to it. The *reed* is a type of the authority given by the Elector John to Luther and the Reformers to preach the Gospel. The *measuring* of the *naos* of the temple and the non-measurement of the outer court Elliott refers to "the measuring or ecclesiastically constituting what was called the Evangelic Church, the mystic temple; of the authorization and introduction throughout the Saxon Churches of new formularies of public worship drawn on Evangelic principles by Luther and Melanchthon; of the removal from the church and church worship of Romish images and superstitions; etc.;" the *two witnesses* are the long line of witnesses for Christ through the 1,260 years of the Papal Antichrist preceding the Reformation; their death signifies the entire cessation of such witness during the few years preceding the Reformation; their bodies *lying unburied for three days and a half*, indicate *"precisely, to a day,"* the 3½ years which elapsed between the ninth session of the Lateran Council, May 5, 1514, and the posting up of the theses of Luther at Wattenberg, Oct. 31, 1517; *their resurrection* was the revival of Gospel preaching by Luther and his associates; their *ascension* indicates the peace of Augsburg (1555) whereby in the fullest measure toleration was accorded to Protestantism. "In short," Elliott adds, "it was the fulfilment of the apocalyptic figuration of the witnesses' ascent into the political heaven in Germany." And the Historical interpretations are all of about the same character. Is it a wonder that the Book of Revelation has fallen largely into disrepute and been regarded as an enigma, when such interpretations are seriously set forth, and considered as bringing out the meaning of God's Word?

III. *The Allegorical Interpretation.* We will select Wordsworth as one of the most sober and conservative among this large class of commentators. This vision of the *measuring* and the *witnessing*, according to Wordsworth, signifies what is now and what has always been going on in the Church. It has been fulfilled "by the preservation of the Holy Scriptures, and of the Sacraments, of Christ, and of an Apostolic Ministry, offering the Incense of Prayer, and ministering the Word and Sacraments." The *reed* represents the Canon of Holy Scripture as *the Rule of Faith;* the *two witnesses* are the *Old* and *New Testaments*, not Enoch and Elijah, or Moses and Elijah, as some of the ancient Fathers thought; the fire coming out of the mouth of the two witnesses is being fulfilled in the insults now offered to the Two Testaments, and it will be fulfilled completely in their future triumph. With him Jerusalem designates the corrupt Church (as with Hengstenberg); the spirit described in this vision is seen in the acts of the rulers of Papal Rome,—especially in the dogma of Papal Infallibility; etc.

IV. *The Futurists.* These maintain that the whole vision refers to the future. The *city* is the literal Jerusalem; the Jews shall return to Palestine; the temple shall be rebuilt; two literal prophets are to be sent to Israel, probably Moses and

Elijah; Jerusalem shall be under the dominion of Antichrist; the Gentiles under Antichrist shall destroy the city; etc.

The Forty and Two Months. Three main views have been maintained: (1) That it represents the whole period from the destruction of Jerusalem by the Romans, 70 A. D., to the Second Coming of Christ; (2) That each day represents a year, so that these periods represent 1,260 years. So nearly all those who accept the Historical scheme (Vitringa, Bishop Newton, Calovius, Faber, Elliott, etc.). Mede brings the end of the period to 1625 or 1715 A. D.; Calovius reckons from the time of Leo the Great (440 A. D.), and so closes with 1700 A. D.; Elliott sees the end of the period 1809 A. D., where the Pope's temporal authority over the Roman States was abolished by Napoleon; etc.; (3) That this period is to be interpreted literally. (So as a rule the Preterists and the Futurists.)

The Two Witnesses. It was the almost unaminous opinion of the Early Church that in the time of Antichrist two prophets would again appear at Jerusalem, and that everything would literally befall them just as it is written in this chapter. All were agreed that *Elijah* would be one of these witnesses, and the large majority of the Fathers considered that *Enoch* would be the second,—and especially since it is directly stated of these two alone of mankind that they had not tasted death. Some however thought that the text more naturally suggested *Moses,* and then it was argued that his passing away, just as in the case of Elijah and Enoch, was also a miraculous one (Deut. 34:5, 6; Jude 9). Victorinus, however, suggests *Elijah* and *Jeremiah,* because Jer. 1:5, "I have appointed thee a prophet unto the *nations*," not having been fulfilled in Jeremiah's former life, must still be fulfilled, after he has

156

been raised from the dead. A few like Tichonius, Primasius, and Bede, followed by some moderns, adopted the figurative interpretation, understanding by the *Two Witnesses* the Old and the New Testaments. Commentators of the Historical School are by no means agreed as to the identity of these two witnesses. De Lyra supposes them to be Pope Silverius and the Patriarch Mennas, others speak of a long line of witnesses or of Huss and Jerome of Prague, or of Luther and Melanchthon. Of modern commentators, including representatives of nearly all schools, who favor the idea that this chapter refers to the still future destruction of Jerusalem, the majority favor the view that Moses and Elijah, or at least two prophets with miraculous powers similar to those once possessed by Moses and Elijah, are the two witnesses referred to in this passage. And this interpretation is most probably the true one.

14. The second Woe is past: behold, the third Woe cometh quickly.

The first Woe ended with the sounding of the fifth trumpet. See notes on 9:12. The second Woe began with the sounding of the sixth trumpet (9:13–21), and continued through the two episodes, the Vision of the Little Book (10:1–11), and the events indicated by the Measuring of the Temple (11:1–13), for these events are closely connected with the events indicated by the sixth trumpet. (See notes introductory to the tenth chapter.) We are still under the seventh seal, for the entire series of trumpet-visions is developed out of the seventh seal (8:1, 2, 6), the first six seals (6:1–17) bringing in preliminary judgments, while the coming seventh trumpet under the seventh seal introduces the final end, partly anticipated under the sixth seal (6:12–17). See notes

157

on 8:1, 2.

36. The Sounding of the Seventh Trumpet, or the Third Woe (11:15–18)

15. And the seventh angel sounded; and there followed great voices in heaven, and they said, The kingdom of the world is become *the kingdom* of our Lord, and of his Christ: and he shall reign for ever and ever (Gr. *unto the ages of the ages*).

It is best to restrict the seventh Trumpet to 11:15–18, and to regard this as the close of the main vision beginning wirh chapter 6. We have here the announcement that the final end has come, although in later visions we will have a fuller description of the details of this consummation. The *great voices* that John heard were probably those of the armies of heaven. The time of the final judgment has come,—in fact, it is conceived as past, for Ps. 2:2 has been fulfilled, "The kings of the earth did set themselves, and the rulers did take counsel together against the Lord and against his Anointed," and Satan, the prince of the world, and Antichrist has been overcome, for "the kingdom of the world is become the kingdom of our Lord, and of his Christ." And His dominion is an everlasting dominion (Dan. 7:14), for *He shall reign for ever and ever.* This is no temporal rule on earth, but eternal in the heavens. The Lord God, the Almighty (11:17), is to reign, but Christ, His Anointed One, shall reign coequal with the Father. Compare 1 Cor. 15:24, 28, "Then cometh the end, when he shall deliver up the kingdom to God, even the Father; ... and when all things have been subjected unto him, then shall the Son also himself be subjected to him that did subject all things unto him, that God may be all in all."

16. And the four and twenty elders, which sit before God on their thrones, fell upon their faces, and worshipped God.

These twenty-four elders represent the Redeemed Church in heaven. See notes on 4:4, 10; 5:8, 9, 14.

17. Saying, We give thee thanks, O Lord God, the Almighty, which art and which wast; because thou hast taken thy great power, and didst reign.

On the titles ascribed here to God, see notes on 1:8; 4:8. The Redeemed Church, represented by the twenty-four elders, gives thanks to Almighty God, that He has now finally assumed the full exercise of the sovereignty and dominion. God is now no longer described as "He which is to come" as in 1:8; 4:8, for His Coming is here regarded as past. He has *now* assumed the *power* which these same twenty-four elders sang that He was *worthy* to receive (4:11).

18. And the nations were wroth, and thy wrath came, and the time of the dead to be judged, and *the time* to give their reward to thy servants the prophets, and to the saints, and to them that fear thy name, the small and the great; and to destroy them that destroy the earth.

We have here a graphic description of the events that will take place at the final day, viewed here as already past: (1) *and the nations were wroth*, i. e. Antichrist and his armies shall rise up against Christ (compare Ps. 2:1–3); (2) *and thy wrath came*, i. e. Christ broke them with a rod of iron, and dashed them in pieces like a potter's vessel (compare Ps. 2:4, 5, 9); (3) the dead shall be raised and judged; (4) believers shall be rewarded according to their works; (5) and the wicked shall be punished. The later visions will describe the events of the last day more in detail, for with this verse the second main vision of the Apocalypse (4:1–11:18) ends. We are not to

159

suppose that what follows (11:19–14:20) is to be regarded as following consecutively in the history of the events of the Last Day. Alford is in the main correct when he says: "The visions are not continuous, but resumptive: not indeed going over the same ground with one another, either of time or of occurrence, but each involving something which was not in a former, and putting the course of God's Providence in a different light."

This seventh Trumpet brought also the third Woe, but for the description of the terrific and woful aspect of this Coming of Christ, which is only implied here, we must turn to the parallel account of the events of the Last Day as given in 6:12–17, for there we have an exhibition of what the wrath of the Lamb signifies, for in our passage here (11:15–18) we have only a description of Christ's glorious Advent as the Deliverer of His people. This, then, is the second time that the events of the Last Day have been definitely brought before us.

37. The Vision of the Woman and the Great Red Dragon (11:19–12:6)

19. And there was opened the temple of God that is in heaven; and there was seen in his temple the ark of his covenant (or, *testament*); and there followed lightnings, and voices, and thunders, and an earthquake, and great hail.

We come now to a new vision which extends from 11:19 to 14:20, and is introduced by *lightnings, and voices, and thunders,* just as the second main vision (4:5), only that here they were accompanied by *an earthquake* and *great hail;* for it is in judgment that God will proceed to restore His people to

160

His favor—judgment upon His enemies, as upon His people (Zech. 12–14.). John now sees the door of the temple of God in heaven standing open, and he beheld *the ark of the covenant.* This ark is the pledge of God's faithfulness to His covenant people, and this symbolizes that the succeeding visions will have special reference to Israel and to His dealings with His people. This verse is properly the transition between the close of the last Vision, ending with the seventh trumpet, and the Visions that follow. All that follows in this Vision may be regarded as the contents of the *Little Book* (10:10, 11).

12

Revelation 12

1. And a great sign was seen in heaven; a woman arrayed with the sun, and the moon under her feet, and upon her head a crown of twelve stars.

Alford is probably correct when he remarks "that the principal details of the present section are rather descriptive than strictly prophetical: relating, just as in the prophets the descriptions of Israel and Judah, to things passed and passing, and serving for the purpose of full identification and of giving completeness to the whole vision." Instead of a continuous narrative, we have now a recapitulation of God's dealings with the Church and the world (see notes on 11:18, 19), especially during that period covered by the last half of Daniel's week (Dan. 9:27), the period of Antichrist, parallel to the sixth and seventh seals. The symbolism is of a different character from that which has hitherto been employed.

John sees the figure of *a woman* in heaven. This figure has a deep meaning and important signification, for it is *a great sign*, bringing with it momentous revelations. "A *sign*, because St. John saw things not in their proper nature, but in figure and enigma, as the Church under the form of a woman, Satan under that of a dragon" (Hengstenberg). The woman is all glorious in appearance, completely enveloped in light,—her garments are the glittering rays of the sun, and she stands as a victor, for her feet rest on the moon, and a crown of twelve stars composed her victor's crown. Compare the picture of the Shulamite in the Song of Songs (6:10), "Who is she that looketh forth as the morning, Fair as the moon, Clear as the Sun?"

2. And she was with child: and she crieth out, travailing in birth, and in pain to be delivered.

A most vivid description of the anguish and pangs that overtake women at the time of child-birth.

It is a difficult question to decide what is represented by *the woman*. There are four leading interpretations:

(1) The *woman* represents the Virgin Mary (so Bernard, Sadler, and others); (2) She represents the O. and N. T. Church in undivided unity (Victorinus, De Wette, Hengstenberg, Auberlen, etc.); (3) She represents the Christian Church (Irenæus, Bede, N. de Lyra, Hammond, Calovius, Vitringa, Bengel, etc.), particularly at the time of Antichrist (C. à Lapide, Stern, Christiani, etc.); (4) The *woman* represents the Old Testament Church (Hofmann, Ebrard, Duesterdieck, Luthardt, etc.). A careful exegesis will show that the last is probably the correct interpretation. We evidently have here the ideal Old Testament Church, as she appears in God's covenant relation to her, destined finally, according to God's purpose, at His appointed time, to attain the victor's crown, as seen in the light of Rom. 11:25–32. With Ebrard and Hofmann we may refer to Isa. 7:14; Micah 4:10; and with Duesterdieck to Micah 5:2–4, as aiding in solving this

difficult problem. The remarks of Fausset are suggestive: "Clothed with the sun, the Church is the bearer of Divine supernatural light in the world.... The woman of whom Jesus was born represents the *Old Testament congregation of God.* The woman's travail-pains (12:2) represent the O. T. believers' ardent longings for the promised Redeemer.... The twelve stars, the crown around her head, are the twelve tribes of Israel." So in substance also Luthardt. *The moon is under her feet,* for the Jewish Church, notwithstanding her trials, will finally "triumph over night, which for her has passed away" (Luthardt).

3. And there was seen another sign in heaven; and behold, a great red dragon, having seven heads and ten horns, and upon his heads seven diadems.

In this same chapter (12:9, 13, 15) we are informed that this *great red dragon* is *the old serpent, he that is called the Devil and Satan.* Unquestionably, there is a reference to Gen. 3:1; as well as to Isa. 27:1. He appears as *fiery red,* because fire is a symbol of destruction, and because *he was a murderer from the beginning* (John 8:44), and as such seeks to destroy the child of the woman (12:4), as well as the rest of her seed (12:17). Satan, as the source of universal hostility to God and of every antichristian power, appears here as the archetype of the beast (or Antichrist) of 13:1 and 17:3, as having *seven heads* and *ten horns.* In 17:9–13 (which see) John gives us an explanation of these *heads* and *horns.* There these heads and horns are explained as so many kings. The fourth beast of Daniel (7:7, 8, 20–24) also had ten horns, signifying ten kings (Dan. 7:24). Fausset calls attention to the fact that in Dan. 7. the antichristian powers up to Christ's Second Coming are represented by four beasts, which have among them *seven*

164

heads; i. e. the first, second, and fourth beasts have *one* head each; the third, *four heads.* It is the fourth beast that has the ten horns. According to Auberlen these *seven heads* of the Dragon are a caricature of the Seven Spirits of God (1:4; 3:1; 4:5; 5:6), and the *ten horns* are a symbol of his worldly power. The *seven diadems* on his *seven heads* indicate Satan's universal dominion as Prince of this fallen world. Note that the Dragon has *seven diadems* on his *heads;* the Beast of 13:1 (Antichrist) has *ten diadems* on his *horns.*

4. And his tail draweth the third part of the stars of heaven, and did cast them to the earth: and the dragon stood before the woman which was about to be delivered, that when she was delivered, he might devour her child.

The dragon's fury is graphically described, for in the lashing of its tail many stars are removed from their places. So *the little horn* in Dan. 8:10, "cast down to the ground some of the host of heaven and of the stars, and trampled upon them." This *third part of the stars of heaven* evidently also has reference to the angels which the Devil drew down with himself to perdition at the time of his fall (see Jude 6) (Victorinus, Williams, Sadler, etc.). This *standing of the dragon before the woman* evidently "symbolizes the enmity of the serpent against the seed of the woman, beginning with the intended treachery of Herod and massacre of the innocents; but including also the malice that pursued Him through life, the temptation, and at last the cross" (Simcox).

5. And she was delivered of a son, a man child, who is to rule all the nations with a rod of iron: and her child was caught up unto God, and unto his throne.

We agree with Alford in his very emphatic comment on the words, *who is to rule* (shepherdize) *all the nations with a rod of iron;* "These words, cited verbatim from the Greek text of Ps. 2:9, leave no possibility of doubt who is here intended. The man-child is the Lord Jesus Christ, *and none other.* And this result is a most important one for the fixity of reference of the whole prophecy. It forms one of those landmarks by which the legitimacy of various interpretations may be tested.... The exigencies of this passage require that the birth should be understood literally and historically, of that Birth of which all Christians know." Duesterdieck remarks: "These words, which are referred also to Christ in 19:15, make it indubitable that the child born of the woman is the Messiah." (So also De Wette, Rinck, Hengstenburg, Ebrard, Lee, Simcox, Currey, Sadler, Boyd-Carpenter, etc.). Any other interpretation is simply made in the interests of some preconceived theory of Apocalyptic interpretation. In vision John saw that the child was caught up *unto God and unto his throne,* and this had been fulfilled when Christ ascended into heaven, and sat down at the right hand of God. John sees in vision the whole history of the O. T. Church and of Israel, in God's covenant relation to His chosen people, down to the very end of time. The thought here, that this *man-child* is to rule *all the nations with a rod of iron,* brings by anticipation this very period of the final end before us, as we see in the next verse.

6. And the woman fled into the wilderness, where she hath a place prepared of God, that there they may nourish her a thousand two hundred and threescore days.

This whole verse is anticipatory. John here briefly summarizes what is described more minutely in the latter part of this chapter (12:13–15). This also shows that *the war in heaven* (12:7–9) does not follow in time after the flight of the woman, but occurs before it,—in fact occurs contemporaneously with the Ascension of Christ into heaven. We believe that the only true solution of this difficult chapter lies in understanding it in its most simple and natural way. The passage 12:1–5 refers to events connected with the life of Christ, and has been fulfilled with Christ's Ascension into heaven; the one verse 12:6 is parallel to 12:13–17, is anticipatory, and lies still in the future, referring evidently to the last 3½ years of Antichrist's reign, the last half of Daniel's week (Dan. 9:27); the passage 12:7–9 refers to events that took place at the time of Christ's ascension; while 12:10–12 is a continuation of the vision and refers to events in connection with the days of Antichrist. This would imply, contrary to the whole scheme of the Continuous-Historical interpreters, that no notice is taken here, or in the Apocalypse anywhere, of what is known as the Historical Church Period, elapsing between Christ's Ascension and the times of the Second Advent. The remarks of Sadler are very suggestive on this point: "I desire to put on record the enunciation of a great principle, which is this: that from the departure of our Lord, at the moment of His Ascension to the moment of His Second Advent, it is not lawful for us to assume that any definite lapse of time intervenes.... I believe that there is no time allotted to the world or to the Church between the disappearance of Christ on Mount Olivet and His return. During the whole of these 1,800 years and more He might have been expected at any moment; so that I think that it is not permitted to us to make the history of the events which have occurred since the visions of the Apocalypse to be the subject of these visions, so that so many centuries should elapse between the time in which St. John saw them and the present time. Where there appears to be visions of successive events, it is only in appearance." And we might add, that with Daniel also there is no time between the close of the 69 weeks when the *Anointed one was to be cut off,* and the final week when *the prince that shall come* shall make *a firm covenant with many for one week,* but *in the midst of the week* he shall cause *the sacrifice and the meat offering to cease* (Dan. 9:26, 27). This also explains why in Christ's prophecy of the signs of His Coming and of the end of the world, there seems to be such a close connection between the destruction of Jerusalem and the final consummation.

The *woman* represents the *remnant of Israel* (see notes on 12:2), now converted by the events connected with the preaching and the resurrection of the two witnesses (see notes on 11:13), and the 1,260 days are the same as *the time, and times, and half a time* of 12:14, and both are to be identified with the last 3½ years of the reign of Antichrist, corresponding to the last half of Daniel's week. For further explanation see the parallel passage 12:13–15.

38. The War between Michael and the Dragon (12:7–9)

7. And there was war in heaven: Michael and his angels *going forth* to war with the dragon; and the dragon warred and his angels.

It is probably best to connect this *war in heaven* with the events recorded in 12:5, as occurring at the time of Christ's Ascension into heaven. Although Satan and his angels had been cast out of heaven at some time previous to the fall of man (see notes on 2 Pet. 2:4; and Jude 6), yet it seems that, in the counsel of God, he was still permitted, in O. T.

times, before Christ's work of Redemption was completed, to enter into the presence of God in heaven. In Job 1:6–12; 2:1–7, he appears before God as the accuser of Job, and in Zech. 3:1, 2, as the accuser of Joshua, the high priest. No matter how mysterious this passage (Rev. 12:7–9) may seem, it is evident that the casting down of Satan from his office of accuser in heaven is connected with the great justifying work of redemption. John here gives us a glimpse into the world of spirits which can be compared with what Christ reveals to us in Luke 10:17, 18, "I beheld Satan falling as lightning from heaven," and John 12:31, "Now is the judgment of this world: now shall the prince of this world be cast out;" with what Peter unfolds in 1 Pet. 3:19, 20, and 4:6 (see *Lutheran Commentary on General Epistles*), and with the revelations given by Paul in Col. 2:15 and Eph. 4:8–10. We have a right to infer that Satan, when he found himself unable to overcome Christ here on earth by subtlety, carried his war into heaven itself, returning thither with his angels, with the vain hope of supplanting Christ on the throne of heaven—God permitting it, in His eternal counsels, for the sake of the glory of His Son. In fact, in the Bible we find that the history of the ever deeper downfall of Satan has *four* periods: (1) From his original fall to the first Coming of Christ, during which time he still had access to heaven as the accuser (*Devil*) and adversary (*Satan*) of man; (2) from Christ's Ascension to His Second Advent, during which time he is still the prince of *this world*, and rages especially during *the short time* immediately preceding Christ's Coming to destroy Antichrist; (3) his being bound during the period of the Millennium (20:1–3); and (4) his final judgment (20:10). The *Archangel Michael* (Jude 9) is not to be identified with Christ,

169

as some commentators maintain. He was the adversary of Satan, in their strife about the body of Moses (see notes on Jude 9), and in the O. T., as the guardian of the Jewish people in their conflict with heathenism, he is represented as the leader of the good angels in their conflict with the power of Satan (Dan. 10:13, 21; 12:1).

8. And they prevailed not, neither was their place found any more in heaven.

Not only were the dragon and his angels defeated, but they were cast out of heaven, no more to enter therein. Satan had now, for the believer, been utterly vanquished, and the great work for which the Son of God had come into the world was accomplished (see notes on 1 John 3:8).

9. And the great dragon was cast down, the old serpent, he that is called the Devil and Satan, the deceiver of the whole world (Gr. *inhabited earth*); he was cast down to the earth, and his angels were cast down with him.

A fuller description of what was meant by the preceding verse. The names here given to the dragon describe his character. First, he is called *the old* serpent, with reference to Gen. 3:1. This is the serpent which beguiled Eve (2 Cor. 11:3), the *old* serpent, because *he was a murderer from the beginning* (John 8:44). Secondly, he is called the *Devil*, that is, *Slanderer* or *Accuser*, because he slanders God to man (Gen. 3:4, 5) and man to God (Job 1:9–11; 2:4, 5; Rev. 12:10), and *Satan*, that is, *Adversary*, because he is the great opposer of God and man. Thirdly, he is described as the *deceiver of the whole inhabited world*, of which he is the prince and god. He does not, indeed, succeed in betraying all, but he endeavors even to deceive the saints. This *casting down* of Satan and his angels to the earth is the consequence of their being cast out

170

of heaven,—and though the *abyss* is the home of Satan and his angels (see notes on 9:11), still as "the prince of this world" (John 12:31; 16:11), he is very active here on earth among men during the time intervening between the Ascension of Christ and the Second Advent, but especially during *the short time* of the days of Antichrist.

39. The Rejoicing in Heaven at the Fall of Satan (12:10–12)

10. And I heard a great voice in heaven, saying, Now is come the salvation, and the power, and the kingdom of our God, and the authority of his Christ: for the accuser of our brethren is cast down, which accuseth them before our God day and night.

In the heavenly choir, no notice is taken of the long period elapsing between Christ's Ascension and His Second Coming to assume His Kingdom. See notes on 12:6. The heavenly song, probably proceeding from the 24 elders as representing the Redeemed Church (the expression *our brethren* suggests this), celebrates the final consummation as at hand, and Christ as entering upon His universal Kingdom. This song is introductory to the final events occurring during the times of Antichrist as described more fully, 12:13–14:20. Duesterdieck calls attention to the fact that the individual ideas of this song are very significant. *The Salvation* refers to "the sum total of all righteousness, blessedness, and holiness, as they have been prepared for the creature by God through His Christ" (7:10; 19:1); *the power* of God has special reference to His victory over the Dragon, not only contemplated as having taken place at Christ's Ascension, but in view of

171

the final and complete victory over Satan, which is here anticipated; *the power* or authority "is ascribed to God's Christ, because it is the definite, supreme power peculiar to God's Christ as such." They rejoice because he who has always had the habit of accusing saints is now cast down. Simcox, Lee, and others correctly see in the present *accuseth* the mark of the habitual act, rather than that of the *present*. The sense is illustrated by the scene in the Prologue of Job and in Zech. 3:1, 2, already referred to.

11. And they overcame him because of the blood of the Lamb, and because of the word of their testimony; and they loved not their life even unto death.

The song now celebrates the victorious faith of those believers who endured the trials of the days of Antichrist, which are here regarded as victoriously overcome. They overcame Satan, not by their own power or might, but the cause on account of which the victory was won was Christ's victory over Satan, won by the shedding of His precious blood, and this victory of believers was also the consequence of their having given a faithful testimony of their faith even unto death. "It is *because* they have given a faithful testimony, even unto death, that they are victorious" (Alford).

12. Therefore rejoice, O heavens, and ye that dwell (Gr. *tabernacle*) in them. Woe for the earth and for the sea: because the devil is gone down unto you, having great wrath, knowing that he hath but a short time.

The inhabitants of heaven are to rejoice, for the final consummation has come. Christ will now enter upon the full exercise of his universal Kingdom. Only *a short time* will elapse. He cometh quickly. But woe to the earth and its inhabitants. For the devil is still the prince of this world, and now in the days of Antichrist he has but *a short time.* Great is his wrath, and it is inflamed anew, for he has but little time to wreak his anger upon those who resist either him, or his beast, or his authority.

40. The Deliverance of the Woman (12:13–17)

13. And when the dragon saw that he was cast down to the earth, he persecuted the woman which brought forth the man *child.*

John now explains more freely the cause of the flight of the woman, to which reference had been made in 12:6. When the dragon saw that he could no longer succeed in destroying the man-child, he turned his hatred towards the mother of the child. No notice whatever is here taken of the time elapsing between the snatching up of the child and its accompanying war, and the final persecution of the woman, the remnant of Israel converted by the preaching of the two witnesses (see notes on 11:13)—in the days of Antichrist. Of course it is implied that the dragon always persecuted Israel from the time of the Ascension of Christ into heaven,—and the whole history of the Jewish people ever since is but the living illustration of the truth of this great fact, for Satan not only stirred up in them a bitterness and hatred against the *Man-Child,* but has even used the professing church as an instrument to punish the Jews during the whole period,—but of this there is no reference here. John describes simply the final end, for we are again at the beginning of the last 3½ years of the reign of Antichrist (13:1), just as we were by anticipation at 12:6.

14. And there were given to the woman the two wings of

the great eagle, that she might fly into the wilderness unto her place, where she is nourished for a time, and times, and half a time, from the face of the serpent.

The two wings of the great eagle. This figure is taken from Ex. 19:4, "ye have seen what I did unto the Egyptians, and how I bore you on eagles' wings, and brought you unto myself," for "as an eagle stirreth up her nest, that fluttereth over her young, he spread abroad his wings, he took them, he bore them on his pinions" (Deut. 32:11). *Two* wings are mentioned to indicate the rapid and sure escape which was made by the believing Jewish remnant. Duesterdieck correctly: "As God formerly bore His people, when they fled from the Egyptians, on eagles' wings, so, for her sure escape, a pair of eagle's wings is given the woman fleeing from the dragon." **Into the wilderness.** Just as Israel was delivered out of Egypt by the flight into the wilderness, so, in the oppression and bondage of the Egypt of Antichrist, will deliverance come to the believing Jewish remnant, by the flight *into the wilderness.* There is nothing incredible in this, and this is in perfect harmony with Ezek. 20:35–38. **Unto her place.** This is the *place prepared of God,* mentioned in 12:6. Just as the wilderness of Sinai had been the place especially prepared for the deliverance of Israel (Ex. 23:20, "Behold, I send an angel before thee, to keep thee by the way, and to bring thee *into the place which I have prepared*"), so God in these last days of trial and tribulation has a special place of deliverance and safety prepared for His suffering people. **Where she is nourished.** Just as God nourished Israel with manna in the wilderness, so shall *the woman* be nourished in the wilderness *for a time, and times, and half a time,* corresponding to the 1,260 days of 12:6, the period of

174

Antichrist referred to in Dan. 7:25; which is the same as the last half of Daniel's week (Dan. 9:27),—all corresponding to the 42 months during which the beast exercises his authority (13:5–7).

15. And the serpent cast out of his mouth after the woman water as a river, that he might cause her to be carried away by the stream.

In contrast to the miraculous preservation of Israel by the waters of the Red Sea and the destruction of the Egyptians by the same, we have here the attempt of Satan to destroy the saints by a flood. Although we do not profess to understand or explain any of these prophecies concerning events still lying in the future, we deem it far better to accept the idea that God will in some way bring about all these events as here indicated, than to adopt the strange and arbitrary fancies with which the allegorists and historical interpreters seek to becloud us. Alford, although he himself is unable to see any definite solution, is, however, clear in his own mind that the historical interpretation given by so many to this whole passage (12:13–17), is utterly wrong. He remarks: "Then the river which the dragon sent out of his mouth after the woman might be variously understood,—of the Roman armies which threatened to sweep away Christianity in the wreck of the Jewish nation,—or of the persecutions which followed the church into her retreats, but eventually became absorbed by the civil power turning Christian,—or of the Jewish nation itself, banded together against Christianity wherever it appeared, but eventually itself becoming powerless against it by its dispersion and ruin,—or again. of the influx of heretical opinions from the Pagan philosophers which tended to swamp the true faith, I confess that not one of these seems

175

to me satisfactorily to answer the conditions: nor do we gain anything by their combination. But anything within reasonable regard for the analogies and symbolism of the text seems better than the now too commonly received historical interpretation, with its wild fancies and arbitrary assignment of words and figures."

16. And the earth helped the woman, and the earth opened her mouth, and swallowed up the river which the dragon cast out of his mouth.

Just as God once miraculously saved His people by their passage through the Red Sea, so now by a similar miracle He will again save His people, but in another way, for the earth shall open its mouth, just as once before it did, when it swallowed up all those concerned in the matter of Korah, Dathan, and Abiram (Num. 16:26–35), and receive the rushing torrent in its gaping mouth

17. And the dragon waxed wroth with the woman, and went away to make war with the rest of her seed, which keep the commandments of God and hold the testimony of Jesus: and he stood upon the sand of the sea.

The woman, as we have seen, represents the converted remnant of Israel, which the dragon sought to destroy, but as she has been delivered out of his hands in a miraculous way by God, Satan now vents his anger against those believers among the Gentiles which remain faithful to God, and keep the testimony of Jesus. How the dragon makes war with the believing Gentiles is more fully related in the next chapter. He is here represented as standing upon the sand of the sea, in order that he may call forth the beast, to whom he will give all his power and authority (13:2).

Synopsis of Interpretations. The *Preterists* as a rule (Herder,

Ewald, Renan, etc.) refer the whole chapter to events preceding the destruction of Jerusalem, 70 A. D., especially to the flight of the Christians from Jerusalem to Pella beyond Jordan. The *Dragon* is the symbol of the Roman Empire. The *Continuous-Historical* interpreters, no matter how they may differ in details, see in this vision a prediction of the triumph of Christianity in the Roman Empire, and the majority of commentators see in it especially the victories of Constantine and Theodosius (Elliott, Mede, Vitringa, Brightman, Bishop Newton, etc.). The *Futurists* as a rule maintain that this chapter sets forth the state of things at the close of the first half of the last week of Daniel, after the general conversion of the Jews.

The Woman.—In addition to the interpretations given under 12:2, we have other theories as to the signification of *the woman*,—as the primitive Church, or the invisible. Church, or the pure Church, or the true visible Church, or humanity, etc.

The Dragon.—(1) Satan inspiring Herod, Judas, and others; (2) the Roman Empire under Nero; (3) the Roman Empire as a persecuting power hostile to Christianity; (4) the rulers of the Roman Empire; etc.

The Man-Child.—(1) Christ formed mystically in His members; (2) all regenerated children of God; (3) the origin of the Christian Empire; (4) Constantine; (5) Christ's kingly dominion; (6) the Nicene Creed; (7) the Roman Catholic Church; etc.

The Woman's Flight.—(1) The flight of the faithful in the days of Antiochus (Doellinger); (2) at the time of the threatened destruction of Jerusalem (the Preterists); (3) the passage of Christianity from the Jews to the Gentiles (Vitringa,

Bengel, Auberlen, and others); (4) the division of the Roman Empire into the Greek and Latin Empires (Isaac Newton); (5) the corruptions of the Church (Cunninghame); etc.

The War in Heaven.—(1) The original fall of Satan and his angels; (2) occurred at the time of the Ascension of Christ; (3) will take place in the future, at the end of days (Ebrard, De Burgh, Stern, etc.); (4) the conflict between paganism and Christianity (Elliott and others); (5) the struggle between a faithful and apostate priesthood (Faber); etc.

The Two Wings of the Great Eagle.—(1) The Old and New Testament (Wordsworth); (2) the two divisions of the Roman Empire, under its successive rulers, protecting the Church (Mede, Bengel, Auberlen, and others); (3) the Roman Empire under Theodosius (Elliott); (4) the faith of Jesus Christ; etc.

The Flood of Water.—(1) The Roman persecution; (2) the deluge of barbarous nations, the Goths and Huns (Wordsworth); (3) the Arian heretics; (4) the Turks; (5) the streams of the migration of nations (Auberlen); (6) the hosts of Antichrist: (7) the French Revolution; etc.

The Rest of her Seed.—(1) Those to whom the woman was to give birth in the wilderness (Mede); (2) the churches of the Dispersion (Renan); (3) the Eastern Church; (4) the Western Church, especially the Waldenses, etc.; (5) faithful witnesses, like Augustine and others; (6) the Gentile Christians (Ebrard, Bisping, and others); etc.

13

Revelation 13

41. The Vision of the First Beast. (13:1–10)

1. And I saw a beast coming up out of the sea, having ten
horns and seven heads, and on his horns ten diadems, and
upon his heads names of blasphemy.

John in his vision saw a beast coming up out of the sea,
evidently called forth by the dragon, who was standing upon
its visible shore (see last verse). To the large majority of
commentators the sea represents the confused multitude of
the nations of the world (Hengstenberg, Ebrard, Kliefoth,
Wordsworth, Lee, and others). This beast is the same already
referred to in 11:7, and more fully described in Rev. 17. He
sees that the beast has *ten horns* and *seven heads*, the same
number each that the dragon had, in whose interests the beast
appears. The *horns* are here mentioned first, because they
are first seen as the beast comes up out of the sea, afterwards
the *heads* are always mentioned first (17:3, 7). There was the
difference, however, between the dragon and the beast—the

dragon had *seven* diadems upon its *seven heads* (12:3), but the beast had *ten* diadems upon its *ten horns*, and upon each of its seven heads there was written a name of blasphemy. Throughout our whole exposition we must keep in mind the Vision of Daniel (Dan. 7), but John's Vision differs in some particulars and supplies details which are not given there.

Daniel saw *four* beasts coming out of the sea (Dan. 7:3), which were explained to him as representing four kings (Dan. 7:17), or kingdoms (Dan. 7:23). We have here to do especially with his *fourth* beast which had *ten horns* (Dan. 7:7, 20), among which the *little horn* came up, having plucked up three of the first horns by the roots (Dan. 7:8, 20), and made war with, and wore out the Saints of the Most High (Dan. 7:21, 25). It was explained to Daniel that *the ten horns* signify that out of the fourth kingdom *ten kings* should arise (Dan. 7:24), and that *the little horn* represents another king who shall put down three kings, and who from the whole presentation may be regarded as the Old Testament type of Antichrist. In John's Vision we are also informed of the meaning of the *seven heads* and *ten horns* of the first Beast, for the angel explains that *the seven heads* are *seven kings,*—"the beast is himself also an eighth, and is of the seven,"—and the *ten horns* are *ten kings* which "receive authority as kings with the beast, for one hour" (Rev. 17:10–12).

2. And the beast which I saw was like unto a leopard, and his feet were as *the feet* of a bear, and his mouth as the mouth of a lion: and the dragon gave him his power, and his throne, and great authority.

Daniel saw *four beasts;* representing four kingdoms (Dan. 7:17, 23); St. John sees *one* beast uniting the characteristics of the four. It is almost certain that the four kingdoms rep-

180

resented by the four beasts of Daniel are, (1) the Babylonian or Assyrian; (2) the Medo-Persian; (3) the Macedonian or Greek; and (4) the Roman.

This is the traditional view and defended by Caspari, Keil, Pusey, Wordsworth, and others. The Preterists as a rule maintain that the four kingdoms are Babylonia, Media, Persia, and Greece. The remarks of Wordsworth are very suggestive: "In the Vision of Daniel—who looks *forward* from the *Assyrian* Dynasty, under which he was living, to the three *succeeding* ones, the Medo-Persian, Greek, and Roman—we see first the Assyrian *Lion* (Dan. 7:4), next the Medo-Persian *Bear* (Dan. 7:5), and then the Greek *Leopard* (Dan. 7:6). In the Vision of the Apocalypse of St. John—who looks *backward* from the *Roman* Dynasty, under which he was living, to the three *preceding* dynasties—we see the *three Animals* of Daniel, mentioned in an *inverted order*, and combined in the first Beast, here displayed."

But this First Beast cannot be identified with the Fourth Beast of Daniel, or the Roman kingdom. The whole description given of the First Beast in Rev. 17:9–13 shows that it corresponds with *the Little Horn* which arises among the ten horns of the Fourth Beast (Dan. 7:20–25). This is very clearly brought out by Williams: "This Beast of John is in itself composed of the four Beasts of Daniel. It has the leopard-likeness of the third, the Grecian or Macedonian; it has the bear-feet of the second, the Persian; the lion-mouth of the first, the Babylonian; and the ten-horned head of the fourth beast, which is the Roman kingdom. Nor is that all, for it has also *seven heads*, which make up the heads of the four beasts, inasmuch as the leopard of Daniel has four heads (Dan. 7:6), which four, together with the other three, form

181

the *seven*. This appears to indicate that he represents some great principle of evil found in all the heathen kingdoms. It is therefore a mistake to suppose that this is the fourth beast of Daniel, or the Roman power; it will rather be found to grow out of that, the last of the four. For it corresponds with the Little Horn which arises among the ten horns.... St. John has a nearer and fuller view of the Little Horn of Daniel, which he sees as this great Beast of universal dominion; and this ten-horned Beast is undoubtedly Antichrist." **The dragon gave him his power.** Satan, as prince of this world (John 12:31; 16:11; Eph. 2:2), will equip Antichrist with all his own diabolical power, in order to use him as an instrument of his wrath against "the rest of the seed of the woman," that is, the Gentile Christians (12:17). Duesterdieck calls attention to the inner relation existing between Satan's *power, throne*, and *authority*. This diabolical authority imparted to Antichrist will be seen in his power over freedom and life (13:7, 10), and over the business of men (13:17), and the mention of a *throne* gives us a more definite view of the *worldly dominion* which will be exercised by the beast (16:10). Simcox: "It is the devil's interest and policy to disguise his working under the forms of the world; at present, he has actually persuaded many to disbelieve in his existence." Antichrist thus becomes the vice-regent and instrument of the devil, his earthly persecuting power.

3. And *I saw* one of his heads as though it had been smitten (Gr. *slain*) unto death; and his death-stroke was healed: and the whole earth wondered after the beast.

Lee remarks: "Nowhere is it more important for the correct interpretation of the Apocalypse to adhere to historical facts than here," but we add, if any one thing is certain, it is this, that every explanation hitherto offered by historical interpreters has utterly failed to satisfy the text or the context. It is evident that when the beast rose from the sea, John saw the deadly wound on one of the heads of the beast, but this death-blow was apparently healed. In 17:10, 11, we read: *The seven heads are seven kings; the five are fallen, the one is, the other is not yet come; and the beast is himself also an eighth, and is of the seven.* This death-blow must have been given to one of the five kings that are fallen. These seven kings or kingdoms have been variously understood: (1) as seven personal Kings or Emperors of Rome (Preterists); (2) as seven world-powers, *either* (1) Egypt, (2) Assyria, (3) Babylonia, (4) Medo-Persia, (5) Greece, (6) Rome, (7) the Roman Empire with its Ten Horns after the Barbaric Invasion, under which we now live (Hengstenberg, Auberlen, Burger, Keil, Alford, and others), *or* (1) Assyria, (2) Babylonia, (3) Persia, (4) Macedonia, (5) Syria under Antiochus Epiphanes, (6) Rome, (7) the future Apocalyptic Kingdom (Hofmann, Ebrard, Füller, Luthardt, and others). Luthardt takes courage to name the five fallen kings as Sennacherib (Assyria), Nebuchadnezzar (Babylonia), Cyrus (Persia), Alexander the Great (Macedonia), and Antiochus Epiphanes (Syria), and favors the idea that the Antichrist of the future will in some form or other be another Antiochus Epiphanes restored to life. And there is nothing incredible in this. The Preterists see in this verse the death of Nero, and his expected re-appearance as Antichrist; others see in it the effect of Christ's death on the Cross; or the fall of Napoleon's Empire (Faber); or the fall of the Roman Pagan Empire and the establishment of the Christian Roman Empire (Alford); or the blow which the Roman Empire received from the

Barbarian invaders, etc. But the manifestation of Antichrist lies still in the future, and when he makes his appearance, the whole earth shall *wonder*, and their wonder leads to worship.

Fausset: "The beast, *healed* of its temporary and external *wound*, returns not only from the sea (13:1) but from the abyss (17:8), whence it draws new anti-christian strength of hell (13:12, 14; 11:7). A new and worse heathenism breaks in upon the Christianized world, more devilish than the old one of the first heads of the beast. The latter was an apostasy only from the general revelation of God in nature and conscience; but this new one is from God's revelation of love in His Son. It culminates in Antichrist, the man of sin, the son of perdition (17:11; 2 Thess. 2:3)," in those grievous times described by Paul (2 Tim. 3:1–4) as being marked with all the characteristics of old heathenism (Rom. 1:29–32).

4. And they worshipped the dragon, because he gave his authority unto the beast; and they worshipped the beast, saying, Who is like unto the beast? and who is able to war with him?

Two effects, awful to contemplate, follow the *astonishment* with which the world beholds the power and success of Antichrist. They will worship Satan and his beast. Such is to be the final issue of modern civilization, of all this vaunted progress in thought, art, science, and methods of education. So blinded will men become that they will no longer be able to discern between what is of Satan and what is of God. Williams: "Our Lord's temptation is renewed in some mysterious manner, so that men worship Satan on account of the wealth and power of the world which he bestows, under this sway of Antichrist." Boyd-Carpenter: "The spirit of the wild beast is adored wherever worldliness

184

prevails. There is nothing so successful as success, and the homage of men is more often paid to power than to principle." Commentators call attention to the fact that even the phraseology in which they express their worship of the beast "seems like a blasphemous parody of the praise with which the O. T. Church celebrated the incomparable glory of the living God" (Duesterdieck). (Compare Ex. 15:11: Ps. 11:3, 5; Micah 7:18.) **Who is able to make war with him?** The reference seems to be to the great battle for which all things in the Apocalypse are preparing (12:17; 13:7; 19:19).

5. And there was given to him a mouth speaking great things and blasphemies; and there was given to him authority to continue forty and two months.

In this verse the words and deeds of the first beast are described. We here find consolation for believers, for the beast has no power beyond what is given to him. "Only in accordance with God's will can the dragon equip his beast, and only within the limits fixed by God can the beast do his works" (Duesterdieck). The *little horn* of Daniel, which is evidently the same as the First Beast in his later stage of existence, i. e. Antichrist, is also described as having "a mouth speaking great things" (Dan. 7:8, 20, 25). This mouth *speaking great things and blasphemies* (2 Thess. 2:4) may be regarded as the outcome of the highest arrogance, self-glorification, and self-deification—the result of the boasted culture and selfish civilization of the last times,—the echoes of which are already resounding in many of the antichristian utterances of the present day. Antichrist will receive power *to continue*, better, as in the margin of the Revised Version, *to do* his works *during* "forty and two months." Compare "*and he shall do* his pleasure "of Dan. 8:24; 11:28, 30. This period

185

of 42 months refers to the last half of Daniel's week (Dan. 7:25; 9:27; 12:7), the well-known period of 3½ years or 1,260 days, during which Antichrist shall persecute the saints. See notes on 11:2; 12:6, 14, and compare Matt. 24:9.

6. And he opened his mouth for blasphemies against God, to blaspheme his name, and his tabernacle, *even* them that dwell (*tabernacle*) in the heaven.

We have here a more particular description of the blasphemies referred to in the last verse. Even if we omit *and* before "them" and read *even* as in the Revised Version, regarding the last clause in apposition with the preceding, we may see here a reference to *three* forms of blasphemy: (1) the blasphemy of God's name,—in that the Beast usurps for himself the names, honor, and worship of God, "exalting himself against all that is called God or that is worshipped" (2 Thess. 2:4)—thus denying the Son of God,—the great characteristic of Antichrist; (2) the blasphemy of the *tabernacle* or dwelling-place of God, whether we regard it on earth—"so that he sitteth in the sanctuary (*naos*) of God, setting himself forth as God" (2 Thess. 2:4)—or in heaven, for Antichrist blasphemes also heaven itself; and (3) the blasphemy of the Redeemed Church in heaven, the gracious work of God,—including the holy angels. Blunt, following Williams and some of the ancient commentators, suggests that the three forms of blasphemy are: (1) against God in His Divine Nature; (2) against the Tabernacle of God, that is, God Incarnate tabernacling in Human Nature, or Christ Himself; and (3) against the Mystical Body of God Incarnate, that is, the Church: and that this blasphemy "represents the extreme form of all words spoken against God, Christ, and His Church."

186

7. And it was given unto him to make war with the saints, and to overcome them: and there was given to him authority over every tribe and people and tongue and nation.

Compare Dan. 7:21, 22, "I beheld, and the same horn made war with the saints, and prevailed against them; until the ancient of days came, and judgment was given to the saints of the Most High; and the time came that the saints possessed the kingdom." Antichrist shall exercise universal dominion, for his empire shall extend over the whole earth,—the four specifications, *tribe, people, tongue*, and *nation*, covering all the inhabitants of the earth. In Dan. 7:22 (quoted above) we find the consolation for true believers on earth at the time of this tribulation. Though many shall fall away and worship the beast even among professing believers (Matt. 24:9–12), the true believers shall be preserved through the great tribulation (Matt. 24:13). In the Providence of God and by His permission "the devil gives to Antichrist what he offered to Christ (Luke 4:6)" (Simcox).

8. And all that dwell on the earth shall worship him, *every one* whose name hath not been written in the book of life of the Lamb that hath been slain from the foundation of the world.

All shall worship the beast, as well as the dragon whom the beast represents (13:4), except the elect, whose names have been written in the book of life. All this points to the great final apostasy predicted by our Lord (Matt. 24:11, 12) and by St. Paul (2 Thess. 2:3). **From the foundation of the world.** These last words may belong either to "written" or to "slain." The former connection is suggested by the similar one in Rev. 17:8, and advocated by Bengel, Hengstenberg, Ebrard, Duesterdieck, Milligan, margin of Revised Version, and American Revisers, and others; the latter seems to be the most natural, according to the order of the words in the Greek text. If not contrary to the analogy of faith, it is always far better to interpret according to the exact language of Scripture. Here there is no doctrinal difficulty, whichever way we translate. If in Biblical phraseology the kingdom was prepared for believers "from the foundation of the world" (Matt. 25:34), and if before the foundation of the world (John 17:24; Eph. 1:4) it was a part of God's plan, known and provided for, that Christ should redeem the world by His blood (1 Pet. 1:20), it is equally biblical to say that in the counsels of God, Christ was *slain from the foundation of the world* (so in substance Bede, Alford, Blunt, Plummer, Lee, Pearson, Wordsworth, Sadler, Boyd-Carpenter, Currey, and others). Wordsworth: "The *Lamb* is said *to have been slain from the foundation of the world*, because in the Divine Mind He was foreseen as our Propitiation, and we were foreknown in Him (Eph. 1:4–11), and His death was represented in Types, and foretold in Prophecies, even from the beginning (Gen. 3:15)."

Lee: "Observe that in this description of the First Beast there is something wanting to complete our idea of Antichrist; there is none of that hypocrisy and deceiveableness which other parts of Scripture lead one to expect. This is supplied by the Second Beast (13:11); see 2 Thess. 2:9–13" (After Williams).

9. If any man hath an ear, let him hear.

For this description of the great apostasy and of the power of the beast demands our most solemn attention. See notes on 2:7. It is also a warning that believers be prepared for the trials that will overtake them in the days of Antichrist.

188

10. If any man *is* for captivity, into captivity he goeth: if any man shall kill with the sword, with the sword must he be killed. Here is the patience and faith of the saints.

Compare Jer. 15:2, "Such as are for death, to death; and such as are for the sword, to the sword; and such as are for the famine to the famine; and such as are for captivity, to captivity." The Greek text of the first clause is somewhat uncertain,—the margin of the Revised Version gives us the alternative reading—*If any man* leadeth *into captivity.* It is difficult to decide whether this verse is designed as a consolation, or as a warning to believers. Some maintain that it is a *consolation*, teaching that God will in due time avenge His elect,—that the persecutors of the Church shall experience the vengeance of God, and suffer the same evils as they had inflicted on the saints. But it is better to regard it as a *warning,* teaching believers to suffer with patience, without having recourse to weapons of carnal welfare, "for all they that take the sword shall perish with the sword," Matt. 26:52. *The patience and the faith of the saints* will be displayed in their confidence in God, and in their meek endurance of the trials through which they will have to pass. If we accept the reading of the text of the R. V., then these words "form a prophetic declaration how it shall fare with the saints in the day of persecution, and declare also that in holy suffering of captivity and death consists their faith and patience" (Alford).

42. The Vision of the Second Beast (13:11–18)

11. And I saw another beast coming up out of the earth; and he had two horns like unto a lamb, and he spake as a dragon.

This Beast *out of the earth* is identical with the False Prophet

189

(16:13; 19:20; 20:10). It seems that the *little horn* of Daniel, the O. T. emblem of Antichrist, is here represented by *two* figures, the *First Beast* and the *False Prophet*, for these two are very closely connected. The *First Beast* evidently corresponds to the "mouth speaking great things" and the *False Prophet* to the "eyes like the eyes of a man" of Dan. 7:8, 20. We have thus a hellish trinity of evil in contrast to the Divine Trinity,—Satan or the Dragon as opposed to God the Father, the First Beast or Antichrist as opposed to Christ, and the Second Beast or the False Prophet as opposed to the Holy Spirit, author and bestower of all true prophecy. Duesterdieck suggests that the Beast arises *out of the earth*, because he is to work upon the inhabitants of the earth, while Milligan and others, regarding *the sea* as the nations as opposed to God (13:1), would refer *the earth* to the Jews, as God's prophetic and priestly people, the Beast thus having a religious, not a secular origin. Lee sees here a symbol of *earthly* wisdom, "earthly, sensual, demoniacal" (James 3:15). This second Beast appears innocent and harmless in appearance, *having two horns like a lamb*, and some commentators suggest that these *two horns* signify that he claims to exercise the power of Christ, but as the Lamb of God is described as having *seven* horns (5:6), the *two* denote the great inferiority of the Beast's power to that of Christ. Others also call our attention to Matt. 7:15, where Christ warns us against "*false prophets*, which come in sheep's clothing, but inwardly are ravening wolves." His speaking *as a dragon* describes the treacherous and seductive character of this demoniacal lamb-like Beast (13:14). Simcox: "He *looks* like Christ and *is* like Satan." Fausset: "The dragon gives his external power to the first beast (13:2), his spirit to the second, so that it *speaks as a dragon*." Williams: "In

190

the description of the *first Beast* there is something wanting to complete our idea of Antichrist; for there is none of that hypocrisy and deceivableness which other parts of Scripture lead one to expect. This is filled up by the *second Beast.* The *Man of Sin* as described by Paul seems to comprehend both of these Beasts (2 Thess. 2:3–12). As Primasius says, 'both Beasts evidently form but one body, practise one course of wickedness.' Both combined describe that intimate connection with religion which we suppose Antichrist to have." So close is the connection between these two Beasts that there are some who would even identify the *Second Beast* with Paul's *Man of Sin*, the personal Antichrist,—regarding the first Beast as the antichristian Empire. But that the first Beast represents Antichrist is evident from 17:11–13. Currey: "The second Beast differs from the first, to which it is auxiliary. The first has the power, the second prompts its exercise. The first is openly overbearing and violent, the second is in appearance mild, but really crafty and cruel. As the first represents the world-power wielded by ungodly rulers, the second signifies the more subtle yet more deadly influence of false teachers." Boyd-Carpenter: "Some see in this second wild beast the Pagan priesthood aiding the imperial power, the embodiment of the first wild beast; others see in it the Papal sacerdotal power, the heir of Pagan rites; others, again, would combine the two, and view the second wild beast as the sacerdotal persecuting power, Pagan and Christian. I believe that, though there is truth in these views, they are too narrow.... All who use their knowledge, their culture, their wisdom to teach men that there is nothing worthy of worship save what they can see, and touch, and taste, are acting the part of the second wild beast; and be

191

they apostles of science, or apostles of culture, or apostles of logical immorality, or apostles of what is called materialism, if their teaching leads men to limit their worship to the visible and the tangible, they are making men worship the beast."

12. And he exerciseth all the authority of the first beast in his sight. And he maketh the earth and them that dwell therein to worship the first beast, whose death-stroke was healed.

This second Beast acts for the first Beast, in his presence, as his representative, and performs all acts of authority, as a prime-minister would serve his king. He uses all his arts of persuasion to cause all the inhabitants of the earth to pay religious service to Antichrist, his lord. Those who worship the first Beast are the worldly minded, including the unfaithful Christians, "whose names are not written in the book of life of the Lamb" (13:8). The first Beast is here described as in 13:3, as the one whose death-stroke was healed, that is in his later stage of manifestation.

13. And he doeth great signs, that he should even make fire to come down out of heaven upon the earth in the sight of men.

In the times of Antichrist, "whose coming is according to the working of Satan, with all power and signs and lying wonders" (2 Thess. 2:9), diabolical miracles shall be visibly performed by the second Beast to lead men astray from God. They will be wrought by the power of Satan, as were those performed by the Egyptian magicians in the time of Moses. Probably this special miracle of calling down fire from heaven is mentioned to suggest that the second Beast is endowed by Satan with the spirit and power of an Elijah, showing how the False Prophet seeks to counterfeit the work of the two witnesses (11:5), as well as of Elijah in the time of Ahab (1 Kings 18). Christ had already foretold this miraculous power which will be displayed in the times of Antichrist (Matt. 24:24). Just as Christ shall again be accompanied by a second Elijah as His witness, so Antichrist has his Elijah in the second Beast. Mere miracles are no criterion of the truth (Deut. 13:1–3). Sadler: "These miracles will deceive, if possible, the very elect. And I cannot help thinking that the widespread denial of the reality of the miracles of the Bible will prepare the way for the ready acceptance of the miracles of Antichrist."

14. And he deceiveth them that dwell on the earth by reason of the signs which it was given him to do in the sight of the beast; saying to them that dwell on the earth, that they should make an image to the beast, who hath the stroke of the sword, and lived.

The worldly-minded are deceived by the diabolical miracles performed by the False Prophet (2 Thess. 2:10–12). This power to perform miracles was given to him by Satan, subject to the will of God. The False Prophet, seeing how he has beguiled the worldly-minded, now suggests that they set up an image of Antichrist, so as to show how greatly they honor and glorify him. For had he not been slain, and by the fact that *he lived* again, established his right to divine majesty! Just as Paul maintains that Jesus Christ was declared to be the Son of God by His resurrection (Rom. 1:4), so in the times of Antichrist stress will be laid on the fact, that though the first Beast had received his death-stroke, nevertheless he had *lived*,—and that this established his right to claim divine majesty and worship. We are reminded of Daniel's narrative respecting the golden image set up by Nebuchadnezzar (Dan.

193

3.).

15. And it was given *unto him* to give breath to it, *even* to the image of the beast, that the image of the beast should both speak, and cause that as many as should not worship the image of the beast should be killed.

To the second Beast was also given power by Satan to put a demoniacal spirit of life into the image of Antichrist, so that it became alive and spoke, and caused those who did not worship the image to be killed. Note that "image" is the subject of both verbs. Probably this image of Antichrist will be placed in the temple at Jerusalem, and it may be that it is to this *abomination of desolation* that Christ refers in Matt. 24:15, and to which Daniel three times refers (Dan. 9:27; 11:31; 12:11). Antichrist however proceeds to more severe measures than Nebuchadnezzar. Wordsworth sees here, as everywhere, the Papacy: "The first Beast itself is the Papacy; and the *image* of it is the *personification* of the Papacy, in the visible form of the *Pontiff for the time being.* Every one who is created Pope is immediately made into an *Image* or *Idol*, and this process has now been continued for many centuries. This verse describes the process by which the *Papal Image* gives utterance to what is *breathed into* it by the *Papal Hierarchy.* A striking specimen how this prophecy is fulfilled in the Papacy has been recently displayed to the world. On the 8th December, 1854, the Pope promulgated the new Doctrine of the Immaculate Conception, and affirmed that it was thenceforth necessary to salvation to believe that the Blessed Virgin was exempt from original sin, and now, on July 18, 1870, *breath has been given* by the *Hierarchy* to the *Image*, which their own hands had made, and had set up to be adored, for the Pope has been declared to be *Infallible*, and

194

to be revered as having the attribute of God; and all who contravene that dogma have been anathematized by him and consigned to perdition."

16. And he causeth all, the small and the great, and the rich and the poor, and the free and the bond, that there be given them a mark on their right hand, or upon their forehead.

The False Prophet, in his zeal for promoting the cause of Antichrist, compels all to receive his mark either upon their right hand or upon their forehead,—that is, upon some conspicuous part of the body, where it can be readily seen by every one. Fausset: "The mark in the right hand and on the forehead implies the prostration of *bodily* and *intellectual* powers to the beast's domination." Blunt: "This 'mark' of Antichrist is plainly imitative of the 'seal of God' which the faithful received 'on their foreheads' (9:4); and as that seal is identified with the 'new Name' of Christ (3:12) and the Name of God (14:1; 22:4), so the mark of the Beast is elsewhere called 'the mark of his name' (14:11)."

17. And that no man should be able to buy or to sell, save he that hath the mark, *even* the name of the beast or the number of his name.

It seems that Antichrist will try to regulate the labor troubles of his day somewhat on the method some agitators seek to solve the problem in our own days. In order to possess the liberty to buy and sell, one must join the organization of which Antichrist is the head, and bear the mark of allegiance to the Beast. Dennett: "Under the mask of the welfare of the empire, all will be subjected to this awful tyranny under the pains and penalties of the deprivation of the commonest liberty of the individual. Foreshadowings of this forgetful abuse of authority are frequently seen even

195

in this tolerant age, affording a sufficient warning to those whose eyes are opened, that the most absolute despotism may often be cloaked under a profession of the most liberal ideas, and giving also an indication of the ultimate goal of modern politics under the concealed guidance and inspiration of Satan." This *mark* which all must receive will be either the name of Antichrist stamped in letters, or the number of the name thus stamped. Most commentators, however, think that we dare not interpret here literally of an actual mark impressed,—that as in the case of the servants of God no actual visible mark is intended, so here the mark "signifies rather conformity and addiction to the behests of the beast" (Alford).

18. Here is wisdom. He that hath understanding, let him count the number of the beast; for it is the number of a man: and his number is Six hundred and sixty and six.

Here is wisdom. He who is able from the number of the beast to find out the name of Antichrist gives evidence of wisdom and deep understanding. "The terms of the challenge serve to show that the feat proposed is possible, and that it is difficult" (Alford). *The number of a man* may mean either "according to man's mode of reckoning" as "the measure of a man" in 21:17, or "the number of a particular individual." It is best to refer it to an individual. In Hebrew and in Greek *letters* are used as numerals, every letter having its proper value as a number. If the numerical values of each letter in a word are added together the sum would represent the word. This process was called by the Jews *Gematria*, a corruption of the Greek *Geometria.* Most commentators maintain that this sum is meant by "the number of a man" or of a name. There are many words, even proper names of men well known in history, the sum of whose letters will amount to 666, whether we use Hebrew, Greek, Latin, or German letters. Over 100 attempted solutions, some very ingenious, may be tabulated. Some insist that as the book was written in Greek and for Greek readers, we must use Greek letters, while others, appealing to the Hebraistic coloring of the Apocalypse, maintain that we must employ the Hebrew alphabet. Among the various attempted solutions we may mention Lateinos, Caligula, Nero, Titus, Trajan, Julian the Apostate, Genseric the Vandal, Mohammed (Maometis), Benedict IX., Paul V. (the Catholics have found to their satisfaction the names of Martinus Lauterus, i. e. *Luther*, Joannes Calvinus, and Beza Antitheos), Louis XIV., Napoleon Bonaparte, and Napoleon III. A great deal of ingenuity has been wasted in manipulating the spelling of words, and in conjuring with numbers, and Dr. Salmon (*Introduction* pp. 230, 231), after having shown how deceptive this whole method of solution is, suggests "three rules by the help of which I believe an ingenious man could find the required sum in any given name. First, if the proper name by itself will not yield it, add a title; secondly, if the sum cannot be found in Greek, try Hebrew, or even Latin; thirdly, do not be too particular about the spelling."

Of the various names that have been suggested, two especially have been accepted by a large number of commentators. The first is *Lateinos*. The numerical value of this word in Greek letters is 666, as follows: $l = 30 + a = 1 + t = 300 + e = 5 + i = 10 + n = 50 + o = 70 + s = 200 = $ total 666. This interpretation is the oldest we know of, and was already mentioned by Irenæus, who, however, prefers *Teitan;* i. e. Titus. *Lateinos* has been accepted in substance as the true interpretation by Calovius, De Wette, Bleek, Ebrard, Duesterdieck, Alford (with much hesitation), Wordsworth, Lee, Schaff, Sadler, Fausset, and others,—some referring it to some individual person, some to the heathen Roman Empire, others to the Latin Empire, and still others to the Papacy.

The second solution, which at present is the most popular interpretation, and which the modern school of rationalism boastingly claims as the only possible solution, and to which some conservatives enthusiastically give their consent, is that the number 666 signifies *Neron Kaisar*, written in Hebrew characters n r o n k s r, and counting according to the numerical value in the Hebrew alphabet, thus: $n = 50 + r = 200 + o = 6 + n = 50 + k = 100 + s = 60 + r = 200$, or in all, 666. So Fritzsche, Benary, Hitzig, Reuss, Ewald, Baur, Hilgenfeld, Volkmar, Hausrath, Gebhardt, Renan, Davidson, Stuart, Cowles, Farrar, and others. Gebhardt suggests that both *Lateinos* and *Nero Caesar* were intended, and both solutions are at one in making the number point to the great Roman Power, though some would refer it to the past, and others still to the future.

But all these attempts to solve the mystery are unsatisfactory. We may be pretty certain that it will be impossible to discover the secret before the beast's appearance, and then believers will be able to recognize him by this number. Deeply significant is the fact, noticed by many commentators, that the number of the name *Jesus*, our Redeemer's personal name, according to the numerical value of the letters in its Greek form, is 888. The number *eight* has a deep significance. It is the number of the resurrection. It has the same relation to the number of Christ, as six has to the number of Antichrist. 8+80+800 is the number of Christ, and six the world number, raised to its tens and hundreds, 6+60+600, gives us the number of Antichrist. When the personal Antichrist comes, then his number will enable believers readily to identify him,—but until he comes the mystery will not be solved.

14

Revelation 14

43. The Vision of the Lamb with the 144,000 (14:1–5)

This is still a continuation of the Vision which extends from 11:19 to 14:20, to the close of this chapter. The Vision brings us down to the very end. It also introduces reference to events which will be more clearly described in later visions.

1. And I saw, and behold, the Lamb standing on the mount Zion, and with him a hundred and forty and four thousand, having his name, and the name of his Father, written on their foreheads.

This is the same Lamb which has been standing in the midst of the throne (5:6). The Lamb is now set as King upon the holy hill of Zion (Ps. 2:6). This Mount Zion here is not in heaven but probably on the earth, for the hour of judgment has come (14:7), and the new Jerusalem has not yet appeared (21:2). The vision is for the comfort and encouragement of those believers who will have to endure the persecutions of the beast. It points to the final victory that shall surely be theirs, and depicts the glory in store for the faithful. These 144,000 are probably identical with the faithful sealed ones of 7:4 (see notes on this passage). They are those from among the Jews who are converted during the times of Antichrist. They are described as 144,000 in number, being the complete and full number, according to the counsels of God. They have the seal of God on their foreheads (7:2, 3), described here as the name of the Lamb of God, and of His Father, so that they can readily be recognized as children of God. Dennett: "In chapter 13. the frightful oppression and persecution of the saints is seen; and in this vision they are displayed as having been tried and come forth as gold. In contrast with chapter 13. this chapter opens like a magnificent sunrise after a stormy night. The vision overleaps all the intervening sorrows and judgments, and, as in the scene on the Mount of Transfiguration, permits us to behold His majesty and glory in the seat of His earthly rule and dominion."

2. And I heard a voice from heaven, as the voice of many waters, and as the voice of a great thunder: and the voice which I heard *was* as *the voice* of harpers harping with their harps.

This voice came from heaven, and the volume sounded like the rushing of many waters (1:15), loud as thunder (6:1), but at the same time it was a charming sound, like the melody of players on the harp, "divinely terrible, yet divinely sweet." Boyd-Carpenter: "The saints stand with their Lord, the Lamb, on Mount Zion, and just as of old a voice came from heaven bearing witness to Christ, so round the abode of the saints heavenly voices are heard, full of majesty, terribleness,

201

and sweetness, as though the sounds of sea and thunder blended with the music of heavenly harps."

3. And they sing as it were a new song before the throne, and before the four living creatures and the elders; and no man could learn the song save the hundred and forty and four thousand, *even* they that had been purchased out of the earth.

The harpers, probably angels, are in heaven, and sing their *new* song before the throne, and in the presence of the four living creatures and the four elders, i. e. in the presence of God Himself, of creation and the Redeemed Church (see notes on 4:2, 4, 6). It is *new*, probably because it is a song of victory to the praise of the Lamb, "the song of Messiah's kingdom" (De Burgh). No one can learn the melody and words of the song, save the 144,000, for "the song has regard to matters of trial and triumph, of deep joy and heavenly purity of heart, which none other among men but these pure and holy ones are capable of apprehending" (Alford). "Amid the world-noises of Babylon, men can neither hear nor sing aright the Lord's song (Ps. 137:4); but the Redeemed (the purchased out of the earth) of the Lord can come with singing unto Zion (Isa. 51:11)" (Boyd-Carpenter).

4. These are they which were not defiled with women; for they are virgins. These *are* they which follow the Lamb whithersoever he goeth. These were purchased from among men, *to be* the firstfruits unto God and unto the Lamb.

In this and the next verse four things are predicated of these 144,000 saints: (1) They had lived the life of virgins while on earth; (2) They have the special privilege of being the personal attendants of our Lord; (3) They are the firstfruits from among the redeemed; (4) Perfect truthfulness had always

202

marked their earthly life. It is probably best to interpret *virgins* in the literal sense. In the trying circumstances peculiar to the days of Antichrist, the sealed among the Jews who have to pass through the great tribulation, "by reason of the distress" of those times (1 Cor. 7:26), will remain unmarried, in order that they may be "careful for the things of the Lord, how they may please the Lord" (1 Cor. 7:32). Not in the sense as if there were any defilement in marriage (Heb. 13:4), or that there was any peculiar sanctity in celibacy, but if "every one that hath left houses or brethren, or sisters, or father, or mother (or wife, Luke 18:28), or children, or lands, for Christ's sake, shall receive a hundredfold" (Matt. 19:29), so shall these, who, for Christ's sake in the times of the great tribulation, renounce all family ties, receive their special reward, and become *the first fruits unto God and unto the Lamb in* the Messianic kingdom. "In the regeneration when the Son of man shall sit on the throne of his glory" (Matt. 19:28), they shall be the consant retinue of the Lamb. Although all the redeemed share in the glory of the Lamb, yet these, in an eminent sense, shall partake of the same. Simcox: "A devout and unselfish celibacy gives special means for serving God, and so we need not be surprised to learn here that it has a special reward from Him."

5. And in their mouth was found no lie: they are without blemish.

It is best to understand *lie* in its general sense. They lived their earthly life in utter truthfulness. Possibly there is a reference to Ps. 15:1, 2, "Who shall dwell in thy holy hill? He that walketh uprightly, and worketh righteousness, and *speaketh truth in his heart.*" The sealed ones among Israel, who endured the persecutions of the days of Antichrist, were noted for their moral perfection, in contradistinction to the impurity and sinfulness of the followers of Antichrist.

Duesterdieck brings out clearly the purpose of this whole vision: "The manifestation of the blessed with the Lamb in eternal glory is intended to give believers who are on earth, and exposed to persecution on the part of the dragon, a pledge inspiring courage and patience, that if they remain faithful they shall also attain to that glory."

44. The Vision of the First Angel of Judgment (14:6, 7)

In verses 6–11 we have the description of three great events which will immediately precede Christ's Coming to destroy Antichrist: (1) The announcement that the "eternal gospel" is to be proclaimed to all men (14:6, 7); (2) The Fall of Babylon (14:8); (3) A warning to all who worship the Beast and his image (14:9–12).

6. And I saw another angel flying in mid heaven, having an eternal gospel to proclaim unto them that dwell on the earth, and unto every nation and tribe and tongue and people.

Another angel, besides those already mentioned (11:15). **Flying in mid-heaven.** See notes on 8:13. The voice of the angel is to reach all dwelling on the earth. **An eternal gospel.** Ebrard: "He brings a message which is eternal as to its contents, and, therefore, is eternal also, according to its announcement, as since the foundation of the world there has been no other message of joy and salvation, and in eternity there will be no other." The judgment is at hand, and as preparatory to it the gospel is to be proclaimed *to all that sit on the earth* (so in *Greek*, probably with reference to their false security, "dwelling in worldliness and carnal indifference," Luke 21:35), in accordance with our Lord's words, "And this gospel of the kingdom shall be preached in the whole world for a testimony unto all the nations: and then shall the end come" (Matt. 24:14). The four-fold enumeration of the inhabitants of the earth shows how universal the proclamation of the gospel shall be (see also 5:9). Fausset: "Here begins the portion relating to the Gentile world, as the former portion related to Israel. Before the *end* the gospel is to be preached for a Witness unto all the nations; not that all nations shall be converted, but all nations shall have the opportunity given them of deciding whether they will be for or against Christ."

7. And he saith with a great voice, Fear God, and give him glory; for the hour of his judgment is come: and worship him that made the heaven and the earth and sea and fountains of waters.

The end is at hand (Matt. 24:14), and the hour of judgment upon the nations, and the time for the destruction of the Beast, even of Antichrist, has come. Just before the end, by supernatural means, as in Apostolic times, the greatest era of Christian missions is inaugurated, and men are everywhere exhorted to repent (Acts 17:30), and "to turn unto God from idols, to serve a living and true God, and to wait for His Son from heaven, whom He raised from the dead, even Jesus, which delivereth us from the wrath to come" (1 Thess. 1:9, 10). No doubt the angel makes this proclamation in opposition to the False Prophet, who during this same period is forcing all the inhabitants of the earth, at the threat of death, to worship the Beast and his image (13:12, 15). Fausset: "This *judgment* is not the general judgment, but that upon Babylon, the beast, and his worshippers (14:8–12)." Simcox calls attention to the fact that "the substance of the angel's message is pure natural theism." It may be the final warning to the ungodly world, reminding them of the utter degradation into which they have fallen (Rom. 1:18–25). There is a four-fold division of creation, probably with reference to 8:7–12,—for as peculiar judgments had been visited upon these objects of creation, so now God will remove every plague, and all His works will glorify Him.

45. The Vision of the Second Angel of Judgment (14:8)

8. And another, a second angel, followed, saying, Fallen, fallen is Babylon the great, which hath made all the nations to drink of the wine of the wrath of her fornication.

This is the second angel of judgment. We have here the first mention of Babylon, in anticipation of a fuller description hereafter (see 16:19; 17:5; 18:2, 10). So sure and near is this impending judgment of the destruction of Babylon, that it is prophetically regarded as already fulfilled. The imagery is taken from Jer. 51:7, 8, "Babylon hath been a golden cup in the Lord's hand, that made all the earth drunken; the nations have drunk of her wine; therefore the nations are mad. Babylon is suddenly fallen and destroyed." Babylon is the type of the world-power which persecutes the Church of God. It is the representative of the world, as Jerusalem is of the Church of God. The history of the Babylon of Jeremiah's time shall be repeated in the times of Antichrist. **The wine of the wrath.** Alford correctly: "Two things are mingled: (1) the wine of her fornication, of which all nations have drunk (17:2); and (2) the wine of the wrath of God which He shall give her to drink (14:10; 16:19). The latter is the retribution for the former; the former turns into the latter; they are treated as one and the same." By *fornication* is meant in the text *idolatry*, the worship of the Beast and his image, and the general unfaithfulness towards God, so prevalent in the days of Antichrist. The Preterists understand by Babylon, Pagan Rome; the Continuous-Historical interpreters refer it to Papal Rome; the Futurists, as a rule, refer it to the chief city of the antichristian world-power of the Last Days—the Capital of Antichrist,—some maintaining it is Rome of the future; others, Jerusalem ruled over by Antichrist. Now is finally fulfilled in its fullest significance the prophecy of Isaiah (Isa. 21:9). Boyd-Carpenter: "Babylon belongs not to one age. Pagan Rome was Babylon to St. John; papal Rome was often Babylon to a later age. Dante, Savonarola, Tauler, Luther, felt her to be so in the days when their eyes were enlightened; but Babylon was not on the Euphrates alone; she has reared palaces on the Seine, and on the Thames, Tiber, and on the Bosphorus. She may yet erect her power in more imposing form."

46. The Vision of the Third Angel of Judgment (14:9–12)

9. And another angel, a third, followed them, saying with a great voice, If any man worshippeth the beast and his image, and receiveth a mark on his forehead, or upon his hand.

This third angel proclaims the Judgment that shall surely overtake all worshippers of the Beast and his image (13:15, 16). Bengel: "This threatening and warning (14:9–11) stands by itself, and is the most dreadful of all contained in the whole of Scripture."

10. He also shall drink of the wine of the wrath of God, which is prepared (Gr. *mingled*) unmixed in the cup of his anger; and he shall be tormented with fire and brimstone in the presence of the holy angels, and in the presence of the Lamb.

He *also*, as well as Babylon and the nations of verse 8, shall have to drink of the foaming cup of the wrath of God, for "surely the dregs thereof all the wicked of the earth shall drain out and drink them" (Ps. 75:8). See also Jer. 25:15. The wine of wrath shall be *unmixed*, pure, working with all its power and heat, not tempered with mercy, "for judgment is without mercy to him that hath showed no mercy" (James 2:13), and the wicked shall feel the full force of God's righteous anger. This wrath of God is nothing more than the manifestation of God's holiness towards sin and those who have continually persisted in abiding in sin. **Tormented.** The punishment of *Gehenna*, of Hell proper, is here described in all its terrible reality (see also 19:20; 20:10; 21:8). The figure seems to be taken from Isa. 34:8–10. An aggravation of their punishment is signified, notes Duesterdieck, by the fact that the holy angels and the despised and persecuted Lamb are spectators; and he refers to 11:12 and Luke 16:23, etc. Note specially that this warning is given to men now, and also to those living in the days of Antichrist, while there is still time to repent.

11. And the smoke of the torment goeth up for ever and ever (Gr. *unto ages of ages*); and they have no rest day and night, they that worship the beast and his image, and whoso receiveth the mark of his name.

The source of this description evidently may be traced to Gen. 19:28; Isa. 34:10; 66:24,—especially to the last two passages. This statement is very emphatic. Every one who receives the mark of the Beast, or who worships him or his image, shall surely suffer eternal torment in *Gehenna.*Williams: "Very awful is every expression in the torments that ensue; for the 'cup of fornication' becomes a *cup of wrath* unmixed and without alloy; no water in the wine, no mitigation, no repentance, no third part smitten, but entire, irremediable. It is, moreover, *in the presence of the angels*, as infinitely increased by the sense of their purity and bliss; and *in the presence of the Lamb*, 'as in remembrance,' Aretas observes, 'of that sacrifice of salvation which they had despised.' And *the smoke ascending* intimates the cloud of wailing which ascends, not for a time only, but for ever; which Isaiah has expressed by 'the undying worm, and the fire which is not quenched' (Isa. 66:24). It is 'the wrath of God *abiding* (John 3:36) on them." It is surprising how little notice is taken by some commentators of the awful truths underlying these verses. Have men become afraid to lay stress upon the eternal realities which underlie all God's revelation, and out of respect to corrupted Reason shirk to expound the plainest truths of God's word? Is the spirit of Antichrist already working, preparing the way for the apostasy of the professing Christian Church? Nothing can be plainer than the truths here taught in the most concrete way. This statement *of the eternity and everlasting duration* of the punishment of the wicked is in strict agreement with the universal teaching of Scripture. There is an eternity of sin as well as an eternity of punishment. There is no foundation whatever in the Bible for the doctrine of

Universalism or Restorationism, nor for Annihilationism. Unending existence in a state of punishment is in multiplied passages asserted of the wicked. Nothing short of absolute immortality and unending existence for the wicked, as truly as for the righteous, will adequately interpret such solemn declarations as Matt. 25:41, 46; Mark 3:29; 9:43, 48; John 3:36; 5:28, 29; Rom. 2:7–9; 2 Thess. 1:8, 9; Jude 7; Rev. 20:10. Dennett: "It is instructive to note, in a day when Universalism is so popular, even among professing Christians, the character of this judgment. True, it falls upon a class; but if there were only some who will have to endure their punishment for 'ages of ages,' and who will 'have no rest day and night,' the contention that there is no such thing as 'eternal punishment' is utterly disproved."

12. Here is the patience of the saints, they that keep the commandments of God, and the faith of Jesus.

"He that endureth to the end, the same shall be saved" (Matt. 24:13). These saints have two marks: (1) they keep the commandments of God, and do not worship the beast nor his image, but patiently endure the persecutions of Antichrist, even death itself; and (2) they keep the faith of Jesus once for all delivered to the saints, and remain faithful in the midst of all temptation. And they shall also receive their reward, for they shall inherit the kingdom and glory of God, while all the worshippers of the beast and his image shall surely suffer eternal punishment. See 13:10, and end of notes there.

47. The Proclamation of the Blessedness of the Holy Dead (14:13)

13. And I heard a voice from heaven saying, Write, Blessed are the dead which die in the Lord from henceforth: yea, saith the Spirit, that they may rest from their labours; for their works follow with them.

We need not determine from whom the heavenly voice comes. It brings consolation to all believers, but especially to those who have to suffer during the persecutions of Antichrist. *From henceforth* belongs to the first part of the sentence, as in the text of the R. V., not as in the *margin.* It is also better to connect it with the verb *die* than with *blessed.* It is true, indeed, that ever since Christ's death and resurrection all who die in the faith of Christ are blessed and immediately are with Christ, and rest from their labors, but the context implies that this verse refers especially to the saints in the days of Antichrist. Those who maintain that the natural meaning of this passage is that this blessedness is affirmed as dating from the utterance of the heavenly voice to John, sever this verse entirely from its context. Those who *die in the Lord* are those who believe in Christ,—and remain faithful to Him even unto death,—which here probably refers mainly to a martyr's death. *From henceforth,* for "the glorious end, which will bring condemnation to enemies and complete blessedness to all believers" (Duesterdieck), is at hand. Alford: "The harvest of the earth is about to be reaped; the vintage of the earth to be gathered. At this time it is that the complete blessedness of the holy dead commences: when the garner is filled and the chaff cast out." **Yea, saith the Spirit.** This is not the utterance of John himself, nor of another voice,

211

but the same voice from heaven still continues. Alford: "The affirmation of the Spirit ratifies the blessedness proclaimed, and assigns a reason for it." **That they may rest.** The conjunction *that* must be connected with *blessed*, not with the previous clause *which die.* Alford: "They *rest* from their labors, because the time of working is over, their works accompanying them not in a life of activity, but in blessed memory; wherefore not labor, but rest is their lot." *Their works follow with them*, not simply, however, only in *memory* (as Alford), but there is evidently a reference to their *reward*. Every work done for Christ and for His sake shall surely be rewarded. Fausset: "Their full *blessedness* is now from henceforth, i. e. *from this time*, when the judgment on the beast, and the harvest-gathering of the elect are imminent.... Their *works* are specified because respect is had to the coming judgment wherein every man shall be judged according to his works" (Rom. 2:6–11).

48. The Vision of the Harvest or Ingathering of the Saints (14:14–16.)

14. And I saw, and behold, a white cloud; and on the cloud *I saw* one sitting like unto a son (*the Son*) of man, having on his head a golden crown, and in his hand a sharp sickle.

John in vision sees Christ sitting on a white cloud, for the Day of His Coming, and of the Judgment upon the nations, has arrived (Dan. 7:13; Matt. 24:30; 26:64; Mark 13:26). He *sits*, because He comes in judgment. His having a *golden crown* on His head implies that the time for His triumphant victory has come, and for the establishment of the Messianic Kingdom. The *sharp sickle* implies that the earth is ripe for judgment, and the time for the harvest is come (Mark 4:29). Just as in 6:12–17 and 11:15–18, we here again come to the end,—a proof that we are not to regard the Apocalypse as a consecutive history of the end of all things. The end is here described under a two-fold aspect: (1) as a harvest, in which the saints are gathered (14:14–16); (2) as a vintage, in which the wicked are gathered for the winepress of the wrath of God (14:17–20). Both these acts of God are combined in one passage in Joel 3:12, 13, "Let the nations bestir themselves and come up to the valley of Jehoshaphat: for there will I sit to judge all the nations round about. Put ye in the sickle, for the harvest is ripe; come, tread ye; for the winepress is full, the fats overflow; for their wickedness is great."

15. And another angel came out from the temple, crying with a great voice to him that sat on the cloud, Send forth thy sickle, and reap: for the hour to reap is come; for the harvest of the earth is over-ripe (Gr. *dried up*).

This angel is represented as coming from the inner sanctuary or *naos*, from the immediate Presence of God, bringing a message from the Father to the Son. Alford rightly remarks that this message is one regarding the times and seasons, which the Father hath kept in His own power (Acts 1:7). This verse reminds us of Christ's words, "When the fruit is ripe, straightway he sendeth forth the sickle, because the harvest is come" (Mark 4:29). Wordsworth: "The *Harvest* is mentioned *first;* and this priority shows that Christ's first desire is that all should be saved (1 Tim. 2:4). The Harvest is the manifestation of God's love in the ingathering of the good wheat into the heavenly barn (Matt. 13:30, 39). In like manner when Christ describes the transactions of the Great Day, He speaks first of the rewards to them on the right hand

213

(Matt. 25:34), and afterwards He pronounces the doom of those on the left hand." Williams: "Judgment first begins at the house of God. The good are taken, the evil left. The harvest precedes the vintage. The righteous are called into the kingdom prepared of the Father; and then the wicked are sent away into condemnation.... It is questionable whether the harvest and vintage are of the final judgment, or some previous coming of Christ."

16. And he that sat on the cloud cast his sickle upon the earth; and the earth was reaped.

The angel who brought the Father's message takes no part in the act of reaping. That act is performed by the Son alone, by Him who sat on the cloud,—not directly, but indirectly,—for the Son of man "shall send forth his angels with a great sound of a trumpet, and they shall gather together his elect from the four winds, from one end of heaven to the other" (Matt. 24:31; Mark 13:27), for "the reapers are angels" (Matt. 13:39). Lange: "The beginning of the judgment, therefore, precedes the actual *Parousia* Christ." Bengel: "By means of *the harvest* a great multitude of the righteous, and by means of *the vintage* a great multitude of the ungodly, are removed from the world." Fausset: "By the *harvest*-reaping the elect righteous are gathered out; by the *vintage* the anti-Christian offenders are removed out of the earth, the scene of Christ's coming kingdom."

49. The Vision of the Vintage or Ingathering of the Wicked (14:17–20)

17. And another angel came out from the temple which is in heaven, he also having a sharp sickle.

Now an angel comes forth from the *naos*, from the very Presence of God, from whom all judgments proceed (11:19). Christ Himself in the Harvest has the sickle and presides over the reaping, but now when the vintage for the winepress of the wrath of God is to be gathered, the vintage is altogether intrusted to angels.

18. And another angel came out from the altar, he that hath power over fire; and he called with a great voice to him that had the sharp sickle, saying, Send forth thy sharp sickle, and gather the clusters of the vine of the earth; for her grapes are fully ripe.

This angel, having power over fire, coming out from the altar beneath which the souls of the martyrs were, crying for vengeance (6:9, 10), is evidently the same as the one mentioned in 8:3–5 as presenting the prayers of the Saints, and as casting some of the fire of the altar upon the earth, introductory to the judgments of the trumpets. This whole description shows that the vintage here spoken of differs from the harvest of 14:14–16. Duesterdieck: "This angel, since he has power over fire, manifests himself as one whose sending brings an answer to the prayers of the martyrs, and thus, by his entire manner and appearance, recalls the blood-guiltiness of the enemies whose blood is to cover the earth (14:20)." The verse refers only to the vintage of the wicked (Joel 3:13; Isa. 63:1–4).

19. And the angel cast his sickle into the earth, and

215

gathered the vintage (Gr. *vine*) of the earth, and cast it into the winepress, the great *winepress*, of the wrath of God.

The vintage is now described. This can only refer to the in-gathering of the wicked. Fausset maintains that the apostate world of Christendom, not the world of heathendom, which has not heard of Christ, is the object of this judgment. We have here (in Greek) in the expression *the great* winepress, a masculine adjective agreeing with a feminine noun, possibly to emphasize the terrible nature of the wrath of God. Weiss holds that God's great wrath is itself the winepress.

20. And the winepress was trodden without the city, and there came out blood from the winepress, even unto the bridles of the horses, as far as a thousand and six hundred furlongs.

This verse describes the terrific nature of the punishment that shall overtake the enemies of Christ at the time of His Coming to destroy Antichrist. The city is evidently earthly Jerusalem, where the whole scene seems to lie (14:1). The whole figurative description is based upon Joel 3:13 and Isa. 63:3, which see. Duesterdieck: "How fearful the bloodshed is, is illustrated by designating it as a stream of blood which is so deep as to reach to the reins of the horses wading therein, while its extent is given as 1600 furlongs." It is probably best to understand the number 1600 in a schematical, or symbolic sense, as indicating the magnitude and completeness of the most terrible punishment ever visited upon man. Why just this particular number 1600 is chosen no one can positively tell. Some have suggested that it is derived from the square of four, the signature of the created world, multiplied by the square of ten, which is the sign of completeness, thus indicating that no created being can escape God's judgments. Ebrard suggests 40 × 40 = 1600 as the symbol of terrible punishment (Num. 14:33; Judg. 13:1; Ezek. 29:11). Wordsworth: "The casting of grapes into a *winepress*, and the act of treading them under the feet, so that the juice flows out of them in purple streams, is emblematic in Holy Scripture of *destruction of enemies* in battle, with great *carnage.*... When the day of grace and salvation is passed, and the Day of Doom is come, and the season of the *World's Vintage*, then will He tread all His enemies *under His feet* (1 Cor. 15:25, 27) with the same ease as the treader of grapes in a winepress tramples the ripe, luscious fruit (Isa. 63:1–6; Joel 3:13)." This vision is evidently parallel to that of 19:11–16. As our Lord has suffered" without the gate "(Heb. 13:12), so this winepress shall be trodden "without the city." Bengel is correct when he maintains that the slaughter of the wicked is here intimated, not their eternal punishment. Williams: "Here, again, we come to the termination of all things and pause. The visions again begin to traverse the same period with another form of prophetic description. This continual hurrying to the end, and then breaking off, as it were, with a pause; and then bringing all things again suddenly to an abrupt conclusion, is surely very striking: and has in it something awful and mysterious."

15

Revelation 15

50. The Vision of the Seven Angels (15:1)

1. And I saw another sign in heaven, great and marvelous, seven angels having seven plagues, *which are* the last, for in them is finished the wrath of God.

This verse briefly describes the contents of this and the sixteenth chapter, referring to events that shall take place on earth immediately before Christ's coming to destroy Antichrist. It maps out more fully the punishment that shall overtake his followers. This vision extends to the end of the sixteenth chapter, and in it we have a recapitulation in some respects of events already referred to in the vision recorded in 11:19–14:20. In 12:1, a *great sign* was seen in heaven, and here *another sign* is seen. It was *great and marvelous*, probably because of the terrible nature of the events signified by these seven vial-angels, which bring upon the earth the seven *last* plagues,—*last* because they introduce the final and victorious Coming of Christ, and because "in them is finished the wrath

218

of God."

51. The Song of the Victors (15:2–4)

2. And I saw as it were a glassy sea mingled with fire; and them that come victorious from the beast, and from his image, and from the number of his name, standing by (or, *upon*) the glassy sea, having harps of God.

A glassy sea. See notes on 4:6. This is evidently the same glassy sea before the throne of God, mention being made in both passages of the *four living creatures* (4:6; 15:7). Here the glassy sea was *mingled with fire*, a symbol of judgment, for all the surroundings have to do with *judgment*. Before the vision of the seven Vial-Angels is continued, another vision, showing the glorious issue of the patient endurance of the persecutions of Antichrist, is interposed. This is given for the encouragement of those who will have to pass through the great tribulation. **From the beast.** See notes on 13:4, 7, 8. **From his image.** See notes on 13:15, 16; 14:9. **From the number of his name.** See notes on 13:17, 18. **Harps of God.** So called because used solely for the praise of God. Compare also 5:8; 14:2. Wordsworth: "Standing on the shore of this heavenly sea are seen those who come *forth* conquerors *out of the* bondage of the *Beast*, that is, those who are delivered from his sway, as the Israelites were in the Exodus from the land of Pharaoh, and from the house of bondage, and who emerged in triumph from the waters of the Red Sea."

3. And they sing the song of Moses the servant of God, and the song of the Lamb, saying, Great and marvellous are thy works, O Lord God, the Almighty; righteous and true

219

are thy ways, thou King of the ages.

They sing a song of victory similar to that sung by Moses and the children of Israel, as recorded in Ex. 15. Moses is here called *the servant of God* as in Ex. 14:31; Num. 12:7; Josh. 22:5; Heb. 3:5. The same song is also called the victorious song of the Lamb, not however because it is composed by Moses and the Lamb, and taught to the victors, as suggested by Duesterdieck, but rather as Gerhard suggests, "Just as the Israelites, after their deliverance from Pharaonic bondage praised God in the song of Moses (Ex. 15), so the blessed, after their deliverance from the tyranny of persecutors, and all the adversities of this life, praise God in the song of the Lamb, or of Christ." For the Lamb has redeemed them, even as Moses has redeemed Israel. This song, like that in 4:8 (which see) is addressed to the *Lord God, the Almighty.* The ground of their praise is the marvelous character of the works of God, especially as seen in the judgments visited upon the oppressors of God's people. The ways of God's government have been vindicated, for though at times they seemed obscure, now that the end has come, they confess that all His ways are both *righteous* and *true.* **Thou King of the ages.** There is no manuscript authority for King of *saints* as in A. V. It is difficult to decide whether *ages* or *nations* is the correct reading. All modern critical editors of the Greek text, save Wescott and Hort, read *nations*, but W. and H. place *ages* in the text (so also Revised Version) and put *nations* in the margin. The reading *nations* would best suit the context, for these judgments especially concern *the nations*, but the reading *ages* would also be biblical. In 1 Tim. 1:17 we have an inscription to "the incorruptible, invisible, the only God, *the King of the ages,*" translated however in the R.

V. "the King *eternal*." Fausset: "The Lamb leads the song in honor of the Father amidst the great congregation. This is the 'new song' mentioned in 14:3. The singing victors are the 144,000 of Israel, 'the first fruits,' and the general 'harvest' of the Gentiles."

4. Who shall not fear, O Lord, and glorify thy name? for thou only art holy; for all the nations shall come and worship before thee; for thy righteous acts have been made manifest.

On the first part of the verse compare Jer. 10:6, 7. The three clauses *for ... for ... for ...* give the reasons for fearing and glorifying God: (1) because God is *holy* (*hosios*, only used of God here and in 16:5); (2) because all nations shall yet worship Him; (3) because His righteous acts in the destruction of His enemies have been made manifest to all. The last clause, however, may give the reason why "all the nations shall come and worship before" God. Milligan suggests that this worship of the nations here referred to is one "of awe, of terror, and of trembling," and illustrates it by Phil. 2:10, 11, but it is probably better to refer this worship of the nations to the events occurring after the Coming of Christ, during the thousand years' reign spoken of in 20:4–8. It is only then that the conversion of the world will take place. Compare Ps. 86:9; Isa. 2:2–4; 66:23; Micah 4:2–4; Zech. 8:22. Bengel: "Here is declared the conversion of all nations, and the moving cause, together with the time of the conversion." De Burgh maintains that this verse proves "that not until the coming of Christ in judgment does the conversion of the world take place," and that it is an error "to expect the conversion of the world as an event" to occur before the coming of Christ to destroy Antichrist. Fausset: "The conversion of *all nations*, therefore, shall be when Christ

221

shall come, and not till then; and the first moving cause will be Christ's *manifested judgments* preparing all hearts for receiving Christ's mercy. He shall effect, by His presence, what we have in vain tried to effect in His absence. The present preaching of the gospel is gathering out the elect remnant; meanwhile 'the mystery of iniquity' is at work, and will at last come to its crisis, and then shall judgment descend on the Apostates. The confederacy of the Apostates against Christ becomes, when overthrown with fearful judgments, the very means, in God's overruling providence, of preparing the nations not joined in the Anti-Christian league to submit themselves to Him."

52. The Seven Angels receive Seven Bowls of Wrath (15:5–8)

5. And after these things I saw, and the temple of the tabernacle of the testimony in heaven was opened.

Compare 11:19, where "the ark of the covenant" was seen, reminding of mercy,—but here although the same ark is seen, it is called *the tabernacle of testimony*, reminding of *judgment*, and of God's faithfulness in avenging His people.

6. And there came out from the temple the seven angels that had the seven plagues, arrayed with *precious* stone, pure *and* bright, and girt about their breasts with golden girdles.

From the presence of the Lord came forth these messengers of His wrath. The office of these seven angels is to usher in the last seven plagues. Their dress is here described. It is very difficult to decide whether the correct reading is *linon* (linen), or *lithon* (stone) as accepted by Lachmann, Tregelles, Wescott and Hort, and the Revisers. Alford,

Tischendorf, and Weiss, accept the reading *linon*, i. e. arrayed *in linen*, "pure and bright,"—a description of the angelic priestly attire. Those who accept the reading *stone*, the more difficult reading, and all other things being equal, therefore, presumably the better reading, refer us to Ezek. 28:13, "every precious stone was thy covering,"—this reading indicating that each angel wore raiment studded with precious stones. They were *girt about with golden girdles*, like our Lord Himself (1:13), possibly because they were clothed with authority and girded by divine righteousness to act for Christ in bringing the plagues upon His enemies (Isa. 22:21).

7. And one of the four living creatures gave unto the seven angels seven golden bowls full of the wrath of God, who liveth for ever and ever.

As the representative of life on the earth, for these plagues pertain to all earthly creatures (16:3), one of the *four living creatures* (see notes on 4:6–9), gives to the seven angels *seven golden bowls* full of the wrath of God. This translation *bowls* is much better than the *vials* of the A. V., for the Greek word designates a shallow bowl or cup, rather broad than deep. It is highly probable that *seven* angels are chosen and *seven* bowls poured out, in order to show that in them is completed the wrath of God (15:1). This figure of pouring out God's wrath in Judgment is taken from the O. T. (Ps. 79:6; Jer. 10:25; Zeph. 3:8). The description of God, as He *who liveth unto the ages of the ages* increases the terribleness of the idea of this wrath of God.

8. And the temple was filled with smoke from the glory of God, and from his power; and none was able to enter into the temple, till the seven plagues of the seven angels should be finished.

In the *smoke* we have a symbol of the glory of the Divine Presence, "the covering of the Divine majesty" (Bengel). The glory and power of God so filled the temple, that God was unapproachable, until the completion of the judgments. Milligan: "God cannot be approached at the moment when He is revealing Himself in all the terrors of His indignation (Ex. 19:21)." The whole description conveys an impression of the awful sacredness of God's presence. Bengel: "When God pours out His fury, it is fit that even those who stand well with Him should withdraw for a little, and should restrain their inquiring looks. All should stand back in profound reverence, till by and by the sky becomes clear again."

16

Revelation 16

53. The First Bowl of Wrath (16:1, 2)

1. And I heard a great voice out of the temple, saying to the seven angels, Go ye, and pour out the seven bowls of the wrath of God into the earth.

Just as the visions of the opening of the seals (6:12–17; 8:1), and those of the sounding of the trumpets (11:15–18), and those of the harvest and vintage (14:14–20), in each case bring us down to the end, so likewise the pouring out of these bowls of the wrath of God brings us a fourth time to the coming of Christ to destroy Antichrist (16:17–21). All these visions are therefore more or less synchronous and depict different aspects of the end, which will be described more in detail in Rev. 17–20.

The Temple was filled with the glory of God (15:8), and now the voice of God is heard commanding the seven angels to begin their work of punishing all who worship the beast and his image. God now begins in a direct way to bring to an end the great tribulation through which his faithful ones are passing, by visiting judgment upon the followers of Antichrist. Blunt: "The pouring forth of these vials belongs altogether to the reign of unfulfilled prophecy, and they are called 'the seven last plagues' (15:1), as belonging to the epoch which is so often described as 'the end' or 'the end of the world'; and they appear to represent those human woes and convulsions of nature to which our Lord refers when He speaks of the signs that will precede His Second Coming (Matt. 24:29; Luke 21:11)." The kingdom of Antichrist will be scourged by plagues like those which fell on Pharaoh and his people. Fausset: "The trumpets shook the world-kingdoms in a longer process; the vials destroy with a swift and sudden overthrow the kingdom of the beast in particular who had invested himself with the world-kingdom … These seven vials (the detailed expansion of the *vintage* (14:18–20), being called *the last*, must belong to the period just when the term of the beast's power has expired (whence reference is made in them all to the worshippers of the beast as to the objects of the judgments), close to the end or Coming of the Son of Man.… The first four are more general, affecting the earth, the seas, springs, and the sun, not merely a portion of these natural bodies, as in the case of the trumpets, but the whole of them; the last three are more particular, affecting the throne of the beast, the Euphrates, and the grand consummation. Some of these particular judgments are set forth in detail in chapters 17–20."

2. And the first went, and poured out his bowl into the earth; and it became (or, *there came*) a noisome and grievous sore upon the men which had the mark of the beast, and which worshipped his image.

226

In vision John sees the first angel leaving heaven and approaching the earth, pouring out his bowl of the incense of God's wrath into the earth. This reminds us of the sixth plague of Egypt (Ex. 9:8–12). For as the ashes of the furnace which Moses sprinkled toward heaven became small dust over all the land of Egypt, and became grievous ulcers breaking forth upon man and beast, so likewise in the last days grievous sores shall be supernaturally brought upon all the followers of Antichrist. Note that the human race alone is smitten, but all the worshippers of the beast and his image are included. Note the use of the prepositions *into* and *upon* (Greek). Wordsworth: "The first three vials are poured *into* the earth, *into* the sea, *into* the rivers; the last four vials are poured *upon* the sun, *upon* the throne of the beast, *upon* the river Euphrates, *upon* the air,"—probably, as Wordsworth suggests, *into* "denoting *infusion into* and *admixture with* the object of punishment;" *upon* "denoting the divine dominion *over* the object which has exalted itself against God." There is no reason why we should spiritualize this plague, as so many do, for there is nothing incredible in its literal fulfilment.

54. The Second Bowl of Wrath (16:3)

3. And the second poured out his bowl into the sea; and it became blood as of a dead man; and every living soul (Greek, *soul of life*) died, *even* the things that were in the sea.

Just as in the first Egyptian plague the waters of the Nile turned to blood and the fish died, and the river stank (Ex. 7:20, 21), so now the whole sea is changed into blood, and becomes tainted with corruption, and every living creature in it dies. What is most horrible of all is that the sea becomes

227

like the clotted and putrefying blood of a dead man. Whether this is to be taken literally or symbollically the future alone can decide, but the Egyptian plague suggests that there may be a literal fulfilment. Most commentators interpret all these vials symbolically,—the *sea* representing nations in a restless state, tossed about by the winds and storms of passion, and this *bowl of wrath* designating the moral and spiritual death among the nations. But this interpretation is very unsatisfactory. Notice the similarity and the difference between this plague and that of the second trumpet (8:8, 9), The judgments of God grow more and more terrible as wickedness increases and the end approaches

55. The Third Bowl of Wrath (16:4–7)

4. And the third poured out his bowl into the rivers and the fountains of the waters; and it became blood.

Some ancient authorities read *and they* (that is *the waters*, neuter plural) *became blood.* This third plague was even more terrible in its nature than the second, for the fresh water of the earth was turned into blood. Compare Ex. 7:19–24, the account of the first Egyptian plague. In the corresponding judgment of the third trumpet (8:10, 11) only a third part of the waters were affected and became bitter.

5. And I heard the angel of the waters saying, Righteous art thou, which art and which wast, thou Holy One, because thou didst thus judge.

This plague is now acknowledged by heavenly voices as a just retribution (16:5–7) visited upon the persecutors of the saints. Probably the angel who celebrates the righteous acts of God is the same one who has poured out the bowl of wrath,

228

and to whom power was given over the waters. **Righteous art thou.** See notes on 15:3, 4. **Which art.** See notes on 1:4; 4:8; 11:17. The attribute *which is to come* (1:4; 4:8) is omitted *here* and in 11:17, probably because the coming to judgment is considered as already in the process of fulfilment. **Thou Holy One.** See notes on 4:8; 15:4. Bengel: "At the beginning and at the close of the Apocalypse the Lord is called *the Almighty;* here where judgments show themselves, He is called *the Holy.*" Craven: "The term *hosios* has reference to the *covenant love and mercy* of Jehovah toward His own people. It is here used as the most fitting ascription to Him who has avenged the blood of His saints or *consecrated ones,* upon their persecutors." The latter part of the verse we can literally translate, "because thou didst judge *these things*"; i. e. the judgments described in verse 4.

6. For they poured out the blood of saints and prophets, and blood hast thou given them to drink; they are worthy.

The punishment visited upon the followers of Antichrist is a just and righteous one, for they persecuted the saints to death, and killed the prophets, notably the two witnesses (11:7). As they poured out blood, so now in retribution they must drink blood as their punishment. They have merited this severe judgment, for **they are worthy,** deserving of just such a punishment.

7. And I heard the altar saying, Yea, O Lord God, the Almighty, true and righteous are thy judgements.

This is an answer to the cry of the souls under the altar, "How long, O Master, the holy and true, dost thou not judge and avenge our blood on them that dwell on the earth?" See notes on 6:9, 10. Wordsworth: "The *Altar speaks,* as the Blood of Abel is said to *cry* (Gen. 4:10; Heb. 12:24), and the *stones* of

Jerusalem to *cry out* (Luke 19:40). The Altar *speaks*, because the souls of the Martyrs, who had been slain by the Beast, are described as *victims* whose *blood* has been poured out upon God's Altar (6:9)."

56. The Fourth Bowl of Wrath (16:8, 9)

8. And the fourth poured out his bowl upon the sun; and it was given unto it to scorch men with fire.

The fourth plague brings great physical suffering upon all who worship the beast and his image. The sun shall shine with intense power and his rays shall produce terrific heat, so as to scorch men with fire.

9. And men were scorched with great heat: and they blasphemed the name of God which hath the power over these plagues; and they repented not to give him glory.

So great will the wickedness of men become in the latter days of Antichrist, that although they perceive that these plagues are a visitation of God, they, like Pharaoh of old, instead of repenting, will only harden their hearts, and curse and blaspheme the name of God. We have a right to infer that there would still be forgiveness, if men only would repent of their sins. But the statement is that they will not repent to give glory to God. Williams sees here a reference to the times of which Daniel speaks, when "many shall run to and fro, and knowledge shall be increased," when "the wicked shall do wickedly, and none of the wicked shall understand" (Dan. 12:4–10).

57. The Fifth Bowl of Wrath (16:10, 11)

10. And the fifth poured out his bowl upon the throne of the beast; and his kingdom was darkened; and they gnawed their tongues for pain.

This fifth plague affected the power and rule of Antichrist himself, and the lands over which he ruled were covered with darkness, as in the ninth Egyptian plague (Ex. 10:21–23). We learn from this and the next verse that these plagues were visited upon the followers of Antichrist so quickly one after another, that they were contemporaneous, and not successive. Their character was cumulative, each one intensifying the terror and suffering of the preceding ones.

11. And they blasphemed the God of heaven because of their pains and their sores; and they repented not of their works.

In addition to the terror of darkness which overspread the whole land ruled over by Antichrist, all his followers will endure great physical suffering, caused by the grievous ulcers inflicted by the first plague, and by the scorching heat of the fourth plague, the effects of which are still most keenly felt. But they only will harden their hearts, and will not repent of their evil works. Lange: "The blasphemy is directed no longer simply against *the name of God*, revelation, but against the *God of heaven*, the primeval revelation of God, and God in his universal revelation—hence, against all that is Divine."

58. The Sixth Bowl of Wrath (16:12–16)

12. And the sixth poured out his bowl upon the great river, the *river* Euphrates; and the water thereof was dried up, that the way might be made ready for the kings that *come* from the sunrising.

The sixth trumpet also had reference to "the great river Euphrates." See notes on 9:14. God in a supernatural way prepares a great highway by which the kings that come from the East may gather together their armies unto the great battle against Christ (16:14), which, however, to their utter amazement, shall turn out so disastrously to the beast, to the false prophet, and to all the followers of Antichrist (19:19–21). Just as the Euphrates was once the means of bringing punishment upon the enemies of God's people, when Cyrus took Babylon (538 B. C.), so now in the last days of Antichrist this river shall again indirectly be the means of bringing punishment upon the enemies of Christ. There is here no reference to the conversion of the Eastern nations, the hundreds of millions that swarm over Eastern and South-Eastern Asia, for these kings *from the sunrising* do not come to worship Christ, but come with their immense armies to assist Antichrist in the final battle at Har-Magedon (16:16) against Christ and his armies (19:19). Blunt: "The drying up of the Euphrates is also connected in the prophecy of Isaiah with some great deliverance of the people of God at the time of our Lord's Second Advent (Isa. 11:15, 16). So also in the prophecy of Zechariah (Zech. 10:10, 11). The drying up of the Euphrates, on which Babylon was situated, may therefore signify the preparation of a way for God's people to come out of her (Rev. 18:4) as well as a way for the kings

232

of the East to follow them, as Pharaoh did God's people of old, on the road to their own destruction."

13. And I saw *coming* out of the mouth of the dragon, and out of the mouth of the beast, and out of the mouth of the false prophet, three unclean spirits, as it were frogs.

During this whole period known as the days of Antichrist, the dragon or the devil is giving his power to the First Beast or Antichrist (13:2–4), and the Second Beast or the False Prophet is deceiving the followers of Antichrist (13:14). In vision John beholds three evil spirits proceeding from this trinity of evil, diabolical in character, and loathsome in appearance, likened unto frogs, sent forth to mislead and deceive the kings and nations of the earth. We must insist that these three spirits are just as real as the dragon and his two beasts, from whose mouths the spirits actually proceed. Milligan: "The spirits are as *frogs*, unclean, boasting, noisy, offensive." There are *unclean* spirits; Burger very aptly refers to the contrast afforded by the dovelike form of the Holy Spirit of God (Luke 3:22). The Second Beast of 13:11 is here for the first time called the *False Prophet* (so also 19:20; 20:10). Currey: "From the *dragon*, or Satan, goes forth the spirit of rebellion; from the beast, or World-power, his agent, the spirit of persecution; from the second beast, the false prophet, their subordinate, the spirit of falsehood (compare Zech. 13:2)."

14. For they are spirits of devils (*demons*), working signs; which go forth unto the kings of the whole world, to gather them together unto the war of the great day of God, the Almighty.

It is here clearly stated that these are *demoniacal* spirits, able to perform Satanic miracles. This is in strict accordance with the teaching of Christ and of Paul, that in the days of Antichrist diabolical miracles shall be performed (Matt. 24:24; 2 Thess. 2:9). In what way these spirits influence the kings of *the inhabited earth* we are not told, but the result is that they array themselves on the side of Antichrist and gather together their armies against God and His Christ. For the details of this war see 19:11–21. Compare also Zech. 14:1–5. Milligan: "The representation may rest upon 1 Kings 22:20–22 when a lying spirit goes forth to persuade Ahab to rush upon his fate. These lying spirits in like manner persuade the kings of the whole godless world to rush upon the fate prepared for them in the last great judgment of God—'His day.' " The remarks of Boyd-Carpenter are very suggestive: "These spirits of demons go forth to gather every world-power to the struggle.... There are three radical foes of Christ, and His righteousness: the dragon, representing the hate of evil spirits; the wild beast, representing the hostility of world-power; the false prophet, representing the antagonism of world-culture and intellectualism—these three send forth each their emissary appealing to the pride and passions of men.... The world-power would have us worship the things seen. It sends forth the spirit of earthliness, the spirit which works in the voluptuary, the ambitious, and the avaricious, the spirit which makes earthly things its end (Phil. 3:19). The world-culture sends forth its spirit of intellectualism, which denies the spiritual nature of man, and substitutes taste and culture for spirituality. The dragon sends forth the spirit of egotism, of proud, self-sufficient independence, which culminates in an utter hatred of the Creator. The three spirits combined make up that wisdom which St. James described as earthly, sensual (unspiritual, psychical), devilish (James

234

3:15)."

15. (Behold, I come as a thief. Blessed is he that watcheth, and keepeth his garments, lest he walk naked, and they see his shame.)

Some think that John is here speaking in the name of Christ, but it is better to refer these words to the Lord Himself. These words of comfort and exhortation contain two main thoughts, (1) the suddenness of Christ's coming, and (2) the destruction which it brings to the ungodly. Alford: "In the spiritual sense, the garments are the robe of righteousness put on by faith in Him who is our Righteousness; and the walking naked is that destitution of these garments which will at that day bring shame before assembled men and angels." On the suddenness of Christ's coming see Matt. 24:42, 44; 1 Thess. 5:2; 2 Pet. 3:10; Rev. 3:3. On *garments* see notes on 3:17, 18; 7:14. The believer must ever be clothed in "the wedding-garment" (Matt. 22:11) of Christ's righteousness, and never lay aside "the whole armor of God" (Eph. 6:13–18).

16. And they gathered them together into the place which is called in Hebrew Har-Magedon.

The evil spirits accomplished their purpose (16:14) and gathered the kings and their armies together to assist Antichrist in his conflict with God and His Christ. This battle, however, does not yet take place. The place of the struggle is mentioned here only by anticipation. The battle itself is described in 19:19–21. There is no reason why we should not regard Har-Magedon as the name of a real place. If we read *Har*, it means *the mountain*, if *Ar, the city*, of Megiddo, or *of slaughter*. In the O. T. we read of the *plain* or *valley* of Megiddo (2 Chron. 35:22; Zeck. 12:11), and of *the waters* of

235

Megiddo (Judg. 5:19), in the plain of Esdraelon, the battle-field of Jewish history. The historical interpretation is more in keeping with the Apocalypse than the etymological, but the latter has also its significance. The plain of Esdraelon has been in O. T. history the scene of four great battles, of which two were great victories, (1) when Deborah and Barak annihilated the host of Sisera and of the kings of Canaan (Judg. 4:4–24; 5:19), (2) when Gideon with his 300 men put to flight and routed the Midianites (Judg. 7:4–25), and two were great disasters, (3) when the Philistines overcame Israel and slew Saul in Mount Gilboa (1 Sam. 31:1–13), and (4) when the Egyptians under Pharaoh Necho overcame and slew Josiah (2 Kings 23:29; 2 Chron. 35:20–24). The historical reference seems to be to Judg. 5:19, for when these antichristian kings assemble against Christ at Har-Magedon, their fate shall be the same as that of the kings of Canaan who fought against Deborah and Barak, for the Lord shall also overcome and discomfit them, and utterly destroy them. Godet: "If the antichristian Jewish Monarchy is hereafter to have its seat in the East, at Jerusalem, the rival of Rome, the choice of this battlefield, normal in Palestine, need not surprise us." It is evident that we must distinguish between the battle of Har-Magedon, and the *Day of Judgment*, for in Zech. 14:4, 5, the Mount of Olives, and in Joel 3:12, the Valley of Jehosaphat, is represented as the scene of that great event.

59. The Seventh Bowl of Wrath (16:17–21)

17. And the seventh poured out his bowl upon the air, and there came forth a great voice out of the temple, from the throne, saying, It is done.

236

This bowl of wrath was poured out *upon the air*, probably because it is the abode of the powers of darkness, as Satan is called "the prince of the power of the air" (Eph. 2:2). The voice of God is now heard saying that the end has come. We are reminded of our Lord's dying words on the Cross (John 19:30). The time has now come for the complete overthrow of Antichrist and of all that opposes Christ and His Kingdom.

18. And there were lightnings, and voices, and thunders; and there was a great earthquake, such as was not since there were men upon the earth, so great an earthquake, so mighty.

See notes on 8:5; 11:19. These are the signs which usually accompany the judgments of God. But the terrors of this earthquake are especially dwelt upon. Although closely connected with the events depicted under the sixth seal (6:12–17), and with those following under the seventh trumpet (11:19), still it seems that this earthquake is specially characteristic of the terrors of the seventh bowl, although all these descriptions are in a certain sense contemporaneous, ushering in the second coming of Christ.

19. And the great city was divided into three parts, and the cities of the nations fell: and Babylon the great was remembered in the sight of God, to give unto her the cup of the wine of the fierceness of his wrath.

By *the great city* is probably meant Jerusalem, as in 11:8 (so Bengel, Hofmann, Milligan, Ebrard, Simcox, and others), not heathen Rome (Ewald, De Wette, Bleek, Hengstenberg), nor Papal Rome, nor is it to be understood as identical with "Babylon the Great," as most commentators hold. Possibly Jerusalem is still at this time the seat of Antichrist, and although Jerusalem is to be converted at the very last (11:13), still this will probably not happen until towards the end of

Antichrist's reign,—so that it is most likely that this judgment takes place upon Jerusalem while it is still antichristian. Zechariah also refers to this division of the city of Jerusalem into three parts, at the coming of the Lord (Zech. 14:4, 5). But also the other cities of the hostile nations shall be overwhelmed by the earthquake. There may be a reference to Micah 5:10–15. In connection with this earthquake, and as a part of the outpouring of the seventh bowl of wrath, judgment shall especially fall upon *Babylon the Great*, whose fate is here referred to by anticipation, as in 14:8, the destruction of which is so vividly depicted in the next two chapters, which see.

20. And every island fled away, and the mountains were not found.

Such were the effects of the great earthquake mentioned in 16:18. The terrors of the last day are described as in 6:14, (which see). Burger: "Islands and mountains disappear, but the earth remains. The case is different in 20:11."

21. And great hail, *every stone* about the weight of a talent, cometh down out of heaven upon men: and men blasphemed God because of the plague of the hail; for the plague thereof is exceeding great.

Hailstones will fall from heaven sixty times heavier than ever known before, masses of ice weighing 57 lbs (Attic talent), or probably 96 lbs. (Hebrew talent) avoirdupois. And still those who are not killed will not repent, but only blaspheme God. Frightened by the earthquake, it seems that men will fly for safety to the open fields, but they cannot escape the just judgment of God. Contrast the result of this earthquake with that in 11:13, when man gave glory to the God of heaven. Josephus speaks of stones which were thrown

238

from machines in the siege of Jerusalem as each of a talent weight, but in the last days hail of so monstrous a size shall fall from heaven. Hailstones are everywhere in Scripture regarded as a symbol of divine wrath. On the history of the interpretation of the *Seven Vials* or Bowls of Wrath, see *Excursus V.*

17

Revelation 17

60. Description of the Great Harlot (17:1–6.)

A new series of Visions begins here, closely connected with what precedes, but we now have a more particular description of the events of the period immediately preceding the Second Coming of Christ. Twice already has the Fall of Babylon been introduced by way of anticipation (14:8; 16:19), and twice also has the Beast by anticipation been referred to (11:7; 13:1–10), but now we obtain a clearer glimpse of the days of Antichrist and of the destruction of Babylon (chapters 17 and 18).

1. And there came one of the seven angels that had the seven bowls, and spake with me, saying, Come hither, I will shew thee the judgement of the great harlot that sitteth upon many waters.

One of the seven angels that brought the last seven plagues,—probably the seventh, because it was during the outpouring of the seventh bowl that reference is made to the fact that God remembered Babylon the Great in the fierceness of his wrath (16:19),—invited John to approach in order to behold the judgment impending, which will surely be visited upon *the great harlot*, which in 17:18 is explained as being a symbol of "the great city which reigneth over the kings of the earth." This *great harlot* is Babylon the Great (17:5), the center of the God-opposing world-power, the city in which the throne of the beast will be set up (16:10). Alford maintains that by the harlot we must understand *Papal Rome*: "God's Church and people that had forsaken Him and attached herself to others." He remarks: "In eighteen places out of twenty-one where the figure occurs, such is its import; viz. in Isa. 1:21; Jer. 2:20; 3:1, 6, 8; Ezek. 16:15, 16, 28, 31, 35, 41; 23:5, 19, 44; Hosea 2:5; 3:3; 4:15 (Micah 1:7). In three places only is the word applied to heathen cities: viz. in Isa. 23:15, 16, to Tyre, and in Nah. 3:4 to Nineveh." So in substance, Vitringa, Wordsworth, Elliott, Barnes, and others. Others, however, maintain that the image of the *harlot* is taken from the O. T. description of the heathen cities of Tyre and Nineveh, and Simcox remarks: "The truth is, the Anti-christian Empire is conceived as embodying the various forms of evil that existed in previous earthly empires." But whether Babylon the Great refers to the Apostate Church of the future, or to a real city on earth, the heathen Rome of John's time, or the papal Rome of the future, or to heathen Rome of the future, or to Jerusalem, or to Babylon rebuilt on the Euphrates, a careful exegesis of these two chapters (17 and 18) will aid us in deciding. In 17:15 the interpreting angel explains that "the waters which thou sawest," (compare Jer. 51:13), "where the harlot sitteth, are peoples, and multitudes, and nations, and tongues,"—thus showing that this city shall

241

have sovereigntyover many nations, "reigning over the kings of, the earth," (17:18).

2. With whom the kings of the earth committed fornication, and they that dwell in the earth were made drunken with the wine of her fornication.

For all the kings of the earth, as well as all the nations, were seduced by the beast (13:7, 8), especially by the sins of the great city, Babylon the Great, wherein was the throne of the beast (14:8; 16:10). The terms *harlot* and *fornication* suggest that this city will seduce men from the worship of the true God to worldliness and sin and to the worship of the beast (Isa. 1:21). Blunt: "The words indicate a great city or community which is entirely given up to worldliness and false worship,—a city exceedingly prosperous, as Tyre was on account of her commerce, and as Rome was on account of her political power, and dangerously opposed to true religion.... That such a power will arise in the future is made certain by this prophecy; and when it revives it may be expected that the great harlot of the last days will be an empire conspicuous for its commercial wealth and for its hatred of Christ's religion; whether it will spring up from the midst of any Christian people, ... or from any heathen people, none can tell; perhaps it may prove in the end to be a new power altogether, of which the elements are as yet scattered far and wide, to be gathered together through the personal influence, the intellectual and political power, of the yet future Antichrist."

3. And he carried me away in the Spirit into a wilderness: and I saw a woman sitting upon a scarlet-coloured beast, full of names of blasphemy, having seven heads and ten horns.

Fausset: "As the dragon is fiery-red, so the beast is blood-red in color; implying its *blood-guiltiness,* and also deep-dyed sin." This beast is the same as the one described in 13:1–9, for it also has *seven heads and ten horns.* In 13:1 it is stated that "upon his heads were names of blasphemy," and here it is stated that the whole beast was also covered with names of blasphemy, for at this stage of development the beast has become tenfold more blasphemous in its titles and assumptions than before. See notes on 13:1. The woman is seen *sitting* upon the beast, not because she exercises control and power over it, but rather because *the woman* relies upon *the beast* for support. In verses 8–12 we have a more definite explanation of the beast or Antichrist.

4. And the woman was arrayed in purple and scarlet, and decked (Gr. *gilded*) with gold and precious stone and pearls, having in her hand a golden cup full of abominations, even the unclean things of her fornication.

We here have a fuller description of the woman her-self. Many Protestant commentators see in this verse a description of the robes of Roman bishops and cardinals, and perhaps not altogether unjustly. *Purple* indicates royal dominion, and the *scarlet* evidently refers to her being stained with the blood of the saints (17:6). We then have a further description of her rich and gorgeous apparel (cf. 18:16), but the *golden cup* in her hand is filled with *the unclean things of her fornication* wherewith she seduces and corrupts the nations of the earth. Compare the description of the King of Tyre (Ezek. 28:13), also Jer. 51:7, "Babylon hath been a golden cup in the Lord's hand, that made all the earth drunken; the nations have drunk of her wine."

5. And upon her forehead a name written, MYSTERY, BABYLON THE GREAT, THE MOTHER OF THE HAR-LOTS AND OF THE ABOMINATIONS OF THE EARTH.

It is difficult to decide whether the word *mystery* is to be regarded as a part of the name, or as indicating the symbolical character of this city, probably the latter. In the ancient world it was customary for harlots to have their names attached to their foreheads. This city, Babylon the Great, is the concrete representative of the whole antichristian empire, in the days of Antichrist, and is the source of all spiritual idolatry and of all corruption, both as to teaching and example. Duesterdieck: "As *the Mother of harlots*, she has made her daughters, i.e. the cities of the Gentiles, harlots, and given them to drink of her own cup of abominations." Lee: "The sins of the World-city—unbelief, superstition, sensuality—are all included under the Harlot's title."

6. And I saw the woman drunken with the blood of the saints, and with the blood of the martyrs (or, *witnesses*) of Jesus. And when I saw her, I wondered with a great wonder.

In his vision, John beholds that the woman is drunken, and he learns, how we are not told, probably by revelation, that the cause of her drunkenness is the blood of the saints which she has caused to be shed, for she has been the tool of the beast or Antichrist in persecuting those who remained faithful to Christ. Stuart: "The phraseology is derived from the barbarous custom (still extant among many pagan nations) of drinking the blood of enemies slain in the way of revenge. Here, then, the fury of the persecutors is depicted in a most graphic character." John, when he saw this woman greatly wondered, for he did not understand this mystery of the woman, nor that of the beast.

61. Explanation of the Scarlet-Colored Beast (17:7-14)

7. And the angel said unto me, wherefore didst thou wonder? I will tell thee the mystery of the woman, and of the beast that carrieth her, which hath the seven heads and the ten horns.

Although there is a distinction between the woman, or World-*city*, and the Beast, or Antichrist (the World-*kingdom*), they are nevertheless so closely united, that there is but *one* mystery, that "of the woman and of the beast." In the verses that follow (8-14) we have a fuller description of the beast with its "seven heads and ten horns," (cf. 13:1-8); and in verses 15-18 and chapter 18, we have a full description of Babylon the Great, and her fall.

8. The beast that thou sawest was, and is not; and is about to come up out of the abyss, and to go into perdition. And they that dwell on the earth shall wonder, *they* whose name hath not been written in the book of life from the foundation of the world, when they behold the beast, how that he was, and is not, and shall come (Gr. *shall be present*).

Four stages are marked in the existence of the Beast or Antichrist: (1) it *was;* (2) it *is not* now; (3) it shall again *reappear;* (4) it shall suffer in the lake of fire (19:20). All the inhabitants of the earth, who do not remain faithful to Christ, shall wonder after the beast, whose death-stroke was healed, and shall worship him (See notes on 13:3, 4, 8). The fuller statement con cerning the beast is given in verses 9, 10. The beast *goeth* into perdition, referred to also in verse 11, but the event is only fully described in 19:20. **Written in the book of life.** See notes on 13:8. **Abyss.** See

245

notes on Rev. 9:1, 2, 11; 11:7. No matter how difficult of interpretation this question of *the beast* may be, this verse contains no reference to Nero, or to his supposed rising from the grave. This prophecy is a continuation of that of Daniel, and refers to greater events than those concerning any single emperor of Rome. Not only is this Beast the same as that described in 13:1–8, but there are so many points of resemblance between it and St. Paul's prophecy concerning "the mystery of lawlessness," "the son of perdition" (2 Thess. 2:3–10), that it is evident that the reference in both cases is to a future Antichrist. Simcox, who accepts the Nero hypothesis, remarks: "On the whole, ancient tradition, where it speaks, and modern criticism agree in the interpretation of these words, *he was, and is not. Nero,* who killed himself in June, 68 a. d., *had been, and was not* at the date of this vision: but his reappearance was looked for by many, with various feelings of hope and fear.... It is possible that John means to tell us, that the Antichrist who is to come will actually be Nero risen from the dead: more probably, Antichrist will be a new Nero in the same way as he will be a new Antiochus, an enemy of God as they were, typified by them inasmuch as they were actuated by his spirit."

9. Here is the mind (or, *meaning*) which hath wisdom. The seven heads are seven mountains, on which the woman sitteth.

As in 13:18, with reference to the number of the beast, so here special wisdom is required to understand what is now revealed. Most commentators maintain that the *seven mountains* of this verse, as well as 17:18, point definitely to Rome as the city designated. Lee: "That the expression *Seven Mountains* points to the City of Rome, seated on the Palatine,

246

Quirinal, Aventine, Cælian, Viminal, Esquiline, and Janiculan hills—in St. John's age the capital of the Universal World-empire to which the imagery points—need not be questioned. This result, indeed, is plainly indicated in verse 18," others again question this interpretation, and Sadler, after quoting a writer, who says, "no one acquainted in the slightest degree with ancient literature can doubt that Rome is the place to which this description points," remarks: "But may I, notwithstanding such confident assertions, be permitted humbly to ask this question: If it undoubtedly fixes the beast to the city of Rome, why should St. John have prefaced what he is about to say with the words, *Here is the mind which hath wisdom*, whereas it requires no divine wisdom to see the city of Rome on the seven hills, for it is described as such in some of the best-known heathen authors, as will be seen in such commentaries as those of Alford and Wordsworth! Evidently by these words the Apostle must allude to something more secret and more mysterious. Now the numeral seven is itself a deeply mysterious number, and may signify here divine completion, and may indicate something far more extensive than Rome." So likewise, Isaac Williams calls attention to the fact that "it requires no divine wisdom to see the City of Rome on the Seven Hills.... but to understand the mystic power of the symbolic language requires Scriptural wisdom. According to the analogy of the allegoric interpretation of the Apocalypse it need not be the city of Rome; but as the ten-horned beast is something far more extensive than Rome, so would its *seven heads* appear to be." He nevertheless adds: "Still it must be allowed that the prophecy does in some awful manner hover, as with boding raven wing, over Rome." Williams also gives us a summary of the explanation given by the Greek interpreters: "The seven heads and seven hills on which the universal Babylon is seated are seven places pre-eminent in power, on which the Kingdom of the world is established: Nineveh, of the Assyrians; Ecbatana, of the Medes; Babylon, of the Chaldeans; Susa, of the Persians; the Kingdom of Macedon; the ancient Rome, and the new Rome. And with these they connect the seven kings, as Ninus, Arbaces, Nebuchodonosor, Cyrus, Alexander, Romulus, and Constantine." Other commentators call attention to the fact that there are many cities which can boast of their seven hills—Constantinople, Brussels, and especially *Jerusalem*, which has *four* larger (Zion, Akra, Moriah, Bezetha) and *three* smaller hills, (Ophel, Castle Antonia, and the hill of the three towers). Zuellig, Hartwig, Herder, and others, therefore maintain that by Babylon the great, Jerusalem is meant. The remarks of Boyd-Carpenter are suggestive: "The description seems to be drawn from Rome, the seven-hilled city. This keeps the reference to Rome before us, but at the same time the further explanation (in verse 10) widens our thoughts, and shows us that the literalism on which the imagery is based is used to convey a broader symbolical meaning. The woman rides on the seven-headed beast, even so Rome dwells on her seven hills, and so also the world-city, seen in vision, sits among the various empires which have risen, like great mountains, in the history of the world."

10. And they are seven kings; the five are fallen, the one is, the other is not yet come; and when he cometh, he must continue a little while.

Alford (condensed): "To interpret these kings as *emperors of Rome*, or as successive *forms of government over Rome*, is to miss the propriety of the symbolism and to introduce utter confusion. They belong to the *beast*, which is not Rome, nor the Roman Empire, but a general symbol of secular antichristian power. They are in substance the same seven crowned heads which we saw on the dragon in 12:3,—the same which we saw, with names of blasphemy on them, on the beast of 13:1, to whom the dragon gave his power and his throne. *The five fell*, i. e. the first five out of seven. If I understand these *five* of individual successive kings, if I understand them of forms of government adopted and laid down on occasion, I can give no account of this verb *fell*, or *are fallen;* but if I understand them of forms of empire, one after another heading the antichristian secular power, one after another violently overthrown and done away, I have this verb in its right place and appropriate sense. *Egypt* is fallen, the first head of the beast that persecuted God's people (Ezek. 29, 30); *Nineveh* is fallen, the bloody city (Nahum 3:1–19); *Babylon* is fallen, the great enemy of Israel (Isa. 21:9; Jer. chaps. 50 and 51); *Persia* is fallen (Dan. 10:13; 11:2); *Græcia* is fallen (Dan. 11:3, 4). *The one is*, the Roman empire; *the other* (required to complete the seven) *is not yet come*. I agree with Auberlen in regarding this seventh as *the Christian* empire beginning with Constantine." Alford also maintains that the true meaning of *he must continue a little while* is not that "of short continuance," but rather *of duration.* On the other hand, Hofmann, Ebrard, Luthardt, and others enumerate Assyria, Babylonia, Persia, Macedonia and Syria under Antiochus Epiphanes, as the *five* fallen kingdoms, and the *Roman* as the sixth kingdom, the *one* existing in John's time. Luthardt also names the representative sovereigns of the five fallen kingdoms—Sennacherib, Nebuchadnezzar, Cyrus, Alexander the Great, and Antiochus Epiphanes. He, however, does not name the representative of the sixth kingdom or the Roman empire, but only mentions "the Roman emperor." As the seventh empire, which shall follow that of the Roman and precede that of Antichrist, Luthardt refers to "the present period of the European systems of government." The Preterists, as a rule, see in these *five fallen kings*, the first five emperors, Augustus, Tiberius, Caligula, Claudius, and Nero. According to their view, when the Apocalypse was written (69 a. d.), these five were fallen, Nero having died the year before. Many see in *the one* who *is*, Vespasian, and in *the other* who *is not yet come*, Titus, who reigned "a little while," that is two years. Wordsworth, who represents the anti-papal school of interpreters, differs in some respect from the Continuous-Historical School, with reference to these kingdoms: "*Six* of these seven kingdoms are described by the prophet Daniel, whose predictions are repeated and continued in the Apocalypse; they are, (1) the Babylonian; (2) the Medo-Persian; (3) the Macedonian or Greek; (4) the Syrian: (5) the Egyptian; (6) the *Roman Heathen Imperial....* The *seventh* king represents some power which was *first extrinsic* to Rome, and was afterwards *added* to Rome.... This was the *Imperial* Power of *Germany.*"

It matters very little whether we refer the *five fallen* king-doms to Egypt, Assyria, Babylonia, Persia, and Macedonia, on the one hand, or to Assyria, Babylonia, Persia, Macedonia, and Syria, on the other, for in either case *the Roman Empire* of John's time would be the sixth kingdom. The *seventh* kingdom was still to come in John's time, and of the various views held concerning the *seventh* kingdom, "the Christian empire beginning with Constantine" (Alford), "the imperial power of Germany" (Wordsworth), "the antichristian World-power which is to succeed the power of pagan Rome" (Lee), "the world-empire which is to come between the Roman empire and Antichrist" (Ebrard), "a new heathen power to rule in the last age of Christianity" (some Roman Catholic writers),—although many of these in general mean the same thing,—still we think it best, with Luthardt, Keil, and others, to regard this *seventh* empire as represented by the world-powers of modern Europe that have taken the place of the Roman empire. See notes on 13:3.

11. And the beast that was, and is not, is himself also an eighth, and is of the seven; and he goeth into perdition.

The beast here referred to is identical with the one named in verse 8. It is the eighth world-power concentrating in itself all the rage and God-opposed spirit of the seven preceding kingdoms, and is the last and worst manifestation of the ungodly power of the world. Its king will be Antichrist, prefigured already by the Little Horn of Daniel, and especially described by Paul in 2 Thess. 2:3–10. This *eighth* kingdom or king is a new power or person proceeding *out of* the seven, embodying all the antichristian features of the preceding seven. **Himself also an eighth.** Fausset: "The *He* is emphatic in the Greek. *He*, peculiarly and pre-eminently answering to 'the little horn' with eyes like the eyes of a man, and a mouth speaking great things, before whom *three of the ten horns were plucked up by the roots* (Dan. 7:8, 20), and to whom the whole ten 'give their power and authority' (17:12, 13, 17). That a *personal* antichrist will stand at the head of the anti-Christian kingdom, is likely from the analogy of Antiochus Epiphanes, the O. T. Antichrist, 'the little horn' in Dan. 8:9–12; also 'the man of sin,' 'the son of perdition' (2 Thess. 2:3–8), answers here to *goeth into perdition*." This last kingdom, and its king, Antichrist, does not fall like the other seven (17:10), but he is overcome by the Lord in person, and cast into *perdition*, "cast alive into the lake of fire that burneth with brimstone" (19:20). Sadler: "It seems as if the world-power in its last stage would not act through some empire, but directly through Antichrist himself." Ebrard refers the *sixth* kingdom to the Roman world-power; the *seventh* world-power to the *ten kings* of verse 12, and the *eighth* world-power to Antichrist, or the Beast from the abyss (17:8), and this seems to be the best interpretation. So also in substance Williams: "For this Apocalyptic Beast corresponds with the Little Horn of Daniel, which arises among the ten horns of the seventh head, and by its rising roots up three, by which it becomes itself *the eighth.*

12. And the ten horns that thou sawest are ten kings, which have received no kingdom as yet; but they receive authority as kings, with the beast, for one hour.

The best commentary on this verse is that given by Daniel (7:23–27): "The fourth beast shall be a fourth kingdom upon earth" (the Roman Empire of John's time), "which shall be diverse from all the kingdoms, and shall devour the whole earth, and shall tread it down, and break it in pieces. And as for the ten horns, out of this kingdom shall ten kings arise: and another shall arise after them; and he shall be diverse from the former" (the kingdom of Antichrist), "and he shall put down three kings. And he shall speak words against the Most High, and shall wear out the saints of the Most High: and he shall think to change the times and the law; and they shall be given into his hand until a time and times and half a time" (the last three and-a-half years of Antichrist's reign. "But the judgment shall sit, and they shall take away

252

his dominion, to consume and to destroy it unto the end. And the kingdom and the dominion, and the greatness of the kingdoms under the whole heaven shall be given to the people of the saints of the Most High; His kingdom is an everlasting kingdom, and all dominions shall serve and obey him." Alford remarks: "Ten kingdoms shall arise out of the fourth kingdom of Daniel: ten European powers, which in the last time, in concert with and subjection to the antichristian power, shall make war against Christ. In the precise number and form here indicated, they have not yet arisen. It would not be difficult to point out the elements and already consolidating shapes of most of them; but in precise number we have them not as yet. What changes in Europe may bring them into the required tale and form, it is not for us to say."

In some way these *ten* horns seem to belong to the beast as represented in the *seventh* kingdom. These *ten kings* had not yet received their power in John's time, for that was still the period of the *sixth* kingdom,—and it seems as if this *seventh* kingdom is simply now in its course of development,—for these ten kings will only receive their authority, about the time that Antichrist's manifestation draws near. They will receive *authority as kings* **with the beast,** at least **for one hour;** i. e. for a short time, at the beginning of Antichrist's appearance. According to Daniel, presupposed but not mentioned by John, Antichrist will overcome *three* of the *ten* kings or kingdoms, and reduce the rest to his rule. These ten kings or kingdoms evidently represent the ultimate kingdoms of the world which will wage war against Christ. Blunt: "The gradual de-Christianization of European governments points to the possibility of a not very distant

253

time when they may become permanently Antichristian, as that of France became so temporarily when it established the worship of Reason in the place of the worship of God." Fausset: "Antichrist is in existence long before the fall of Babylon; but it is only at its fall he obtains the vassalage of the ten kings. He, in the first instance, imposes on the Jews as the Messiah, coming in His own name; then persecutes those of them who refuse his blasphemous pretensions. Not until in the latter part of his reign does he associate the ten kings with him in war with the Lamb, having gained them over by the aid of the spirits of demons working miracles. His connection with Israel appears from his sitting 'in the temple of God' (2 Thess. 2:4), and as the antitypical 'abomination of desolation standing in the holy place' (Dan. 9:27; 12:11; Matt. 24:15), 'in the city where our Lord was crucified' " (Rev. 11:8).

13. These have one mind, and they give their power and authority unto the beast.

We have here a description of the universal antichristian character of these future kingdoms. They are one in their opposition to God and His Christ, and they become allies of the Beast or of Antichrist, and act in concert with him, whether his enmity is directed against the Lamb (17:14), or against the harlot (17:16).

14. These shall war against the Lamb, and the Lamb shall overcome them, for he is Lord of lords, and King of kings; and they *also shall overcome* that are with him, called and chosen and faithful.

This gathering together of the beast and the kings of the earth to make war against the Lamb is described in 19:19 (which see). The victory of the Lord over the beast, the false prophet, and their hosts, is graphically depicted in 19:20, 21 (which see). It is here stated that not only the Lamb, because He is Lord of lords, and King of kings, but also the saints who are with the Lamb, shall share in this victory over these kings. The redeemed are represented as sharers in the victory. The order of the description of the redeemed, as *called, chosen*, and *faithful*, is significant. The *elect*, or chosen, are first *called*, and they prove that they are *the elect* in that they remain *faithful* unto the end. Plummer: "These three epithets describe the progressive life of those who share Christ's victory. They are *called*—as all men are—to serve Him; having heard the call, they dedicate their lives to His service, and become His *chosen* servants; finally, having remained *faithful* to Him, they share in His victory." Sadler: "It seems incredible that men should gather themselves together and fight against Christ Himself appearing personally; but men opposed Him when He came the first time ... why may they not go a step further and fight against Him when He rides on the white horse leading the armies of the saints?"

62. The Mystery of the Woman (17:15–18)

15. And he saith unto me, The waters which thou sawest, where the harlot sitteth, are peoples, and multitudes, and nations, and tongues.

We have now an explanation of the symbol of the *harlot sitting upon many waters* (17:1). The waters signify the sum total of the inhabitants of the earth, for the great city Babylon *shall reign over the kings of the earth* (17:18). See notes on 17:1–6.

16. And the ten horns which thou sawest, and the beast,

these shall hate the harlot, and shall make her desolate and naked, and shall eat her flesh, and shall burn her utterly with fire.

We have here by anticipation a statement of the cause of the fall of Babylon the Great, the theme of the next chapter. The kings of the earth shall rebel against her dominion, and the Beast, by their aid, shall utterly destroy her. Alford: "Her former lovers shall no longer frequent her nor answer to her call; her rich adornments shall be stripped off. She shall lose, at the hands of those whom she formerly seduced with her cup of fornication, both her spiritual power over them and her temporal power to adorn herself." The moving cause of this terrible catastrophe which shall overtake this world-city is God (17:17), but the immediate occasion is not revealed; it is simply stated that the beast and his allied kings *shall hate the harlot.* It is evident that Antichrist and these kings continue after the Fall of Babylon. It seems as if the reign of Antichrist and the development of his power immediately follows on the fall of Babylon.

Those who regard the Harlot or Babylon the Great as signifying *the Apostate Church* see here a description of what is in store for the faithless. So Fausset: "As Jerusalem used the world-power to crucify her Saviour, and then was destroyed by that very power, Rome; so the church, having apostatized to the world, shall have judgment executed on her first by the world-power, the beast and his allies; and these afterward shall have judgment executed on them by Christ Himself in person." Wordsworth, on the other hand, maintains that "the Harlot sitting on the beast is the City of Rome.... This verse reveals the wonderful results, that the Horns of the Beast, that is, some Powers that have grown out of the Roman Empire,

256

will one day be alienated from the Papacy, and will *hate the Harlot* and *devour her flesh* ... The ruin of Papal Rome will not be effected by Protestant Nations, but by Papal Princes and people rising against her." Godet maintains that the last political power of which Antichrist shall be the head is Israel; Babylon the Great denotes the city of Rome; at Rome the Monarch of Israel (Antichrist) shall first take up his abode; but as God has made use of Rome to chastise Israel, so now He will make use of Israel to judge Rome. His exact words are: "It is the old antagonism between Jew and Pagan—the most profound antithesis of history—which now attains to its supreme crisis. Rome is reduced by triumphant Israel to the actual state of Nineveh or of Babylon. After this act of vengeance, Antichrist will go to establish as we have seen (11:7, 8), at Jerusalem, his natural capital;" then, according to Godet, follows the struggle of the Beast with the Two witnesses (12:7, 8), and the conversion of Israel (11:13), which had already been restored politically.

17. For God did put in their hearts to do his mind, and to come to one mind, and to give their kingdom unto the beast, until the words of God should be accomplished.

Here it is directly stated that God used Antichrist and his allied kings as instruments to punish Babylon. In three things did this confederation agree: (1) in determining the destruction of the city, and thus carrying out the righteous will of God; (2) in their hatred of the harlot; (3) in giving all their authority unto Antichrist. This unanimity of sentiment prevailed until the words of God concerning the destruction of Babylon were fulfilled. The great influence of this great city became oppressive to Antichrist, and so he determined to destroy it, and thus was an instrument of God to punish

257

Babylon the Great, the harlot.

18. And the woman whom thou sawest is the great city, which reigneth (*hath a kingdom*) over the kings of the earth.

If we interpret this verse grammatically there seems to be no difficulty in deciding what is meant by *the great city* or *the woman*. The statement is—this *woman* which John saw sitting upon many waters (17:1, 15), is *the great city*, and this city is *the one having a kingdom over the kings of the earth*. The present participle *the one having* points to the time when the words were uttered, and to the dominion then exercised by the city. It is evident that when John wrote, Rome was just such a city as this verse describes. It is highly probable, almost certain, that the City of Rome is here referred to. The only question that can arise is whether by *the great city* is meant Pagan Rome, or Papal Rome, or Rome under both aspects, or Rome as it shall be in the future days of Antichrist. There can be only one answer, it is Rome as it shall be in the future time to which this vision refers. That *the Woman* of this Vision, under the symbol of Babylon, represents Rome in some form, has been the common opinion of the great majority of commentators of all schools. This has been the case since the days of Tertullian and Jerome. In the Middle Ages, Rome is often styled "the Western Babylon." Currey: "Luther, and others before him, in their earnest struggles against the corruptions of a dominant Church, and suffering under its persecutions, found in Babylon the symbol of their foe, and applied to Papal Rome all the epithets and adjuncts here attached to Babylon; and many still insist upon this view of the Apocalypse." Luther speaks of the Pope as "the very Antichrist" (*Art. Smalc.* IV.) and Melanchthon writes—"the marks of Antichrist plainly agree with the Kingdom of the

258

Pope and his adherents" (*Power and Primacy of the Pope*). Some of the other Reformers (Calvin), as many moderns, identified the Harlot with the Apostate Church, and maintained that this corresponds with the Papacy. In opposition to this Protestant interpretation, there arose in the Church of Rome a school of expositors, which with the Protestants, identified Babylon with Rome, but with Rome of the future, Rome again become Pagan. Stern, a representative of this Roman Catholic school, remarks: "Babylon is really the City of Rome, not only, however, according to the old-heathenish, but also according to the new-heathenish signification of the World's history. So long as Rome maintains Christianity, so long God forgets, humanly speaking, her ancient guiltiness. But in the last times of the New Testament World-history, many inhabitants of the Roman obedience will abandon their holy Catholic faith; will unite with the revolutionists of all lands; nay, unmeasured wickedness will rear its throne in Rome, after the Holy Father with his faithful Bishops and priests and the pious believers shall have been hunted into the desert."

Those who maintain that Babylon the Great represents the Apostate Church may be right in so far that it is certain that the Babylon of the days of Antichrist will be utterly antichristian in its character, and its inhabitants may be largely apostates from a professed worldly Christianity; and they who refer it to Papal Rome may be right in a certain sense, for the Papacy may have been the great factor and instrument in the development of the Antichristian spirit of those days; and they who refer it to a heathen or pagan Rome of the future, may be right in so far that the spirit of Babylon, in the days of Antichrist, before its destruction, represents a type of wickedness more diabolical than the worst kind ever known in heathenism.

18

Revelation 18

63. The Fall of Babylon Announced (18:1–3)

1. After these things I saw another angel coming down out of heaven, having great authority; and the earth was lightened with his glory.

Another angel. Besides the one who showed John the mystery of the Woman and the Beast (17:1–7). He had *great authority*, and may be the instrument of carrying out God's will in the punishment of Babylon, which however is not acted out before the Seer, but only described. His *authority* was manifested in his very appearance, for the glory of the Lord accompanied Him, so that the earth shined with His glory (Ezek. 43:2).

2. And he cried with a mighty voice, saying,

Fallen, fallen is Babylon the great,

And is become a habitation of devils (Gr. *demons*).

And a hold (or, *prison*) of every unclean spirit,

And a hold (or, *prison*) of every unclean and hateful bird.

See notes on 14:8. Compare Isa. 21:9, "Babylon is fallen, is fallen." The fall of Babylon had also been foretold in 16:19; and 17:16. The description of the destruction of Babylon the Great is largely based upon the writings of the O. T. prophets. In describing the future desolation of Babylon the very words which Isaiah and Jeremiah used concerning the ancient Babylon on the Euphrates are here employed. Compare especially Isa. 13:19–22; 34:14, 15; Jer. 50:39; 51:37. So complete will also be the desolation of this future Babylon after it has been destroyed by Antichrist and his allied kings (17:16). As the prophecies concerning ancient Babylon were exactly fulfilled, this fact is a pledge that the prophecies of this book shall also be fulfilled in the case of the Babylon of the days of Antichrist. Some have thought that this future Babylon might be the old Babylon rebuilt, but the prophecy is that Babylon of old "shall be no more inhabited forever" (Jer. 50:39, 40).

A more graphic description of the utter desolation of Babylon can scarcely be conceived of—beasts and birds of prey dwelling in the deserted ruins, and demons (evil angels) making their abode there. We are reminded how our Lord speaks of unclean spirits passing through waterless places seeking rest, and finding it not (Matt. 12:43).

3. For by the wine of the wrath of her fornication all the nations are fallen;

And the kings of the earth committed fornication with her,

And the merchants of the earth waxed rich by the power of her wantonness (or, *luxury*).

Some authorities omit *the wine of,* and some read *all the nations have drunk.* We have in this verse a statement of the cause of the fall of Babylon. See notes on 14:8; 17:2. So great shall be the wealth, luxury, and resources of this great city of the future, that all the merchants of the earth shall be enriched thereby. **Wantonness.** "This word signifies overweening pride and insolence and wantonness, arising from superfluity of wealth, and gifts." (Plummer). "It is applied to describe insolence and voluptuousness breaking out into boastful vauntings of pride, and dissolute riot and revelry; like those of Babylon of old on the eve of her fall" (Wordsworth). "Rome was in St. John's day a wealthy and luxurious city, not a commercial city *primarily*, in the same sense as ancient Tyre and modern London, but a city with an immense commerce ... What Rome was then it may, and probably will, be again: and there is thus no need to look elsewhere than at Rome for the literal fulfilment of St. John's description" (Simcox).

64. Warning to the Saints (18:4–8)

4. And I heard another voice from heaven, saying,
     Come forth, my people, out of her,
     That ye have no fellowship with her sins,
     And that ye receive not of her plagues.
  The apostle hears an angel's voice warning God's people to come out of Babylon. Compare Jer. 50:8; 51:6, 45. We have a right to infer that some of the saints will be dwelling in the midst of the wicked city even almost up to the time of her fall, "and that there will be danger of their being, through a lingering fondness of the city, partakers in the coming Judgment" (Alford). Two reasons are given why they should come out of Babylon, (1) that they may not participate in her sins, and (2) that they may not participate in her punishment.

263

At all times in the history of the development of God's kingdom on earth have the people of God been warned to flee from the City of Destruction. See Gen. 19:15, 22; Num. 16:26; Isa. 48:20; 52:11; Matt. 24:16. "Remember Lot's wife" (Luke 17:32). Sadler: "This, of course, will not come as an audible voice from heaven, but it will be a secret, yet universal intimation to all that are in the mystical Babylon, that they are to leave her society, her fellowship, and it may be, as of course it was in the case of the Babylon of old, to leave the city, if it is Rome or any other city." Williams: "The period of this command in the Apocalypse appears to be on the great rising of Antichrist above all; and on the destruction apparently of the outward and visible frame and form of Christianity, which is to precede the end."

5. For her sins have reached (*clave together*) even unto heaven,

And God hath remembered her iniquities.

So great will be the accumulation of the sins of Babylon, that these sins being heaped up, they will reach unto heaven (see Jer. 51:9). Wordsworth: "the Babel-tower of *sin* is a tower which man builds in pride, and when its top reaches to heaven, then it is suddenly thrown down (18:19)." **Remembered.** Compare 16:19.

6. Render unto her even as she rendered,

And double *unto her* the double according to her works:

In the cup which she mingled, mingle unto her double.

The words of this and the next verse are addressed to those who are the executioners of God's judgments, and probably refer to Antichrist and his allied Kings, who are the instruments by which God punishes Babylon (17:16). The words are based upon Jer. 50:15, 29, "as she hath done, do

264

unto her"; Jer. 16:18, "I will recompense their iniquity and their sin double." A double share of the wine of the wrath of God shall be her portion (14:8; 17:2, 4), The punishment shall be proportioned to the sin (Jer. 17:18).

7. How much soever she glorified herself, and waxed wanton,
So much give her of torment and mourning:
For she saith in her heart, I sit a queen,
And am no widow, and shall in nowise see mourning.

The thought is still of retribution. We have here a reecho of the prophecies against Babylon of old (Isa. 47:7–9), and against Tyre (Ezek. 27:3; 28:2). According to the degree of her boasting and wantonness, so shall punishment and sorrow overtake her.

Therefore in one day shall her plagues come,
Death, and mourning, and famine;
And she shall be utterly burned with fire;
For strong is the Lord God which judged her.

Compare the prophecy against ancient Babylon (Isa. 47:9–11). Alford: "The judgments here are more fearful; death, for her scorn of the prospect of widowhood; mourning, for her inordinate reveling; famine, for her abundance; fire, as the punishment of the fornicatress." See also 17:16. The reason of the severity of the judgment lies in the fact that the Lord God is *the Almighty* (1:8). Antichrist and the allied Kings are the executors of the judgment but, they are really carrying out the will of God (17:16, 17). Williams: "This suddenness is the great characteristic carried out from the Babylon of old, whose destruction came upon her suddenly as a snare and a net; how to be fulfilled in this, the antitype, is a great mystery." Fausset: "Literal fire may

265

burn the literal city of Rome, which is situated in the midst of volcanic agencies.... Bengel is probably right in thinking Rome will once more rise to power. The carnal, faithless, and worldly elements in all churches, Roman, Greek, and Protestant, tend toward one common centre, and prepare the way for the last form of the beast, i. e. Antichrist."

65. The Lament of Kings, Merchants, and Mariners over the Fall of Babylon. (18:9–19)

Three classes of persons are now introduced as bewailing the fall of Babylon—kings (verses 9, 10), merchants (verses 11–17a), and mariners (verses 17b–19). Note that the lamentations are all of a selfish character.

9. And the kings of the earth, who committed fornication and lived wantonly (or, *luxuriously*) with her,

Shall weep and wail over her,

When they look upon the smoke of her burning.

See notes on 17:2. Lee: "Compare the dirge over Tyre (Ezek. 26:15; 27:36), into which the description here passes imperceptibly." We have here the lamentation of *the Kings of the earth* who have been the instruments of God in destroying Babylon (17:16, 17). Milligan: "The deeds of the wicked, even when effecting the purpose of God, bring no joy to themselves." Wordsworth, who everywhere sees the Papacy, remarks: "A marvelous prophecy. Some of those very Powers, who were once vassals of Rome, will one day rise against her; they will be instruments in God's hands of His retributive justice upon her; ... And yet when they have done the deed, they will *weep over her.* The reason of this is, that the *Fall* of Papal *Rome* will be followed by a triumph of Anarchy and an outbreak of Infidelity." It is very likely that the fall of Babylon will occur before the greatest development of the power of

Antichrist. Dennett: "Babylon, with its outspreading roots, will have interlaced itself with almost every social fibre of the life of the nations; and her fall, therefore, will spread universal dismay and confusion as well as render human governments unstable and powerless. This will account for the wail of these kings."

10. Standing afar off for the fear of her torment,

Saying, Woe, woe, the great city, Babylon, the strong city!

For in one hour is thy judgment come.

Very graphic is this description of the lamentation of the kings. They are represented as standing at a distance from the burning city, afraid that the destruction might also reach them. The reference to the greatness and power of the city, and her sudden destruction, only heightens the impression made by the awful catastrophe. Compare Ezek. 26:16, 17. Blunt: "As regards its future fulfillment it seems to apply to some immense maritime city such as London or New York. Should a distinct and professed Antichristianity ever gain the upper hand in either of these cities, the elements of wealth and wickedness which they contain would be greatly developed, and a vast Babylon or Tyre would be the result, one which would fully meet the terms of the prophecy."

11. And the merchants of the earth weep and mourn over her,

For no man buyeth their merchandise (Gr. *cargo*) any more.

We come now to the lament of the merchants of the earth (11–17*a*). The sorrow of these merchants is even more purely selfish than that of the kings. The description is based upon the lament over Tyre in Ezek. 27, and in Isa. 23. The merchants can no longer find purchasers for their *cargo*, or *ship's burden*, as in Acts 21:3,—*their freight*, and this

267

only emphasizes how immense the traffic of this luxurious city will be. Relying on the meaning of the word *cargo*, many commentators think that Babylon does not refer to the future city Rome, because it does not lie on the sea, and cannot have a large maritime commerce. But the answer is very simple. What Rome was once in the past, the centre of all commerce by sea and land, it may again become in the future. For this very reason we may question the statement of Alford: "I leave this difficulty unsolved ... For Rome never has been, and from its very position never could be, a great commercial city ... The details of this mercantile lamentation far more nearly suit London, than Rome at any assignable period of her history." Wordsworth sees here the *spiritual* traffic of Papal Rome. Williams: "The lamentation passes imperceptibly into that which is descriptive not of Babylon, but of Tyre; the depth and breadth of meaning in the Apocalypse is such that it must indicate some especial reference in the latter ages to maritime nations, in which the corruption of the Church will extend ... The Tyre of the last ages is to be restored, and sing as an harlot."

Merchandise (Gr. *cargo*) of gold, and silver,

And precious stone, and pearls,

And fine linen, and purple, and silk, and scarlet;

And all thyine wood, and every vessel of ivory,

And every vessel made of most precious wood,

And of brass, and iron, and marble.

Compare Ezek. 27. The various articles of merchandise, representative of the great commercial activities of the world, are mentioned in suitable groupings, "a gorgeous picture of worldly riches and extravagances" (Milligan). Zuellig arranges them into seven classes of articles of luxury: (1) of

268

precious wares; (2) of materials of rich attire; (3) of materials for costly furniture; (4) of precious spices (verse 13*a*); (5) of articles of food (verse 13*b*); (6) of merchandise for agricultural and domestic uses (verse 13*c*); (7) of the traffic in men (verse 13*d*). **Thyine wood.** Possibly the white cedar or *citrus* of the Romans, used for costly doors, fine tables, panels, and ceilings, noted for its sweet scent.

13. And cinnamon, and spice,

And incense, and ointment, and frankincense,

And wine, and oil,

And fine flour, and wheat,

And cattle, and sheep; and *merchandise* of horses and chariots,

And slaves (Gr. *bodies*); and souls (or, *lives*) of men.

Spice. Greek *amomum*, a precious ointment made from an Asiatic shrub, used for the hair. **Chariots.** The luxurious carriages used in the Rome of John's time by the wealthy and the nobles. **Slaves ... Souls of men.** The most probable explanation is that these words refer to two classes of slaves, the *first* to such slaves (the grooms or coachmen of the last times) as have to do with horses and chariots, and the *second* (souls of men), to slaves in general. Boyd-Carpenter: "The climax of wicked worldliness is reached in this last; it gives the finishing touch to the picture of society wholly engrossed in pleasure and indolence and selfishness, which lays every market under tribute to add to its luxuriousness, and sacrifices not only the happiness, but the lives and liberties of their fellow-creatures, to their own enjoyment." What Rome was in the past, the Babylon of the future shall be, only on a larger scale. Many commentators interpret this merchandise spiritually, and refer these things to the Papacy, but Sadler correctly remarks: "Not one of these commodities can be connected particularly with any ecclesiastical state of things. It is impossible, as regards the greater part of them, to interpret them spiritually."

14. And the fruits which thy soul lusted after are gone from thee,

And all things that were dainty and sumptuous are perished from thee,

And *men* shall find them no more at all.

This verse seems to be addressed to Babylon either by the merchants in their lamentation, or (which is probably the better interpretation) by the voice from heaven (18:4). Babylon of the future will seek all the merchandise and sumptuous things of earth for selfish enjoyment, and to satisfy earthly lust and worldly glory. But the day of reckoning shall come.

15. The merchants of these things, who were made rich by her,

Shall stand afar off for the fear of her torment,

Weeping, and mourning.

Just as in 18:9, 10, the kings of the earth made their lament, so here the merchants who were enriched by the trade of Babylon will make their lament over the sudden and awful punishment visited upon Babylon. See notes on 18:10.

16, 17*a*. Saying, Woe, woe, the great city,

She that was arrayed in fine linen and purple and scarlet,

And decked (Gr. *gilded*) with gold and precious stone and pearl!

For in one hour so great riches is made desolate.

Woe. See notes on 18:10. **Arrayed.** Compare 17:4; 18:12. **One hour.** Compare 18:10. Stress is laid upon the luxurious glory of the city, and its sudden desolation. The expression *in one hour* is thrice repeated (18:10, here, and 19). In each case the lamentation is not only over the loss of riches, but their sudden and unforseen ruin.

17*b*. And every shipmaster, and every one that saileth any whither,

And mariners, and as many as gain their living by sea,
Stood afar off.

The description includes all who in any way make their living by the sea, whether as pilots, captains, sailors sailing merchants, fishermen, divers for pearls, etc. Compare Ezek. 27:25–36. Like the kings (18:10) and the merchants (18:15), they are represented as standing afar off, to avoid being overwhelmed in the destruction of the city.

18. And cried out as they looked upon the smoke of her burning,

Saying, What *city* is like the great city?

Smoke of her burning. See notes on 18:9. **What … great city.** Compare Ezek. 27:32. Boyd-Carpenter: "The outcry of those who call to mind, with pain, a glory that was great, but now is gone. It is not to be taken as meaning *what city has suffered as she has?*… The lingering of the mind over delights now vanished is one subtle element of misery."

19. And they cast dust on their heads,

And cried, weeping and mourning, saying,

Woe, woe, the great city,

Wherein were made rich all that had their ships in the sea by reason of her costliness!

For in one hour is she made desolate.

Cast dust on their heads. A sign of their great mourning. See Ezek. 27:30. The Babylon of the future will become the

271

source of great wealth to all sea-merchants, on account of the extravagance and luxury which marks her inhabitants,—her *costliness.* The splendor of her buildings and palaces shall make levy on all parts of the world (18:11–13), **One hour desolate....** Compare notes on 18:10, 17.

Sadler seems to be correct when he maintains that this description of Babylon given in this chapter cannot refer to Papal Rome,—"these references to cargoes, to freights, to ships, ship-owners, etc., lead us to look to a collapse of a great commercial system.... It is as if London and Liverpool and Glasgow and New York were all amalgamated together and involved, as in a moment, in one common and irreversible ruin." Dennett: "All this description is symbolical, the import of which is that the whole commercial system of the empire is utterly deranged, if not destroyed, by the judgment upon Babylon. The blow that falls upon her destroys with her the prosperity of the habitable world; and hence the universal sorrow; for men are ever ready to bewail the loss of the means of their comforts, wealth, and affluence."

66. The Angel calls upon the Inhabitants of Heaven to Rejoice (18:20)

20. Rejoice over her, thou heaven,
    And ye saints, and ye apostles, and ye prophets;
    For God hath judged your judgment on her.

The saints, and apostles, and prophets, are regarded as being in heaven. The answer to the prayer of the saints has now been given (6:10), for the judgment of God upon the guilty city is supposed to have taken place. Blunt: "It is plain that the words have a comprehensive character, relating to

272

the martyrs who suffered under Roman dominion in the Apostolic age, and to those who shall fall as martyrs in the Great Tribulation of the last times." **Your judgment.** Alford: "God hath exacted from her that judgment of vengeance which is due to you."

67. Symbolic Proclamation of Babylon's Fall (18:21–24)

21. And a strong angel took up a stone as it were a great millstone, and cast it into the sea, saying,

Thus with a mighty fall shall Babylon, the great city, be cast down, and shall be found no more at all.

A symbolical act, immediately explained by the angel, presenting in a most vivid manner the suddenness and completeness of the destruction of Babylon. Both the *might* of the angel and the *greatness* of the millstone are emphasized. At the basis of this passage lies Jer. 51:63, 64. Andreas of Crete has already given us the true meaning: "Just as the millstone sinks by its impulse into the sea, so also the destruction of this Babylon shall be all at once, so that not a trace of it shall be preserved for posterity."

22. And the voice of harpers and minstrels and flute-players and trumpeters shall be heard no more at all in thee;

And no craftsman, of whatsoever craft, shall be found any more at all in thee;

And the voice of a millstone shall be heard no more at all in thee.

For the imagery see Jer. 25:10 (which denunciation, however, refers to Jerusalem) and Ezek. 26:13 (where the reference is to Tyre). Milligan: "The destruction spoken

273

of is enlarged on in strains of touching eloquence, but it is unnecessary to dwell on the particulars. They include everything belonging either to the business or to the joy of life." The phrase *"no more at all"* occurs six times in *verses* 21–23. In this verse, emphasis is laid upon the fact that three kinds of the activities of life have ceased—the life of pleasure, the life of business, and domestic life.

23. And the light of a lamp shall shine no more at all in thee;

And the voice of the bridegroom and of the bride shall be heard no more at all in thee;

For thy merchants were the princes of the earth;

For with thy sorcery were all the nations deceived.

Compare the denunciation against Babylon in Isa. 47:9–12. In the latter part of this verse and *verse* 24 we have a threefold statement of the sins of Babylon and of the cause of her downfall: (1) her covetousness, luxury, wealth, and extravagance—her *"merchants were the princes of the earth"*; (2) her idolatry and licentiousness—*"with her sorcery were all the nations deceived";* and (3) her persecution of the saints (*verse* 24).

Sadler: "No one can read these verses over without being struck with their extraordinary sublimity and beauty. It is as if the Apocalyptic seer lamented with all his heart the desolation which it was laid upon him to foretell."

24. And in her was found the blood of prophets and of saints,

And of all that have been slain upon the earth.

The future Babylon, the great world-city of the Last Days, will be the central power from which all the persecutions of the saints will arise, especially in the earlier part of

Antichrist's rule, before Babylon is destroyed by him and his allied kings (17:6).

Here, as everywhere, Wordsworth sees *Papal Rome*. He thinks that the awful words of this divine prophecy demand some practical application: "The Book of Revelation delivers a warning from Almighty God to the world. It proclaims the peril and unhappiness of those who are enthralled by Rome, and its prophetic and comminatory uses ought to be pointed out by Christian ministers, and to be acknowledged by Christian congregations. We may forfeit a great blessing and incur great danger, if we neglect these divinely-appointed uses of the Apocalypse, particularly in the present age, when the Church of Rome is busily employed in spreading her snares around us, to make us victims of her deceits, prisoners of her power, slaves of her will, and partners of her doom."

19

Revelation 19

68. The Song of Triumph in Heaven (19:1–8)

1. After these things I heard as it were a great voice of a great multitude in heaven, saying, Hallelujah; Salvation, and glory, and power, belong to our God.

In the former chapter the Fall of Babylon was announced. In this chapter it is assumed to have taken place, and now the overthrow is celebrated in heaven, by a Song of Victory. As in 18:20 the angel calls upon Heaven and its inhabitants to rejoice, so now here, in 19:1–8, we have the response. This Hallelujah, from the heavenly hosts, the Redeemed Church, and the four living creatures (19:4) representing Creation, celebrates the first act of the final sentence upon the antichristian world manifested in the utter destruction of Babylon. Lee calls attention to the fact that from this point onwards the Apocalypse follows the course of the closing chapters of Ezekiel from Ezek. 36 to the end: "There the land of Israel is comforted, and a resurrection of the dead is described (Ezek. 36, 37); then comes the Gog-catastrophe (Ezek. 38, 39); then we read of a new Heaven and a new Jerusalem in a new Holy Land resembling Paradise."

This *great multitude* evidently consisted of the heavenly hosts of angels standing round about the throne, and about the elders and the four living creatures (see 7:11). **Hallelujah.** That is, *Praise ye, Jah or Jehovah*, an exalted ascription of praise, common to the Psalms, repeated in this song four times, and only found here in the whole N. T. **Salvation ... power.** See notes on 7:10; 12:10. Songs of praise are also found in 4:8–11; 5:9, 12, 13; 7:10, 12; 11:15, 17; 15:3, 4; 16:5–7.

2. For true and righteous are his judgments; for he hath judged the great harlot, which did corrupt the earth with her fornication, and he hath avenged the blood of his servants at her hand.

True and righteous. See notes on 15:3; 16:7. **Her fornication.** See 14:8; 17:2, 4; 18:3, Alford: "The vengeance is considered as a penalty exacted, forced out of the reluctant hand (Ezek. 33:6)." The judgments of God correspond to reality and propriety of things. Note how this verse is an answer to the prayer of 6:10.

3. And a second time they say, Hallelujah. And her smoke goeth up for ever and ever (*unto the ages of the ages*).

The smoke of the burning Babylon (18:8, 9, 18) shall ascend for ever and ever. Her punishment shall never cease. Lange: "This far surpasses modern sentimentalities." It is probably best to refer this to the temporal destruction of Babylon and her worldly glory. This implies, however, that her wicked inhabitants shall suffer everlasting punishment (see notes on 14:10, 11).

277

4. And the four and twenty elders and the four living creatures fell down and worshipped God that sitteth on the throne, saying, Amen: Hallelujah.

See notes on 4:8, 10; 5:8, 11–14; 7:11, 12; 14:3. The representatives of the Redeemed Church and of Creation confirm the praise given by the heavenly host. The mind of heaven is one, both in praising God, and in rejoicing over the vengeance that has overtaken Babylon.

5. And a voice came forth from the throne, saying, Give praise to our God, all ye his servants, ye that fear him, the small and the great.

It is not necessary to decide whose voice it was that calls upon all servants of God to praise Him. Compare Ps. 134:1; 115:13.

6. And I heard as it were the voice of a great multitude, and as the voice of many waters, and as the voice of mighty thunders, saying, Hallelujah: for the Lord our God, the Almighty, reigneth.

There is an immediate response to the call for praise, given in the last verse. The description of the sound heard suggests an innumerable number of heavenly voices. Compare 1:15; 14:2. Basil and Ambrose compare the full harmonious response of the congregations in their day to the noise of the sea on the shore; Jerome likens it to "the heavenly thunderings." **Almighty.** See notes on 1:8. **Reigneth.** Though the Greek verb is in the *aorist* tense, this can only be here properly translated by the present; or, we might translate, *did take the kingdom.* Compare also 11:15, 17. Boyd-Carpenter: "This anthem expresses the exultation of the servants of God that the Kingship of their God is manifested, and vindicated against those who denied, or hated His rule....

278

Their joy arises also from the prospect of the nearer union between the Lamb and His Bride. This close union is more fully spoken of later; here the glorious close is for a moment anticipated: the morning glow announces the coming day; it is near even at the doors." The things hereafter to take place are here spoken of as if they were already accomplished (see 14:8 and 16:19). Christ is prophetically considered as already reigning, for His Advent follows so soon after the fall of Babylon.

7. Let us rejoice and be exceeding glad, and let us give the glory unto him: for the marriage of the Lamb is come, and his wife hath made herself ready.

Alford probably gives the true relation of this verse to what follows in the Apocalypse: "These words introduce to us, transitionally, a new series of visions respecting the final consummation of the union between Christ and His Church, which brings about the end (21:1, 2): the solemn opening of which now immediately follows (19:11–16). This series, properly speaking, includes in itself the overthrow of the kings of the earth, the binding of Satan, the thousand years' reign, the loosing of Satan, the final overthrow of the enemy, and the general judgment: but is not consummated except in the entire union of Christ and His Church with which the book concludes." In its prophetic aspect it is assumed that the time of the marriage of the Lamb is come, though it has not yet occurred in the vision, and will not happen until after the events foretold in Rev. 19:11; 20:15, have taken place. But it is in perfect harmony to speak of this event as having come, for an actual beginning of its fulfilment has been made, for Babylon, the great Harlot, has now in vision received already her merited punishment. This marriage is not here described, and is not fully consummated until after the final judgment (21:2, 9, etc.).

Others, however, maintain that the song of triumph has not reference to the *entire* future, but only to the *immediate* future, and that this *marriage of the Lamb* takes place at the beginning of the millennial period, and that 21:2, 9, 10, do not refer to this marriage but to a *new manifestation* of the Bride. This view implies (1) that the Bride consists only of those saints (the quick and the dead) who have believed on Christ up to the time of His Second Advent and the beginning of the Millennium; (2) that the marriage consists in the union of these saints (the subjects of the First Resurrection) with Christ in the glory and government of the millennial kingdom; (3) that the New Jerusalem state (21:2, 9, 10) is not a simple continuance of the millennial kingdom, but the kingdom of Christ raised to a higher plane,—or as Craven presents it (in Lange): "The millenial kingdom is the reign of the saints over a race and earth freed indeed from the assaults of Satan, but still in measure, in sin and under a curse; the New Jerusalem period is that of the reign of the saints over a race and earth perfectly purified." A careful exegesis of the passages here in question can alone help us to decide whether there is any foundation for such an interpretation.

The *rejoicing* in this verse is in anticipation of the events that will now occur, there being evidently a reference also to the punishment to be visited upon the Beast and the False Prophet, as well as to the near approach of *the marriage of the Lamb.* This marriage is the blessed union of the Lord with His chosen Bride, the Church. The figure of marriage is borrowed from the O. T. (Isa. 54:1–8; Ezek. 16:7, 8; Hos. 2:19, 20). Compare also Matt. 9:15; 22:1–14; 25:1–13; John

3:29; Eph. 5:25–32. Respecting the marriage itself, see 21:2, 9, etc. **His wife hath made herself ready.** For the Bride, His Church, has arrayed herself in a becoming manner. In what her raiment consists, we learn from the next verse.

8. And it was given unto her that she should array herself in fine linen, bright *and* pure: for the fine linen is the righteous acts of the saints.

It is difficult to decide whether these words are a part of the song, or an explanation given by the angel, or by John himself. That this garment of *fine linen, bright and pure,* is bestowed upon the Church by the grace of God is implied in the expression *it was given unto her.*

The reference here is not so much to the robe of Christ's righteousness imparted to the believer by faith, as to the *righteous acts* of the saints, the *inherent* righteousness, the fruit of the new life, which, however, is also the work of God. This reference to the *deeds* of the saints is very appropriate here, for the question is of reward to be given to the saints for their fidelity. See also 14:13. Fausset: "Though in one sense *she* 'made herself ready,' having by the Spirit's work in her put on 'the wedding garment,' yet in the fullest sense it is not *she*, but her Lord, who makes her ready by granting to her that she be arrayed in fine linen. It is He who by giving Himself for her, presents her to Himself, a glorious Church, not having spot, but holy and without blemish. It is He also who sanctifies her, naturally vile and without beauty, and with the washing of water by the Word, and puts His own comeliness on her, which thus becomes hers."

69. The Blessedness of those Bidden to the Marriage Supper of the Lamb (19:9)

9. And he saith unto me, Write, Blessed are they which are bidden to the marriage supper of the Lamb. And he saith unto me, These are true words of God.

The speaker is probably the angel of 17:1. This blessedness is affirmed particularly of the individual, for he shall have blessed communion with the Lord. This is one of the six benedictions of the Apocalypse (1:3; 14:13; 19:9; 20:6; 22:7, 14). On the *marriage supper* compare the Parable of the Wedding Garment (Matt. 22:1–14), and of the Ten Virgins (Matt. 25:1–13). **These are true words of God.** Referring especially to what has been revealed concerning Babylon and the Bride (18:1–19:9). Milligan: "After the marriage will come the marriage supper, the fulness of blessing to be enjoyed by the redeemed. It may be a question whether we are to distinguish between the bride herself and those who appear rather to be spoken of as guests at the marriage supper. But the analogy of Scripture, and especially of such passages as Matt. 22:2; 26:29, leads to the conclusion that no such distinction can be drawn. Those who are faithful in the Lord are at once the Lamb's bride, and the Lamb's guests."

70. The Angel Forbids John to Worship Him (19:10)

10. And I fell down before his feet to worship him. And he saith unto me, See thou do it not; I am a fellow-servant with thee and with thy brethren that hold the testimony of Jesus; worship God: for the testimony of Jesus is the spirit of prophecy.

John was so overcome by the awfulness of the vision that out of undue reverence to the angel who showed him these latter visions (17:1), he fell at his feet to adore him. But the answer came—Worship God alone: I am also a servant of God as thou art. The argument of the angel is somewhat as follows: Both he and John are engaged in the same work, prophesying concerning Christ, and as in both cases the witness borne to Jesus is *the spirit of prophecy*, the result of the Spirit working in them (1 Pet. 1:11), so both stand on the same footing before God, and both must worship God alone. Lee: "*Worship God*, whose servants we both are (see 22:6, 9)—of whose prophetic Spirit we alike partake in this our common ministry; and therefore one of us may not worship the other."

71. The Vision of the Second Advent (19:11–16)

11. And I saw the heaven opened; and behold, a white horse, and he that sat thereon, called Faithful and True; and in righteousness he doth judge and make war.

Although the opening words of this vision are the same as that recorded in 6:2, the two do not refer to the same event (see notes on 6:2). Here we have a description of the *Revelation* of Christ to destroy Antichrist, and He is represented as sitting on a white horse, as the Conqueror. As in 3:7, 14, so here Christ is called and described as the *Faithful* and *True, faithful* because He will keep His promises to those who have remained faithful, and *true*, for He manifests Himself as their true Saviour, the Messiah announced in the O. T. *Righteousness* also marks His progress in war, as clearly foretold in Isa. 11:3–5, for "he shall not judge after the sight of his eyes," "and with the breath of his lips shall he slay the wicked, and righteousness shall be the girdle of his loins, and faithfulness the girdle of his reins." Compare also Ps. 45:3–5.

Fausset calls especial attention to the fact that we must distinguish between this Coming of Christ to destroy Antichrist (Matt. 24:27, 29, 30, 37, 39), and the *end* or final Judgment (Matt. 25:31; 1 Cor. 15:23, 24; Rev. 20:11–15). Dennett: "Until this point, from chapter 4 and onwards, we have been occupied with actings and events, whether in heaven or on earth, which take place between the rapture of the saints at the coming of the Lord, as described in 1 Thess. 4, and His public appearing in glory. The time of His patience has now ended; and heaven opens for Him to come forth in judgment, when 'every eye shall see Him, and they which pierced him; and all the tribes of the earth shall mourn over him' (1:7). It may also be remarked, as helping to understand this section of the book, that from 19:11 to 21:8, we have a consecutive history, beginning with the appearing of Christ, and closing with the eternal scene in the new heaven and the new earth.'

12. And his eyes *are* a flame of fire, and upon his head *are* many diadems; and he hath a name written, which no one knoweth but he himself.

His eyes a flame of fire. A type of purity and judgment.

See notes on 1:14. **Many diadems.** Probably because He is King of kings (19:16). The true Heir waited till the time determined by the Father, and now, after His long sitting at the right hand of God, He comes forth, crowned with many crowns, to take His inheritance, and to reign till He hath put all His enemies under His feet (1 Cor. 15:25). **A name written.** Evidently the *new name* referred to in 3:12 (which see). It cannot be the name given in 19:13 or in 19:16, for both these names are known. Currey: "This betokens that there is in the Nature and the Person of our Lord that which it is beyond the capacity of man to comprehend. It is not so much *the name*, as the *full import* of the name, which no man can know." "No one knoweth the Son, save the Father" (Matt. 11:27).

13. And he *is* arrayed in a garment sprinkled with blood: and his name is called The Word of God.

Now the prophetic description of Isaiah (63:1–6) receives its true fulfilment: "Who is this that cometh from Edom, with dyed garments from Bozrah?... I have trodden the winepress alone.... I trod them in mine anger, and trampled them in my fury; and their lifeblood is sprinkled upon my garments, and I have stained all my raiment. For the day of vengeance was in mine heart, and the year of my redeemed is come...." The reference here in Isaiah as well as in the Apocalypse is to the blood of the enemies of Christ. Some ancient authorities read "garment *dipped* in blood." **The Word of God.** Only used by St. John,—a strong argument in favor of his authorship of the Apocalypse. Lee: "At His first coming, in humility, He is known as 'The Son of Man'; at His Second Coming, in glory, as 'The Word of God.' "

14. And the armies which are in heaven followed him upon

white horses, clothed in fine linen, white *and* pure.

These armies will consist of myriads of holy angels and all the glorified saints, who were raised and translated at the time of the Rapture (1 Thess. 4:15–17), which will precede the great Tribulation. This mighty host is not equipped for war, they have no armor, neither do they wear crowns. They are but spectators of the glories of their Lord and triumph with Him, and no blood is sprinkled upon *their* garments. Compare also Ps. 110:3–6. By the linen, *white* and *pure*, is symbolized the holiness and purity of the armies of heaven.

15. And out of his mouth proceedeth a sharp sword, that with it he should smite the nations: and he shall rule them with a rod of iron: and he treadeth the winepress of the fierceness of the wrath of Almighty God.

This *sword* is the word of God in its judging power. See notes on 1:16. The whole symbolism is descriptive of warfare, victory and judgment. **He shall rule them.** See notes on 2:27; 12:5. All these passages are based on Ps. 2:9. **Treadeth.** See notes on 14:10, 19, 20. Compare also Isa. 63:2–6. The two images of the "cup of his anger" and of the "winepress" in 14:10, 19, 20, are here combined. Dennett: "In these few brief sentences the coming of Christ in judgment, the execution of God's vengeance, the establishment of His throne, the subjection of all kings and all nations to His sway, and His supreme exaltation in the earth, are all comprised. It is the complete fulfilment of the second psalm. The *sharp sword* is the Word of God, according to which the nations will be judged, and with which they will be judicially smitten. The *rod of iron* expresses the absolute and inflexible character of His government, while the *winepress*, as the context shows, as well as the vintage judgment of chapter 14, speaks of

286

the unsparing and unmitigated vengeance which will be poured out upon that awful day." Body-Carpenter: "The power of this Word found an illustration in the falling back of the hostile band which came to take Him in the day of his humiliation (John 18:5); yet more gloriously will the power of His Word now be felt (compare Isa. 11:4; Jer. 23:29; 2 Thess. 2:8) when He will slay the wicked with the word of His wrath. The passage in Ps. 2:9 must be borne in mind. Christ comes as king; His is a rule in righteousness; those who oppose this kingdom of righteousness find the shepherd's staff as a rod of iron; the stone rejected falls upon the builders, and grinds them to powder. It is thus that the winepress of God's wrath is set up, and the righteous king appears as one who treads it (Isa. 63:1–3). *He* Himself (the emphasis lies here) treads it. We have again the figure of the vintage made use of (14:20). It is the harvest of retribution; the wicked are filled with the fruit of their own doings." **The wrath of Almighty God.** Fausset: "The fierceness of Christ's wrath against His foes will be executed with the resources of omnipotence."

16. And he hath on his garment and on his thigh a name written, king of kings, and lord of lords.

It is probably best to regard the name written partly on the garment, and partly on the thigh itself, at the part where, in an equestrian figure, the robe drops from the thigh. The name itself was a pledge that He will conquer all the kings of the earth, and manifest Himself King of all kings. See notes on 17:14. Boyd-Carpenter: "The King rides at the head of His host. On His robe, where it spreads out from the waist, His title is inscribed; it proclaims Him to be the one who is the true supreme King of all.... The title anticipates the final victory; His power is irresistible, His kingship is universal."

287

The whole context shows that in this section we have a description of the Second Advent, and that it takes place before the Millennium spoken of in 20:4–6. This question, however, has been the occasion of much discussion during the last two hundred years. For the view of the Futurists, which as a rule are Pre-Millennialists, see pages xxix.–xxxv. of the *Introduction*, and also *Excursus* I., where nearly all the scripture passages are given upon which the greatest stress is laid. Those who wish to make this subject a special study will find an excellent presentation of the view held by Pre-Millennialists in Blackstone's *Jesus is Coming*, a small volume of 160 pages.[1] The ablest presentation of the view held by the Post-Millennialists is that given in Dr. David Brown's *Christ's Second Coming*, the standard work on this subject. For the presentation of the view of the Post-Millennialists see *Excursus* VI.

72. The Victory over the Beast and the False Prophet (19:17–21)

17. And I saw an angel standing in the sun: and he cried with a loud voice, saying to all the birds that fly in mid-heaven, Come *and* be gathered together unto the great supper of God.

Verses 17 and 18 emphasize the vastness, universality, and terribleness of the slaughter that will take place in this final conflict with Antichrist and his armies. Both verses are based upon Ezek. 39:17–21, which is in substance here reproduced. Compare also Matt. 24:28. **In the sun.**Duesterdieck: "Because from this standpoint, and at the same time with the glory suitable to an angel, he can best call to the fowls flying in mid-heaven." **The great supper of**

God. Not the supper spoken of in 19:9, but rather just the very opposite, the *supper* which is reserved for the ungodly, in which they are the prey. We have here one aspect of "the war of the great day of God, the Almighty" (16:14).

18. That ye may eat the flesh of kings, and the flesh of captains, and the flesh of mighty men, and the flesh of horses and of them that sit thereon, and the flesh of all men, both free and bond, and small and great.

Such is the terrific nature of the awful slaughter that shall overtake Antichrist and his armies. Compare Ezek. 39:17–21. **Flesh.**Wordsworth calls attention to the fact that the word *flesh* is repeated five times "to denote the *completeness* and *universality* of God's retribution, and the destruction of all His *carnal* foes." **All men.** That is, all the ungodly. Compare the parallel description of the Coming of Christ in 6:15–17. Dennett: "The flower of Europe in men and arms will be gathered together, and in anticipation of their dreadful fate this angelic summons resounds in the heavens."

19. And I saw the beast, and the kings of the earth, and their armies. gathered together to make war against him that sat upon the horse, and against his army.

This is the same beast mentioned in 13:1 and in 17:11, 13, 14, even Antichrist himself. This is the war of the great day of God (16:14), the war against the Lamb (17:14), that shall take place at Har-Magedon (16:16). The kings of the earth are the same as those spoken of in 17:12–14. The armies of the Lord are referred to in 19:14, spoken of here in the singular "in order to mark the holy unity of the entire army of Christ, in contrast with the great body of his enemies" (Duesterdieck). A clear summary is given by Wordsworth:

289

"Here is an ampler description of the battle pre-announced in the Sixth Vial (16:13–16). See also 17:13, 14. The battle itself does not take place till now. Thus we are now brought again to the eve of the end. Observe the sequence of events. The mystical Babylon is now fallen (18:2; 19:2). After her fall, the Beast and False Prophet still survive, and they muster their forces against Christ, and rise up against Him in a great rebellion, called the conflict of Har-Magedon (16:16). They are there routed by Christ and His army; and the Beast and false Prophet are seized and cast into the Lake of fire (19:20). And now there remains one great enemy, the Dragon.... This will be the final struggle." Sadler: "Is the *Beast*, then, to be distinguished as one personal entity from the kings of the earth and their armies? It would seem so, and yet, where all is so involved in mystery, it is impossible to speak certainly. Many things in this book would lead us to believe that he is not a mere figure, a mere impersonation of the world-power. He cannot be any Kingdom, for the kings and kingdoms are distinguished from him." Sadler, however, belongs to that class which holds that *the false prophet* is Antichrist, and hence his dilemma.

20. And the beast was taken, and with him the false prophet that wrought the signs in his sight, wherewith he deceived them that had received the mark of the beast, and them that worshipped his image: they twain were cast alive into the lake of fire that burneth with brimstone.

The beast was taken. In what way, the future alone can reveal. On **the false prophet,** who is identical with the Second Beast, see notes on 13:11–17. Both the Beast and the False Prophet will be cast into Gehenna, or Hell proper (Matt. 5:22, 29, 30; 10:28; 18:9; Mark 9:43, 45, 47), See *Excursus* II.

on *Hades*. Into this Gehenna, Satan also will be cast after the Millennium (20:10), and it is also distinctly stated, that after the Final Judgment all those whose names are "not found written in the book of life" shall be "cast into the lake of fire," which is "the Second Death" (20:14, 15). **Were cast alive.** This heightens the idea of the terror and awfulness of their punishment. Two men in Old Testament times passed alive into heaven, and here these two archenemies of God and His Christ are cast alive into the lake of fire. De Wette: "They are judged earlier than Satan because their existence and activity have attained their end; whilst, on the other hand, Satan, by virtue of the course of development of things, still has a root in the world, and must again make his appearance, although bound for a thousand years." Fausset makes a very suggestive comment: "Many expositors represent the first beast to be the secular, the second beast to be the ecclesiastical power of Rome.… I think it not unlikely that the false prophet will be the successor of the spiritual pretensions of the Papacy: while the beast, in its last form, as the fully revealed Antichrist, will be the secular representative and embodiment of the fourth world-kingdom, Rome, in its last form of intensified opposition to God. (Compare with this prophecy, Dan. 2:34, 35, 44; 11:44, 45; 12:1; Joel. 3:9–17; Zech. 12, 13, 14) The first Beast is a political power; the second, a spiritual power. But both are *Beasts*, the worldly antichristian wisdom serving the worldly antichristian power.… Between the judgment on Babylon, and the Lord's destruction of the Beast, will intervene that season in which earthly-mindedness will reach its culmination, and antichristianity triumph for a short time. It is characteristic that Antichrist and his kings, in their blindness, imagine that they can wage war against the

291

King of heaven with earthly hosts."

21. And the rest were killed with the sword of him that sat upon the horse, *even the sword* which came forth out of his mouth; and all the birds were filled with their flesh.

By *the rest* are meant "all the followers of Antichrist," the armies of verse 19, not "all the inhabitants of the earth." Probably they all suffered bodily death, and their souls went into Hades, there to await the resurrection of the wicked and the Final Judgment (20:13–15). They may have been stricken down by the word of Christ, like Ananias and Sapphira (Acts 5). On this verse compare Isa. 11:4; 2 Thess. 2:8; and notes on 19:17, 18. Alford: "All this must not be spiritualized. For if so, what is this gathering? what is indicated by the coming forth of the Lord in glory and majesty? Why is His personal presence wanted for the victory?"

The Scriptures very plainly teach that this Second Advent of Christ will be *visible* and will *precede* the Millennium. Thus Auberlen: "This coming of Christ to establish His kingdom of glory upon earth must be carefully distinguished from His coming to the Final Judgment. It is this coming which both Daniel and John describe (Rev. 19:11, 12; Dan. 2:44; 7:9–14, 26, 27); it is this coming by which all shall be fulfilled which the prophets of the O. T. have prophesied concerning the Messianic time of peace and prosperity; it is this coming which the Lord Jesus refers to in His discourse, Matt. 24:29–31, as distinguished from that spoken in Matt. 25:31.

Duesterdieck maintains that the allegorical exposition of this chapter arrays itself against the whole context, and he gives a brief history of its interpretation. Some think that *the fowls* of verses 17 and 21 are the Goths and Vandals,

others, the Turks; some see in *the kings* of verse 19, Julian
and his nobles, etc.; others, as C. à Lapide, have thought
that the fulfilment of this prophecy could be shown in
the horrible death and burial of heretics, and the latter, a
Roman Catholic, "cites authors who report of Luther that he
committed suicide, and that at his burial not only a multitude
of ravens, but also the Devil, who had come from Holland,
appeared."

* * *

[1] Craven (in *Lange*, pp. 339, 340) gives a concise summary
of the Premillennarian view: "The Premillennarians rely
principally on two classes of passages: (1) Those which
seem to connect the future Advent with the restoration of
Israel, the destruction of Antichrist, or the establishment
of a universal kingdom of righteousness on earth, such as
Isa. 11:1–12:6; 57:20, 21, compared with Rom. 11:25–27;
Jer. 23:5–8; Ezek. 43:2, etc.; Dan. 7:9–27; Joel 3:16–21:
Zech. 14:1–21; Rom. 11:1–27; 2 Thess. 1:1–8; Acts
3:19–21; (2). Those passages which speak of the coming
of the Lord as imminent (in connection with those which
declare that there is to be a period of generally diffused peace
and righteousness preceding the final consummation), such
as Matt. 24:42–44: Mark 13:32–37; Luke 12:35–40; 1 Thess.
5:2, 3; Tit. 2:11–13; James 5:7, 8.

In a special note on Acts 3:19–21, Dr. Craven maintains
that a careful study of all Scripture passages bearing on the
restoration here spoken of seems to warrant us in affirming:
(1) A restoration of the hearts of the fathers to the children

(Mal. 4:6). (2) The restoration of the rejected seed of Jacob to holiness and the consequent favor of God (Isa. 1:25; Jer. 24:7) (3). The restoration of Israel to their own land. (4) The establishment of Israel, not again to be dispersed (Jer. 24:6, 7). (5) The establishment of the kingdom of righteousness as a visible kingdom, in power and great glory, with its seat at Jerusalem (Isa. 1:25, 26; 2:2, 3; 58:12–14; Jer. 23:5–8; 33:7–13. (6) The gathering of all nations as tributary to Israel or the Church. (7) The Palingenesia, the new heavens and the new earth (Isa. 11:1–9; 65:17–25).

Dr. Craven, in order to give due stress to the Scripture passages on which the Post-Millennialists base their arguments for the view that Christ will not come until after the Millennium and at the time of the Final Consummation, suggests that it is evidently the teaching of Scripture "that *two* Advents still future are predicted—the one for the establishment of the kingdom (at which shall take place a partial resurrection and judgment); the other at the final consummation, at which time shall take place the general judgment."

294

20

Revelation 20

73. The Binding of Satan (20:1–3)

1. And I saw an angel coming down out of heaven, having the key of the abyss and a great chain in his hand.

This *angel* is a real angel, not Christ Himself, probably Michael, who once before had conquered Satan. See notes on 12:7–9. *The key of the abyss* is here given by Christ (1:18) to a powerful angel to carry out God's purpose with reference to Satan. On *abyss*, see notes on 9:1, 2, 11. This abyss is the present abode of Satan and his angels, and is to be distinguished from the lake of fire (20:10), the final place of Satan's punishment. **A great chain.** *Upon* his hand, and hanging down on both sides, lay a great and heavy chain, in order that Satan might be bound securely,—a very concrete picture, suggesting the power and craftiness of the Devil.

It seems almost certain that we have here a continuous narrative, beginning with the event recorded in 19:11, and closing with 21:8.

2. And he laid hold on the dragon, the old serpent, which is the Devil and Satan, and bound him for a thousand years.

This is the same great dragon mentioned in 12:9. (See notes on 12:7–9.) Milligan: "The *binding* is more than a mere limitation of Satan's power. It puts a stop to that special evil working of his which is in the Seer's eye." Blunt: "If we ask why the Evil One should not be bound forever, so that he should be able to do no more harm to God's people, the question is but a reopening of the ancient problem of the world's spiritual history, the mystery of God's permission of the presence of evil in the world at all. But there is also the answer that all events await the times destined for them in the Divine Providence; and that it is also clearly represented as His purpose for Satan to be overthrown by successive stages, and not at one blow."

3. And cast him into the abyss, and shut *it*, and sealed *it* over him, that he should deceive the nations no more, until the thousand years should be finished: after this he must be loosed for a little time.

Notice with what clearness and correctness the description of the fate of Satan is given in these two verses—he is laid hold of, then bound, then cast into the abyss, then shut in, then sealed in, that he should deceive the nations no more until the end of a certain definite period. It is clearly presupposed and implied here, that after the destruction of the hosts of Antichrist in 19:21, there will remain nations on earth who did not take part in that conflict, and that these same nations shall continue on earth during the period in which Satan is bound, and that at the end of this period, when Satan is loosed again, he will again deceive some of these nations, especially those "which are in the four corners of the earth, God and Magog" (20:8). Bengel: "This period itself, of a thousand years, is distinguished by a new, great, pure, and long-continued exemption from internal and external evils, since the authors of these evils are removed, and by an abundance of varied happiness, such as the Church hitherto has not beheld.... *He must deny the perspicuity of Scripture altogether who persists in denying this, and who endeavors to refute it.*... There is no error, much less danger, in maintaining that the thousand years are *future*, but rather in interpreting these years, whether future or past, in a carnal sense. The doctrine respecting the *Son* of God is a mystery, His *cross* is a mystery, and lastly, His *glory* also."

Most commentators, since the time of Augustine, suppose that this binding of Satan for a thousand years began when Christ gained the victory over Satan by His death on the cross, or that it began at some definite period in the past. But such an interpretation is inconsistent with the whole teaching of the Apocalypse, with the history of the Church in the past, and with Christian experience. If any one thing is clear, it is this, that the power of Satan has not as yet been bound. This binding still lies in the future. Satan will not be bound until after Christ's victory over Antichrist, and until after His Second Coming. There is every reason to maintain that this chapter follows the preceding one in chronological order, and that there is no recapitulation here.

Sadler: "All this is evidently in the future.... Now let the reader remember that no matter what meaning—spiritual or literal—we give to this *sealing* and this *chain*, yet, if we are to be guided by Scripture, the abyss is evidently a real, actual place (Luke 8:31). With respect to his deceiving the nations no more, this cannot signify that sin is put an end to, because the nations have not yet risen again in their sinless bodies: so that in each person there yet remains original sin (and sin must involve deception), but there is no longer that combination on the side of evil which it is the especial prerogative of Satan to bring about." Luthardt: "The thousand years of the binding of Satan cannot lie in the past—say, for example, in the time of the German Empire, from Charlemagne 800 A.D. to 1806; for Satan was not then bound, but loose in Rome and elsewhere, and Luther himself caused the Church to sing:

" 'And check the stroke of Pope and Turk.'

Consequently, here a period of the future is meant, in which no longer sin, but Christ and His Word, shall be the controlling power in history, although the obedience shown by all may not be the inner obedience of the heart."

74. The Millennial Kingdom of Christ (20:4–6)

4. And I saw thrones, and they sat upon them, and judgement was given unto them: and *I saw* the souls of them that had been beheaded for the testimony of Jesus, and for the word of God, and such as worshipped not the beast, neither his image, and received not the mark upon their forehead and upon their hand; and they lived, and reigned with Christ a thousand years.

Compare Dan. 7:9, "I beheld till thrones were placed, and one that was ancient of days did sit;" Matt. 19:28, "Ye which have followed me, in the regeneration when the Son of man shall sit on the throne of his glory, ye also shall sit upon twelve thrones, judging the twelve tribes of Israel;" Dan. 7:22, "Until the ancient of days came, and judgment was

298

given to the saints of the Most High; and the time came that the saints possessed the kingdom." John **saw thrones,** where it is not definitely stated, but evidently in heaven, although some would place their thrones on earth. The number of these thrones is not given, probably many, including the thrones for the Apostles. **They sat upon them.** Who these were, we are not expressly told, probably the Apostles, and such saints as are worthy,—possibly those mentioned in this verse as reigning with Christ. **Judgment was given unto them.** The reference can only be to a judicial rule over the nations on the earth during the thousand years, the nature of which we cannot explain. Two special objects are seen in this vision, (1) thrones; and (2) souls, that lived and reigned with Christ. **The souls.** Two classes of souls are here spoken of as *living again* and *reigning* with Christ: (1) all martyrs who were beheaded for Christ's sake; and (2) all martyrs who suffered during the great persecution raging during the times of Antichrist. **They lived.** *They revived, lived again.* Luthardt: "The words can only be understood of a bodily resurrection, but of course in a glorified body." Alford: "I cannot consent to distort words from their plain sense and chronological place in the prophecy, on account of any consideration of difficulty, or any risk of abuses which the doctrine of the millennium may bring with it. Those who lived next to the Apostles, and the whole Church for three hundred years, understood them in the plain literal sense: and it is a strange sight in these days to see expositors who are among the first in reverence of antiquity complacently casting aside the most cogent instance of consensus which primitive antiquity presents. As regards the text itself, no legitimate treatment of it will extort what is known as the spiritual interpretation

299

now in fashion. If in a passage where *two resurrections* are mentioned, where certain *souls lived* at the first, and the rest of the *dead lived* only at the end of a specified period after the first,—if in such a passage the first resurrection may be understood to mean *spiritual* rising with Christ, while the second means *literal* rising from the grave;—then there is an end of all significance in language, and Scripture is wiped out as a definite testimony to anything. If the first resurrection is spiritual, then so is the second, which I suppose none will be hardy enough to maintain; but if the second is literal, then so is the first, which in common with the whole primitive Church and many of the best modern expositors, I do maintain, and receive as an article of faith and hope." **And reigned with Christ.** This passage gives us no foundation for the view that the Lord Himself, with His risen and glorified saints, shall be visibly present on earth during this period. The reigning of the saints with Christ over this earth takes place from heaven. The *thrones* which the Apostle saw are not on earth, but in heaven. In Rev. 4:4 the thrones are in heaven, so also in 11:16, we have the same scene repeated, and 3:21 helps us to determine more definitely the place, "I will give to him to sit down with me in my throne, as I sat down with my Father in his throne." The Father's throne, and Christ's throne is in heaven, and it is best, therefore, to regard these thrones which John saw as in heaven, and the risen saints will therefore reign with Christ *from* heaven, for they partake of His Glory and Kingdom. So also Delitzsch: "Is it conceivable that the glorified Lord will permanently dwell upon the old unglorified earth?... Bengel could not conceive of that; and as little could Jacob Boehme, the German philosopher, whose tendency was

realistic, and whose mind was also given to mystery. I have always preferred the exegesis of Bengel, according to which, Rev. 20:4, 'they lived, and reigned with Christ a thousand years,' indicates a reigning of ascended saints who rule, with Christ, from heaven." Auberlen, who discusses this subject very fully, takes the same view of the reigning of these Risen Saints: "They likewise reign with Christ a thousand years. After having gathered His Church, and after having taken His bride to Himself, Christ returns with her to heaven. Earth is not as yet transfigured, and can, consequently, not be the locality meet for the transfigured Church. But from heaven the saints now rule the earth, whence we may conclude, that one of the glories of the millennium shall consist in the much freer and more vivid communion of the heavenly and earthly churches in particular, and the lower and higher world in general; a type of which state may be seen in the forty days of the Risen Saviour, during which He appeared to His disciples.... In this respect we must view the millennial kingdom as a time of new divine revelations, which reappear after the long pause during the Church-historical period."
A thousand years. This number, as the duration of the millennial kingdom, is peculiar to the Apocalypse. Whether it is to be regarded as denoting with chronological accuracy the duration of the kingdom, or is to be used in its symbolical signification, as denoting that the world will now during a certain definite period be penetrated perfectly by the divine element, will always remain an open question, but there is no reason why we should reject the literal meaning. See also *Excursus* VII. on the *Millennium.*

5. The rest of the dead lived not until the thousand years should be finished. This is the first resurrection.

If we accept the Futurist view that all the believing dead, including the O. T. saints, are raised at the time of the Rapture, when the saints are caught up to meet Christ in the air (1 Thess. 4:15–17),—all this occurring before the tribulation,—then the *first resurrection* refers to the Tribulation Saints alone. The remaining dead are not raised until the day of the Final Judgment, as described in 20:11–15. In the first resurrection here referred to, only the two classes of dead believers take part, in order to reign with Christ during a thousand years. See *Excursus* VIII. on the *First Resurrection.*

6. Blessed and holy is he that hath part in the first resurrection; over these the second death hath no power; but they shall be priests of God and of Christ, and shall reign with him a thousand years.

Those who become partakers of this first resurrection shall be eternally holy and blessed; before the final judgment and their abode in the new heavens and new earth, they shall already, during the thousand years of the Millennium, partake of a regal and priestly glory. They shall not come *into* the judgment (John 5:24), for the *Second death* hath no *authority* over them, but they shall be present at the Judgment (Rom. 14:10; 2 Cor. 5:10), and in some mysterious way even take part in the judgment, for Paul twice asks: "Know ye not that the saints shall judge the world?" "Know ye not that we shall judge angels?" (1 Cor. 6:2, 3). **The second death.** This is "the lake of fire" (19:14), the eternal punishment of the whole man, body and soul united (Matt. 25:46). This does not mean annihilation, the blotting of the soul and body out of existence. See notes on 14:11. **Priests of God.** See notes on 1:6; 5:10. **Shall reign.** See notes on 5:10;

302

20:4; and *Excursus* VII. on the *Millennium.* Sadler: "We are assured by the words of the most Apocalyptic book of the O. T. that angels take a part, of course under God, in the direction of kingdoms (Dan. 10:5–7, 13, 20, 21; 12:1).... And if angels, why not glorified saints? In the few places in which the Son of God speaks of the future state of the saints, He speaks of it as a state of rule, and nothing better brings into exercise the whole intellectual, moral, and spiritual powers of redeemed man than such a state." **A thousand years.** See notes on 20:4. Luthardt: "Here, consequently, is taught the so-called Chiliasm; i. e. the rule of Jesus Christ and His glorified Church of faithful confessors over the rest of mankind, which is to follow the present course of the world and the resurrection of the righteous. By the thousand years is meant a great world-day. Not a fleshly rule (compare *Augsburg Confession*, Art. XVII.), but a spiritual, heavenly reign of peace, and state of blessedness on earth—of which, indeed, inasmuch as it does not pertain to the present order of things, we have no conceptin, nor can we frame any idea. But we may be satisfied that we shall ever be with Christ, and that He will glorify His Church before the world—a doctrine which in the first centuries belongs to orthodoxy, but was allowed to decline subsequently. For, as Bengel says: 'When Christianity had attained, through Constantine, the upper hand in the world, the hope of the future became greatly weakened by the enjoyment of the present.' The doctrine thereby fell into the hands of the fanatics, and was basely perverted."

75. The Final Victory over Satan (20:7–10)

7. And when the thousand years are finished, Satan shall be loosed out of his prison.

After the completion of the Millennium, during which time Satan has been bound, he shall be loosed for a little time. See notes on 20:3. In the providence of God, Satan is once more permitted to turn his demoniacal power against the Church, that the glory of God may be manifested in his irrecoverable overthrow. The reign of the saints with Christ does not cease, and it is highly probable that this final struggle will be as brief as it is fierce.

8. And shall come forth to deceive the nations which are in the four corners of the earth, Gog and Magog, to gather them together to the war: the number of whom is as the sand of the sea.

When Satan is set loose he shall deceive those nations who are furthest removed from the centre of Christ's kingdom, and stir them up in rebellion against Christ and His Church. Now the prophecies of Ezekiel (38 and 39) receive their final and complete fulfilment. Magog in Ezek. 38:2 seems to be a general name for the northern nations, and Gog is their prince. Ever since Ezekiel's time, the names Gog and Magog have been used to designate the enemies of Christ, who shall come up against Jerusalem, in the last day, to destroy it. In the Targum (of Jerusalem) on Num. 11:27 we read: "At the end of the extremity of the days shall Gog and Magog, and their army, come up against Jerusalem; but by the hand of King Messiah shall they fall, and seven years of days shall the children of Israel kindle their fires with their weapons of war" (quoted by Duesterdieck). Gebhardt: "After the course

304

of a thousand years, the personal principle of all ungodliness will be loosed from his prison, and, according to the purpose of God, will again become active on earth; the Devil has still a footing there; evil yet exists, and must show its activity in opposition to God and His kingdom. Christianity has spread and triumphed even to the end of the earth; but there are yet nations who are not subject to it, but who, enslaved and led by the Devil, seek to destroy it."

9. And they went up over the breadth of the earth, and compassed the camp of the saints about, and the beloved city: and fire came down out of heaven, and devoured them.

So large will be the armies of these nations, that in their march they overspread the land of Palestine, and will sweep everything before them, until they surround the armies of the saints encamped round about Jerusalem. Then the final catastrophe, like a flash of lightning, shall suddenly strike them (Ezek. 38:22; 39:6). Jerusalem shall again be rebuilt and is destined yet to play a most glorious part in the history of the kingdom of God on earth. The Jerusalem here spoken of is not yet the *new* Jerusalem, of which we will hear in the next chapter.

10. And the devil that deceived them was cast into the lake of fire and brimstone, where are also the beast and the false prophet; and they shall be tormented day and night for ever and ever (Gr. *unto the ages of the ages*).

The devil. Compare notes on 2:10; 12:9, 12; 20:2. **Deceived.** Now that judgment will overtake the devil, stress is laid upon his peculiar guilt. **Lake of fire.** See notes on 19:20. **Beast and the false prophet.** See notes on 19:20. **Tormented.** See notes on 14:10, 11. *They* shall be tormented; i. e. the devil, the beast, and the false prophet.

The three great enemies of God's kingdom have now been judged and punishment awarded to them. Satan has now been cast into that *Gehenna* of which our Lord declared that it had been "prepared for the devil and his angels" (Matt. 25:41). See also *Excursus* II. on *Hades*.

76. The Final Judgment of the Wicked (20:11–15)

11. And I saw a great white throne, and him that sat upon it, from whose face the earth and the heaven fled away; and there was found no place for them.

The day of judgment and of the final consummation has come. In vision John beholds the awful scene—a *great* throne, *great* corresponding to the glory of the Judge, and *white*, as symbolizing the purity of His justice. He sees the Father sitting on the throne, for the Day of Judgment has now come. Although the Father hath given all judgment to the Son (John 5:22), nevertheless all must receive their judgment before the Father. This does not conflict with Matt. 25:31, for the Son sitteth with the Father on His throne (Rev. 3:21), and there is only one throne, that "of God and of the Lamb" (22:1). **The earth and the heaven fled away.** In 2 Pet. 3:10–12 we have a full statement of the manner in which this occurs, for this passing away of the earth and heaven shall be by fire. The whole description implies that now the final consummation takes place. The heavens and earth of this corruptible world shall be dissolved, and a new heavens and a new earth, glorious and incorruptible, shall appear (2 Peter. 3:13). The old earth and heavens will be completely destroyed, for *there was found no place for them.*

12. And I saw the dead, the great and the small, standing

306

before the throne; and books were opened: and another book was opened, which is *the book* of life: and the dead were judged out of the things which were written in the books, according to their works.

In vision John now sees the Judgment. As the first resurrection referred to believers alone, it seems that this resurrection refers to unbelievers alone. John sees "the rest of the dead" of verse 5, who rose as described in verse 13, standing before the throne. **Books were opened.** Compare Dan. 7:20, "the judgment was set, and the books were opened." In Scripture books are spoken of as the register of all human actions (Ps. 56:8; Mal. 3:16; Matt. 12:37). All these dead are judged according to the words recorded in these books. There are therefore degrees of punishment, as well of reward. In contradiction to the books there is *the book of life,* one book, which contains only the names of those who will become partakers of the eternal blessed life in heaven (20:15). It is highly probable that Hengstenberg and others are correct in maintaining that *the books* are "those of guilt, condemnation, and death," and that "a name cannot be written both in the *books,* and in the *Book* of the Lamb." This then would also favor the view that this judgment refers to unbelievers alone. Milligan: "The *dead* are here the wicked alone; and *the books* contain a record of no deeds but theirs. There is not the slightest indication that *the book of life* was opened for judgment. The only purpose for which it is used is that mentioned in verse 15. It will be observed, moreover, that no *works* are referred to except those of the *wicked.* So far, therefore, from being led by a *vicious literalism* to confine the judgment before us to the wicked, such an interpretation appears to be demanded by a plain

and natural exegesis of the text." The remarks of Faussett are
very suggestive: "The wicked who had died from the time
of Adam to Christ's Second Advent, and all the righteous
and wicked who had died during and after the Millennium,
shall then have their eternal portion assigned to them. The
godly who were transfigured and reigned with Christ during
the Millennium shall also be present, not indeed to have
their portion assigned as if for the first time, but to have
it *confirmed* for ever, and that God's righteousness may be
vindicated in the presence of the assembled universe. The
living saints are not specially mentioned; as these all shall
probably first (before the destruction of the ungodly of v. 9)
be transfigured and caught up with the saints long previously
transfigured; and though present for the confirmation of
their justification by the Judge, shall not then first have their
eternal state assigned to them, but shall sit as assessors with
the Judge." These remarks of Fausset raise two questions,
which the curious are anxious to have answered: First, What
becomes of the wicked who die after the first resurrection,
either during the Millennium or during the rebellion led
by Satan? The answer would be—Their souls descend to
Hades to await their resurrection at the Final Judgment, as
described in the next verse. The second question is, Do
any believers die after the first resurrection, either during
the Millennium or afterwards? Various answers have been
given by Pre-Millennialists, of which one kind is represented
by the remarks of Fausset. Some maintain, however, that
few deaths of believers will occur, and if they should die
they will be immediately glorified, and that before the
passing away of the heavens and the old earth, the living
are transfigured. But nearly all these questions are mainly

matters of speculation, for we know, after all, very little of the nature of the Millennium.

13. And the sea gave up the dead which were in it; and death and Hades gave up the dead which were in them: and they were judged every man according to their works.

All the ungodly dead, whether buried on earth or drowned in the sea, over whom Death had gained his victory, arose. Death and Hades are both personified. See notes on 1:18; 6:8. Hades is the place of Death, and all these souls were in Hades. This is another evidence that the resurrection here is of the wicked alone. See *Excursus* II. on *Hades*. **According to their works.** The constant teaching of Scripture, repeated from verse 12,—the burden of the Judgment. Compare Rom. 2:6; etc.

14. And death and Hades were cast into the lake of fire. This is the second death, *even* the lake of fire.

Death and Hades are here personified, and Hades is regarded as the receiver of the prey of death. See *Excursus* II. on *Hades*. **The lake of fire.** The Gehenna, the final abode of punishment for the wicked. See notes on 20:10. **Second death.** The intensified death, the coming of sinners in their risen bodies to eternal death or perdition (Rev. 17:8, 11). See notes on 2:11; 20:6. There is no final restoration for the unbeliever. The great conflict between heaven and hell, between God and the Devil, finally comes to an end.

The crisis has come, but it ends in an *absolute dualism.* God and Heaven have obtained the victory. The Devil and Hell have been defeated and overcome. But the Devil is not changed, Hell is not purified, nor are they destroyed in the sense of ceasing to exist. The wicked are not annihilated, but after the day of judgment continue eternally in the lake of fire and brimstone. Death for believing and glorified humanity has now been abolished for ever (1 Cor. 15:26); but for unbelieving humanity it exists for ever as the second death, as eternal fire.

15. And if any was not found written in the book of life, he was cast into the lake of fire.

Milligan: "Here, then, is the purpose, and the only one, for which *the book of life* is spoken of as used at the judgment before us. It was searched in order that it might be seen if any one's name was *not* written in it; and he whose name could not be discovered in the pages was cast into the lake of fire."

21

Revelation 21

77. The Vision of the New Heavens and New Earth (21:1–8)

1. And I saw a new heaven and a new earth: for the first heaven and the first earth are passed away; and the sea is no more.

The final judgment has taken place, as well as the final consummation of all things. What follows in these last two chapters refers to the eternal kingdom of God in the new heavens and new earth. The purified and renewed earth has now become the abode of glorified humanity, and the tabernacle of God is with men. Now Isa. 65:17; 66:22, have received their fulfilment. See also 2 Pet. 3:13. Alford: "The vision does not necessarily suppose the annihilation of the old creation, but only its passing away as to its outward and recognizable form, and renewal to a fresh and more glorious one. And though not here stated on the surface, it is evident that the method of renewal is that described in 2 Pet. 3:10–12, namely, a renovation by *fire*. This alone will account for the unexpected and interesting feature here introduced, that the sea exists no longer." Bengel: "It is not a flourishing state of the Church in the last time which John here describes, but he speaks of all things entirely new and perfect for eternity."

2. And I saw the holy city, new Jerusalem, coming down out of heaven from God, made ready as a bride adorned for her husband.

In vision John had seen the new heavens and the new earth, prepared by God as the new and eternal abode for His Redeemed, and now in vision John sees the glorified Church coming down out of heaven from God upon the renewed earth. John sees the glorified Church coming as the bride of the Lamb, but this idea passes over into the identifying of the bride with the holy city, the new Jerusalem, the dwelling-place of the bride. Lange: "The new Jerusalem, as the sum of perfected individuals, is the *city of God;* in its unity, it is the *bride of Christ.*" Bengel: "This new city has no connection with the Millennium, but belongs to the state of perfect renovation and eternity, as is shown by the series of visions, the magnificence of the description, and the opposition to the second death (20:11, 12; 21:1, 2, 5, 8, 9; 22:5)." The description of the holy city, Jerusalem, given in verses 10–27, reproduces in a condensed and transfigured form the corresponding vision of Ezekiel. Hengstenberg: "A threefold Jerusalem is peculiar to the N. T.: (1) The heavenly community of the righteous (Gal. 4:26; Rev. 14:1–5); (2) The Church in her militant state (11:2; 20:9); (3) The New Jerusalem on the renovated earth, as here; after whose descent from heaven the two other forms are seen no more. In this *third* form Jerusalem combines the heavenly character of the *first* and the earthly existence of the *second*." On *the holy city* Faussett comments: "There is no longer merely a Paradise as in Eden, no longer a mere garden, but now *the city of God* on earth, costlier, statelier, and more glorious, but at the same time the result of labor and pains such as had not to be expended by man in dressing the primitive garden of Eden."

3. And I heard a great voice out of the throne saying, Behold, the tabernacle of God is with men, and he shall dwell with them, and they shall be his peoples, and God himself shall be with them, *and be* their God.

This voice, coming from the throne of God, describes the blessed condition of the glorified humanity on the renovated earth, for God Himself shall then dwell with His people, composed not only of the Jews—as when in symbol He dwelt in an earthly tabernacle among His chosen people, on the old earth—but now including also the nations (Gentiles), for they also shall partake of the glory of God (21:23, 24). Wordsworth: "This realization *began* when the Son of God came down from heaven and *tabernacled* in our flesh (John 1:14). It will be consummated in the new Jerusalem, as had been pre-announced in the *sixth seal*, the language of which supplies the best exposition of the present vision." See 7:15–17. C. a Lapide: "As a king is with his people, a father with his children, a master with his disciples, so God will be for ever with the blessed in Heaven, refreshing, feeding, gladdening, blessing them." On this verse compare Rev. 20:11, 12; Ezek. 37:27, 28.

4. And he shall wipe away every tear from their eyes; and death shall be no more; neither shall there be mourning, nor crying, nor pain any more: the first things are passed away.

John now describes the eternal consolation of the re-deemed. All this is revealed to encourage believers who are yet on earth. **Every tear.** Compare Isa. 25:8. **Death.** See notes on 20:14. **Mourning.** Compare Isa. 35:10. **Crying.** Compare Isa. 65:19. Milligan: "From all sorrow, whether sharp or dull; from all burdens, whether proceeding from the body or the mind, the dwellers in the New Jerusalem shall be for ever free. These trials belonged to the *first things*, to the old earth; and the old earth, the first things, have passed away."

5. And he that sitteth on the throne said, Behold, I make all things new. And he saith, Write: for these words are faithful and true.

He who sat on the throne is the same before whom the Judgment took place (see notes on 20:11). It is possible that the words, *Write ... true,* may have been spoken by an angel, but it is probably best to regard God Himself as the speaker. He assures John that His *words are faithful and true,* that "the new heavens and the new earth are the end towards which He has been always working" (Milligan). On *faithful and true,* see notes on 3:14. On the words, *I make all things new,* BLUNT remarks: "This New Creation may be viewed chiefly with regard to the bodies and souls of men and their spiritual work. (1) The *Body* will be re-created in such a manner that it shall be incorruptible (1 Cor. 15:50). Such bodies as are suitable for the work of this world will not be suited for the immediate Presence-chamber of the all-glorious and all-holy God.... In the new heaven and the new earth we cannot imagine hunger, thirst, and the capacities and desires which are not characteristic of bodily life as it now is to have any place ... for He 'shall fashion anew the body of our

314

humiliation, that it may be conformed to the body of His glory' (Phil. 3:21). (2) The *Soul* of man will also be re-created in such a manner that it may be fitted for the highest form of spiritual life, that of uninterrupted communion with God by unhindered consciousness of His presence.... From the perpetual shining upon the soul of that light which no man in his mortal condition can approach unto, there must ensue a never-ceasing growth of saintliness and intelligence. (3) The *spiritual work* of man will also be renovated; its one object and purpose will be the worship and contemplation of God; and whether or not adoration be the sole work of a future life, it is undoubtedly the typical form of the spiritual work in which all the redeemed will be engaged. The occupations of the saints will be in accordance with their new condition, occupations which will engage them wholly in a service of obedience and of adoration." In general agreement with this presentation we find the words of our Saviour: "The sons of this world marry, and are given in marriage: but they that are accounted worthy to attain to that world, and the resurrection from the dead, neither marry, nor are given in marriage; for neither can they die any more: for they are equal unto the angels; and are sons of God, being sons of the resurrection" (Luke 20:34–36; also Matt. 22:30; Mark 12:25). This teaching of Christ holds true, not only during the Millennium, but also after the Final Consummation, in the new heavens and new earth.

6. And he said unto me, They are come to pass. I am the Alpha and the Omega, the beginning and the end. I will give unto him that is athirst of the fountain of the water of life freely.

It matters very little whether we regard the Father as

315

speaking, or Christ, probably the latter, for the throne is that "of God and of the Lamb" (22:1). **They are come to pass.** *All things* determined by God, the passing away of *the first things* (21:4), the making of all things *new* (21:5). The end to which all things pointed is reached. **The Alpha.** See notes on 1:8. **The beginning.** See notes on 1:17; 2:8. **That is athirst.** It is true, as Milligan maintains, that these words are neither a call nor a promise to those in search of the fountain of life, but are spoken rather of those who have already drunk of the living water, nevertheless, we may regard these words, including verses 7 and 8, as written for the warning and encouragement of believers yet in this life. Compare also 22:13–17. Fausset: "This is added lest any should despair of attaining to this exceeding weight of glory. In our present state we may drink of the stream, then we shall drink at the *Fountain.* Even in heaven our drinking at the Fountain shall be God's *gratuitous* gift." Compare also Isa. 55:1. Bengel: "Twice it is said in this book, 'It is done.' First at the completion of the wrath of God (16:17), and *here* at the making of all things new."

7. He that overcometh shall inherit these things; and I will be his God and he shall be my son.

Overcometh. See notes on 2:7, 11, 17. **These things.** The glories of the New Jerusalem. This inheritance includes all the joys of the eternal life in the new heavens and new earth. **His God ... my son.** Compare 21:3. The perfect fulfilment of Lev. 26:12; 2 Sam, 7:24,—now fulfilled not only for the house of David, but for all the Redeemed.

8. But for the fearful, and unbelieving. and abominable, and murderers, and fornicators, and sorcerers, and idolaters, and all liars, their part *shall be* in the lake that burneth with fire and brimstone; which is the second death.

316

In the preceding verses we have had a description of the blessed condition of the righteous in the new heavens and earth, and now, in contrast with this, and as a terrible warning, we have a brief statement of the punishment that shall befall the ungodly. First the ungodly are described in general terms, and then classified according to the particular sins which they commit. The sins specified are much the same as those mentioned in the sixth Trumpet (9:21). **Fearful.** *Cowards*, who are afraid to do their duty. **Unbelieving,** The *unfaithful* are also included. **Abominable.** This means more than "polluted with idols,"—it includes the foul and abominable sins committed in the licentious rites practised in idol-worship. **The lake that burneth with fire.** See notes on 20:14. **The second death.** See notes on 2:11; 20:6, 14.

78. The Vision of the New Jerusalem (21:9–27)

9. And there came one of the seven angels who had the seven bowls, who were laden with the seven last plagues; and he spake with me, saying, Come hither, I will shew thee the bride, the wife of the Lamb,

One of these seven angels had shown to John the vision of the great harlot, Babylon the Great (17:1–3). Compare the great contrast between these two visions. In 17:1–3 the woman represents the worldly city, Babylon the Great, and here the bride, the wife of the Lamb, is the holy city Jerusalem. Milligan: "The combination of the terms *bride* and *the Lamb's wife* is remarkable. The Church is not only espoused but married to her Lord, yet she remains for ever in a virgin purity."

317

10. And he carried me away in the Spirit to a mountain great and high, and shewed me the holy city Jerusalem, coming down out of heaven from God.

Note the sharp contrast between the scene of this vision and that of 17:3. There it was a *wilderness*, here a *mountain, great and high.* Compare the parallel vision in Ezek. 40:1, 2. Alford: "The city must not be conceived of as *on* or covering the mountain, but as seen descending to a spot close by it," so also in Ezek. 40:2, whether we read *by which* (A. V.), or *whereon* (R. V.). The *height* of the mountain "assures the seer of the complete view of the city spread out before him, which at all events does not lie upon the mountain" (Duesterdieck). Here in 21:9–27 we have a closer view of the holy city, a glimpse of which John saw in 21:2. It is probably best, with Duesterdieck, to understand this in such a way, that while the city is descending from heaven to earth, John is carried away in the Spirit by the angel to the mountain, and thence gazes upon the holy city lying before him. Some, relying on Ezek. 40:2; Isa. 2:2; Heb. 12:22, think that the city itself was situated upon "the mountain," or at least upon some outlying peaks. **Coming down out of heaven.** Fausset: "Even in the millennium, the earth will not be a suitable abode for transfigured saints, who, therefore shall then reign in heaven over the earth. But after the renewal of the earth at the close of the millennium and judgment, they shall *descend* from heaven to dwell on an earth assimilated to heaven itself." Zuellig gives us an interesting analysis of this whole vision: "The interpreting Angel shows the Seer the new City of God,—its appearance as a whole (verses 10, 11); its walls with their gates and foundations (12–14); its measurements (15–17); its special features also,—such as its magnificence

(18–21), its unique character (22, 23), the life-movement within it (24–27)."

11. Having the glory of God: her light (Gr. *luminary*) was like unto a stone most precious, as it were a jasper stone, clear as crystal.

The glory of God, His abiding presence, did lighten the city; for it hath no need of the sun, neither of the moon to shine upon it (21:23). Her *light* is the Lamb, for "the lamp thereof is the Lamb" (21:23). Compare Isa. 60:19. This brilliancy, the most glorious conceivable, likened unto the crystalline clearness of the jasper stone, probably the diamond (see notes on 4:3), irradiates the whole city and makes the deepest impression upon John. There shall be no night in the City of God (21:25; 22:5). Lee: "Here begins the description of the city, following Ezek. 48:30–35. In verses 11–23 are described the structure and plan; in verses 24–27 what takes place within its walls; in 22:1–5 the felicity of the life within it."

12. Having a wall great and high; having twelve gates, and at the gates twelve angels; and names written thereon, which are *the names* of the twelve tribes of the children of Israel.

The description of the city and of its gates is based upon Ezek. 48:30–35. The wall is a type of the absolute security of the heavenly city. The *gates* were twelve in number, arranged like the gates of the encampment of Israel around the Tabernacle. These *gates*, Greek *portals*, include the gate-towers under which the traveller passes to this day into many Eastern cities. The *twelve angels* typify the heavenly protection bestowed on the people of God. Upon the gates, as on the stones of the ephod (Ex. 28:9), and on the breastplate (Ex. 39:14), were written the names of the Twelve Tribes

319

(Ezek. 48:31), as representing the whole people of God. Lee: "Each *gate* bears the name of one of the Twelve Tribes. It is thus denoted that the Church made perfect is no confused multitude, but an organized body, each member has its special vocation and peculiar glory." The gates being never shut (21:25) imply perfect liberty and peace. Sadler: "The names of the Patriarchs occurring here startle us, seeing that in the citizenship of this city there is neither Jew nor Greek—all are one in Christ, and so we should have supposed there would be in such a city no remembrance of Reuben or Simeon, or Levi or Judah, but God's thoughts are not our thoughts. In some way unknown to us, and which all will acknowledge to be just and right, there will be an association of the Israel of God with the former Israel."

13. On the east were three gates; and on the north three gates; and on the south three gates: and on the west three gates.

In Ezekiel the gates on the east are those of Joseph, Benjamin, and Dan (48:32); on the north, those of Reuben, Judah, and Levi (48:31); on the south, those of Simeon, Issachar, and Zebulun (48:33); on the west, those of Gad, Asher, and Naphtali (48:34). In Num. 2:1–31 the order of encampment is different. See notes on Rev. 7:5–8. Some commentators see in this fact that the city faces to each of the four quarters of heaven, an emblem of the universality or œcumenical character of the New Jerusalem.

14. And the wall of the city had twelve foundations, and on them twelve names of the twelve apostles of the Lamb.

It seems that the wall around the city was in twelve sections, each of which was supported by a visible foundation, the splendor of which could be seen (verses 19, 20), as well as

320

the inscriptions thereon. Four of these foundation stones were evidently the four corners of the wall. On these foundation stones the names of the Twelve Apostles were written, because they by their doctrine founded the Church, and it rests upon them as on an immovable foundation (Eph. 2:20) (after Calovius). Those who raise the question whether the name of Matthias or of Paul is substituted for that of Judas altogether miss the significance of this symbol. Some think that we are to understand these foundations as twelve courses of stones, each course encompassing the city, and constituting one foundation (21:19). It does not follow from this verse that the writer was not himself one of the twelve Apostles. Blunt calls attention to the fact that "the continuity and unity of the Church of God are symbolized by the names of the twelve tribes on the gates and those of the twelve Apostles on the walls; this being analogous to the unity symbolized by the four and twenty elders."

15. And he that spake with me had for a measure a golden reed to measure the city, and the gates thereof, and the wall thereof.

The angel wishes to give John a clear idea of the great size of the city by measuring it. The reed was *golden* because of the splendor of the objects to be measured. Now follows the measurement of the city (verse 16), the wall (17–20), and the gates (21). Sadler: "What is intended by this elaborate measuring? Evidently, I think, to impress upon us that the things revealed are not spiritual visions, beautiful dreams, signifying some spiritual grace and moral character in those who, being pure spirits, need no local habitation, but the exact contrary."

16. And the city lieth foursquare, and the length thereof

is as great as the breadth: and he measured the city with the reed, twelve thousand furlongs: the length and the breadth and the height thereof are equal.

The city forms a perfect square. It is difficult to decide whether the entire circuit of the city was twelve thousand stadia, three thousand to a side, or that the city was an enormous cube, which measured twelve thousand stadia in length, in breadth, and in height. The last is the plain meaning of the text. If we would interpret this literally it would mean that the city was about 1,400 miles long, 1,400 miles wide, and 1,400 miles high. Probably Plumner is correct when he remarks: "The plain meaning seems to be that the city forms a vast cube, and this is typical of its perfect nature. The account given is that of a vision, and not of a reality, and therefore there is no need to attempt to reduce the enormous dimensions given here, as is done by some writers." No doubt there is a reference to the Holy of Holies, which was also cubical in shape. The original of the symbolism seems to be Ezek. 48:16. Fausset: "The city being measured implies the entire consecration of every part, all things being brought up to the most exact standard of God's holy requirements, and also God's accurate guardianship henceforth of even the most minute parts of His Holy City.... The stupendous height, length, and breadth, being exactly alike, imply its faultless symmetry, transcending in glory all our most glowing conceptions." Williams: "*Equal* every way in *length* and *breadth* and *height*, as setting forth the love of God infinite and perfect on every side (Eph. 3:18)."

17. And he measured the wall thereof, a hundred and forty and four cubits, *according to* the measure of a man, that is, of an angel.

Probably the thickness of the wall is now given. In the measuring, that of the angel is the same as if a man had taken the measure. Milligan: "It is hardly possible to think that we have here the *height* of the wall.... The wall is a part of the city as strictly as the foundations are, and is itself, like them, radiant with the light which shines forth from the city as a whole. It seems better, therefore, to think here of the *breadth* of the wall. Its length and height had been measured, and its thickness is now added, to complete the description of its strength." This may be the case. Lange: "The figure of the wall approaches the idea of Zechariah (2:5), 'For I, saith the Lord, will be unto her a wall of fire round about, and I will be the glory in the midst of her.' The prodigious extent of the city is expressive of the ideal fact that it extends, with unseen limits, through the universe, and towers up into the height of eternity; that it belongs to Heaven, whence it has descended to earth." Burger comments: "The sacred *twelve*, the *signature* of the Church, which we have already met in the *Twelve* gates, the *Twelve* foundations, the *Twelve* thousand stadia, is here multiplied by itself. The *wall* is intended for the protection of the city; and its true defence consists in this, that it is the City of the perfected Church of Christ, of which the *number* is 144." Williams; "The *measuring* of the *wall* must be of its thickness.... But everything by multiples of the Sacred Twelve."

18. And the building of the wall thereof was jasper: and the city was pure gold, like unto pure glass.

Duesterdieck calls attention to the fact that in verses 18–21 the splendor of the holy city "is described with the greatest glory whereof human fantasy is capable." The material used in the building of the wall was *jasper* (see notes on 4:3), and that for the city itself was *pure gold*, but not of the kind known now on earth, but far surpassing this in splendor, for it is *transparent* gold. Milligan: "*Pure gold*, the most precious metal known, but in this case transfigured and glorified, for it was *like unto pure glass.*"

19. The foundations of the wall of the city were adorned with all manner of precious stones. The first foundation was jasper; the second, sapphire; the third, chalcedony; the fourth, emerald.

Foundations. See 21:14. **Adorned.** These precious stones were not merely set upon the foundations, but it seems the foundations *consisted* of them. **Jasper.** Probably the diamond. See notes on 4:3. **Sapphire.** Probably the modern *lapis lazuli*, of a clear blue color, and very precious. **Chalcedony.** Probably an agate, sky-blue, with stripes of other colors, brought from the mines of Chalcedon. **Emerald.** The same as the modern stone, of a green color peculiarly pleasing to the eye. See notes on 4:3. Lange: "The general symbolic significance lies in the *nature* of the precious stones, and also, particularly, in their *colors.*" Wordsworth: "Some ancient expositors have proceeded to distinguish the symbolical meaning of these several jewels as follows: *jasper*, an emblem of the brightness of faith; *sapphire*, of hope; *chalcedony*, the flame of love. Their meaning may be more fully revealed hereafter in the Heavenly City itself. It is now enough to know that the City is adorned with *every precious stone;* that nothing is wanting in the Church for her growth in grace here and for her everlasting glory hereafter."

20. The fifth, sardonyx; the sixth, sardius; the seventh, chrysolite; the eighth, beryl; the ninth, topaz; the tenth, chrysoprase; the eleventh, jacinth; the twelfth, amethyst.

On this verse compare Ezek. 28:13. **Sardonyx.** A kind of *onyx*, valued for its use in engraving into cameos. **Sardius.** Probably our *carnelian* (see notes on 4:3). **Chrysolite.** A variety of the gem known as the topaz, of yellow color. Some have suggested that it is identical with the modern amber. **Beryl.** A variety of emerald, of a bluish-green color, like the pure sea. **Topaz.** Our topaz is yellow and transparent, but the topaz of the ancients seems to have been of a yellowish-green color. **Chrysoprase.** Probably a variety of the emerald, of a yellowish pale-green hue. **Jacinth.** Probably a stone of yellow amber color. **Amethyst.** Probably the purple stone now known by that name. Milligan: "Two things are especially noteworthy in regard to these precious stones when they are taken as a whole. (1) All are precious, fitly representing the splendor of the celestial city. (2) All are different from each other, though they blend into a harmonius unity." The stones here mentioned are nearly the same as the twelve in the breastplate of the High Priest (Ex. 28:17–20)." Sadler: "It is impossible to attempt to give a separate spiritual or moral meaning to each of these foundation stones, though we may be sure that they represent every spiritual grace bestowed upon God's faithful servants.... Equally impossible is it to assign to each of these stones the name of an Apostle.... The one thing to keep in mind is that these stones are the most precious things of the earth; they are as rare as costly, and are assigned as the foundations of the city in order to illustrate how God builds it up with what must be new creations of His power."

21. And the twelve gates were twelve pearls; each one of the several gates was of one pearl: and the street of the city was pure gold, as it were transparent glass.

This whole description only emphasizes the surpassing splendor of the city. We are not to think of only one street, for a city so large, and with so many gates, must have many streets, and all are of pure transparent gold.

22. And I saw no temple therein: for the Lord God, the Almighty, and the Lamb, are the temple thereof.

The inhabitants of the holy city need no fixed places of worship, for the Lord God the Almighty and the Lamb are ever present with them. The glory of God fills the New Jerusalem, and the City itself is the bride of the Lamb. The people of God dwell in His presence, ever worshipping and adoring Him. See notes on 21:3. Lee: "The City is in form a perfect cube, like the Holy of Holies in the Temple of Jerusalem. The entire City is now that which the Holy of Holies had formerly been—the locality of the immediate presence of God." Boyd-Carpenter: "In Ezekel's vision the vast and splendid proportions of the Temple formed a conspicuous part: its gigantic proportions declared it to be figurative (Ezek. 48:8–20); but the present vision passes on to a higher state of things. *I saw no temple*: Ezekel's vision declared that the literal temple would be replaced by a far more glorious spiritual temple." Williams: "In the vision of Heaven throughout the Apocalypse, the temple and the temple service has supplied the figures, as denoting that it spoke of the Church as yet militant on earth before the final judgment; but this has now ceased, the temple is no more, there is none seen in Heaven."

23. And the city hath no need of the sun, neither of the moon, to shine upon it: for the glory of God did lighten it, and the lamp thereof *is* the Lamb.

Such is the glorious brilliancy of the glory of God and of

Christ that all other light in comparison is without lustre. See notes on 21:11. Compare Isa. 60:19, 20. Lee: "The glory of God is the Sun which illumines the New Jerusalem; and His light is reflected from the Lamb, who is 'the brightness,'—'the effulgence,'—'the reflexion,' of the Father's glory (Heb. 1:3)." Sadler: "In the intense splendor and joy of that city of light, the remembrance of Him who was 'led as a *lamb* to the slaughter' gives depth and fulness to its joy."

24. And the nations shall walk amidst the light thereof: and the kings of the earth do bring their glory into it.

This description is based entirely upon the language of Old Testament prophecy. Isaiah prophesies of this when he says: "Nations shall come to thy light, and kings to the brightness of thy rising; thy gates also shall be open continually; they shall not be shut day nor night; that men may bring unto thee the wealth of the nations, and their kings led with them; the sun shall be no more thy light by day; neither for brightness shall the moon give light unto thee; but the Lord shall be unto thee an everlasting light, and thy God thy glory" (60:3, 11, 19).

We are not to interpret this as if besides the glorified saints in the holy city there shall still be dwelling on the renewed earth, nations, organized under kings, who shall, from time to time, visit the Holy City and bring their treasures unto her, and be saved (22:2) by means of the influence of the heavenly city, as Alford suggests. Some would also refer this whole section (21:9–27) to the period of the Millennium, but as to this question, there can be only one answer. This holy city which John saw coming down out of heaven from God (21:10) is the same city which is referred to in 21:2, and belongs to the new heavens and new earth of 21:1. The final

327

consummation has taken place, and on this renewed earth there shall be no other inhabitants save the glorified saints, which compose the Holy City Jerusalem, even the bride, the wife of the Lamb (21:9). Any other interpretation is contrary to the whole context, and belongs to the crudities of exegesis. This verse (24), from the prophetic standpoint of the time of the vision, portrays the blessed fact that Gentiles also shall be among the glorified saints of that New Jerusalem, and among them shall be some of the greatest of earth, even those who in this earthly life had ruled as kings. The interpretation of Duesterdieck is the correct one: "In the tone and language of the ancient prophets, John describes the people who are to find entrance into the future city. In general, as is said in verse 27 in a decisive way, they are only such as are written in the Lamb's book of life; but here, in verses 24–26, the Gentiles are expressly designated as those who, according to the ancient prophecies, are to find admission into the city. The Gentiles, just as the Jews receive full citizenship in the new Jerusalem, and, in like manner, participate in the blessed glory of the holy city." This interpretation is not in any way affected, even if we should maintain that Isa. 60:3, 11, will receive their fulfilment, in a certain manner, already in the Millennium. Fausset: *"The kings of the earth, who once had regard only to their own glory, having been converted, now in the new Jerusalem do bring their glory into it to lay it down at the feet of their God and Lord."* It is surprising to what extremes some students of prophecy are led. They see things that the prophets never saw, and expound most definitely and positively what the apostles themselves did not understand. Like Dante they describe the future with the accuracy of eyewitnesses and ear-witnesses.

It is one thing to maintain that there will be nations on earth, and a perpetuation of the race, during the Millennium, for that period still on earth belongs to the Militant Church, the glorified saints reigning with Christ, from heaven, over the earth,—but it is quite a different matter to teach that there shall be nations on the renovated earth, outside of the New Jerusalem, and that there shall be a perpetuation of humanity, by the propagation of a holy race, after the final consummation, and after the appearance of the new heavens and new earth, wherein dwelleth righteousness. There is no Scripture foundation whatever for the view suggested by some that nations shall still dwell on the renewed earth, outside of the New Jerusalem, and not inhabitants thereof, and "that, even after the new creation, the human race is to be continued (ever propagating a holy seed, such as would have been begotten had Adam never sinned), under the government of the glorified Church" dwelling in the New Jerusalem.

25. And the gates thereof shall in no wise be shut by day (for there shall be no night there).

The reason why the gates of the New Jerusalem are always open is because it is always day. An emblem of peace and security. This prophetically also implies the readiness with which the Gentiles are admitted into the kingdom, both before and during the Millennium, up to the final consummation.

26. And they shall bring the glory and the honour of the nations into it.

They need not necessarily refer to the *kings* of verse 24. See notes. The verb is used impersonally. All these are among those whose names are found "written in the Lamb's Book of Life" (21:17; 20:15), before the final day of judgment. The New Jerusalem possesses for ever the glory and the honor of the Gentiles and the kings of the earth, converted before the final day of judgment.

27. And there shall in no wise enter into it anything unclean, or he that maketh an abomination and a lie: but only they which are written in the Lamb's book of life.

Just as in the last three verses, we have a prophetic statement describing the persons who shall find admission into the Holy City, so now we have in this verse a definite statement describing those who shall not find admission. And it is definitely affirmed that only those whose names were found written in the book of life before the final judgment can be admitted. It is thus evident that *the nations* of verse 24 are among the redeemed, and that our interpretation of that verse is the correct one. Blunt: "This verse may be said to be retrospective, referring to the times preceding the last judgment, since all evil was then destroyed."

Lee: "In the picture here given of the New Jerusalem we have once more before us the descriptions given in Isa. 60, and in Ezek. 40–48. St. John, however, follows the order in Ezekiel, who, after his account of Gog and Magog, exhibits, in vision, the Holy City and the Temple, and the return to it of God's glory."

22

Revelation 22

79. The Paradise of God (22:1–5)

1. And he showed me a river of water of life, bright as crystal, proceeding out of the throne of God and of the Lamb.

In this Paradise of God "there is a river, the streams whereof make glad the city of God" (Ps. 46:4), here called the *water of life.* The whole description is based upon Ezek. 47:1–12; Zech. 14:8. Compare Gen. 2:10; Joel 3:18. This river proceedeth from one and the same throne (3:21). In John 7:38, 39, Christ speaks of "rivers of living water," and John remarks "this spake he of the Spirit, which they that believed on him were to receive," and so many commentators think that we have here a reference to the Holy Ghost. But we need not take it here in a purely spiritual sense. Lange: "It denotes the spiritual-corporeal life-power which, as an eternal renewing power, ensures the imperishability and vital freshness of the new world (Ezek. 47:1; Zech. 14:8). The properties of the *river of paradise,* which operated as a purely

331

natural blessing (Gen. 2), and those of the *spiritual fountain of healing*, first promised by the prophets, and subsequently opened in Christ, are united in this river.... As the *trees of life* are ensured by this eternally clear river, so the river is ensured by the Divine throne itself." Blunt: "Water so constantly signifies the grace of God and the work of God the Holy Ghost (Isa. 55:1; John 7:37–39), that it cannot be doubted its signification here is the same also; the grace of God still flowing to His redeemed people as the means for renewing their spiritual life day by day."

2. In the midst of the street thereof, and on this side of the river and on that was the tree (or, *a tree*) of life, bearing twelve *manner* of fruits, yielding its fruit every month: and the leaves of the tree were for the healing of the nations.

Compare Ezek. 47:7, 12, "upon the bank of the river were very many trees on the one side and on the other.... On this side and on that side, shall grow every tree for meat, whose leaf shall not wither, neither shall the fruit thereof fail: it shall bring forth new fruit every month, because the waters thereof issue out of the sanctuary: and the fruit thereof shall be for meat, and the leaf thereof for healing." John seems to see the main street of the Holy City through which the river is flowing. On both banks of the river he sees the trees of life—a mass of trees, the fruit of which serve the blessed for food. The Greek does not say *the tree* of life, but *tree* of life, and it is best to regard *tree* as collective. Duesterdieck correctly remarks: "The expression designates the entire mass of trees in general. In eternity, the continually growing fruits of the tree of life serve the blessed for food." Just as it is implied that the fruits of the tree of life are for the nourishment of the inhabitants of the new Jerusalem in general, so it is stated that the leaves of the tree are especially for the converted Gentiles who are among the glorified saints. Duesterdieck very clearly brings out the meaning: "The expression *for the healing of the nations* is as little to be pressed, in the sense that a still present sickness of the heathen were presupposed, as it is to be inferred that the tears which God will wipe away from the blessed (21:4) are the sign of pains still endured; but as the tears which are wept because of earthly sorrow are wiped away in eternal life, so the healing leaves of the tree of life serve for the healing of the sickness from which the heathen have suffered in their earthly life, but shall suffer no longer in the new Jerusalem. If they were previously hungry and thirsty, now they are also to be satisfied; if they were previously blind, miserable, and without the power of life, now they are to share in the enjoyment of all glory, holiness, and blessedness." Sadler: "According to all analogy of God's dealings, the various forms of life have to be sustained by nourishment, and here God provides the water of life as well as the fruit of the tree of life to sustain the eternal life of His people." **Bearing twelve** *manner* **of fruits** or *twelve crops of fruit.* "Signifying," notes Ebrard, "the ever new enjoyments of the Blessed." The idea is rather that of continuous nourishment than of variety of blessings.

3. And there shall be no curse any more; and the throne of God and of the Lamb shall be therein: and his servants shall do him service.

Better as in the margin of R. V., *there shall be no more anything accursed,* for everything evil has been judged, and punishment has been meted out (20:15). Compare Zech. 14:11. Nothing evil can come into the city, for within it are found only the throne of God and of the Lamb and

333

the glorified saints, the servants of God, who do His good pleasure.

4. And they shall see his face; and his name *shall be* on their foreheads.

For they shall be so near God, in His glorious Presence. **Name ... foreheads.** See notes on 3:12; 14:1. Blunt: "Beyond all the blessedness which belongs to the mystical presence of God Incarnate in the Church militant, and His visible presence in Paradise, there is yet further reserved for the glorified people of God that they will be admitted to His immediate Presence and have the Beatific Vision of His unveiled glory. Thus will the pilgrimage of the saints be ended in a restored Paradise, where the voice of God will be heard as it was heard by our first parents before the Fall, and where there will be a more glorious privilege than that of Paradise, that of 'seeing God as He is.' "

5. And there shall be night no more; and they need no light of lamp, neither light of sun; for the Lord God shall give them light: and they shall reign for ever and ever (Gr. *unto the ages of the ages*).

Compare notes on 21:23, 25. **They shall reign.** In a far higher sense than during the Millennium. They sit down with their Lord in His throne, even as He overcame, and sat down with His Father in His throne (3:21). Sadler: "Over whom shall they reign? Perhaps over countless worlds which God has created, and will create. Again, let us remember that the one great distinctive employment of those who have overcome will be reigning. An employment which will exercise throughout eternity their highest and best faculties."

With this verse the Apocalypse proper (4:1–22:5) comes to a close.

334

80. An Assurance of the Truth of the Apocalypse (22:6, 7)

6. And he said unto me, These words are faithful and true: and the Lord, the God of the spirits of the prophets, sent his angel to shew unto his servants the things which must shortly come to pass.

The angel, probably the one mentioned in 1:1, now informs John that he can rely that the visions he has seen will surely come to pass. There is an absolute certainty that the testimony here vouchsafed about the future is trustworthy and true. See also, 3:14; 19:11; 21:5. The angel evidently refers to the whole of the Apocalypse. The same God who worked upon *the spirits of the prophets*, who spake from God, being moved by the Holy Ghost (2 Pet. 1:21), also sent His angel to reveal these things to John. See notes on 1:1. It is best by the *spirits* of the prophets to understand the *spirit* of each prophet, which God inspires and guides by His divine spirit.

We come now to the concluding part of the Apocalypse, and the practical lessons of the book are now enforced. There is a close correspondence between this Epilogue and the Introduction. Bengel seems to have the true idea of this Epilogue when he remarks: "There is a wonderful disagreement between interpreters respecting the distribution of the speeches in this Epilogue. But if my interpretation pleases any one, there speaks—the angel (22:6), Jesus (7), John, respecting his own action, and his correction by the angel (8, 9). Again, in the same order, the angel (10, 11), Jesus (12–17), John (18, 19), John and Jesus, and again John (20, 21)."

7. And behold, I come quickly. Blessed is he that keep eth

335

the word of the prophecy of this book.

Alford thinks the speech now passes into the words of Christ Himself reported by the angel. At least we must insist that the first part of the verse are the words of Christ. **I come quickly.** So also in 22:12, 20. See 3:11. **The prophecy of this book.** Probably spoken by the angel. The command given in 1:11, 19, is now supposed to have been carried out. See also notes on 1:3. Williams: "The expression *I come quickly* intimates the shortness of the time, in the sight of God, between the first and second coming of our Lord; and of the space in which all these things occur."

81. The Testimony of John Himself (22:8, 9)

8. And I John am he that heard and saw these things. And when I heard and saw, I fell down to worship before the feet of the angel which shewed me these things.

John now bears witness to the reality of the visions which he has seen. The reference is to all the events narrated in the Apocalypse. **I fell down to worship.** Mulligan: "Once before (19:10) he had done the same thing, and had been corrected for it. We need not wonder that he should do it again. Such had been the glory of the revelations that a mistake of this kind might easily be made more than once." It may be possible, however, that there is no repetition of the act of worship, but that now at the close of the whole vision John refers again to the event recorded in 19:10.

9. And he saith unto me, See thou do it not: I am a fellow-servant with thee and with thy brethren the prophets, and with them which keep the words of this book: worship God.

See notes on 19:10. The words are almost the same save

that here the thought is added that the angel is a fellow-servant of God, just as *believers* themselves are. Blunt: "The words of the angel also confirm those of St. Paul respecting angels: 'Are they not all ministering spirits, sent forth to do service for the sake of them that shall inherit salvation?' (Heb. 1:14), for he declares himself to be a fellow-servant of the Apostle, of his brethren the prophets, and of all the faithful who shall keep the words of the book." Sadler: "This incident is very decisive against anything approaching to saint or angel worship, but it yields a still deeper lesson suited to our times, which is this, that the best, the most devout, the holiest of men may be betrayed into thus falling." Fausset; "Rapturous emotion, gratitude and adoration at the prospect of the Church's future glory transport Him out of Himself, so as all but to fall into an unjustifiable act."

82. The Final Message of the Angel (22:10, 11)

10. And he saith unto me, Seal not up the words of the prophecy of this book; for the time is at hand.

To Daniel the directions were given to seal up the book, even to the time of the end (Dan. 12:4, 9), because the vision belonged *to many days to come* (Dan. 8:26). But here the words are not to be sealed up, *for the time is at hand* (1:3). Duesterdieck: "The nearer the time is, the more the churches need warning and consolation with respect to what is contained in this revelation."

11. He that is unrighteous, let him do unrighteousness still: and he that is filthy, let him be made filthy still: and he that is righteous, let him do righteousness still: and he that is holy, let him be made holy still.

Alford brings out the meaning very clearly: "The saying has solemn irony in it: the time is *so* short, that there is hardly room for change—the lesson conveyed in its depth is 'change while there is time.' " Compare Matt. 26:45, "Sleep on now, and take your rest; behold, the hour is at hand;" also Ezek. 20:39, "Go ye, serve every one his idols, and hereafter also, if ye will not hearken unto me."Hengstenberg: "If men will not sanctify Him, He will sanctify Himself upon them. If they will have it so, let it be so;—if it is right in their view, so it is also in God's." Fausset: "The punishment of sin is sin, the reward of holiness is holiness. Eternal punishment is not so much an arbitrary law as a result necessarily following in the very nature of things, as the fruit results from the bud. No worse punishment can God lay on ungodly men than to give them up to themselves." The exhortation to the righteous is probably best explained in the way that Sadler suggests: "No matter how short the time is, slacken not in your efforts to preserve righteousness and holiness. The Lord has not come yet; take care that when He comes you may be found of Him as He would have you to be."

83. The Testimony of Jesus (22:12–17)

12. Behold, I come quickly; and my reward is with me, to render to each man according as his work is.

Addressed to believers, for their encouragement. Compare also Isa. 40:10; 62:11. We shall be *saved* by faith alone, but *rewarded* according to our works.

13. I am the Alpha and the Omega, the first and the last, the beginning and the end.

See notes on 1:8, 17; 21:6. The Lord Jesus plainly speaks

here. The three clauses used before in the Apocalypse, Christ here applies to Himself, a manifest proof of His divinity.

14. Blessed are they that wash their robes, that they may have the right *to come* to the tree of life, and may enter in by the gates into the city.

Wash their robes. See notes on 7:14. Compare also 1:5. All those whose sins are forgiven, and whose names are written in the book of life (21:27) have a right to eat of the tree of life (22:2), and to enter into the city. Blunt: "Cleansed in the blood of Christ they enter into the Paradise of God, and there eat of the tree of life in the midst of it and live for ever (2:7)."

15. Without are the dogs, and the sorcerers, and the fornicators, and the murderers, and the idolaters, and every one that loveth and maketh a lie.

See notes on 21:8, 27. **Dogs.** Impure, filthy persons. All these have no right to enter the city. This verse pronounces a sentence of eternal exclusion of all such from the City of God. Bossuet (quoted by Lee): "I am not sure if any portion of Scripture can be found in which terrors and consolations are better intermingled than they are in these last two chapters. There is everything to attract in this most blessed City; all in it is rich and glorious; but everything also is fitted to inspire one with dread,—for we perceive still more of purity than of grandeur."

16. I Jesus have sent mine angel to testify unto you these things for the churches. I am the root and the offspring of David, the bright, the morning star.

Angel. The one spoken of in 1:1. **For the churches.** Luthardt: "A book for the congregation; not a book merely for the few and for a select circle, is this book of prophecy.

339

And Jesus Himself expressly confirms the fact that it is from Him. Who will dare to contradict Him?" **Root ... of David.** See notes on 9:5. Compare Rom. 1:3, "Who was born of the seed of David according to the flesh." **The morning star.** See notes on 2:28.

17. And the Spirit and the bride say, Come. And he that heareth, let him say, Come. And he that is athirst, let him come: he that will, let him take the water of life freely.

The Holy Spirit, working in the Prophets and in the Church, and the Bride, the Church herself, say, *Come, Lord Jesus.* Let each individual say, *Come.* Milligan maintains that the latter part of the verse must be taken in the same sense as the similar words in 21:6. "The thirst referred to is not the first thirst after salvation. It is the constant longing of one who has already been refreshed for deeper and fuller draughts. The persons referred to are already believers, within the city, within the reach of the water of life." It is best, however, to understand this passage, as if Christ here for the last time gives the invitation to the weary and heavy laden, and the thirsty, to come unto Him and partake of the water of life freely. "It is the last, full evangelic tone in the New Testament," comments Lange. In this verse there seems to be a double meaning to the word *Come.* In the first half, it is, *Come, Lord Jesus;* in the last half, *Come to Me,* the Water of Life. On the latter Bengel remarks: "By thirst, which in itself is no act of the will, each one is moved to long, to pray, to cry, to take. O gracious invitation! Take and be filled—acknowledge it as a mere gift of grace, and take freely."

84. Conclusion (22:18–21)

18. I testify unto every man that heareth the words of the prophecy of this book, If any man shall add unto them, God shall add unto him the plagues which are written in this book.

We have here the final solemn warning of the Apostle. This is addressed to every one who becomes acquainted with the contents of the Apocalypse. Compare notes on 1:3. Wordsworth: "Here is a prophetic protest against the spurious Revelations forged by false teachers in the name of Apostles. Here, also, is a prophetic protest against all *additions* to the words of *Holy Scripture;* whether those additions be made by unwritten traditions, or by Apocryphal books, as of equal authority with Holy Scripture." Bengel: "To change, is at once to add and to take away. An unskilful *expounder*, who is blind and rash, offends, and especially if he deems himself to be endowed with a singular prophetical gift and faculty."

19. And if any man shall take away from the words of the book of this prophecy, God shall take away his part from the tree of life, and out of the holy city, which are written in this book.

Compare Deut. 4:2; 12:32. We may refer also to a similar denunciation of St. Paul (Gal. 1:8, 9). Luthardt: "As Paul, Gal. 1:8, 9, invokes the curse on the man who corrupts the doctrine of *faith,* so John invokes the curse here on the man who corrupts the doctrine of *hope;* for the subject-matter here is the true consolation and light of the Church in the heaviest tribulation, and also the Word which has power to preserve the faithful so that they may not fall in the great Temptation, and perish." Alford: "This is at least an awful warning both to those who despise and neglect this

341

book, and to those who add to it by irrelevant and trifling interpretations."

20. He which testifieth these things saith, Yea: I come quickly. Amen: come, Lord Jesus.

It seems as if Christ Himself was the speaker of the first part of the verse. The last part is the reply of the Apostle. We have here the last recorded words of the Lord Jesus.

21. The grace of the Lord Jesus be with the saints. Amen.

With the benediction of grace the Apocalypse opens, and with the same benediction it closes. Compare 1:4. To this, his last prayer and blessing, may be added St. John's own words: "And now, my little children, abide in Him; that, if He shall be manifested, we may have boldness, and not be ashamed before Him at His coming" (1 John 2:28).

UNTO HIM THAT SITTETH ON THE THRONE, AND UNTO THE LAMB, BE THE BLESSING, AND THE HONOR, AND THE GLORY, AND THE DOMINION, FOR EVER AND EVER, AMEN.

23

Excursus: The Kingdom of God

T*he Kingdom of God.*—The expressions "the kingdom of God," "the kingdom of heaven" (used only by Matthew), "the kingdom," "the kingdom of Christ" (Eph. 5:5), are evidently synonymous. But these different phrases have been used in various senses, and often by the same writer. Sometimes the kingdom of God is spoken of as existing now, in the heart of the believer, or in the Church (visible or invisible), having been established by Christ at His First Advent, and again it is referred to as something to be established at Christ's Second Advent. All are agreed that Scripture teaches that the fulness and consummation of this kingdom still lies in the future, but here two different views must be sharply distinguished,—(1) that which maintains that by *the kingdom* is meant the future kingdom of glory in a new heaven and earth, and (2) that which maintains that by *the kingdom* is meant an earthly kingdom, like that of David, to be established here on earth by the glorious Second Advent of Christ, to continue during the millennial era. The Futurist interpreters of the Apocalypse, as a class and almost unanimously, maintain that not only is the kingdom prophesied by Daniel[1] future, but that this prophecy cannot mean simply a spiritual reign in the hearts of Christians, but that the true and proper signification is that the Lord Jesus Christ will yet have a kingdom on this earth, with universal dominion.

1. They maintain that our Lord and His Apostles at every stage of the N. T. referred to the establishment of this kingdom as still future. (*a*) Indefinitely as being *at hand*, but not yet established. The principal passages quoted are Matt. 4:17; (Mark 1:14); Matt. 6:10; (Luke 11:2); Luke 10:9; (Matt. 10:7); Luke 19:11; 22:18, 29, 30; (Matt. 26:29; Mark 14:25); Acts 1:3, 6, 7; James 2:5.[1] (*b*) By representing that this kingdom should be established at the time of Christ's Second Coming. The principal passages quoted are Matt. 16:28; (Matt. 8:28; 9:1; Luke 9:27); Luke 21:31; especially our Lord's last discourse (Matt. 24, 25; Mark 13; Luke 21), in which they claim that He had the prophecies of Daniel (7:9–27; 9:27; 12:1–13) in view throughout.[1]

2. They maintain that Christ brought the kingdom, but His being rejected by the Jews altered the character of the kingdom for the time being, and postponed the establishment of it in power and glory. The kingdom is now in a sort of interregnum. The King came and was rejected. He has now, like the nobleman of the Parable of the Pounds, gone forth "to receive for himself a kingdom, and to return" (Luke 19:12). When He will come the second time he will execute judgment upon His enemies and establish His Kingdom, for "the kingdom of the world shall become the Kingdom of our Lord, and of His Christ; and He shall reign for ever and ever" (Rev. 11:15). The principal passages quoted (in connection

344

with those already given under the preceding head) are Luke 19:41–44 (the weeping over Jerusalem) and the subsequent addresses in the temple as recorded in Matt. 21:23–23:39, especially Matt. 21:42, 43; 23:37–39.[2]

Dr. Craven, whose valuable and scholarly note in Lange's *Commentary on Revelation* (pp. 93–100) we have been closely following, maintains that if we interpret the prophetic passages referring to *the kingdom*, as any other Scripture passages, especially as the N. T. interprets all prophecies in the O. T. bearing on the First Advent of Christ, we will find that the following characters of the future kingdom of our Lord are emphasized:

(1) It was a government to be established in a glorious visible advent of "the Son of man" (Dan. 7:13, 14). The only passage which really seems opposed to this is Luke 17:20, 21; but this Dr. Craven maintains can be satisfactorily explained.

(2) This kingdom shall be established in "the time of the end" (Dan. 9:27; 12:4, 13). This was directly taught by Christ and in manifest reference to the prophecy of Daniel (Matt. 24:3, 6, 13; Mark 13:7; Luke 21:9, 31).

(3) It shall be established after a period of great tribulation (Dan. 12:1; 7:25–27).[1] This is strictly confirmed in the N. T. (Matt. 24:21, 29; Mark 13:19, 20; etc.).[2]

(4) The members of this kingdom are to be *governors* (the subject nations were *under*, not *members* of the kingdom), Dan. 7:18, 22, 27.[1] Dr. Craven maintains that this doctrine was never controverted by our Lord, but He always took its truth for granted. Witness Matt. 19:28; 24:47; 25:21, 23; Luke 12:44; 19:17, 19; Luke 22:29, 30.[2] See also 1 Cor. 6:2, 3; Rev. 3:21; 5:10; 20:6; 22:5.[3]

(5) This kingdom or government shall be *over all* the earth

345

(Dan. 7:14, 27; etc.).[4] No one affirms that this characteristic was ever denied by our Lord.

(6) This kingdom is described in the prophets as a political one, in the proper sense of the term, indicating an external government over persons and things. It is also universally admitted that the Jews were expecting such a kingdom of the Messiah, an expectation which was shared by the Apostles. Throughout His whole ministry he never corrected them if they were in error, and often used language which must have confirmed them in their belief on this point (Luke 22:29, 30; Acts 1:3–7).[1]

(7) The members of this kingdom shall be the *risen* and *changed* Saints of a former dispensation. Dr. Craven refers to the passages already quoted, Dan. 7:18, 22, 27; 12:4, 13; especially Luke 13:28; 1 Cor. 15:50–52, compared with 1 Thess. 4:14–17. Only glorified saints will inherit the kingdom.

(8) This kingdom shall be a government in which righteousness (spiritual and external) shall prevail. Into this kingdom nothing impure shall enter.

According to this presentation of the *nature of the kingdom*, the Futurists draw a distinction between the Church and the kingdom. They maintain that the Church militant which really began its true existence on the Day of Pentecost will be caught up to meet Christ in the air (the *Rapture* of 1 Thess. 4:15–17) before the great Tribulation, that the kingdom begins only with the Revelation of Jesus Christ, at the close of the Tribulation (2 Thess. 1:7–10). In Peter's *Theorcatic Kingdom* (3 vols. New York, 1884) will be found a verbose exposition of this whole subject, with allied topics, gathered from all kinds of sources. If the substance of these 2,100

346

pages were succinctly presented in a readable volume of about 450 pages, there would be considerable merit in the work.

[1] Dan. 2:44, "And in the days of those kings shall the God of heaven set up a kingdom, which shall never be destroyed, nor shall the sovereignty thereof be left to another people; but it shall break in pieces and consume all these kingdoms and it shall stand forever;" 7:13, 14, 18, "And behold there came with the clouds of heaven one like unto a son of man, and he came even to the ancient of days, and they brought him near before him. And there was given him dominion, and glory, and a kingdom, that all the peoples, nations, and languages should serve him: his dominion is an everlasting dominion, which shall not pass away, and his kingdom that which shall not be destroyed.... The saints of the Most High shall receive the kingdom, and possess the kingdom for ever, even for ever and ever."

[1] Matt. 4:17, "Repent ye; for the kingdom of heaven is at hand."

Matt. 6:10, "Pray ye: ... Thy kingdom come."

Luke 10:9, "Say unto them, The kingdom of God is come nigh unto you."

Luke 19:11, "He spake a parable (*Of the Pounds*), because they supposed that the kingdom of God was immediately to appear."

Luke 22:18, "I say unto you, I will not drink from hence-forth of the fruit of the vine, until the kingdom of God shall come; Luke 22:29, 30, "I appoint unto you a kingdom, even as my Father appointed unto me, that ye may eat and drink at my table in my kingdom; and ye shall sit on thrones, judging the twelve tribes of Israel."

Acts 1:3, 6, 7, "Appearing unto them … and speaking the things concerning the kingdom of God.… They therefore asked him, saying, Lord, dost thou at this time restore the kingdom to Israel? And he said unto them, It is not for you to know times or seasons, which the Father hath set within his own authority."

James 2:5, "Heirs of the kingdom which he promised to them that love him."

[1] Matt. 16:28, "Verily I say unto you, there be some of them that stand here, which shall in no wise taste of death, till they see the Son of man coming in his kingdom."

Luke 21:31, "Even so ye also, when ye see these things coming to pass, know ye that the kingdom of God is nigh."

[2] Matt. 21:43, "Therefore say I unto you, The kingdom of God shall be taken away from you, and shall be given to a nation bringing forth the fruits thereof.'

Matt. 23:37–39, "O Jerusalem, Jerusalem, which killeth the prophets, and stoneth them that are sent unto her! how often would I have gathered thy children together, even as a hen gathereth her chickens under her wings, and ye would not. Behold, your house is left unto you desolate. For I say unto you, Ye shall not see me henceforth, till ye shall say, Blessed is he that cometh in the name of the Lord."

[1] Dan. 12:1, "And there shall be a time of trouble, such as never was since there was a nation even to that same time: and at that time thy people shall be delivered, every one that shall be found written in the book."

Dan. 7:25–27, "And he shall speak words against the Most High, and shall wear out the saints of the Most High.… And the kingdom and the dominion, and the greatness of the kingdoms under the whole heaven, shall be given to the people of the saints of the Most High."

[2] Matt. 24:21, "There shall be great tribulation, such as hath not been from the beginning of the world until now, no, nor ever shall be."

Matt. 24:29, "But immediately, after the tribulation of those days, … then shall appear the sign of the Son of man in heaven."

Mark 13:20, "And except the Lord had shortened the days, no flesh would have been saved; but for the elect's sake, whom he chose, he shortened the days."

[1] Dan. 7:18, "But the saints of the Most High shall receive the kingdom, and possess the kingdom for ever, even for ever and ever."

Dan. 7:22, "And the time came that the saints possessed the kingdom."

[2] Matt. 19:28, "Verily I say unto you, that ye which have followed me, in the regeneration when the Son of Man shall sit on the throne of his glory, ye also shall sit upon twelve thrones, judging the twelve tribes of Israel."

[3] 1 Cor. 6:2, 3, "Know ye not that the saints shall judge the world?… Know ye not that we shall judge angels?"

Rev. 5:10, "Thou madest them *to be* unto our God a kingdom and priests; and they reign upon the earth."

Rev. 20:6, "They shall be priests of God and of Christ, and shall reign with him a thousand years."

Rev. 22:5, "And they shall reign for ever and ever."

[4] Dan. 7:14, "That all the peoples, nations, and languages should serve him."

Dan. 7:27, "And the greatness of the kingdoms under the whole heaven, shall be given to the people of the saints of the

Most High."

[1] Acts 1:6, 7, "They asked him, saying, Lord, dost thou at this time restore the kingdom to Israel? And he said unto them, It is not for you to know times or seasons, which the Father hath set within his own authority."

24

Excursus: The New Testament Teaching on Hades

T he *N. T. Teaching concerning Hades.*[1]—Of the many treatises written on this topic we know of none that develops the biblical teaching more clearly than the presentation made by Dr. Craven in his long *Excursus on Hades* in Lange's *Commentary on Revelation* (pp. 364–377). Our aim in this note will be to give the substance of his discussion, and on the basis of his article to present what we deem the N. T. teaching.

1. *The Difficulties in the Way.* There are three reasons why such diverse views have been held. (1) The impression has been that little has been revealed in Scripture on this point. But more is revealed than is generally supposed. (2) The whole matter has been obscured by a mistranslation in the Authorised Version. The words *Sheol* in the O. T., and its Greek equivalent *Hades* in the N. T., have a fixed and definite meaning indicating *the place of departed spirits*, distinct from both Heaven and Hell (*Gehenna*), yet in the A. V. the word *Sheol* (which occurs *sixty-five* times in the O. T.) is translated

thirty-one times by *grave, thirty-one* times by *Hell*, and *three* times by *pit;* and *Hades* (which occurs *eleven* times in the N. T.) is translated *once* by *grave* and *ten* times by *Hell.* In but a few instances has the true biblical idea been clearly and distinctly presented by the A. V., although the attempt has been made to remedy this in the Revised Version. (3) It has been the general impression that the Bible teaches that the dwelling-place of the souls of the *righteous* dead has been the same *since* the Resurrection and Ascension of Christ that it was *before* that event. This has led to two serious errors: first, of those who affirm the existence of an intermediate place, located in Hades, into which the souls of those who *now* die in the Lord are carried; and secondly, of those who deny that there is now a Hades, or ever has been, into which the souls of the wicked at death must enter.

2. *Hades is not the Grave.* (*a*) Old Testament Teaching. Dr. Craven, in his scholarly examination of all the passages in which *Sheol* occurs in the O. T., most conclusively shows that the term *Sheol* was not used by the O. T. writers to designate *the literal grave.* (1) The word *Sheol* is never construed as *qebher* (grave), the place of the burial of the body. (2) It is spoken of with expressions of comparisons utterly inconsistent with the idea of the literal grave (Deut. 32:22; Ps. 86:13; Prov. 9:18; Ezek. 32:21). (3) In two instances *Sheol* is clearly distinguished from *the grave* (Gen. 37:33, 35; Isa. 14:15, 19). (4) It is used in antithesis with Heaven under circumstances which show that the literal grave cannot be intended (Job 11:8; Ps. 139:8; Amos 9:2). (5) *Sheol* is used as synonymous with two other terms (*pit* and *nether parts of the earth*) which cannot be regarded as indicating the literal grave. The word *bôr* (pit) occurs fifteen times, and that it is

352

synonymous with Sheol, or indicates a compartment thereof, is abundantly evident. (See especially Ps. 30:3; Prov. 1:12; Isa. 14:15; Ezek. 31:14–18.) The Hebrew for *nether parts of the earth* in Ezek. 31:14, 16, 18; 32:18, 24; 26:20, is manifestly synonymous with *Sheol.* So likewise Ps. 63:9; Isa. 44:23. (6) Those in *Sheol* are spoken of as being in a state of conscious existence, which never occurs in the case of those in *the grave* (Isa. 14:9–17; Ezek. 32:21–25; 2 Sam. 22:6; Ps. 18:5; 116:3).

(*b*) New Testament Teaching. Still clearer is the teaching of the N. T. on this point, for there is not a single instance in which the word *Hades* means *the grave.* In the Revised Version *Hades* occurs *ten* times, textual authority being in favor of the reading *death* in 1 Cor. 15:55 instead of Hades. That the word will not bear the translation *grave* is evident from the mere reading of these passages:

Matt. 11:23, "And thou, Capernaum, shalt thou be exalted unto heaven? thou shalt go down unto Hades."

Matt. 16:18, "Thou art Peter, and upon this rock I will build my church; and the gates of Hades shall not prevail against it."

Luke 1:15, "And thou, Capernaum, ... thou shalt be brought down unto Hades."

Luke 16:23, "And the rich man ... was buried. And in Hades he lifted up his eyes, being in torments."

Acts 2:27, "Because thou wilt not leave my soul in Hades, neither wilt thou give thy Holy One to see corruption."

... 2:31, David "foreseeing spake of the resurrection of the Christ, that neither was he left in Hades, nor did his flesh see corruption." That is, the body of Christ did not see corruption although it was placed in a *sepulchre*, and His soul was not left in Hades,—implying that His soul had gone

353

down to Hades at His death.

Rev. 1:18, "I am alive for evermore, and I have the keys of death and of Hades."

Rev. 6:8, "And I saw, and behold, a pale horse: and he that sat upon him, his name was Death; and Hades followed with him."

Rev. 20:13, "And death and Hades gave up the dead which were in them."

Rev. 20:14, "And death and Hades were cast into the lake of fire."

Hades, therefore, neither in the O. T. nor in the New ever has the meaning of *the literal grave.*

3. *Hades is not Hell* (Gehenna) *regarded as the Place of Final Punishment.*—In the Parable of the Rich Man and Lazarus (Luke 16:19–31), we have the clearest revelation in the N. T. of the state of the dead before Christ's death and resurrection. This parable, taken in connection with Luke 23:43 and Acts 2:24–32, implies that the generic Hades was a world into which the souls of all the dead entered before Christ's resurrection, having two compartments—one of joy and comfort (Paradise, Luke 23:43), and the other of misery (specific Hades, Luke 16:23), separated by an impassable gulf (Luke 16:26). The specific Hades, as the place of misery, received all the souls of the wicked, and Paradise, as the place of joy, received all the souls of the pious; and these two parts were embraced in that one place, generally known in the O. T. as *Sheol,* and in the N. T. as *Hades.* Into this Sheol or Hades, antecedent to the resurrection of Jesus, descended all the righteous dead, but into that part of Hades which Christ calls Paradise (Luke 23:43). Thither descended the patriarch Jacob (Gen. 37:35), the pious Job (Job 17:13), the inspired

David (Ps. 16:10), the righteous Hezekiah (Isa. 38:18), and our Lord and Saviour Himself (Luke 23:43; Acts 2:31).

But this Hades is *not Hell or Gehenna*, the place of final punishment. The word *Gehenna* properly translated *Hell*, occurs *twelve* times in the N. T., and is always used by Christ to describe the place or condition where the wicked, with body and soul re-united, after the judgment, shall suffer everlasting punishment. Christ speaks of a *Gehenna* or hell as "the unquenchable fire" (Mark 9:43, 45, 47), "where their worm dieth not, and the fire is not quenched" (Mark 9:48), and *Gehenna*, is represented as the place of the destruction of the body (Matt. 5:29, 30); as a place of destruction to both soul and body (Matt. 10:28); as the place of wickedness for the children of hell (Matt. 23:15); as the place of damnation (Matt. 23:33); and God is represented as that Supreme Being who has power to cast into Gehenna, and who will assign to it the wicked (Matt. 10:28; 18:9; Luke 12:5; Matt. 23:33).

All admit that the ungodly are at present in *Hades*, but they are not yet in their place of final and everlasting punishment—they are not yet in *Gehenna* or *Hell*. Not until after the final judgment shall the wicked enter therein.

4. *Hades does not include Heaven as the blessed abode of the righteous.* We must sharply distinguish between Hades as existing before the resurrection of Christ, in two parts (Paradise as the abode of the pious, and specific Hades as the home of the ungodly), and Hades as it now exists after Christ's Resurrection and Ascension, as the present abode of the disembodied spirits of the wicked. Before Christ's resurrection all the souls of the pious descended to Hades, but into that part of Hades known as Paradise.

(1) It is unquestionable that the idea of the *Sheol or Hades of*

355

the good presented in the O. T. is that of a *subterranean* place, distinct from Heaven. Of Elijah (implied also in Enoch's case) alone of all the O. T. saints is it said that he *ascended*, and of him alone it is said that he went into *Heaven.*

(2) That the *Sheol or Hades of the good* was not Heaven is evident from the fact that it was always spoken of as a place of imperfect happiness—a place to be delivered from. The inspired Psalmist exclaims, "But God will redeem my soul from the power of Sheol" (Ps. 49:15), as of deliverance from a prison, and David, who had bright visions of a future glory, wrote not only prophetically concerning the Messiah (Acts 2:31), but also concerning himself, "For thou wilt not leave my soul to Sheol" (Ps. 16:10). So also Paul, speaking of the condition of the O. T. worthies, makes reference to the incompleteness of their blessedness antecedent to Christ's death and resurrection (Heb. 11:39, 40).

(3) That the *Hades of the righteous* was not Heaven is proved by the fact of their deliverance therefrom at the time of the Resurrection and Ascension of our Lord. In connection with Christ's descent into Hades as the risen and glorified God-Man (immediately after His revivification and before His visible manifestation to His disciples in His resurrection body) and as the result of His descent, great changes took place in the kingdom of Hades. (See my notes on 1 Pet. 3:19 and 4:6 in *Lutheran Commentary.*) Then took place that wondrous scene to which Paul refers, when Christ "put off from himself the principalities and the powers, and made a show of them openly, triumphing over them in it" (Col. 2:15), and it was in connection with His ascension into heaven that another great triumphal act of the risen Christ took place, when that part of Hades, which had been known

356

as Paradise before Christ's descent as the risen God-Man, yielded up its captives, for Paul also distinctly states, that "when Christ ascended on high, he led captivity captive, and gave gifts unto men" (Eph. 4:8). Christ opened the prison-house of Hades for the righteous of the O. T., and the gifts which the exalted Christ gave to them were freedom from the dominion of Hades, and the glory of being with Him in heaven, for from this time, according to the constant testimony of the N. T., the souls of the blessed dead are in heaven with Christ—and the souls of all believers who now die enter immediately into heaven, and not into Hades, to be with Christ in joy and glory,—there in blessedness to await the glorious resurrection, when with body and soul re-united, they shall enter upon their eternal glory. That our Lord descended into Hades is admitted by all, and equally clear is the teaching that between the period of His death and ascension He delivered from Hades a captivity detained therein, and that the place to which our Lord ascended, leading "captivity captive," was Heaven, none deny, and to the writer it is equally clear that the "captivity" consisted of the pious dead of Old Testament times. Hades therefore was a place distinct not only from Gehenna or Hell proper, but also from Heaven. All that we can say is that Hades for the believer has been conquered, and that the souls of believers no longer enter into Hades,—but that Hades as such still remains, only that now it is a fore-hell as it were, the abode of the ungodly dead (Rev. 20:13), into which the souls of all unbelievers still enter, reserved under punishment until the day of judgment (2 Pet. 2:9), and it evidently will finally become the Gehenna, the Hell proper, where, after the resurrection, the ungodly shall suffer eternal punishment.

357

(4) That this interpretation is the true and scriptural one is shown from the fact that (a) it brings into perfect harmony two apparently discrepant classes of scripture passages, and that (b) it sheds light on several obscure passages in the Bible. (a) The two views that seemed to be antagonistic are now harmonized. For there are many passages, as we have already shown, written before the death and resurrection of Christ, in which it is clearly taught that Hades was a place distinct from Heaven, to which the souls of the righteous as well as of the wicked were consigned, and all these statements are true, for such was Hades before Christ Himself descended thither to conquer death, Satan, and Hades. But all the N. T. teachings given since the resurrection of Christ, most clearly teach that the souls of believers at their death do immediately enter Heaven to be with Christ in glory. The testimony of the Apostles as to the immediate entrance of the redeemed at death on their heavenly state is very explicit, we need only quote a few:

John 17:24, "Father I will that where I am, they also may be with me; that they may behold my glory."

2 Cor. 5:6–7, "Knowing that, whilst we are at home in the body, we are absent from the Lord ... we are willing rather to be absent from the body, and to be at home with the Lord."

Phil. 1:23, "But I am in a strait betwixt the two, having the desire to depart and be with Christ; for it is very far better."

That the souls of believers enter now immediately into Heaven and are with God, is also distinctly implied in Rev. 6:9–11; 7:9–17; etc.

(b) It sheds light on many obscure passages. (1) It enables us to enter more deeply into Christ's saying to His disciples, John 14:2, "In my Father's house are many mansions; if it were not so, I would have told you; *for I go to prepare a place for you.*" Christ did prepare a place, and the pious dead are now no longer in Hades, but in Heaven, whither Christ ascended. (2) So likewise our interpretation throws light upon Heb. 11:39, 40. "These all," i. e., the O. T. worthies, "received not the promise, God having provided some better thing concerning us, that apart from us, they should not be made perfect," taken in connection with Heb, 12:22, 23, "but ye are come unto Mount Zion, ... and to the spirits of just men made perfect, and to Jesus the mediator of a New Testament." When Christ led "captivity captive" (Eph. 4:8), these "spirits of just men" received their heavenly blessedness and the promise. (3) Our interpretation also throws light upon 1 Pet. 3:19 and 4:6, and illustrates, as has been shown, the great importance of these passages as bearing upon the mystery of Christ's work of redemption. (4) It gives a new and higher meaning to all the O. T. passages in which the word *Sheol* occurs. (5) It sets forth in clearer light the N. T. teaching concerning Christ's relation to his saints.

* * *

[1] See also Weidner's *Biblical Theology of the New Testament.* Vol. I. pp. 94–101, 184–195; vol. II. pp. 37–40, 265, 283.

25

Excursus: The First Six Seals

The *First Six Seals.*—We did not regard it as wise to introduce into our notes an account of all the various views held by commentators, believing it to be far better for the student and reader of these annotations that we develop what we regard to be the plain biblical teaching of the book, and allow the testimony of God's word to speak for itself. But it may be of interest to many to know what the different interpretations are, which have been advocated by the different schools as represented by the Preterists, the Continuous-Historical School, and the Spiritualists. To give a historical setting to the brief outline, we will also add the views of the Early Church.

I. *The Early Church.*—Maitland: "Down to the year 1120 every writer that had handled the seals had agreed on the meaning of the *first, sixth,* and *seventh.* The *first* had been taken to mean the Gospel Triumph; the *sixth* the precursor of the last Judgment; the *seventh* the beginning of the eternal rest." There was also a general agreement that the *second, third,* and *fourth* seals signified wars, famines, and pestilences, but with some divergences in their application. So, in general, Victorinus (about 290 A. D.), Tichonius (about 380 A. D.), Primasius (about 553 A. D.), Bede (about 735 A. D.), and others. Some of these referred these wars to the *persecutions,* and the *famines* to *heresies.* Wordsworth, who lays much stress on the ancient interpretation, says: On the whole, we may acquiesce in the ancient interpretation of *the first three seals.* The early expositors may be safely followed *here,* because they are speaking of prophecies which *had been fulfilled* in their day. Their judgment on this matter is thus expressed in the commentary published under the name of *Aquinas:*

" 'The first seal represents the primitive state of the Church.

" 'The second seal displays the *persecution* of the Church by the *heathen,* in the days of the martyrs.

" 'The third seal unfolds the persecution of the Church by heretics.' " Andreas explains the *fifth* seal as the martyrs' cry for vengeance; the *sixth* as a transition to the days of Antichrist, or, he adds, as some hold, the siege of Jerusalem under Vespasian. Tichonius and Primasius refer the *fifth* seal to martyrdom generally, and the *sixth* to the last persecution.

II. *The Preterist School.*—We may select Grotius, Bossuet, Moses Stuart, and Renan as representatives of this class (see *Introduction,* p. xxvi).

Grotius regards the first horseman as Christ, identical with the horseman of 19:11–13 (so Victorinus, Bede, Lyra, Vitringa, Calovius, Hengstenberg, Ebrard, Boehmer, Kliefoth, Duesterdieck, etc.); the *second* seal refers to the Jewish war (also Wetstein, Herder, Boehmer, Eichhorn, etc.); the *third* to the famine under Claudius (Wetstein, Herder, Boehmer, etc.); the *fourth* to the diseases and rapine and sufferings of

361

the Jewish war (Wetstein, Herder, Boehmer, etc.); the *fifth* refers to the sufferings of the Jews in Judæa; and the *sixth* seal relates to the events during the siege of Jerusalem by Titus (Wetstein, Herder, Boehmer).

Bossuet (*died* 1704) finds the fulfilment of the Apocalypse in the conquest of pagan Rome by Alaric. The rider of the first horse is Christ; the *second* seal represents war: the *third* famine; the *fourth* pestilence; the altar of the *fifth* seal is Christ (Col. 3:3, 4); the *sixth* seal designates the divine vengeance, which is to fall first on the Jews, and then on the persecuting empire.

Moses Stuart held that the Apocalypse was written *before* the destruction of Jerusalem, and that the greater portion of the book, including chapter 19, referred to that great catastrophe. According to him the *first four seals* indicate the assembling and preparing of an awful array against the enemies of the Church. A mighty conqueror leads on the hosts of destruction. In the train comes *famine, Death, Hades,* and the *wild beasts.* The *fifth* seal presents the persecuted and slaughtered martyrs as crying aloud to the God of justice; while in the *sixth* "calamitous events" are foretold.

According to Renan the *first* seal represents the Roman Empire; *the second,* war, the revolt of Judæa; the *third,* the famine of the year 68 A. D.; the *fourth,* death; the *fifth,* the cry of the souls of the martyrs of the year 64; the *sixth,* the convulsion of the universe at the last judgment.

III. *The Continuous-Historical School.*—As representatives of this class we select Mede, Vitringa, Bengel, Elliott, and Wordsworth, noting incidentally also the views of the most important modern commentators.

Mede (*died* 1638) regards the seven seals as a syllabus of

362

Roman History. The same general view is adopted by Bishop Newton, Fleming, Daubuz, Scott, Lowman, Doddridge, Hales, and others. Lee gives a good summary of Mede's views: In the seven seals we see (1) the Empire in peace, after the Jewish war under Vespasian; (2) the Empire under Trajan and Aurelian; (3) the balance of justice under Septimius and Severus; (4) the evils under Decius, Gallus, and Valerian; (5) the persecution under Diocletian; (6) the overthrow of paganism and the changes under Constantine; and (7) the last seal, as explained by the seven trumpets, reveals the inroads of the barbarians, and the fall of the Empire.

Vitringa (*died* 1722) regards the *first* Seal as describing the peaceful condition of the Apostolic primitive Church prior to persecutions (so Bede, de Lyra, C. à Lapide, Calovius, etc.); the *second*, persecutions (Bede, de Lyra, Calovius, Wordsworth, etc.); the *third*, the heresies and calamities from Constantine to the ninth century (in general Bede, C. à Lapide, Stern, Wordsworth, Lord, etc.); the *fourth*, the Saracenic and Turkish inroads (à Lapide); the *fifth*, the sufferings of the Albigenses and Waldenses and others; the *sixth*, the fall of the Jewish nation; *or* the changes under Constantine; *or* the commotions at the time of the Reformation; *or* the destructions of Antichrist. Bengel (*died* 1752) maintains that the *first four seals* denote the bloom of imperial power and refer to what is *visible* and *past;* the last *three* Seals relate to things *invisible;* the *fifth* Seal, to the blessed dead, the Apostolic Martyrs, including also the Waldenses; the *sixth* Seal, the unrighteous dead; and the *seventh* Seal, to the holy angels with their service. Elliott identifies the Horses of the first four Seals with the Roman Empire at different times, and the *Riders* with Emperors.

The first *six* seals extend from the date of the Apocalypse (95 or 96 A. D.) to 395 A. D., the year in which Augustine became Bishop of Hippo. *The first* Seal, the golden age, extends from Nerva to the second Antonine; the *second*, from Commodus to the accession of Diocletian (183–284 A. D.). the *third*, overlapping the last, taxation under Caracalla's Edict (212 A. D.); the *fourth*, fearful mortality from War, Famine, Pestilence, and Wild Beasts (248–268 A. D.); the *fifth*, the persecution under Diocletian (303–312 A. D.); the *sixth*, the destruction of the political supremacy of heathenism at the time of Constantine (323 A. D.). Barnes adopts the same interpretation for the first *five* Seals, but refers the *sixth* to the invasions of the Northern hordes of Goths and Vandals.

According to Wordsworth, the Seals represent a prophetic view of the history of the Christian Church from the first Advent of Christ to the end of the world. The *first Seal* displays the marvellous success of Christianity; the *second* Seal represents the ten successive persecutions, (1) under Nero; (2) under Domitian; (3) under Trajan; (4) under Marcus Aurelius Antoninus; (5) under Septimius Severus; (6) under Maximus: (7) under Decius; (8) under Valerius; (9) under Aurelian; (10) under Diocletian; making a period of 240 years, from 64 to 304 A. D.; the *third* represents the machinations of heresy against the Church; the *fourth* Seal shows that the evil is *multiform*, the *sword* representing the violence of the Goths (410 A. D.), the Huns (452 A. D.), the Vandals (455 A. D.), the ravages of Mohammedanism (622 A. D.),—*famine* and *death* signify the woes consequent on heresies and schisms; the *fifth* Seal discloses the blessed condition of the faithful departed in Paradise (Luke 23:43); the *sixth* Seal "reveals the crisis of greatest suffering for the Church; it is the Friday of *her* Passion Week. But it is also the eve of the *Sabbath of her* rest. It brings us down to the *last age* of the Church and the world. It appears to be now being fulfilled in the confusions, conflicts, and convulsions of kingdoms and states at this time."

General Synopsis

The First Seal. Christianity Conquering. So in general, Duesterdieck, Hengstenberg, Ebrard, Kliefoth, Lange, Alford, Lee, Currey, Sadler, etc.

The Second Seal. War and Bloodshed. So in general, Hengstenberg, Ebrard, Duesterdieck, Lange, Lee, and most commentators. Some think that the *red horse* is Nero (de Lyra); some, the devil (Bede, Calovius, etc.).

The Third Seal. Scarcity and Famine. The general interpretation. Some would refer it to a particular dearth (Calovius, Bengel, Huschke, etc.), others some kind of plague (Duesterdieck, De Wette, Hengstenberg, Ebrard).

The Fourth Seal. General Plagues. So Duesterdieck, Lange, etc.

The Fifth Seal. The Souls of Martyrs. So commentators in general.

The Sixth Seal. The Day of Judgment. Still future. So Duesterdieck, Lange, Ebrard, Wordsworth, Alford, Lee, Currey, etc. *Figurative descriptions of events pertaining to the development of the Church.* So Victorinus, Bede, de Lyra, Vitringa, Hengstenberg, and others.

IV. *The Spiritual System.*—Milligan is the best representative of this school. He remarks: "The reader must observe that throughout the whole of this section we have to deal with principles, not with particular historical events.… The seven seals are divided into two groups of four and three.… At the opening of the fifth seal, we pass from the visible to the invisible world (6:9)." In *the first* Seal he sees our Lord in His cause and kingdom "riding prosperously" as in Ps. 45; in the *second* seal Christ comes in war and with the sword; the judgment of the *third* seal is famine; in *the fourth* death is the judgment that comes upon the world. The *first four seals* must be viewed ideally. They refer to no specific war or famine or pestilence, nor do they even necessarily follow one another in chronological succession. They express the great principle borne witness to by the whole course of human history—that the world draws down upon itself the righteous judgments of God. The martyrs of the *fifth* seal are the saints of the O. T. Dispensation waiting for the completion of their happiness; in the *sixth* Seal we reach the beginning of the end, but the end is not yet described.

26

Excursus: The First Four Trumpets

T*he First Four Trumpets.*—In the exposition of the *first four trumpets*, as has been seen in our notes, we meet with the greatest variety of interpretations. It may be of interest to the reader to summarize these views:

I. The *Rationalistic* Preterists, as represented by Volkmar and Renan. The first four trumpets refer to the times before the Apocalypse was written,—to the fearful storms and eclipses of the years 63, 68, and 69. The eagle is the standard of the Roman Empire.

II. *Ordinary* Preterists, represented by Bossuet, Herder, and Farrar. In these four judgments respectively Bossuet sees (1) The desolation of the Jews under Trajan; (2) under Hadrian; (3) the great star was Barchochab; (4) the darkening was the malice of the Jews: Christ being the *sun*, the Church the *moon*, the Apostles the *stars.* Herder regards the first four trumpets as the signals of tumults, massacres, and wars in Judæa. Farrar maintains that the times of Nero furnished abundant instances to satisfy these judgments. The language is obviously that of daring symbolism.

III. *Symbolical* Interpretation. De Lyra sees in the four trumpets *heresies:* (1) Arius, (2) Macedonius, (3) Pelagius, (4) Eutyches; Luther, however, sees here: (1) Tatian, (2) Marcion, (3) Origen, (4) Novatus.

Many who combine the symbolical and historical interpretation refer the third trumpet to *heresies* (Wordsworth, Arianism (Bengel), Arius, Eutyches, Apollonaris, Sabellius, Nestorius (Williams), etc.

IV. The *Historical* School. The greatest divergence appears among the commentators who adopt the historical method of interpretation, with reference to the four trumpets.

1. *The First Trumpet.* (1) Williams sees in it the fall of Jerusalem; (2) Bengel, the wars of Trajan and Hadrian; (3) Frere, Cunninghame, etc., maintain it ends with the death of Theodosius, 395 A. D.; (4) Mede, Keith, Elliott, Barnes, Wordsworth, maintain that it begins with the death of Theodosius; (5) Birks sees in it the invasion of the Eastern Roman Empire (250–365 A. D.); (6) Vitringa recognizes the pestilence and famine under Decius and Gallus, etc.

2. *The Second Trumpet.* There seems to be a general consent on the part of many that this trumpet refers to the invasion of the Goths, Vandals, and Visigoths, but there is much disagreement in details. So in general Mede, Bengel, Vitringa, Newton, Keith, Elliott, Barnes, Wordsworth, Faber. Sander sees in it the Arian controversy.

3. *The Third Trumpet.* Some refer this to the Vandals, others to Attila and the Huns, others to various heresies.

4. *The Fourth Trumpet.* (1) Mede sees in it the final desolation of Rome (542 A. D.); (2) Birks, the eclipse of the Greek Empire (540–622 A. D.); (3) Bengel, the general devastation of the Roman Empire in the fifth century; (4)

Wordsworth, the confusion of the seventh century; (5) Cunninghame, Whiston, and others refer it to the fall of the Empire (476 A. D.), etc.

Faber, who belongs to the continuous-historical school, referring to the fact that scarcely any two expositors agree, observes: "So curious a circumstance may well be deemed the opprobrium of Apocalyptic interpretation, and may natrually lead us to suspect that the true key to the destined application of the first four trumpets has never yet been found, or, if found, has never yet been satisfactorily used." Sadler, who also belongs to this same school in general, is candid enough to say: "I cannot find anything in human history which can with any probability be identified with the four visions at the sounding of the first four trumpets, and so I must content myself with giving the interpretations of various expositors, not one of which I can accept as the undoubtedly true meaning."

Those who have carefully followed us in our exposition will have seen that a careful exegesis of each passage, step by step, has led us to accept at least so much of the Futurist system of interpretation, as to maintain that these judgments represented by the four trumpets are to be regarded as of the same general character as the plagues of Egypt, and that they will usher in the great tribulation of the days of Antichrist. They disclose more clearly the events immediately preceding the coming of Christ, and set forth more fully the end as already depicted by the opening of the sixth seal.

27

Excursus: The Bowls of Wrath

he Seven Bowls of Wrath.—As a rule the Expositors of *the Early Church* referred the Vials or Bowls of Wrath to events occurring in the times of Antichrist, still future. Modern expositors may be classified here in their interpretations as (1) Ordinary *Preterists;* (2) Rationalistic *Preterists;* (3) *Continuous-Historical;* (4) *Anti-Papal;* (5), *Allegorical,* and (6) *Futurists.*

1. *Ordinary Preterist Interpretation.* One of the best representatives of this view is Moses Stuart, who regards these Bowls as a series of judgments upon the enemies of the Church, terminating primarily in the death of Nero and the destruction of Jerusalem, and finally in the destruction of the Pagan power under Constantine.

2. *The Rationalistic Preterists.* All these maintain that these Seven Bowls of wrath refer to the days of Nero.

3. *Continuous-Historical View.* Most of the interpreters of this School, with many variations, refer these Bowls of Wrath to different events between 1494 and the Present Day. According to Bengel, the *seventh* concerns Antichrist,

and should have occurred between 1832 and 1836. *Glasgow* thinks the *first* Bowl was poured out by the preaching of Luther (1517); the *second*, in the Protest of 1529; the *third is* the shedding of Protestant Martyrs' blood, beginning in 1546; the *fourth* began at the rising of the Council of Trent; the *fifth*, at the Thirty Years' War; the *sixth* began with the French Revolution; the *seventh* is the present period, to terminate in the destruction of the systems of the heathen world and of the power of Romanism. All of the Anti-Papal expositors also belong to this School, but their exposition has a special polemic character directed against Roman Catholicism.

4. *The Anti-Papal Expositors.* We will present the views of two representative commentators. Elliott holds that 11:15–19; 14:6–8; 16:1–14, relate to the same period, and that the first six Vials cover the era of the French Revolution, extending from 1789 A. D. to 1848 A. D. The *first* Vial is the outbreak of social and moral evil which marked the French Revolution of 1789; the *grievous sore* is traceable to the corruptions of Papal Rome, etc. According to Elliott, 16:15–22:15, together with 14:9–20, refers to "the present and the future, from 1849 A. D. to the Millennium and Final Judgment." Barnes, in the main, agrees with Elliott. Wordsworth: *The First Vial.* "The contempt of God's Holy Word has already brought forth many foul boils, and blotches, and eruptions upon those who are subject to the Papacy," such as enforced celibacy, the Confessional, desecration of Holy Things. *The Third Vial.* "This may be applied to the traffic of the Papacy in Indulgences and Legendary Fables, and Miracles, which were for many centuries like wells and rivers of wealth to the See of Rome." *The Fourth*

371

Vial. "The temporal splendor of the Papacy has already had an effect similar to that which is here described.... The usurpations and corruptions of the Papacy have already produced a baneful harvest of Infidelity and Blasphemy." *The Fifth Vial.* "This vision is now in course of fulfilment in the dethronement of the Pope by the Italian People (1871)." *The Sixth Vial.* "Probably now being poured out.... The drying up of the stream of Papal Supremacy.... Thus St. John foreshows that the Papacy, when distressed by the drying up of its Euphrates, will resort for help to superstitious means, such as false Miracles, Apparitions, Pilgrimages, and other impostures." *The Seventh Vial.* "The *great city* Babylon is divided into three parts, and the cities of the Nations or Gentiles fall. This prophecy is being fulfilled. The Papal World is now divided into *three parts:* (1) Those who accept the dogma of Infallibility; (2) the Old Catholics, who reject it; (3) those who are driven by it to *unbelief,* called here *the cities of the nations,* i. e. States (like Italy, France, Spain), which lapse into Secularism and infidelity, and are torn asunder by Anarchy (Red Republicanism, Communism, etc.) and *fall.*"

5. *Allegorical or Symbolical Interpretation.* Milligan: "These plagues cannot be literally understood, for literal interpretation is wholly inapplicable to the sixth bowl, and all the bowls must be interpreted on the same principles." Boyd-Carpenter: (1) "The plague of the *evil sore* denotes some throbbing and hateful sore, perhaps spiritual or mental." (2) "The *sea* represents the tumultuous impulses and passions of the masses." (3) The rivers and the fountains "are the powers and influences which go to the making up of the great popular sentiment; these are smitten by the same corruption." (4) "Not only the pleasant gifts and influences, which, like

streams, were made to gladden men, grow corrupt, but the very source of light and knowledge become a power to destroy.... The fierce pride of vaunted light which scorches." (5) "When men shut out the higher light, the smoke of their own candles will soon obscure the whole heaven." (6) The kings *from the sunrising* "represent the forces of rude and open evil which have been long restrained;" etc.

6. *Futurists.* According to Todd, these bowls of wrath do not bring us "to the great Day of final account, but to the fall of Babylon, and to the consequences of that event which are immediately to usher in the Day of Christ's Coming." De Burgh: "I need not state that I consider them one and all as unfulfilled." Craven: "The vision of the Seven Vials relates to events still future—events the last of which will immediately precede the advent of Christ for the establishment of His Millennial Kingdom. The plagues predicted are to be executed upon the opposers of Christ and His true followers—upon the followers of the Beast (i. e. the world-power) and Babylon (i. e. the Apostate or world-allied Church).... By *the frogs* (16:13, 14) we may understand *teachers of evil*, instigated by Satan, and some having *civil* and others *ecclesiastical* authority, and working miracles, who shall seduce the nations into an assault on Christ and His true Church.... The *seventh* Vial poured out upon *the air* may indicate an effect produced upon the literal atmosphere, at once universal in its influence, and producing fearful convulsions in the realms of nature and in human society (comp. Isa. 13:6–10; Joel 2:1, 2, 10, 30, 31; 3:15; Matt. 24:29; Mark 13:24, 25; Luke 21:25, 26; Acts 2:19, 20; Rev. 6:12–17).

28

Excursus: Postmillennialism

P*ost-Millennialism.*—To present the view of those who maintain that the Second Advent will not take place until the time of the general Resurrection and Final Judgment, it will be best to give a summary of the argument in David Brown's famous work, *Christ's Second Coming,* to which reference has already been made. We follow very closely the summary given by Craven in Lange:

(1) The Church will be absolutely complete at Christ's Coming (1 Cor. 15:23; Eph. 5:25–27; 2 Thess. 1:10; Jude 24; Col. 1:22; 1 Thess. 3:13).

(2) Christ's Second Coming will exhaust the object of the Scriptures, in reference—(a) to the Saints (Luke 19:13; 2 Pet. 1:19; James 5:7; 1 Pet. 1:13; 2 Tim. 4:8; Phil. 3:20); (b) to sinners (2 Thess. 1:7–10; 2 Pet. 3:10; Luke 12:39, 40; 17:26, 27, 30).

(3) The Sacraments will disappear at Christ's Second Coming (Baptism, Matt. 28:20; The Lord's Supper, 1 Cor. 11:26).

(4) The Intercession of Christ, and the work of the Spirit

374

for saving purposes, will cease at the Second Advent—(a) the Intercession of Christ stands intermediate between His first and second Coming; (b) the work of the Spirit is dependent upon the Intercession, and terminates with it (John 7:38, 39; 14:16, 17, 26; 15:26; 16:7, 14; Acts 2:33; Tit. 3:5, 6; Rev. 3:1; 5:6).

(5) Christ's proper kingdom is already in being; commencing formally on His Ascension to the right hand of God, and continuing unchanged, both in character and form, till the final judgment (Acts 2:29–36 with Zech. 6:12, 13; Rev. 3:7, 8, 12 with Isa. 22:22; 9:6, 7; Acts 3:13–15, 19–21; Acts 4:25–28 with Ps. 2; Acts 5:29–31; Ps. 110:1 compared with Acts 2:34–36; Heb. 10:12, 13; 1 Cor. 15:24–26).

(6) When Christ comes, the whole Church of God will be "made alive" at once—the dead by resurrection, and the living immediately thereafter by transformation (1 Cor. 15:20–23; John 6:39, 40; 17:9, 24).

(7) All the wicked will rise from the dead, or be "made alive," at the Coming of Christ (Dan. 12:2 with John 5:28, 29; 1 Cor. 15:15, 52 with 1 Thess. 4:16; Matt. 13:43 with Dan. 12:3; Rev. 20:11–15).

(8) The righteous and the wicked will be judged together, and both at the coming of Christ (Matt. 10:32, 33; Mark 8:38; Rev. 21:7, 8; 22:12–15; Matt. 16:24–27; 7:21–23; 25:10, 11, 31–46; 13:30, 38–43; John 5:28, 29: Acts 17:31; Rom. 2:5–16; 2 Cor. 5:9–11; 1 Cor. 4:5; 2 Thess. 1:6–10; 1 Cor. 3:12–15; Col. 1:28; Heb. 13:17; 1 Thess. 2:19, 20; 1 John 2:28; 4:17; Rev. 3:5; 1 Tim. 5:24, 25; Rom. 14:10, 12; 2 Pet. 3:7, 10, 12; Rev. 20:11–15; 2 Tim. 4:1).

(9) At Christ's Second Appearing "the heavens that now are, and the earth," "the elements being dissolved with fervent

heat," shall give place to "new heavens and a new earth, wherein dwelleth righteosuness without any mixture of sin (2 Pet. 3:7, 10–13; Rev. 20:11; 21:1).

Such is Dr, Brown's argument, but a careful examination of all these passages only shows how weak the case of the Post-Millennialists is, for in most cases the interpretation insisted on, though it may be true in itself, presents only one part or aspect of the truth, and in many other cases, the true meaning of the passages harmonizes far better with the view as held by the Pre-Millennialists.

29

Excursus: The Millennium

The *Millennium.*—This word, from the Latin *mille*, "thousand," and *annus*, "year," designates the thousand years' reign of Christ mentioned in 20:4–6. Those who hold to the view that Christ will yet establish His kingdom on earth after the destruction of Antichrist, and who distinguish between two resurrections, one of the saints, for the kingdom of a thousand years, and one of the rest of the dead, at the Final Judgment, are in general known in English as Millennarians, but the usual German designation is Chiliasts. In general, those who adopt this view may be divided into two classes: (1) Those who maintain that the Millennial period belongs to the past; and (2) those who look for it in the future.

(1) Of the *Preterist* theories it may be of interest to mention what are known as the Augustinian and Grotian views. The best modern representative of the *Augustinian* theory is Wordsworth, who very ably defends this view in his *Commentary.* Its main elements are: (1) This Vision (20:1–6) is not a *continuation* of Rev. 19, but a *Recapitulation*, beginning

at Christ's *First Advent;* (2) "The commencement of the *thousand years* here mentioned,—whatever that period may signify,—is, therefore, to be dated from the First Coming of Christ; (3) The number, a thousand years, has a prophetical value and spiritual significance, and expresses *completeness,*—the whole time of the Gospel Dispensation from the First Advent of Christ until the time of the last persecution, when Satan will be loosed, and will rage with impious fury against God and His Saints; (4) The *first* Resurrection is the Spiritual Resurrection of the soul, begun in Baptism; (5) The *second* Resurrection is that of the *body*, and its re-union with the soul, at the time of the general Resurrection.

The *Grotian* theory, first propounded in the sixteenth century, finds its best modern representative in Bush, and is briefly condensed by Craven (in Lange): (1) "By the *Beast* is denoted Pagan Rome, whose destruction under Constantine was predicted in Rev. 19; (2) The power of Satan was then broken, as was manifested in the establishment of the Christian religion as the religion of the state; (3) The Millennial period began in that establishment, and continued to the fourteenth century and closed with the attack on Christendom by the Ottoman Turks; (4) Gog and Magog denote the Mohammedan power, at the close of whose gradual destruction will take place—the universal resurrection, the general judgment, and the eternal blessedness of the saints in heaven.

(2) Of the *Futurist* theories we need to speak also only of two—the Post-Millennial and the Pre-Millennial views. The *Post-Millennial* view was first fully developed by Whitby (*died* 1726) and has been largely adopted by English-speaking Protestant Theologians since his time, and among moderns,

David Brown, Barnes, and Cowles, are good representatives. Although there are great diversities of views among Post-Millennialists, there seems to be a general agreement on the following points: (1) The Millennium of Rev. 20:1–6 can hardly be identical with the whole period of the Gospel dispensation, but still lies in the future; (2) it seems to denote an extended season of tranquillity and prosperity which the Church shall enjoy before the Coming of Christ and the end of time; (3) it will be brought about by the Divine blessing upon the means employed by the Church for the conversion of the world; (4) this glorious revival, which may include the conversion of the Jews, is called a resurrection, not because the bodies of the saints shall be raised, as that will not take place till the last day, but because it is a spiritual resurrection of "souls"; (5) at the close of this period there will be a sharp but short and unsuccessful attack upon the Church, soon suppressed; (6) immediately after this, Christ will come the second time corporeally to the earth, in glorious majesty, to judge both the quick and dead; (7) there is to be but one literal resurrection, and that is to take place "at the last day"—"the just and unjust" shall be raised simultaneously, and together stand before God (Rev. 20:11–15); and this is to be after the Millennium; (8) when Christ makes His Second Advent it will not be to reign a thousand years upon the earth, but to burn up the earth and the works that are therein; (9) then will take place the Final Judgment, and the good and bad will be assigned to their eternal destinies; (10) to be followed by the new heavens and new earth.

As a rule, those who hold this view are amazed that a subject so simple should have bewildered so many minds and occasioned so much controversy.

For the *Pre-Millennial* view held by many moderns see *Introduction* (pp. xxix–xxxv), but probably the interpretation given by Auberlen represents more clearly the Pre-Millennarianism of the German School of theologians, represented by such writers as Rothe, Ebrard, Delitzsch, Hofmann, and others. Auberlen presents his view most fully in *Daniel and Revelation* (pp. 324–358); "After the destruction of the antichristian power of the beast and of the false prophet (19:17–21), the history of the world assumes a character totally different from its character hitherto. In place of the kingdom of the Beast comes the kingdom of the Son of Man, and of His Saints. Dan. 2:35, 44; 7:14, 27, contains a short summary of all O. T. prophecy, and Rev. 20:1–6, a summary of all N. T. prophecy, concerning this kingdom of glory on earth, but a great number of prophetic passages, and many beautiful and deep passages in gospels and epistles, serve to fill up these grand general outlines ... The kingdom of God has different periods; it is come in Christ (Matt. 12:28); it spreads in the world by internal spiritual, hidden processes (Matt. 13:33); but as a kingdom, in the strict sense of the word, in royal glory, it shall only come with the Parousia of Christ (Luke 19:11, 12, 15). And hereby is not meant the eternal blessedness after the final judgment, which is, indeed, the last and perfect consummation of the Kingdom (Matt. 25:34); but anterior to that event, it shall come as an earthly, Jewish, although not carnal, kingdom of glory. Thus the prophets described it, and Jesus does in no way contradict them, but, on the contrary, pre-supposing their prophecies, His own prophecies start from them (Matt. 19:28; Acts 1:6–8).... In the millennium, humanity will be freed, as it were, from the nightmare which weighed upon

380

it. Though sin will not be absolutely abolished,—for men will be still living in the flesh upon earth,—sin will no longer be a universal power, for the flesh is not any longer seduced and assisted by the powers of Satan. This is the difference between *this æon* and the *coming æon;* in this æon the devil is still ruling on earth (2 Cor. 4:4); in the future, Christ shall reign with his saints.... Of the saints' participation in the glory and reign of Christ, the N. T. throughout speaks often and fully ("glorified with him," Rom. 8:17; "reign with him," 2 Tim. 2:12; 1 Cor. 4:8; Luke 12:32; 22:29). To this refer also sayings concerning the inheritance of the children of God, the inheriting of the kingdom (Rom. 8:17; Matt. 5:5; Acts 20:32; 1 Cor. 6:9, 10; 15:50; Gal. 5:21; etc.).... Of the *first resurrection* our Saviour likewise speaks (Luke 14:14), and designates it as the resurrection of the just; and Paul also (1 Cor. 15:23), where he evidently distinguishes three gradations of resurrection: Christ, the firstfruits, rose first; then they who belong to Him at His appearing; then—*eita* corresponding to *epeita* that preceded, and again introducing a considerable interval—the end, that is, the general resurrection, the judgment of the world, the separation of the wicked;—the end, when Christ delivers the Kingdom to the Father, and God will be all in all.... The reign of the saints will be essentially a reign of priests (20:6). Christ and His saints will, by their spiritual rule, direct all external relations and circumstances.

"It is now that Christianity will pervade the world and all relations of life in spirit and in truth; the union of the royal and priestly office, in the ruling saints, will be mirrored in their kingdom upon earth, in the union of Church and State. Spiritual-mindedness will manifest itself everywhere

381

in corresponding forms. All poetry, all art, all science, all social life will be Christian; for the kingdoms of the world are now become the Kingdom of our Lord and His Christ.

"The majority of humanity living at the destruction of Antichrist were neither followers of Antichrist, nor were they followers of Christ, they remain after the Parousia on earth and consist of Jews and heathens. At the beginning of the millennial kingdom humanity will be in a condition similar to that in which it was at the commencement of the church-historical time after the ascension of Christ. But everything is now on a higher degree of development. The wonderful events attending the appearance of our Lord, the coming of Christ in glory, the destruction of all antichristian power, the transfiguration of the Church of believers, the binding of Satan and the ceasing of his influences, necessarily produce an unspeakably deep impression on the nations. Now the veil of Moses is taken from Israel (2 Cor. 3:14–16). Israel is again to be at the head of all humanity. Israel shall be the chosen people through which God executes His plans concerning humanity. The O. T. predictions concerning the conversion and glorious re-establishment of Israel in the Holy Land, have not yet been exhaustively fulfilled. The curse lies even this day on the Jewish nation, and the promised restoration awaits yet its fulfilment and realization. The doctrine of the future glorious restoration of Israel is such an essential and fundamental idea of all prophecy, that the difficulty is not so much to find passages in which it is taught, as to select from the great number. We point out as specimens, Isa. 2:2–4; 4:2–6; 9:2–6; 11:1–16; 12:1–6; 24:6; Jer. 30:1–33:26; Ezek. 34:23–31:36:1–37:28; Hos. 2:16–23; 3:4, 5; 11:8–11; Joel, 3:1–5, 16–21; Amos 9:11–15; Obad. 17–21; Micah 2:12,

382

13; 4:1–13; 5:1–15; 7:12–20; Zeph. 3:14–20; Zech. 2:4; 8:7; 9:9; 10:8–12; 12:2–13:6; 14:8–21. Israel, brought back to its own land, will now be the people of God in a much higher and more internal sense than it was before, for now the power of sin is checked, the knowledge of God fills the whole land, and the Lord dwells again among His people at Jerusalem. A new time of divine revelation will begin, the Spirit of God will be poured out abundantly, and a fulness of gifts of grace (*charismata*) be bestowed,—even as the apostolic church possessed it typically. In the millennium, Jews and Gentiles are united, and all humanity, the whole organism united under the firstborn brother, walks in the light of God, and thus the true and full life of humanity is at last realized (Rom. 11:30–32). And this blessed state of general salvation will extend even to the kingdom of nature; the soil will bring forth with inexhaustible and ennobled fertility; the animal world be freed from murder and fury,—even heaven and earth be united in corresponding harmony. In agreement with this is moreover a circumstance, which may be inferred from Isa. 65:20–25,—people of a hundred years are called children, the days of men are to be as the days of trees—that men will not have to leave their life-work unfinished and unenjoyed (what a glorious, beautiful feature).

"The upper and the lower congregation, although separate during the millennium, are yet closely connected; and it is to this that the Lord refers in the promise which He gives to the twelve (Matt. 19:28; Luke 22:28–30). After the millennial kingdom—after the universal judgment, when heaven and earth are renewed, and the New Jerusalem descends from heaven, then all limitations shall disappear and cease. To this time the Apocalypse looks in the twenty-first and twenty-second chapters.

"But not even the millennial kingdom is the final end of the development of God's kingdom. For even during the millennium, there is a separation between heaven and earth—between humanity transfigured and humanity still living in the flesh. Hence it is possible that an apostasy should take place at the end of the millenium. This kingdom is not yet the new world."—[*Condensed.*]

The *Pre-Millennial* theory, in its general features, is the most ancient, and has been taught with various modifications in all ages of the Church. We may briefly state the main elements of this view as follows: (1) The Millennium is to begin in the glorious personal advent of Christ, immediately after the destruction of Antichrist; (2) Satan is to be bound; (3) The duration is to be one thousand years (literal or symbolical); (4) The first resurrection is to be a literal resurrection of saints (either of martyrs alone, or of all saints); (5) Christ and His risen and transformed saints shall rule over the earth; (6) The Jews and all nations having been converted to Christ, Jerusalem shall become the capital of Christ's kingdom; (7) At the close of this period there shall be a great apostasy under the leadership of Satan; (8) Then follows the destruction of the rebels (20:7–10); (9) Then comes the universal resurrection of the remaining dead; (10) The Final Judgment; (11) The new heavens and the new earth.

30

Excursus: The First Resurrection

T *he First Resurrection.*—If we accept the clear and distinct teaching of scripture in Rev. 20:4–6, 11–15, and interpret literally, we must conclude that John speaks of two resurrections, with the Millennium intervening—the first of believers alone, and the second of the general resurrection to judgment. There is no conflict here with the teaching of Jesus, only a clearer statement of what was already taken for granted by Christ Himself. There may be a reference to the *first* Resurrection in Luke 14:14, "Thou shalt be recompensed in the resurrection of the just," at least there is no conflict, but in Luke 20:35, 36, "They that are accounted worthy to attain to that *æon,* and the resurrection from the dead," this reference has a peculiar significance, and can best be explained, if we regard it the teaching of Jesus that the resurrection here referred to is a special privilege granted only to faithful believers. The passage in John 5:28, 29, is also not against the view of a *first resurrection* of believers alone, for the passage does not necessarily teach that all men shall be raised *at the same time.* Those who object to this teaching on account of Christ's statement that he will raise the believer "at the last day "(John 6:39, 40, 44, 54), are simply laboring under the idea that the last day is one of twenty-four hours. It is true that the resurrection of believers takes place at the last day, but it is at the beginning of the last day, immediately after the destruction of Antichrist, while the general resurrection takes place at the end of the last day, for the last day is a longer period than is generally conceived, and it has a beginning and an end. Nor does their doctrine of the first resurrection come in conflict with Christ's description of judgment as recorded in Matt. 25:31–46; for this description is in harmony with Rev. 20:11–15, for all the risen saints shall be present at the final judgment, although they do not come *into* the judgment (John 5:24), and shall even in some way take part in the judgment (1 Cor. 6:2, 3). And it is only after the final judgment recorded in Rev. 20:11–15 that the saints shall enter upon their complete and full glory and inheritance in the new heavens and the new earth (Rev. 21:1).

Nor is there a conflict with the teaching of St. Paul. In 1 Thess. 4:16, 17, Paul, on the one hand, does not draw a distinction between the *first* resurrection of believers and the *second* resurrection of unbelievers, but on the other hand, this passage does not exclude such a distinction. In 1 Cor. 15:22–26, Paul marks the time when Christ's people shall be raised from the dead as "at Christ's coming"—"each in his own order": (1) Christ; (2) *then* they that are Christ's; (3) "then the end." We know that the interval marked by the "then" between the rising of Christ as the first-fruits, and the rising of those "that are Christ's," at His coming, is for certain more than eighteen hundred years, and we ought not to find fault if John in 20:4–6 reveals to us that there is an

386

interval of a period described as "a thousand years" between the resurrection of believers at the coming of Christ, and the time of the resurrection of unbelievers unto judgment. The most definite reference, however, to the first resurrection of believers in Paul's writings is formed in Phil. 3:11, "if by any means I may attain unto the resurrection from the dead." If St. Paul had been referring simply to the general resurrection, he need not have been so anxious, or made any sacrifice to attain to that, for to it all men must come;—but to attain to the first resurrection he had need to press forward for the prize of that calling. This peculiar expression suggests very plainly the *first* resurrection, which includes only true believers. It is therefore a mistake to maintain that the doctrine of the first resurrection rests solely upon Rev. 20:4–6.

Made in the USA
Coppell, TX
12 February 2022

73481404R00270